# CRIMINALIZING
# WOMEN

# CRIMINALIZING WOMEN

Gender and (In)justice in Neo-Liberal Times

*2nd Edition*

Edited by
**Gillian Balfour &**
**Elizabeth Comack**

Fernwood Publishing
Halifax & Winnipeg

Editing: Robert Clarke
Cover art: Jackie Traverse
Text design: Brenda Conroy
Cover design: John van der Woude
Printed and bound in Canada by Hignell Book Printing

Published by Fernwood Publishing
32 Oceanvista Lane, Black Point, Nova Scotia, B0J 1B0
and 748 Broadway Avenue, Winnipeg, Manitoba, R3G 0X3
www.fernwoodpublishing.ca

Fernwood Publishing Company Limited gratefully acknowledges the financial support of the Government of Canada through the Canada Book Fund and the Canada Council for the Arts, the Nova Scotia Department of Communities, Culture and Heritage, the Manitoba Department of Culture, Heritage and Tourism under the Manitoba Publishers Marketing Assistance Program and the Province of Manitoba, through the Book Publishing Tax Credit, for our publishing program.

    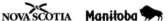

Library and Archives Canada Cataloguing in Publication

Criminalizing women : gender and (in)justice in neo-liberal times
/ edited by Gillian Balfour and Elizabeth Comack. -- 2nd edition.

Includes bibliographical references and index.
ISBN 978-1-55266-682-1 (pbk.)

1. Female offenders--Canada. 2. Women prisoners--Canada. 3. Sex discrimination in criminal justice administration--Canada. 4. Criminal justice, Administration of--Canada. 5. Women's rights--Canada.
I. Balfour, Gillian, 1965-, editor  II. Comack, Elizabeth, 1952-, editor

HV6046.C75 2014          364.3'740973          C2014-905176-X

# Contents

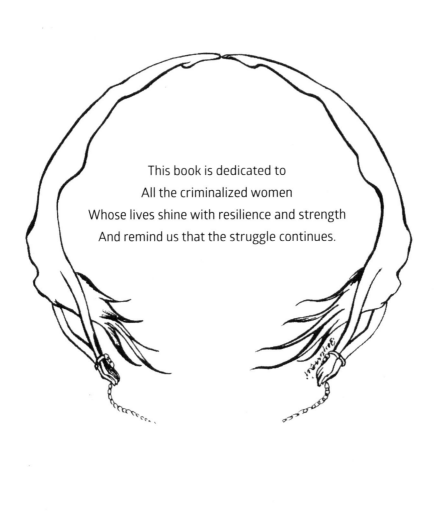

This book is dedicated to
All the criminalized women
Whose lives shine with resilience and strength
And remind us that the struggle continues.

# Contributors

**Gillian Balfour** is an associate professor in Sociology at Trent University, where she teaches in the areas of critical criminology and sociology of law. She has examined how sentencing law reforms have not addressed the overincarceration of Indigenous women. Her current research is an archival study of discipline and prisoner resistance inside the Prison for Women. Gillian is also an ally of the Wall to Bridges Collective and an instructor with Inside/Out Prison Education.

**Chris Bruckert** is an associate professor in the Department of Criminology at the University of Ottawa. Over the past twenty years she has devoted much of her energy to examining diverse sectors of the sex industry. To that end, she has undertaken qualitative research into street-based sex work, erotic dance, in-call and out-call sex work, clients, male sex workers, and management in the sex industry. Chris endeavours to put the principles of committed scholarship into practice and is active in the sex-worker rights movement. Her engagement includes being an extremely active member of POWER (Prostitutes of Ottawa-Gatineau Work, Educate, and Resist), Ottawa's first by-and-for sex-worker rights group.

**Dorothy E. Chunn** is a professor emerita of Sociology at Simon Fraser University. She has published widely in the areas of feminism, law and social change, politics of family, sociology of crime, madness, and welfare, and media depictions of "social problems." Her publications include *Racialization, Crime and Criminal Justice in Canada* (co-authored with Wendy Chan, 2014) *The Legal Tender of Gender: Welfare, Law, and the Regulation of Women's Poverty* (co-edited with Shelley A.M. Gavigan, 2010), and *Reaction and Resistance: Feminism, Law, and Social Change* (co-edited with Susan B. Boyd and Hester Lessard, 2007). Dorothy's recent projects include a collaborative study of the history of autonomous, unmarried motherhood in Canada. She is also co-leader of a team working in the thematic area, "Criminal Justice System, Mental Health, and Substance Use" at the SFU Centre for the Study of Gender, Social Disparities and Mental Health.

**Elizabeth Comack** is a professor of Sociology at the University of Manitoba, where she teaches courses in the sociology of law and feminist criminology. Her recent publications include *Racialized Policing: Aboriginal People's Encounters with the Police* (2012) and *"Indians Wear Red": Colonialism, Resistance, and Aboriginal Street Gangs* (co-authored with Lawrence Deane, Larry Morrissette, and Jim Silver, 2013). She is also the editor of *Locating Law: Race/Class/Gender/Sexuality Connections* (third edition, 2014).

**Colleen Anne Dell** is a professor and research chair in substance abuse in the Department of Sociology and School of Public Health at the University of Saskatchewan. She is also a Senior Research Associate with the Canadian Centre on Substance Abuse, Canada's national addictions agency.

**Nahanni Fontaine** is the Special Advisor on Aboriginal Women's Issues for the Aboriginal Issues Committee of Cabinet of the Manitoba Government.

**Monica Freitas** is a member of the Walls to Bridges Collective at Grand Valley Institution. While incarcerated, Monica has focused on completing her university education and empowering other women inside.

**Jenny Gardipy** is a Masters of Public Health graduate of the University of Saskatchewan and the program co-ordinator at the White Buffalo Youth Inhalant Treatment Centre at Sturgeon Lake First Nation.

**Shelley A.M. Gavigan** is a professor at Osgoode Hall Law School, York University, and Academic Director of the Intensive Program in Poverty Law at Parkdale Community Legal Services. In addition to teaching in the area of poverty law and clinical education, she also teaches in the areas of criminal law, family law, law and poverty, and children and the law. Shelley has published numerous articles in the areas of legal form, legal history, and socio-legal regulation of familial relations, welfare law, lesbian parenting, and abortion law reform and is co-author (with Jane Jenson and Janine Brodie, 1992) of *The Politics of Abortion*, co-editor (with Dorothy E. Chunn, 2010) of *The Legal Tender of Gender: Law, Welfare, and the Legal Regulation of Women's Poverty*, and author of *Hunger, Horses, and Government Men: Criminal Law on the Aboriginal Plains* (2012).

**Amanda Glasbeek** is an associate professor of Criminology and Graduate Socio-Legal Studies in the Department of Social Science at York University. She is the author of *Feminized Justice: The Toronto Women's Court, 1913–34* (2009) and the editor of *Moral Regulation and Governance in Canada* (2006). Her research interests, anchored by feminist criminology and socio-legal studies, include gender and surveillance, women's urban security, and Canadian women's legal history.

**David Hugill** is a Ph.D. candidate in the Department of Geography at York University and an instructor in the Department of Canadian Studies at Glendon College. His research examines the urban legacies of settler colonialism, with an emphasis on North American inner-city geographies. He is author of *Missing Women, Missing News: Covering Crisis in Vancouver's Downtown Eastside* (2010) and a member of *Canadian Dimension* magazine's editorial collective.

**Jennifer M. Kilty** is an associate professor in the Department of Criminology, University of Ottawa. Much of her research centres on the intersection between health and law, including analyses of self-harm, substance use, and most recently the criminalization of HIV non-disclosure. She has also examined the social construction of dangerous girls and women and the gendered nature of incarceration. In addition to a number of book chapters, her research has been published in *Canadian Journal of Law and Society, The Prison Journal, Feminism & Psychology, Qualitative Sociology Review, International Review of Victimology, Criminologie, Contemporary Justice Review, Criminology and Public Policy,* and *Women and Criminal Justice.*

**Nicki Kirlin** is a graduate of the University of Saskatchewan Masters of Public Health program and a researcher in the Office of the Research Chair in Substance Abuse at the University of Saskatchewan.

**Nyki Kish** is a member of the Walls to Bridges Collective at Grand Valley Institution in Kitchener–Waterloo, where she is serving a life sentence. Nyki is a writer, activist, and musician.

**Bonnie McAuley** is an Inside-Out student at Grand Valley Institution in Kitchener–Waterloo, working toward her undergraduate degree. She also a member of the Walls to Bridges Collective, and is a proud mother and grandmother. Bonnie, a federally sentenced woman, had by 2014 served nineteen years of a twenty-five-year sentence.

**Robert Menzies** is a professor of Sociology at Simon Fraser University. His interests include the history and sociology of mental health, criminality, and legal regulation. He is co-founder of the research and education website *History of Madness in Canada* (historyofmadness.ca/). His most recent book (co-edited with Brenda A. LeFrançois and Geoffrey Reaume, 2013) is *Mad Matters: A Critical Reader in Canadian Mad Studies.*

**Joanne C. Minaker** teaches and researches in the Sociology Department at MacEwan University in Edmonton. She studies care, human connection, and social justice. In particular, her work concerns transforming the processes through which marginalized women and criminalized youth are excluded, silenced, and dehumanized. Joanne is the co-author (with Bryan Hogeveen, 2009) of *Youth, Crime, and Society: Issues of Power and Justice.*

**Violet Naytowhow** is a Cree from Sturgeon Lake First Nation and graduated from the First Nations University of Canada with a Bachelor of Indian Social Work. She is a certified Indigenous Addictions Specialist II by the FNWACCB and is working as an Integrated Wellness Coordinator at the Prince Albert Grand

Council Holistic Wellness program, where she shares Indigenous teachings with families. She is also a voice actor, theatre actress, and musician nominated for eight country, folk, and roots awards as a singer/songwriter across Canada and the United States.

**Jennifer J. Nicol** is an associate professor at the University of Saskatchewan with additional credentials as an accredited music therapist and registered doctoral psychologist. She teaches courses in counselling psychology and qualitative research and has an active research program on the health and wellness benefits of music.

**Colette Parent** is a professor in the Department of Criminology of the University of Ottawa. She writes in the areas of the criminalization of women, sex work, and violence against women as partners, and on the contribution of feminism to criminology. She has completed empirical research on different types of sex work (on the streets, in massage parlors and erotic establishments, in erotic bars, and on escorting by women, men, and trans). She has devoted herself to researching the theoretical debates on "prostitution" and on developing our understanding of sex work as a form of labour in the service sector of the economy.

**Shoshana Pollack** is a professor in the Faculty of Social Work, Wilfrid Laurier University. She has been working in the area of women and imprisonment for twenty-five years as a therapist, advocate, and researcher and most recently as an educator.

**Jackie Traverse** is an Ojibway artist from Lake St. Martin, Manitoba. She is a graduate of the School of Art at the University of Manitoba. Her paintings, drawings, documentaries, and sculptures speak to the realities of being an Aboriginal woman.

**Emily van der Meulen** is an assistant professor in the Department of Criminology at Ryerson University. Her research interests include gender and surveillance, the criminalization of sexual labour, and prison health and harm reduction. She is co-editor (with Elya Durisin and Victoria Love, 2013) of *Selling Sex: Experience, Advocacy, and Research on Sex Work in Canada*, an anthology of writing by sex workers, allies, and academics.

# Acknowledgements

We started this journey of producing the second edition of *Criminalizing Women* over a year ago. In the wake of the death of Ashley Smith inside one of Canada's newly designed gender-responsive prisons, we recognized how important it was to renew critical discussion of criminalized and incarcerated women. As with the first edition, we are ever so mindful that the process of producing an edited book depends on a great many resources and friendships.

We thank each of the chapter contributors, whose scholarship and activism on behalf of criminalized women inspired us to imagine the possibility of this book. We truly appreciate their willingness to manage tight deadlines and frenetic emails amid their own busy schedules of work and family life. We're especially thankful to Monica Freitas, Nyki Kish, and Bonnie McAuley for sharing their reflections on the conditions of their confinement and their experiences with the Inside/Out Prison Exchange Program.

We also thank Jackie Traverse, whose artistic talent is (once again) featured on the front cover of the book. Her powerful image of the imprisoned heart so ably captures what this book is about. Jackie was also generous in allowing us to reproduce her piece on scars. We are grateful as well to Gayle Horii for providing the artwork for the dedication page.

As university professors we have the privilege of working with some incredibly talented students. One in particular is Dan Levin, whose indispensable skill in tending to details was put to good work in sorting out the citations, references, and index for the book.

We also had the privilege of working with our talented book editor, Robert Clarke, who once again managed to make the words flow more smoothly.

As always, we owe a special thanks to the folks at Fernwood Publishing for working so tirelessly to produce critical books for critical thinkers. We are especially indebted to our publisher, Wayne Antony, for his commitment over the years to this project, and for putting his trust in our abilities to deliver the final product. We are also thankful to Beverley Rach for coordinating production, Debbie Mathers for inputting the editorial changes, and Brenda Conroy for proofing the final copy. Books don't sell themselves, so we acknowledge the concerted labour of Errol Sharpe, Jessica Antony, Curran Faris, Nancy Malek, and Stacey Byrne in making that happen.

Of course, our families have once again persevered alongside of us as we completed this project. To Quinn and Anastasia — who have become amazing young women over the past seven years — your challenges have inspired me to keep writing about the lives of young women. To Wayne, Jess, and Arth, I hope you know that I couldn't do this work without your support and encouragement — and your ability to keep me grounded.

In keeping with the collective and political nature of this project, the royalities from this book will be donated to groups working in support of criminalized women.

— Gillian Balfour and Elizabeth Comack

# Introduction

*Gillian Balfour & Elizabeth Comack*

In 1990, after decades of activism outside of Canada's notorious Prison for Women and a number of tragic deaths of women inside the prison, an Ottawa task force released the first ever national survey of federally sentenced women (Shaw et al. 1991). The survey exposed the prevalence of physical and sexual abuse among criminalized women (and especially Aboriginal women) and their chronic cross-addictions to alcohol and prescription and street drugs combined with a lack of education and paid work. Based on these significant findings, Canada's federal government set about reforming the conditions of women's imprisonment.

*Creating Choices* — the blueprint for change — outlined a woman-centred correctional model that called for women's prisons to be wholly redesigned, rooted in principles of women's empowerment, respect and dignity, shared responsibility, and meaningful choices (TFFSW 1990). In the following years, however, the implementation of *Creating Choices* proved to be a retrenchment and expansion of carceral power, albeit one defined as "gender-responsive," with women inmates housed in cottages rather than on prison ranges. Simply put, after 1990 more and more women were sentenced to prison in Canada and the conditions of their confinement — especially for Aboriginal women — deteriorated (see Arbour 1995). By 2005 Canada's expanding criminalization and incarceration of women had become part of a "global lockdown" (Sudbury 2005a). In 2006 the International Centre for Prison Studies issued its first ever global study of women's imprisonment rates, reporting that female incarceration had grown on all continents (Walmsley 2006). In the wake of these troubling global trends, feminists re-engaged with the state, this time through the lens of human rights litigation — documenting violations of UN conventions on torture and citing state abuses of women prisoners' human rights (see CAEFS 2003, 2006; CHRC 2003).

The first edition of this book, published in 2006, was intended to take stock of the implications of feminist engagement with the criminal justice system in the face of the failure of *Creating Choices* and the increasing rates of women's criminalization and incarceration. The book was situated against a backdrop of media and public backlash against feminists who sought to expose the prevalence of violence against women (Johnson 1996; DeKeseredy

1999). Starting in the 1990s, media accounts proclaimed that "sugar and spice is not so nice" and that women were now men's "equals in violence" (Laframboise 1997, 1999). Adding fuel to such pronouncements were the tragic deaths of three young women in Canada in the 1990s. The convictions of Karla Homolka for her part in the deaths of Kristen French and Lesley Mahaffy in Ontario and Kelly Ellard for hers in the beating death of Reena Virk in British Columbia were the bread and butter of media tabloids at the turn of the century. Even Hollywood got into the action, releasing the blockbuster film *Monster* — the story of Aileen Wuornos, a woman executed in the United States after robbing and killing seven men, deeds which had earned her the label of America's first female serial killer.

In the years after the first edition of *Criminalizing Women* was published, rates of women's incarceration only continued to increase. Women remain the fastest-growing segment of the prison populations in Western industrialized countries such as Canada, the United States, Britain, and Australia (Currie 2013; Sudbury 2005a). In the news media, stories of women's violence continued to attract attention and public condemnation in the early twenty-first century.

In April 2010, eighteen-year-old Terri-Lynne McClintic pleaded guilty to first-degree murder in the death of eight-year-old Tori Stafford. Young Tori had been abducted by McClintic and then repeatedly raped by McClintic's boyfriend, twenty-eight-year-old Michael Rafferty, before McClintic used a hammer to kill her. Media reports poured over McClintic's history — of how she had been raised by a former stripper and dropped out of school in Grade 8, and her penchant for violent gangsta rap and illicit drugs. The media continue to report on McClintic's status as a maximum-security prisoner inside the Grand Valley Institution for Women (GVIW) in Kitchener–Waterloo, where she began serving a life sentence.

After she was released from prison in July 2005 following a twelve-year sentence, Karla Homolka continued to be the subject of media scrutiny, especially in June 2010 when the Conservative government furthered its "tough on crime" agenda by passing a pardon reform bill that prolonged the period of being ineligible for a pardon for anyone convicted of a serious personal injury offence from five years to ten years after their release from prison. The bill was deliberately aimed at Homolka's case. In 2012 the Canadian press reported that Homolka was living with her new husband and three children on a Caribbean island. Public acrimony was high, with published online comments such as "I find it amazing the double standard for women vs men. Women get away with having no moral compass but men end up vilified, thrown on the sex offender registry for life and all that good stuff. It's as if women can pretend to be childlike and take no personal responsibility for anything if they like" (Thanh Ha 2012).

Meanwhile, high -production film and television continued their fascination with women prisoners with the series *Orange Is the New Black*, which features the daily lives of imprisoned women whose lesbian sex and tight prison garb are most likely intended to titillate the imagination of viewers. The series' popularity suggests that the public appetite for voyeuristic accounts of criminalized women remains high.

But feminists working as advocates for criminalized women inside courtrooms and jails, and in university classrooms, know there is another story to be told. These feminists recognize that despite the media attention devoted to such cases, women who commit unspeakable acts of violence are an extreme rarity. Men, although far more likely to be criminalized for violent offences, do not capture the public imagination or engender public condemnation as much as those few women convicted of serious offences (Jiwani 2006). Sadly, the stories of these anomalous women overshadow the harsh lives of the vast majority of criminalized women — and the conditions of their confinement. Criminalized women in Canada are deeply disadvantaged through poverty, victimization, untreated mental illness, and addictions. Women prisoners also spend more time in segregation ("the hole") than do men prisoners, oftentimes because of self-injurious behaviour or disruptive behaviour linked to untreated mental illness. Consider the lives of these young women:

- In August 2007 Ashley Smith, at age nineteen, arrived at Grand Valley Institution for Women. Her conflicts with the law began as a young teenager. After repeated stints of confinement within Nova Scotia's facilities for young offenders for offences related to public disturbances, breaching probation conditions, and institutional infractions, when she turned eighteen Ashley was transferred to adult custody to serve a six-year sentence for her accumulated youth convictions. She continued to accumulate charges, most of which related to her self-harming behaviour. Throughout her time in adult custody, Ashley was never properly assessed by a psychologist or given a treatment plan to address her complex mental health needs. Instead, she was heavily sedated, constrained by chemical agents, and strapped to a Pinel board (used to physically restrain prisoners). During the eleven-and-one-half months spent in federal custody, she was moved seventeen times between various facilities and spent almost all of that time in administrative segregation. In response to this brutalizing treatment, Ashley became increasingly suicidal. Her self-harming behaviour included self-asphyxiation in an attempt to have guards enter her cell so that she could have some kind of human contact. Eventually the warden of Grand Valley Institution ordered that security officers were not to enter Ashley's cell unless they were certain she was no longer breathing. On October 19, 2009, as the guards looked on, Ashley died on the floor of her segregation cell of self-asphyxiation. A coroner's inquest called to investigate her death ruled that her death was a homicide (see Davidson 2013; Sapers 2008; Richard 2008).

- Tona Mills entered the criminal justice system as a young teenager, charged with minor offences and unruly behaviour. Although her adoptive mother sought help for Tona, the pleas were dismissed by doctors and psychologists, who said that the girl was just spoiled and badly behaved or, even worse, a hopeless cause. Tona entered the federal prison system at age twenty-one after being handed a four-year sentence for discharging a firearm (her father's hunting rifle). In the following years she received no proper diagnosis or treatment; instead the four-year sentence extended to ten years as she accumulated new charges for acting out and assaulting prison staff. To manage her self-injurious behaviour and assaultive outbursts, Tona was confined in segregation on suicide watch. Her ten years in the federal system included six spent in segregation. She was also frequently transferred to various institutions. She was often strapped to a Pinel board or sedated to control her actions. When she was convicted of assaulting another inmate while confined in a men's maximum-security prison, the sentencing judge finally recognized that Tona required appropriate psychiatric care. She was then sent to a psychiatric hospital, where she was diagnosed with schizophrenia. After four years in treatment Tona was released into the community under a mental health supervision order. She was now able to live independently (Brosnahan 2013).

- In December 2013, Lucia Vega Jiménez, a young Mexican woman, was transferred to the detention centre at Vancouver International Airport awaiting deportation to Mexico. She committed suicide at the centre, which was run by the Canadian Border Services Agency (CBSA). The British Columbia Civil Liberties Association (BCCLA) has stated that it has reasons to believe that the cell monitoring of inmates was contracted to a private company, which failed to adequately monitor detention cells. Lucia had been found unconscious in her cell and rushed to an outside hospital where she later died. The Executive Director of the BCCLA, Josh Patterson, stated that the CBSA asked the surviving family to sign a confidentiality agreement, which would prevent them from speaking publicly of Lucia's death (BCCLA 2014a).

- In February 2014, Avery Edison, a British citizen, was detained at Toronto International Airport by the CBSA, which charged that she had overstayed her student visa when she had previously been in Canada attending Humber College. Although legally a woman, Avery was considered to be male by the CBSA officers as she still has male genitalia. They refused to detain her in a woman's facility, and Avery was transferred to a men's prison in Maplehurst, Ontario, where she was held in solitary confinement for her own protection. Following a public outcry against her detention in a men's jail, Avery was transferred to the Vanier Institution for Women. Unlike Lucia Vega Jimenez, Avery is a young white successful woman, with strong public support for her rights as a transgendered woman (Jeffords 2014).

- BobbyLee Worm, an Aboriginal woman who grew up experiencing extreme sexual and physical abuse, entered the federal correctional system at age nineteen as a first offender. She spent three and one-half years in segregation under management protocol, a correctional practice designed for "high-risk" women that allows for indeterminate periods of segregation and denies access to programming, human contact, or fresh air. Almost all women held on management protocol have been Aboriginal. The BCCLA successfully litigated her case, with the court finding that BobbyLee was illegally confined and that management protocol was an illegal practice that violated her constitutional rights (BCCLA 2014b). In 2011, in light of the Worm case, the Correctional Service of Canada (CSC) announced that it would rescind the use of the management protocol that allowed "high-risk" women to be placed in segregation for indefinite periods (Quan 2011).

The pathways of poverty, racism, and the trauma of sexual violence as a journey into crime and criminalization were not new to feminist criminologists, who since the 1980s had been documenting how social conditions framed women's choices. However, at the end of the first decade of the twenty-first century something was different. It seemed that despite two decades of dogged activism, research, and policy-making, feminist criminologists were losing ground. Following the engineered global financial market crash of 2008, the decades-long neo-liberal political rationality took firmer hold as governments proclaimed the need for deep cuts to public services that, they said, harboured unproductive citizens and, even worse, potential terrorists (Krishnamurti 2013). In Canada, provincial governments sought to limit the collective bargaining rights of workers such as teachers and nurses. They cut food-security programs for the poor — most of them single mothers — and starved legal aid budgets, limiting access to legal representation in cases of domestic violence, child protection, housing disputes, and family law, among other matters. At the same time, a neo-conservative political rationality took hold as the federal government began to implement its "tough on crime" agenda, passing more crime-control legislation than had any other previous government and introducing a blueprint for the expansion of prison construction (Mallea 2010; Piche 2011). In particular, Bill C-10, an omnibus bill enacted in 2013, increased the number of mandatory minimum sentences of incarceration for certain offences and restricted the use of community-based conditional sentencing options.[1] Social science experts and constitutional lawyers strenuously opposed the legislation, pointing to the impact of longer sentences on offenders and the overall expense of confining more prisoners (see, for example, Yalkin and Kirk 2012).

Bill C-10 will undoubtedly have a gendered and racialized impact. Women are more likely to be arrested and convicted for non-violent offences (such as fraud and theft under $5,000) than men are (see the Introduction to Part II here). As a result, despite women's already proportionately higher rate of incarceration, more women will be imprisoned as a result of these amendments. Aboriginal women are more likely to be criminalized for violent offences (see chapter 1 for a discussion of the complex reasons that underpin Aboriginal women's violence). Thus, Bill C-10's removal of conditional sentences as an option in some violent offence cases will contribute to higher rates of incarceration for Indigenous women.

While women inside and outside the criminal justice system share a proximity to violence and poverty and experience the failure of the state to remedy conditions of inequality, politicians and policy-makers increasingly consider criminalized women — especially those who live with mental illness — as "too few to count" (Adelberg and Currie 1987a) or "more mad than bad" (Allen 1987). Clearly, we need to counter this dismissive viewpoint by engaging in a more thoughtful and detailed interrogation of the historical and contemporary issues that bear down on the lives of criminalized women. We need to look at the state's response to women in trouble, and consider possibilities for making meaningful change.

Part I of the book begins (chapter 1) with an intellectual history of feminist criminology that highlights the various ways in which criminalized women have been represented and understood. Feminist criminology has assumed different epistemological positions over the decades and has provided several analytical tools that reveal who criminalized women are and how they come to be criminalized. The chapter opens with an outline of the invisibility of women in the research and theory-building of orthodox criminologists. Disenchanted with conventional approaches of criminology, feminists began to transgress the boundaries of the discipline through the use of standpoint methodologies that revealed the prevalence of male violence against women and poverty in the lives of criminalized women, and a postmodern epistemology that drew attention to questions of how women were constituted or defined by professional discourses and how particular techniques of governance (in a number of different sites) work to contain, control, or exclude those who are marginalized in society.

The chapter also discusses how the knowledge produced about criminalized women is always framed by the socio-political context. In these terms, the shift from a social welfare to neo-liberal and neo-conservative rationalities has had a profound impact on the governance of women and their cultural representations in public discourse. This shifting socio-political context created a powerful backlash against feminist knowledge claims, especially the efforts by feminist criminologists to draw connections between women's experiences of marginalization and victimization and their involvement in crime. In response, feminists have asserted the need for an intersectional analysis that takes into account the interconnections of race/class/gender in framing women's lives and choices and a sensitivity to the victimization-criminalization continuum.

Part II moves to an investigation of the nature and extent of women's involvement in crime and explores the issues of women and poverty and the overrepresentation of Aboriginal women and women of colour in the criminal justice system so that we can better understand how class, race, and gender intersect in the lives of criminalized women. Each of the chapters in Part II takes up an issue that enables us to question the common-sense understandings and representations that prevail about criminalized women and girls. In their discussions of the "erring female" of an earlier era, women who work in the sex trade, Aboriginal women's and girls' participation in "street gangs," and the media representations of murdered and missing Indigenous women, the authors also allow us to reconnect the choices that women make to the conditions of their lives.

Part III focuses on the various techniques of regulation — including psychiatric, welfare, public surveillance, and penal regimes — that have been used against women and girls from the early twentieth century until now. In particular, we see how certain representations of women as incorrigible, dangerous, dependent, and risky frame the changing modes of regulation. Throughout the chapters we are reminded of the implications of engaging with the state. It would seem that neo-liberal governments are likely to appropriate feminist knowledge claims to construct women as damaged and in need of therapy rather than providing affordable housing and meaningful employment to end the cycle of violence and poverty. Feminists are caught in the paradox of relying on the legitimacy and resources of the criminal justice system to provide safety and assistance to women, while important public resources such as income assistance, shelters, food banks, and day-care centres are collapsing under the ruinous economic policies of neo-liberal governments. Fuelled by an anxious middle class fixated on their own economic uncertainty, governments have successfully launched new neo-conservative crime-control strategies, such as welfare-fraud snitch lines, that disproportionately place women at greater risk of being criminalized.

Finally, in Part IV, we are left to explore the possibilities for making change in these neo-liberal times. Much has happened in the nearly fifty years since the first feminist scholarship emerged in Canadian criminology. Feminist criminology has gained importance in the specific contexts of university teaching and research. However, feminists remain on the margins of important political discussions about what to do about the issue of "law and order." As Laureen Snider points out, feminist academics and activists have yet to become "authorized knowers." Snider maintains that feminists are on the defensive as they face the brunt of powerful neo-liberal and neo-conservative claims-making. The task now is to re-imagine a feminist criminology that can capture the necessary institutional resources — and the moral and social capital — required to draw attention to the perilous impact of neo-liberal and neo-conservative policies on women. Nonetheless, authors in this part of the book also offer us some strategies — using song and music as a means for Indigenous women to (re)claim their identity and culture and education "inside" the prison walls — as possibilities for making meaningful change.

In sum, this book is about trying to make sense of the impact on women and girls of neo-liberal economics and concomitant "get tough" crime-control agendas. It seeks to provide a space for "subversive tales" (Ewing and Silbey 1995) about criminalized women to be told as a way of countering the hegemony of women as "misfits" or "monsters." In the process, the chapters in this collection provide a thoughtful yet rigorous accounting of the gendered conditions of poverty, violence, racism, and the regulation of women in Canada.

## Note

1.  Conditional sentences are prison terms of less than two years served in the community with onerous conditions, including house arrest, community service, treatment orders, and curfews. This sentencing option was created in 1996 to remedy the overincarceration of Indigenous peoples, as well as to recognize the need for restorative justice principles to be considered in sentencing Indigenous peoples (see Roberts and LaPrairie 2000).

# Part I

# Women, Criminology, and Feminism

# 1

# The Feminist Engagement with Criminology

*Elizabeth Comack*

The feminist engagement with criminology began almost fifty years ago, when pioneers in the discipline such as Marie-Andrée Bertrand (1967) and Frances Heidensohn (1968) first called attention to criminology's amnesia when it came to women. Heidensohn (1968: 171), for instance, described the analysis of women and crime as "lonely uncharted seas" and suggested that what was needed was a "crash programme of research which telescopes decades of comparable studies of males." Since that time, feminist work in this area has developed at a fast pace, to the point where it has become increasingly difficult to keep abreast of the research and publications on women and crime.

There is little doubt about the validity of Heidensohn's claim that women traditionally have been neglected in criminology. Like other academic disciplines, criminology has been a decidedly male-centred enterprise. Despite the use of generic terms — such as "criminals," "defendants," or "delinquents" — criminology has historically been about what men do, so much so that women have been invisible in mainstream criminological theory and research. This is not to say, however, that women have been completely ignored. From criminology's inception, there have been some (rather dubious) efforts to make sense of women and girls who come under the purview of the criminal justice system. Variously referred to as monsters, misfits, and manipulators, women — and especially women who engaged in criminal activity — were relegated by early criminologists to the status of "Other."

Historically, feminist engagement with criminology emerged out of the various ways in which women as an object of knowledge production were understood (or ignored) by the criminological discipline over time. Feminists have not only challenged these understandings but also promoted alternative claims about women and their involvement in crime. This kind of intellectual history is wide-ranging. Much has happened over the past five decades — both within academia and the wider society — that has played a role in instigating and contouring the kinds of work that feminists have undertaken in this area. Like all knowledge production, therefore, the rendering of an intellectual history in this chapter will at best be partial.

## The Invisible Women of Mainstream Criminology

To a certain extent the male-centredness of criminology makes sense when you examine the official statistics on crime. In 2011 women comprised only 21 percent of adults charged with Criminal Code offences in Canada, while men made up the lion's share — 79 percent — of those charged (Brennan 2012: 20). In Australia, females made up 25 percent of individuals charged in three states (Victoria, Queensland, and South Australia) in 2009–10 (Australian Institute of Criminology 2011: 69). A similar percentage exists for the United States, where females made up 25 percent of those arrested in 2010 (Snyder 2012: 2). Yet, even though this sex/crime ratio has long been recognized in the discipline, most mainstream criminologists have never really stopped to question it. Instead, they proceeded to develop theories of crime causation that took men — or, more accurately, poor inner-city Black men — as their subject, even when the theorist was intent on framing a general theory of crime ostensibly applicable to the whole population.

This invisibility of women can be easily demonstrated by examining some of the mainstream theories that make up the criminological canon. Robert Merton's (1938) anomie theory, for example, was offered as a general theory explaining crime in relation to the strain that results from the disjunction between culture goals (like monetary success) and institutionalized means (education, jobs). While Merton's theory reflected sensitivity to class inequalities, the same could not be said with regard to an awareness of gender inequalities. If lower-class individuals were more likely to engage in crime because of a lack of access to the institutionalized means for achieving monetary success, it follows, then, that women — who as a group experience a similar lack of access — should also be found to commit their share of crime as a consequence of this strain. But the statistics tell us that this is not the case.

Like anomie theory, Edwin Sutherland's (1949) differential association theory was presented as a general theory of crime. Sutherland focused on the processes by which individuals learn definitions of the legal code as either favourable or unfavourable, and posited the existence of a "cultural heterogeneity" in society with regard to social assessments that were pro- and anti- criminal. Yet, this "general" theory only applied to half the population. Sutherland suggested that while men were individualistic and competitive, women were more altruistic and compliant. So, while cultural heterogeneity could account for men's involvement in crime, it did not seem to apply to women, leading Sutherland to surmise that women were an exception or anomaly in his theory because they displayed a "cultural homogeneity."

Travis Hirschi's (1969) control theory was also characterized by a neglect of the female. While other criminologists focused their attention on explaining deviance, Hirschi turned the tables and set out to explain conformity. Since women appear to be more conformist than men (given, for example, their underrepresentation in crime statistics), it would have made sense for Hirschi to treat women as central to his analysis. Nevertheless, despite having collected data on females, he simply set these data aside and — like his colleagues — concentrated on males.

With the advent of labelling and conflict theories in the 1960s and 1970s, the potential for a more gender-inclusive approach to crime increased. Nonetheless, while Howard Becker's (1963) labelling theory raised the question of "Whose side are we on?" and advocated an approach to deviance that gave voice to those who were subjected to the labelling process, it was never fully realized in the case of women. Similarly, Ian Taylor, Paul Walton, and Jock Young's *The New Criminology* (1973), which offered up a devastating critique of traditional criminological theories, failed to give even a mention to women.

## Women as Other: Monsters, Misfits, and Manipulators

Women were not completely ignored in criminological thought. A small body of work, dating back to the nineteenth century, attempted to account for women's involvement in crime. What could be classified as the early approaches to explaining women's crime began in 1895 with Cesare Lombroso and William Ferrero's *The Female Offender*, followed by W.I. Thomas's *The Unadjusted Girl* in 1923, Sheldon Glueck and Eleanor Glueck's *500 Delinquent Women* in 1934, and Otto Pollak's *The Criminality of Women* in 1950. While differences exist between these approaches, they all share in common the view of women as "other" than men, and women who engage in criminal activity as even more so. For these theorists, it is women's "inherent nature" that accounts for both the nature and extent of their criminality. In particular, women are cast as sexual beings, and women's sexuality is at the root of their involvement in crime.

Lombroso and Ferrero based their theorizing on an examination of the physical characteristics of a group of 119 "criminal" women, which they compared with a control group of fourteen "non-criminal" women. In applying the concepts of atavism (the idea that some individuals were born criminals) and social Darwinism (the idea that those who get ahead in society are the most fit to survive), they suggested that women as a group possessed limited intelligence. Women were also less sensitive to pain than men, full of revenge and jealousy, and naturally passive and conservative. These traits had a physiological basis. For instance, Lombroso and Ferrero (1895: 109) assert that women's passivity was demonstrated by the "immobility of the ovule compared to the zoosperm." Atavistically, women offenders were considered to display fewer signs of degeneration than men. The reason, according to Lombroso and Ferrero, was that women (and non-white males) had not advanced as far along the evolutionary continuum as (white) males, and so could not degenerate as far. Given that women were relatively "primitive," the criminals among them would not be highly visible. However, those women who were criminal were cast as excessively vile and cruel in their crimes. They ostensibly combined the qualities of the criminal male with the worst characteristics of the female: cunning, spite, and deceitfulness. Lacking "maternal instinct" and "ladylike qualities," criminal women were deemed to be "monsters":

> The born female criminal is, so to speak, doubly exceptional as a woman and as a criminal. For criminals are an exception among civilized people, and women are an exception among criminals.... As a double exception, the criminal woman is consequently a *monster*. Her normal sister is kept in the paths of virtue by many causes, such as maternity, piety, weakness, and when these counter influences fail, and a woman commits a crime, we may conclude that her wickedness must have been so enormous before it could triumph over so many obstacles. (Lombroso and Ferrero 1895: 151–52; emphasis added)

Like Lombroso and Ferrero, W.I. Thomas (1923/1967) framed his theorizing about women on presumed "natural" or biological differences between men and women. Thomas suggested that human behaviour is based on four wishes: desires for adventure, security, response, and recognition. These wishes corresponded to features in the nervous system that were expressed as biological instincts of anger, fear, love, and the will to gain status and power. However, Thomas asserted that men's and women's instincts differed both in quantity and quality. Since women had more varieties of love in their nervous systems, their desire for response was greater than men's. According to Thomas, it was the need to feel loved that accounted for women's criminality, and especially for their involvement in prostitution.

Sheldon Glueck and Eleanor Glueck (1934) continued in this same tradition with their book *500 Delinquent Women*. The Gluecks described the women in their study as a "sorry lot. Burdened with feebleminded-ness, psychopathic personality, and marked emotional instability, a large proportion of them found it difficult to survive by legitimate means." The view of criminal women as Other is clearly evident: "This swarm of defec-tive, diseased, antisocial misfits ... comprises the human material which a reformatory and a parole system are required by society to transform into wholesome, decent, law-abiding citizens! Is it not a miracle that a proportion of them were actually rehabilitated?" (Glueck and Glueck 1934: 299, 303).

Two decades later, Otto Pollak attempted to account for what he de-scribed as the masked nature of women's crime. Sceptical of the official data on sex differences in crime, Pollak (1950) suggested that women's crime was vastly undercounted. He put forward the view that female criminality was more likely to be hidden and undetected. According to Pollak, women were more often the instigators than the perpetrators of crime. Like Eve in the Garden of Eden, they manipulated men into committing offences. Women, he claimed, were also inherently deceptive and vengeful. They engaged in prostitution and blackmailed their lovers. As domestics they stole from their employers, and as homemakers they carried out horrendous acts on their families (like poisoning the sick and abusing children). According to Pollak, woman's devious nature was rooted in her physiology. While a man must achieve erection in order to perform the sex act (and hence will not be able to conceal orgasm), a woman can fake orgasm (Pollak 1950: 10). This ability to conceal orgasm supposedly gave women practice at deception.

Pollak also argued that the vengefulness, irritability, and depression that women encountered as a result of their generative phases caused female crime. For example, menstruation drove women to acts of revenge by re-minding them of their inferior status (and their ultimate failure to become men). The concealed nature of their crimes, the vulnerability of their vic-tims, and their chivalrous treatment by men who cannot bear to prosecute or punish them combined to mask women's offences. When these factors are taken into account, according to Pollak, women's crimes are equal in severity and number to those of men.

For these early criminologists, then, the women involved in crime were monsters, misfits, or manipulators. While we can look back on these con-structions of women with some amusement, it bears noting that these kinds of knowledge claims about women and the reasons for their involvement in crime have not disappeared. Throughout the 1960s, researchers continued to rely on the assumptions and premises of the earlier approaches. John Cowie, Valerie Cowie, and Eliot Slater (1968), for example, in the tradition of Lombroso and Ferrero, looked for "constitutional predisposing factors" to explain female delinquency. In a similarly disparaging manner the same authors (1968: 167) characterized delinquent girls as "oversized, lumpish, uncouth and graceless." Gisella Konopka (1966), in extending Thomas's analysis, equated sexual delinquency in girls with a desperate need for love. Following on the footsteps of Otto Pollak, a more contemporary version of these theories links hormonal changes associated with women's menstrual cycles to their involvement in crime.

Premenstrual syndrome (PMS) has been described as a condition of "irritability, indescribable tension" and a "desire to find relief by foolish and ill-considered actions," something that is thought to occur during the week or two prior to the onset of menstruation (Frank, cited in Osborne 1989: 168). With no biomedical tests for determining its existence, PMS is the only "disease" not dependent on a specific type of symptom for its diagnosis. Nevertheless, PMS has been argued to be a cause of violent behaviour in women who suffer from it. Premenstrual syndrome gained popularity as an explanation for women's criminality in the 1980s, when it was introduced in two British court cases as a mitigating factor in homicide (Luckhaus 1985). Research linking PMS to women's criminality has been criticized for its methodological deficiencies (Morris 1987; Kendall 1991, 1992). As an explanation for women's involvement in crime, however, PMS clearly locates the source of the problem in women's "unruly" bodies. Because of their "nature," women are supposedly prone to madness once a month.

## Enter Feminism ...

In its initial stages, feminist criminology took the form of a critique of the existing approaches to explaining crime. Writers such as Dorie Klein (1973), Carol Smart (1976, 1977), Eileen Leonard (1982), Allison Morris (1987), and Ngaire Naffine (1987) took issue with the sexism of criminological theories — socially undesirable characteristics were attributed to women and assumed to be intrinsic characteristics of their sex.

With regard to the early approaches to explaining crime (offered by Lombroso and Ferrero, Thomas, the Gluecks, and Pollak), Heidensohn (1985: 122) noted how they lent an aura of intellectual respectability to many old folk tales about women and their behaviours. Their constructions of the "female offender" reflected the widely held assumptions about "women's nature," including the good girl/bad girl duality and a double standard that viewed sexual promiscuity as a sign of amorality in women but normality in men. Relying on common-sense, anecdotal evidence, and circular reasoning — that is, "things are as they are because they are natural, and they are natural because that is the way things are" (Smart 1976: 36) — the early theorists failed to call into question the structural features of their society and the gendered roles of men and women. For these early criminologists, sex (a biological difference) and gender (a cultural prescription) were equated as one and the same, with the "ladylike" qualities of the middle-class and upper-class white woman used as the measuring rod for what is inherently female. Feminist criminologists castigated these early theories for being not only sexist, but also racist and classist.

Mainstream theories of crime (such an anomie, differential association, social control, labelling, and conflict theories) came under a similar scrutiny. The invisibility of women and the failure to adequately explain or account for women's involvement in crime led feminist criminologists to label such theories as not just mainstream but "malestream." As Lorraine Gelsthorpe and Allison Morris asserted:

> Theories are weak if they do not apply to half of the potential criminal population; women, after all, experience the same deprivations, family structures and so on that men do. Theories of crime should be able to take account of *both* men's and women's behaviour and to highlight those factors which operate differently on men and women. Whether or not a particular theory helps us to understand women's crime is of *fundamental*, not marginal importance for criminology. (Gelsthorpe and Morris 1988: 103; emphasis added)

Kathleen Daly and Meda Chesney-Lind (1988) refer to one issue raised by the feminist critique of the mainstream theories as the "generalizability problem": can theories generated to explain males' involvement in crime be modified to apply to women? Several feminist criminologists responded to this problem by attempting to make the mainstream theories of crime "fit" women.

Eileen Leonard (1982), for example, in a reformulation of Merton's strain theory, suggested that females are socialized to aspire to different culture goals than are males, in particular relational goals concerning marriage and having children. Following this line of reasoning, women's low rate of criminal involvement compared to men could be explained by the relatively easy manner in which females can realize their goals. Nevertheless, as Allison Morris (1987) notes, such a formulation relies on an idealized and romanticized version of women's lives. Not only does it display an insensitivity to the strains and frustrations associated with women's familial role (raising children and maintaining a household), it fails to acknowledge the very real and pressing economic concerns that women confront in the process (making ends meet and paying the bills).

Such efforts to revise mainstream theories of crime to include women have been referred to as the "add women and stir" approach (Chesney-Lind 1988a). Part of the difficulty with this project is that women are presented merely as afterthoughts, not as integral to the arguments being developed (Gelsthorpe and Morris 1988). Naffine (1997: 32) captures a more significant problem with this effort: "The point of these exercises has been to adapt to the female case, theories of crime which purported to be gender-neutral but were in fact always highly gender specific. Not surprisingly, the results have been varied and generally inconclusive."

A second issue raised by the feminist critique of mainstream criminology is one that Daly and Chesney-Lind (1988: 119) refer to as the "gender-ratio problem." Why are women less likely than men to be involved in crime? What explains the sex difference in rates of arrest and in the variable types of criminal activity between men and women? Attention to the gender-ratio problem sparked a multitude of studies in the 1970s and 1980s on the criminal justice system's processing of men and women (see, for example, Scutt 1979; Kruttschnitt 1980–81, 1982; Steffensmeier and Kramer 1982; Zingraff and Thomson 1984; Daly 1987, 1989). Much of this research was guided by Pollak's assertion of chivalry on the part of criminal justice officials. Are women treated more leniently than men? As in the generalizability problem, the results were mixed. For instance, research that supported this chivalry hypothesis indicated that when it does exist, chivalry benefits some women more than others — in particular, the few white, middle-class or upper-class women who come into conflict with the law. It also appears to apply only to those female suspects who behave according to a stereotypical female script, that is, "crying, pleading for release for the sake of their children, claiming men have led them astray" (Rafter and Natalizia 1981: 92). In this regard, Nicole Rafter and Elena Natalizia argue that chivalrous behaviour should be seen as a means of preserving women's subordinate position in society, not as a benign effort to treat women with some special kindness. Naffine (1997: 36), however, points to a larger problem with this research. By turning on the question of whether women were treated in the same way as men, or differently, the chivalry thesis (and its rebuttal) took men to be the norm: "Men were thus granted the status of universal subjects, the population of people with whom the rest of the world (women) were compared."

At the same time, in the 1970s and 1980s, another thesis was attracting considerable criminological attention. The "women's liberation thesis" posited that women's involvement in crime would come to resemble men's more closely as differences between men and women were diminished by women's greater participation and equality in society. As reflected in the work of Rita Simon (1975) and Freda Adler (1975), the thesis suggested that changes in women's gender roles would be reflected in their rates of criminal involvement. Simon argued that the increased employment opportunities that resulted from the women's movement would also bring an increase in opportunities to commit crime (such as embezzlement from employers). Adler linked the apparent increase of women in crime statistics to the influence of the women's movement and suggested that a "new female criminal" was emerging: women were becoming more violent and aggressive, just like their male counterparts.

The women's liberation thesis "captured the imagination of the media and practitioners" (Morris and Gelsthorpe 1981: 53, cited in Gavigan 1993: 221). While law enforcement officials were quick to affirm its tenets, charging that the women's movement was responsible for triggering a massive crime wave, the media had a heyday with its claims, featuring headlines such as "Lib takes the lid off the gun moll" (*Toronto Star* 15 May 1975, cited in Gavigan 1993: 222). Nevertheless, representations of emancipated women running amok in the streets and workplaces did not hold up under closer scrutiny (see, for example, Chesney-Lind 1978; Weiss 1976; Steffensmeier 1980; Naffine 1987). Smart (1976), for one, noted that the women's liberation thesis was premised on a "statistical illusion" in that the supposed increases in women's crime were being reported as percentages. Given the small base number of women charged with criminal offences, it did not take much of a change to show a large percentage increase. Holly Johnson and Karen Rodgers (1993: 104) provided an example of this problem using Canadian data. Between 1970 and 1991, charges against women for homicide increased by 45 percent, but that figure reflected a real increase of only fifteen women charged. As well, while the women's movement was primarily geared toward privileged white women, poor women and women of colour were most likely to appear in police and prison data. These women were not inclined to think of themselves as "liberated" and — far from considering themselves as feminists — were quite conventional in their ideas and beliefs about women's role in society. For many feminist criminologists, the main difficulty with the women's liberation thesis — similar to the chivalry thesis — was that it posed a question that took males to be the norm: were women becoming more liberated and thus more like men, even in their involvement in crime? In Naffine's (1997: 32) judgment, the thesis that women's liberation causes crime by women has been "perhaps the most time-consuming and fruitless exercise" in criminology.

Another effort to attend to the gender-ratio problem was put forward by John Hagan and his colleagues (Hagan, Simpson, and Gillis 1979, 1987; Hagan, Gillis, and Simpson 1985), who combined elements of feminist theory with Hirschi's control theory to fashion a power-control theory of sex and delinquency. Focusing attention on the gender roles and differential socialization of males and females, power-control theory was designed to explain the sex differences in delinquency by drawing linkages between the variations in parental control and the delinquent behaviour of boys and girls. More specifically, Hagan and his colleagues suggested that parental control and adolescents' subsequent attitudes toward risk-taking behaviour are influenced by family class relations. They distinguished two ideal types of family: the patriarchal family, in which the husband is employed in an authority position in the workforce and the wife is not employed outside the home; and the egalitarian family, in which both husband and wife are employed in authority positions outside the home. Hagan and his colleagues suggested that in the former a traditional gender division exists, whereby fathers and especially mothers are expected to control their daughters more than their sons. Given the presence of a "cult of domesticity," girls will be socialized to focus their futures on domestic labour and consumption activities, while boys will be prepared for their participation in production activities. In the egalitarian family, parents will redistribute their control efforts such that girls are subject to controls that are more like the ones imposed on boys. "In other words, in egalitarian families, as mothers gain power relative to husbands, daughters gain freedom relative to sons" (Hagan, Simpson, and Gillis 1987: 792). As such, the authors predicted that these different family forms will produce differing levels of delinquency in girls: "Patriarchal families will be characterized by large gender differences in common delinquent behaviours, while egalitarian families will be characterized by smaller gender differences in delinquency" (Hagan, Simpson, and Gillis 1987: 793).

While Hagan and his colleagues endeavoured to place delinquency by girls in a broader structural context (by attending to the labour force participation of parents), they made an important assumption: if a woman is working for wages, there will be "equality" within the household. Their formulation does not pay enough attention to the nature of women's paid work and to other variables that might be in operation (such as how power and control may be exercised between males and females within the household). As well, Chesney-Lind regards power-control theory as a variation on the women's liberation thesis because it links the emergence of the egalitarian family with increasing delinquency among girls. In effect, "mother's liberation causes daughter's crime" (Chesney-Lind 1989: 20, cited in Boritch 1997: 71).

## Feminist Empiricism: Countering Bad Science

In their engagement with criminology during the 1970s and 1980s, feminists tended to work within the confines of positivist social science. In other words, they subscribed to the belief that the methods of the natural sciences (measurement and prediction) could be applied to the study of social life. Their critiques of mainstream work in the discipline amounted to the claim that what was being produced was "bad science." In her elaboration of different feminist epistemologies, philosopher Sandra Harding (1990) named this approach "feminist empiricism." Feminist empiricists in criminology held that bringing women into the mix and attending more rigorously to the methodological norms of scientific inquiry could rectify women's omission from the criminological canon. Feminist empiricism is very much reflected in the attempts to reformulate the mainstream theories of crime to include women. It is also reflected in the empirical research conducted to test the chivalry hypothesis and women's liberation thesis.

Yet, given the difficulties encountered in the efforts to respond to the generalizability and gender-ratio problems — in particular, the tendency to take men as the standard or measuring rod — many feminist criminologists saw the need to "bracket" these issues for the time being in order to understand better the social worlds of women and girls (Daly and Chesney-Lind 1988: 121). Maureen Cain (1990) took this suggestion further. She noted that while feminist criminologists needed to understand women's experiences, existing criminological theory offered no tools for doing this. Therefore, feminists needed to transgress the traditional boundaries of criminology, to start from outside the confines of criminological discourse. In carrying out this project, feminist criminologists drew inspiration from the violence against women movement.

## Transgressing Criminology:
## The Issue of Male Violence against Women

At the same time as feminists were fashioning their critiques of criminology, the women's movement in Canada and other Western countries was breaking the silence around the issue of male violence against women. This violence was understood as a manifestation of patriarchy — the systemic and individual power that men exercise over women (Brownmiller 1975; Kelly 1988).

As a political movement united around improving the condition and quality of women's lives, feminism in the 1970s took as one of its key issues the provision of support to women who had been victimized by violence. One of the first books ever published on the subject of domestic violence was Erin Pizzey's (1974) *Scream Quietly or the Neighbours Will Hear You.* Pizzey is also credited for opening, in England in 1971, one of the first refuges for battered women and their children. Rape crisis centres and shelters for abused women also began to appear in Canada in the 1970s. With their establishment came the recognition that male violence against women was a widespread and pervasive phenomenon.

In the early 1980s the Canadian Advisory Council on the Status of Women (cacsw) estimated that one in every five Canadian women will be sexually assaulted at some point in her life, and one in every seventeen will be a victim of forced sexual intercourse. In 1981 cacsw released a report, *Wife Battering in Canada: The Vicious Circle.* Linda MacLeod, author of the report, noted, "Women are kicked, punched, beaten, burned, threatened, knifed and shot, not by strangers who break into their houses or who accost them on dark streets, but by husbands and lovers they've spent many years with — years with good times as well as bad" (MacLeod 1980: 6). She estimated that, every year, one in ten Canadian women who is married or in a relationship with a live-in partner is battered.

More recently, in 1993 Statistics Canada released the findings of the Violence Against Women (vaw) Survey. The first national survey of its kind anywhere in the world, the vaw Survey included responses from 12,300 women (see Johnson 1996). Using definitions of physical and sexual assault consistent with the Canadian Criminal Code, the survey found that one-half (51 percent) of Canadian women had experienced at least one incident of physical or sexual violence since the age of sixteen. The survey also confirmed the results of other research in finding that women face the greatest risk of violence from men they know. "Almost half (45%) of all women experienced violence by men known to them (dates, boyfriends, marital partners, friends, family, neighbours, etc.), while 23% of women experienced violence by a stranger (17% reported violence by both strangers and known men)" (Statistics Canada 1993: 2). The vaw Survey also found that 29 percent of ever-married women had been assaulted by a spouse.

A pivotal moment in the violence against women movement occurred on December 6, 1989, when a man entered a classroom at the École Polytechnique in Montreal, separated the men from the women students, proclaimed, "You're all a bunch of feminists," and proceeded to gun them down. He killed fourteen women and wounded thirteen others that day. The gunman's suicide letter explicitly identified his action as politically motivated: he blamed "feminists" for the major disappointments in his life. Police also found a hit list containing the names of prominent women. The "Montreal Massacre" served in a most profound way to reinforce what women's groups across the country had been arguing for two decades: that violence against women is a serious social problem that takes many forms, including sexual harassment in the workplace, date rape, violent sexual assaults, and wife abuse.

The violence against women movement had a number of implications for the work of feminist criminologists. First, the movement allowed feminists to break away from the confines of mainstream criminology, which had been complicit in the social silencing around male violence against women. Official statistics suggested that crimes like rape were relatively infrequent in their occurrence. Victim surveys — which asked respondents whether they had been victimized by crime — indicated that the group most at risk of victimization was young males, not women. Most mainstream criminologists took these data sources at face value. They seldom questioned whether (and why) acts like rape might be underreported, undercharged, or underprosecuted, or the extent to which victim surveys had been constructed in ways that excluded the behaviours that women feared most. When criminologists did turn their attention to crimes like rape, the focus was on the small group of men who had been convicted and incarcerated for the offence, and these men were typically understood as an abnormal and pathological group. Much of traditional criminology also tended to mirror widely held cultural myths and misconceptions about male violence against women (such as women "ask for it" by their dress or their behaviour; see Morris 1987; Busby 2014). In his "classic" study of forcible rape, for example, Menachem Amir (1967, 1971) introduced "victim precipitation." This concept states that some women are "rape prone" (because of their "bad" reputation) and others invite rape by their "negligent and reckless" behaviour (by going to bars or hitchhiking) or their failure to react strongly enough to sexual overtures. Amir's work blamed the victim for the violence she encounters. In these terms, the issue of male violence against women pointed to significant knowledge gaps in mainstream criminology and encouraged a host of studies by feminist criminologists intent on rectifying this omission (see Dobash and Dobash 1979; Klein 1982; Stanko 1985; Gunn and Minch 1988).

Second, the violence against women movement brought to the fore the issue of engaging with the state to address the issue — especially in light of law's role historically in condoning the violence, for example, by granting husbands the right to consortium (which legally obligated wives to provide sexual services to their husbands such that there was no such thing as, let alone a crime of, rape in marriage) and the right to chastise their wives (which meant that husbands had the authority to use force in order to ensure that wives fulfilled their marital obligations) (Dobash and Dobash 1979; Edwards 1985; Backhouse 2002). While some feminist criminologists joined with other women's advocates and academics in lobbying the state to reform laws relating to sexual assault and domestic violence, others engaged in critical treatises on the wisdom of engaging the criminal justice system to promote feminist concerns (see Snider 1985, 1991, 1994; Smart 1989; Lös 1990; Faith and Currie 1993; Comack 1993a; Martin and Mosher 1995).

Finally, in pointing to the widespread and pervasive nature of male violence against women, the movement raised the issue of the impact that violence has on women who come into conflict with the law. Several quantitative studies in the 1990s began to expose the extent of abuse experienced by women caught up in the criminal justice system. In interviewing women serving federal sentences, Margaret Shaw and her colleagues (1991) found that 68 percent had been physically abused as children or as adults, and 53 percent were sexually abused at some point in their lives. Among Aboriginal women, the figures were considerably higher: 90 percent said that they had been physically abused, and 61 percent reported sexual abuse (Shaw et al. 1991: vii, 31). Another study of women in a provincial jail (Comack 1993a) found that 78 percent of the women admitted over a six-year period reported histories of physical and sexual abuse. To address this issue of the relation between victimization and criminalization, several feminist criminologists adopted the position known as "standpoint feminism" (Harding 1990).

## Standpoint Feminism: Women in Trouble

Influenced by Cain's call to transgress the boundaries of criminology and discover more about the lives of the women who were coming into conflict with the law, standpoint feminists began to dig deeper into the lives of women who came into conflict with the law. As Naffine (1997: 46) notes, while standpoint feminism assumed a number of forms — ranging from the assertion that women are the "experts" of their own lives to the proposal that an adequate social science must be capable of grasping the forms of oppression that women experience — the overall intention was "to place women as knowers at the centre of inquiry in order to produce better understandings of women and the world." Central to much of this research were links between women's victimization and their criminal involvement.

In the United States, Mary Gilfus (1992) conducted life history interviews with twenty incarcerated women to understand their entry into street crime. Most of these women had grown up with violence; thirteen of them reported childhood sexual abuse, and fifteen had experienced "severe childhood abuse" (Gilfus 1992: 70). Among the women Gilfus interviewed were eight African-Americans. While there were no race-based differences in reported abuse, the African-American women were more likely than their white counterparts to grow up in economically marginalized families. Violence, loss, and neglect were prevalent themes in their narratives about their childhoods. Violence was also a common feature of their relationships with men: sixteen of the twenty women had lived with violent men. Repeated victimization experiences, drug addiction, involvement in the sex trade, relationships with men involved in street crime, and the demands of mothering: these themes marked the women's transitions from childhood to adulthood.

Beth Richie's (1996) study focused on African-American battered women in prison. Richie (1996: 4) developed a theory of "gender entrapment" to explain the "contradictions and complications of the lives of the African-American battered women who commit crimes." According to her, gender entrapment involves understanding the connections between violence against women in their intimate relationships, culturally constructed gender-identity development, and women's participation in illegal activities. In these terms, battered Black women were "trapped" in criminal activity in the same way that they were trapped in abusive relationships.

Working in Canada, Ellen Adelberg and Claudia Currie (1987a, 1993) reported on the lives of seven women convicted of indictable offences and sentenced to federal terms of imprisonment. Regularly occurring themes in these women's lives included "poverty, child and wife battering, sexual assault, and women's conditioning to accept positions of submissiveness and dependency upon men," which led Adelberg and Currie to conclude: "The problems suffered by women offenders are similar to the problems suffered by many women in our society, only perhaps more acutely" (Adelberg and Currie 1987b: 68, 98).

My own work, *Women in Trouble* (Comack 1996), was built around the stories of twenty-four incarcerated women. The women's stories revealed complex connections between a woman's law violations and her history of abuse. Sometimes the connections are direct, as in the case of women sent to prison for resisting their abusers. Janice, for instance, was serving a sentence for manslaughter. She talked about how the offence occurred:

*I was at a party, and this guy, older guy, came, came on to me. He tried telling me, "Why don't you go to bed with me. I'm getting some money, you know." And I said, "No." And then he started hitting me. And then he raped me. And then [pause] I lost it. Like, I just, I went, I got very angry and I snapped. And I started hitting him. I threw a coffee table on top of his head and then I stabbed him.* (Cited in Comack 1996: 96)

Sometimes a woman's law violations are located in the context of her struggle to cope with the abuse and its effects. Merideth, for example, had a long history of abuse, beginning with her father sexually assaulting her as a young child, and extending to several violent relationships with the men in her life. She was imprisoned for bouncing cheques — she said she was writing the cheques to purchase *"new things to keep her mind off the abuse."*

*I've never had any kind of conflict with the law. [long pause] When I started dealing with all these different things, then I started having problems. And then I took it out in the form of fraud.* (Cited in Comack 1996: 86)

Sometimes the connections are even more entangled, as in the case of women who end up on the street, where abuse and law violation become enmeshed in their ongoing, everyday struggle to survive. Another incarcerated woman, Brenda, described her life on the street:

*Street life is a, it's a power game, you know? Street life? You have to show you're tough. You have to beat up this broad or you have to shank this person, or, you know, you're always carrying guns, you always have blow on you, you always have drugs on you, and you're always working the streets with the pimps and the bikers, you know? That, that alone, you know, it has so much fucking abuse, it has more abuse than what you were brought up with!... I find living on the street I went through more abuse than I did at home.* (Cited in Comack 1996: 105–6)

This kind of work subsequently became known as "pathways research" — a term that has been applied to a variety of different studies, all of them sharing the effort to better understand the lives of women and girls and the particular features that helped lead to their criminal activity (see, for example, Chesney-Lind and Rodriguez 1983; Miller 1986; Arnold 1995; Heimer 1995; and Chesney-Lind and Shelden 1998; DeHart 2008). In considering this research, Kathleen Daly (1992, 1998) suggests that there is a feminist composite or "leading scenario" of women's lawbreaking:

Whether they were pushed out or ran away from abusive homes, or became part of a deviant milieu, young women began to engage in petty hustles or prostitution. Life on the streets leads to drug use and addiction, which in turn leads to more frequent lawbreaking to support their drug habit. Meanwhile, young women drop out of school because of pregnancy, boredom or disinterest in school, or both. Their paid employment record is negligible because they lack interest to work in low-paid or unskilled jobs. Having a child may facilitate entry into adult women's networks and allow a woman to support herself in part by state aid. A woman may continue lawbreaking as a result of relationships with men who may also be involved in crime. Women are on a revolving criminal justice door, moving between incarceration and time on the streets. (Daly 1998: 136)

Daly maintains that although this leading scenario draws attention to the gendered contexts that bring girls to the streets, and to the gendered conditions of their survival once they get there, questions continue to linger. In particular, "What lies in the 'black box' between one's experiences of victimization as a child and criminal activities as an adult? Is there something more than economic survival which propels or maintains women in a criminalized status?" (Daly 1998: 136–37). Drawing on pre-sentence investigation reports dealing with the cases of forty women convicted in a New Haven felony court between 1981 and 1986, Daly maps out five different categories: street women, harmed and harming women, battered women, drug-connected women, and a final category that she labels "other women." Arguing for a more multidimensional approach to why women get caught up in crime, she proposes three other routes — in addition to the leading scenario of the street woman — that lead women to felony court: 1) abuse or neglect suffered as a child, an "out of control" or violent nature; 2) being (or having been) in a relationship with a violent man; and 3) being around boyfriends, mates, or family members who use or sell drugs, or wanting more money for a more economically secure and conventional life (p. 148).

Overall, these efforts to draw out the connections between women's victimization experiences and their lawbreaking activities had the benefit of locating law violations by women in a broader social context characterized by inequalities of class, race, and gender.

## Intersectionality

While gender was the starting point for analyzing criminalized women's lives, it soon became apparent to feminist criminologists that they needed to somehow capture the multiple, fluid, and complex nature of women's identities and their social relations. Much of the impetus for this recognition came from the critiques offered by women of colour and Indigenous women of the tendency for white feminists to theorize "Woman" as a unitary and homogeneous group. As Marcia Rice (1990: 57) noted, while feminist criminologists had succeeded in challenging stereotypical representations of female offenders, Black women and women from developing countries were "noticeably absent in this discourse," and when attempts were made to incorporate Black women's experiences into feminist writings there were few attempts "to develop perspectives which take into account race, gender and class simultaneously." As Mohawk scholar Patricia Monture-Angus (1995: 177–78) tells us, "It is very difficult for me to separate what happens to me because of my gender and what happens to me because of my race and culture. My world is not experienced in a linear and compartmentalized way. I experience the world simultaneously as Mohawk and as woman.... To artificially separate my gender from my race and culture forces me to deny the way I experience the world."

In response to this critique, feminist criminologists embraced "intersectionality," a concept first highlighted by Kimberlé Crenshaw (1989) to theorize the multiple and complex social relations and the diversity of subject positions involved. Crenshaw argues that the experience of oppression is not singular or fixed but derives from the relationship between interlocking systems of power. With regard to the oppression of Black women, Crenshaw explains, "Because the intersectional experience is greater than the sum of racism and sexism, any analysis that does not take intersectionality into account cannot sufficiently address the particular manner in which Black women are subordinated" (1989: 140). Adopting the notion of intersectionality, therefore, means that rather than viewing class, race, and gender as additives (that is, race + class + gender), we need to think about these concepts — and the relations and identities they represent — as simultaneous forces (that is, race x class x gender) (Brewer 1997).

In contrast to the women's liberation thesis, which argued that women's involvement in crime was a consequence of their "emancipation," feminist criminologists adopted an intersectionality approach to connect women's involvement in crime to poverty. In recent decades, poverty has increasingly taken on a "female face" — especially in terms of the number of single-parent families headed by women (Gavigan 1999; Little 2003; Chunn and Gavigan here). As more and more women are confronted with the task of making ends meet under dire circumstances, the link between poverty and women's lawbreaking has become more obvious. But so too has the move by the state to criminalize those who must rely on social assistance to get by.

Using an intersectionality approach, Kiran Mirchandani and Wendy Chan (2007) document the move in British Columbia and Ontario to criminalize welfare recipients through the pursuit of "fraudulent" claimants. In the process, they argue that this "criminalization of poverty" is also racialized and gendered in that women of colour have borne the brunt of this attack.

A focus on the intersections of gender, race, and class also helped to explain some forms of prostitution or sex trade work (Brock 1998; Phoenix 1999). According to Holly Johnson and Karen Rodgers (1993: 101), women's involvement in prostitution is a reflection of their subordinate social and economic position in society: "Prostitution thrives in a society which values women more for their sexuality than for their skilled labour, and which puts women in a class of commodity to be bought and sold. Research has shown one of the major causes of prostitution to be the economic plight of women, particularly young, poorly educated women who have limited *legitimate* employment records." Maya Seshia's (2005) research on street sexual exploitation in Winnipeg revealed that poverty and homelessness, colonialism and the legacy of residential schools, and gender discrimination and generational sexual exploitation all combined to lead women and transgenders to become involved in the sex trade.

In learning more about the lives of women and the "miles of problems" (Comack 1996: 134) that brought them into conflict with the law — problems with drugs and alcohol use, histories of violence and abuse, lack of education and job skills, and struggles to provide and care for their children — feminist criminologists took pains to distance their work from formulations that located the source of women's problems in individual pathologies or personality disturbances. Instead, the intersecting structural inequalities in society — of gender, race, and class — that contour and constrain the lives of women provided the backdrop for understanding women's involvement in crime. As British criminologist Pat Carlen (1988: 14) noted, "Women set about making their lives within conditions that have certainly not been of their own choosing."

## Blurred Boundaries:
## Challenging the Victim/Offender Dualism

Efforts to draw connections between law violations and women's histories of abuse led to a blurring of the boundaries between "offender" and "victim" and raised questions about the legal logic of individual culpability and law's strict adherence to the victim/offender dualism in the processing of cases (for not only women, but also poor, racialized men). Blurring the boundaries between offender and victim also had a decided influence on advocacy work conducted on behalf of imprisoned women. For instance, *Creating Choices*, the 1990 report of the Canadian Task Force on Federally Sentenced Women, proposed a new prison regime for women that would incorporate feminist principles and attend to women's needs (see TFFSW 1990; Shaw 1993; Hannah-Moffat and Shaw 2000a; Hayman 2006). The near-complete absence of counselling services and other resources designed to assist women in overcoming victimization experiences (see Kendall 1993) figured prominently in the Task Force's recommendations.

As Laureen Snider (2003: 364; chapter 10 here) notes, feminist criminologists at that time succeeded in reconstituting the female prisoner as the "woman in trouble." Less violent and less dangerous than her male counterpart, she needed help, not punishment. When women did engage in violence, it was understood as a self-defensive reaction typically committed in a domestic context (Browne 1987; Jones 1994; Dobash and Dobash 1992; Johnson and Rodgers 1993). Heidensohn (1994) considers this feminist work to be a positive contribution. In comparing her research in the 1960s and 1990s, she argues that the later female prisoners were better equipped to share their standpoints. In the past, not only did women "not easily find voices, there were only limited discourses in which they could express themselves and few places where such expressions could be made" (p. 31). According to Heidensohn, feminist research provided these women "with a particular language, a way of expressing themselves" (p. 32).

Nevertheless, while the concept of blurred boundaries and the construct of the woman in trouble were important feminist contributions to criminology, they were to later have particular ramifications for the ability of feminist criminologists to counter competing knowledge claims — ones founded on representations of women not as victims but as violent and dangerous.

## Postmodern Feminism: Criminalized Women

In addition to feminist empiricism and standpoint feminism, a third position has informed the work of feminist criminologists over the last decade or so. "Postmodern feminism" emerged largely as a critique of the other two positions. In particular, postmodern feminists reject the claims to "truth" proposed by scientific objectivity. "Reality," they say, is not self-evident, something that can simply be revealed through the application of the scientific method. While the postmodern critique of empiricism does not negate the possibility of doing empirical research — that is, of engaging with women, interviewing them, documenting their oral histories (Smart

1990: 78–79) — postmodernists are sceptical of attempts to challenge male-centred approaches by counterposing them with a more accurate or correct version of women's lives. Given the differences within female perspectives and identities, they question whether such diversity can be formulated or expressed in a single account or standpoint of women.

Feminist empiricism and standpoint feminism are still very much firmly grounded on a modernist terrain. Postmodern feminism, however, "starts in a different place and proceeds in other directions" (Smart 1995: 45). While modernist approaches are characterized by the search for truth, the certainty of progress, and the effort to frame grand narratives about the social world, postmodernism draws attention to the importance of "discourse" — "historically specific systems of meaning which form the identities of subjects and objects" (Howarth 2000: 9). Discourses are contingent and historical constructions. As David Howarth describes it, their construction involves "the exercise of power and a consequent structuring of the relations between different social agents" (p. 9). Through the method of deconstruction — which involves taking apart discourses to show how they achieve their effects — postmodernists endeavour to reveal how certain discourses (and their corresponding discursive practices or ways of acting) come to dominate in society at particular points in history.

Adopting a postmodern epistemology has led feminist criminologists to interrogate the language used to understand women's involvement in crime. Carol Smart (1989, 1995), Danielle Laberge (1991), and Karlene Faith (1993), among others, point out that crime categories (such as "crimes against the person," "crimes against property," or "public order offences") are legal constructions that represent one way of ordering or making sense of social life. In these terms, the offences for which women are deemed to be criminal are the end result of a lengthy process of detection, apprehension, accusation, judgment, and conviction; they constitute the official version of women's actions and behaviours. As well, crime categories are premised on a dualism between the criminal and the law-abiding, which reinforces the view of women involved in crime as Other and thereby misses their similarities with non-criminal women. In this respect, women who come into conflict with the law are in very many ways no different from the rest of us. They are mothers, daughters, sisters, girlfriends, and wives, and they share many of the experiences of women collectively in society. Given that crime is the outcome of interactions between individuals and the criminal justice system, Laberge (1991) proposed that we think not in terms of criminal women but of criminalized women.

Throughout the 1990s, in addition to the increasing influence of a postmodern epistemology, feminist criminologists also began to draw heavily on the ideas of the French poststructuralist theorist Michel Foucault. Much of Foucault's (1977, 1979) writing was concerned with the relation between power and knowledge. Rejecting the notion that power was a "thing" or commodity that can be owned, Foucault concentrated on the mechanisms of power that came with the development of what he called the "disciplinary society," characterized by the growth of new knowledges or discourses (such as criminology, psychiatry, and psychology) that led to new modes of surveillance of the population. For Foucault, knowledge is not objective but political; the production of knowledge has to do with power. A reciprocal relation exists between the two: power is productive of knowledge, and knowledge is productive of power. In his later work, Foucault (1978a) replaced his notion of power/knowledge with the concept of "governmentality" to address the specific "mentality" of governance — the links between forms of power and domination and the ways in which individuals conduct themselves.

Australian criminologist Kerry Carrington (1993) employed Foucault's notion of power/knowledge to explore how certain girls come to be officially defined as delinquents. Critical of feminist work depicting male power over women as direct, monolithic, coercive, and repressive, Carrington emphasized the fragmented, fluid, and dispersed nature of disciplinary power. In a similar fashion, British criminologist Anne Worrall (1990) adopted a Foucaultian approach to explore the conditions under which legal agents (judicial, welfare, and medical) claim to possess knowledge about the "offending woman" and the processes whereby such claims are translated into practices that classify, define, and so domesticate her behaviour. Taking a critical view of feminist studies of women's punishment because of their failure (among other things) to take gender seriously as an explanatory variable, Adrian Howe (1994) argued for the need to consider the gendered characteristics — for both women and men — of disciplinary procedures in advancing the project of a postmodern penal politics.

Feminist postmodernism has had a decided impact on the trajectory of feminist criminology. Not interested so much in the task of explaining *why* women come into conflict with the law, those who work in this area raise important *how* questions, such as how women and girls are constituted or defined by professional discourses, and how particular techniques of governance (in a number of different sites) work to contain, control, or exclude those who are marginalized in society. The postmodern attention to discourse has also opened the way to a questioning of the kinds of language used by criminologists and criminal justice officials. Under the tutelage of postmodernists, terms such as offenders, inmates, clients, and correctional institutions — although still widely disseminated — are no longer uncontested.

Nevertheless, at the same time as feminist criminologists were being influenced by the epistemological and theoretical shifts occurring within academia during the 1990s, shifts in the socio-political context and a series of notable events relating to the issue of women and crime were having a significant impact on the work of feminist criminologists. More specifically, as the century drew to a close, neo-liberal and neo-conservative political rationalities had begun to take hold and were readily put to work in the construction of women and girls as violent, dangerous — and downright "nasty."

## The Shifting Socio-Political Context: Neo-Liberalism and Neo-Conservatism

In the initial phases, the efforts of the women's movement to address women's inequality in society were fed by a sense of optimism. Given the expressed commitment by the Canadian state to the ideals of social citizenship (what came to be called the Keynesian welfare state) — that all citizens had a right to a basic standard of living, with the state accepting responsibility for the provision of social welfare for its citizenry — the prospects of realizing substantive change on issues like violence against women and women's treatment by the criminal justice system seemed bright. This change was made all the more possible with the entrenchment of the Canadian Charter of Rights and Freedoms in 1982, and especially the invoking of section 15 (the equality section) in 1985, which prohibited discrimination on the basis of sex. In a climate that appeared to be favourable to hearing women's issues, feminists and women's advocates organized and lobbied throughout the 1980s to bring about a number of changes (including reforms to rape legislation and the provision of resources for women in abusive relationships) and launched human rights and Charter challenges to address the unfair treatment of imprisoned women. With regard to women in prison, many observers took the government's acceptance of the *Creating Choices* report in 1990 as a sign that a sea change was underway, that substantive reform was possible.

Yet, the 1980s also saw a distinct shift in the socio-political terrain. Under the sway of globalization, the state's expressed commitment to social welfare was being eroded. In its place, neo-liberalism became the new wisdom of governing. "Neo-liberalism" is a political rationality founded on the values of individualism, freedom of choice, market dominance, and minimal state involvement in the economy. Under neo-liberalism, the ideals of social citizenship are replaced by the market-based, self-reliance, and privatizing ideals of the new order. As political scientist Janine Brodie (1995: 57) explains it:

> The rights and securities guaranteed to all citizens of the Keynesian welfare state are no longer rights, universal, or secure. The new ideal of the common good rests on market-oriented values such as self-reliance, efficiency, and competition. The new good citizen is one that recognizes the limits and liabilities of state provision and embraces her or his obligation to work longer and harder in order to become more self-reliant.

In this era of restructuring, government talk of the need for deficit reduction translated into cutbacks to social programs (McQuaig 1993), and gains that the women's movement had realized in the previous decade were now under serious attack (Brodie 1995; Bashevkin 1998; Rebick 2005).

In the criminal justice arena, these economic and political developments ushered in an extraordinary expansion in the scope and scale of penalization. Rising crime rates and a growing economic recession in the 1980s gave way to a crime-control strategy that rejected rehabilitation and correction as the goals of the criminal justice system and replaced them with a concern for "risk management": the policing and minimization of risk that offenders pose to the wider community. Under this neo-liberal responsibilization model of crime control (Hannah-Moffat 2002), criminals are to be made responsible for the choices they make: "Rather than clients in need of support, they are seen as risks that must be managed" (Garland 2001: 175).

But neo-liberalism was not the only ideology to inform criminal justice practices. Subjecting the economy to market forces and cutting back on social welfare meant that increasing numbers of people were left to fend for themselves, without the benefit of a social safety net. As well, the precariousness of middle-income families engendered a social anxiety that easily translated into fear of crime — especially of those groups and individuals left less fortunate by virtue of the economic transformations. Calls for more law and order became louder. In tandem with neo-liberalism, therefore, a "neo-conservative rationality," premised on a concern for tradition, order, hierarchy, and authority, fostered crime-control policies aimed at "getting tough" on crime. Zero-tolerance for domestic violence, "super max" prisons, parole-release restrictions, community notification laws, and boot camps for young offenders increasingly became the order of the day (Comack and Balfour 2004: 42–43).

This broader neo-liberal and neo-conservative socio-political context proved to be significant in framing how a number of events that occurred in the 1990s came to be understood. These events — and the ways in which they were being framed in the public discourse — were instrumental in assertions about women and girls that had much in common with constructions that had prevailed in earlier times.

## Violent Women and Nasty Girls

One decisive event was the Karla Homolka case. In July 1993 Karla Homolka was sentenced to twelve years in prison for her part in the deaths of two teenaged girls, Kristen French and Leslie Mahaffy. Homolka's sentence was part of a plea bargain reached with the Crown in exchange for her testimony against her husband, Paul Bernardo. The Crown had entered into this plea bargain prior to the discovery of six homemade videotapes that documented the sexual abuse and torture of the pair's victims — including Homolka's younger sister, Tammy. Bernardo was subsequently convicted of first-degree murder, kidnapping, aggravated sexual assault, forcible confinement, and offering an indignity to a dead body. He was sentenced to life imprisonment in September 1995 (McGillivray 1998: 257).

During Bernardo's trial the real challenge came in trying to explain the role of Homolka, the prosecution's key witness. As Helen Boritch (1997: 2) notes, "Among the various professionals who commented on the case, there was a general agreement that, as far as serial murderers go, there was little that was unusual or mysterious about Bernardo. We have grown used to hearing about male serial murderers." Homolka, however, was the central enigma of the drama that unfolded, transforming the trial into an international, high-profile media event.

The legal documents and media accounts of the case offered two primary readings of Homolka. The first reading constructed her as a battered wife, one of Bernardo's many victims (he had also been exposed as "the Scarborough rapist"). A girlish seventeen-year-old when she first met the twenty-three-year-old Bernardo, Homolka had entered into a relationship that progressed to a fairytale wedding (complete with horse-drawn carriage) and ended with a severe battering (complete with darkened and bruised raccoon eyes). According to this first reading, Homolka was under the control of her husband, having no agency of her own. Like other women who find themselves in abusive relationships, she was cast as a victim and diagnosed as suffering from the Battered Woman Syndrome, a psychological condition of "learned helplessness" that ostensibly prevents abused women from leaving the relationship (see Walker 1979, 1987). The representation of Homolka as a battered wife and "compliant victim" of her sexually sadistic husband (Hazelwood, Warren, and Dietz 1993) was meant to bolster her credibility as a prosecution witness and validate her plea bargain.

This first reading was met with strong resistance in the media and public discourse, leading to the second reading. Journalist Patricia Pearson (1995), for one, vigorously countered the picture of "Homolka as victim" and instead demonized her as a "competitive narcissist" willing to offer up innocent victims (including her own sister) to appease the sexual desires of her sociopathic husband. In a similar fashion, other writers offered diagnoses such as "malignant narcissism": "This personality cannot tolerate humiliation. It is capable of destroying others in the service of meeting its ego needs" (Skrapec, cited in Wood 2001: 60).

Despite their divergent viewpoints, both of these readings relied on the discourse of the "psy-professions" (psychology, psychotherapy, and psychiatry) to make sense of Homolka. Feminist criminologists offered competing knowledge claims, for instance, by pointing out that women are seldom charged with the offence of murder and, when they do kill, women are most likely to kill their male partners — or that while Homolka's middle-class background and lifestyle set her apart from the vast majority of women charged with criminal offences, her efforts to conform to the standard feminine script (dyed blond hair, fairytale wedding) put her in company with a host of other women. But these claims were seldom heard. Instead, the cry that "Women are violent, too!" grew louder, even to the point of arguing that women's violence was quantitatively and qualitatively equal to that of men's.

In a widely publicized book, *When She Was Bad: Violent Women and the Myth of Innocence*, Pearson (1997; see also Dutton 1994; Laframboise 1996) argued not only that "women are violent, too," but also that their violence can be just as nasty as men's. Following on the footsteps of the 1950s criminologist Otto Pollak, Pearson (1997: 20–21) suggested that women's violence was more masked and underhanded than men's: women kill their babies, arrange for their husbands' murders, beat up on their lovers, and commit serial murders in hospitals and boarding houses. Nevertheless, argued Pearson (1997: 61), when their crimes are discovered, women are more likely to receive lenient treatment from a chivalrous criminal justice system. In a fashion that hearkened back to other early criminologists, Pearson (1997: 210) also stated: "Female prisoners are not peace activists or nuns who were kidnapped off the street and stuck in jail. They are miscreants, intemperate, willful and rough."

Pearson drew support for her position from studies that utilize the Conflict Tactics Scale (CTS) to measure abuse in intimate relationships. Most criminologists who use this scale have found equivalent rates of violence by women and men (Straus 1979; Straus and Gelles 1986; Straus, Gelles, and Steinmetz 1980; Steinmetz 1981; Brinkerhoff and Lupri 1988; Kennedy and Dutton 1989). Despite the scale's popularity, however, it has been subject to extensive critiques (DeKeseredy and MacLean 1998; DeKeseredy and Hinch 1991; Dobash et al. 1992; Johnson 1996). Nevertheless, Pearson argued that such critiques amounted to unwarranted attacks by feminists and their supporters, who were invested in a gender dichotomy of men as evil/women as good. In this regard, unlike earlier conservative-minded criminologists, Pearson asserted that women were no different than men. While feminists were intent on gendering violence by drawing its connections to patriarchy, Pearson (1997: 232) was adamant that violence be de-gendered: violence was simply a "human, rather than gendered, phenomena." Framing the issue in neo-liberal terms, violence was a conscious choice, a means of solving problems or releasing frustration by a "responsible actor imposing her will upon the world" (p. 23).

While the Homolka case generated extensive media attention on the issue of women's violence, the spectre of the "nasty girl" was added into the mix with the killing of fourteen-year-old Reena Virk by a group of mostly teenaged girls in November 1997. Early on, in 1998, six girls were convicted of assault for their part in Virk's death. In 1999 Warren Glowaski was convicted of second-degree murder. In April 2005, after three trials, Kelly Ellard was convicted of second-degree murder.

According to the court documents, Virk was confronted by a group of girls under a bridge in Victoria, B.C., and accused of stealing one of their boyfriends. When she tried to leave she was punched and kicked, and one of the girls stubbed out a cigarette on her forehead. Glowaski testified at his trial that he and Ellard had followed Virk across the bridge and confronted her a second time. The pair kicked and stomped her until she was unconscious and then dragged her body to the water's edge, where she subsequently drowned. While Ellard admitted to being an active participant in the initial attack on Virk, she denied any involvement in the second attack. Asked in court whether the thought of seeing Reena left crumpled in the mud made her upset, Ellard replied, "*Obviously — I am not a monster*" (Armstrong 2004: A7).

Ellard's statement notwithstanding, events like the beating and murder of Reena Virk generated a series of media exposés on the "problem" of girl violence. As one CBC documentary, *Nasty Girls* (airing on March 5, 1997), put it: "In the late 1990s almost everything your mother taught you about polite society has disappeared from popular culture, and nowhere is this more apparent than in what is happening to our teenage girls. Welcome to the age of the nasty girls!" (cited in Barron 2000: 81). Girls, so we were told, were not "sugar and spice" after all — but "often violent and ruthless monsters" (McGovern 1998: 24).

These depictions of women and girls as violent, dangerous, and downright nasty were also playing out in relation to what was then the only federal prison for women in Canada — the P4W.

## Lombroso Revisited? Framing the P4W Incident

In February 1995 CBC-TV's *Fifth Estate* aired a video of an all-male Institutional Emergency Response Team (IERT) entering the solitary confinement unit at the Prison for Women (P4W) in Kingston, Ontario, and proceeding to extract women from their cells, one by one. The video showed the women's clothing being removed (in some cases the men forcibly cut it off) and the women being shackled and taken to the shower room, where they were subjected to body cavity searches. The program reported that after the segregation cells were completely emptied (including beds and mattresses), the women were placed back in the cells with only security blankets for clothing.

Some of the women were kept in segregation for up to eight months afterward. They were given no hygiene products, no daily exercise, no writing materials, and no contact with family. Their blankets were not cleaned for at least a month. As part of the program, reporter Ann Rauhala also interviewed several of the women, who recounted their feelings of violation and degradation and drew similarities to their past experiences of being raped and sexually victimized.

When the report of Justice Louise Arbour (1996) into the events of April 1994 was released two years later, the CBC's news program *The National* re-televised segments of the program, including the IERT video. Emails posted on *The National's* discussion site in response to the segments revealed pieces of the public discourse that prevailed around women prisoners:

> While I can see how some of the pictures shown could be disturbing to some viewers, I am more disturbed at your handling of the story.... These women were not ordinary citizens.... They are in a correctional facility because they are CONVICTED FELONS, not Sunday School Teachers.

Myself, I would see nothing wrong with a guard beating these inmates every once in a while! After all they lost their rights when they committed their crimes in the first place.

Don't give me the bleeding heart crap. This is what has screwed up society. These women created their own situation — let them deal with the fallout.

The women involved in this incident were the creators of their own misfortune — both in the short term and the long term.... In recent years, it seems that the courts and government have become too lenient with the likes of these women, and men for that matter. The special interest groups and the "politically correct" that are constantly fighting for the rights of prisoners only undermine the rights of law-abiding citizens.

Clearly, the neo-conservative calls to "get tough on crime" — especially in relation to women — were finding supporters in the public at large. Much like the early criminological constructions of women involved in crime, these CBC viewers rejected the depiction of the women as victims and instead saw them as Other, roundly deserving of the brutal treatment they received.

Such law and order populism was no doubt instrumental in bolstering a neo-liberal realignment by the Correctional Service of Canada when it came to implementing the *Creating Choices* recommendations (TFFSW 1990). *Creating Choices* had been silent around the issue of women's violence. According to Shaw (2000: 62), "Overall, the report portrayed women as victims of violence and abuse, more likely to injure themselves than others as a result of those experiences." The April 1994 event, however, was held out as evidence to the contrary. The CSC maintained that calling the male IERT to the women's prison had become necessary to contain "unruly women" after a fight had broken out between six of the prisoners and their guards. In 1996, in a move that marked an about-turn from the Task Force's women-centred approach and the attendant focus on addressing women's needs, CSC adopted a new scheme for managing women prisoners, the Offender Intake Assessment Scheme, designed for male prisoners. Now, women's needs — including the need to recover from experiences of victimization — were to be redefined (in neo-liberal terms) as risk factors in predicting a woman's likelihood of reoffending. That same year the CSC announced that all women classified as maximum security would not be allowed at the new regional centres (including the Aboriginal healing lodge) that had been constructed on the basis of the *Creating Choices* recommendations. Instead, the women were to be housed in maximum-security facilities located inside men's prisons. As well, CSC implemented a new mental health policy for women thought to be experiencing psychological and behavioural problems. In contrast to its initial endorsement of the *Creating Choices* report, therefore, the government was clearly moving in a different direction.

## Feminist Criminologists Respond to the Backlash

The apparent ease with which the neo-conservative and neo-liberal readings of events like the Homolka case, the Virk killing, and the P4W incident took hold in the public discourse was emblematic of the dramatic shifts in the socio-political context that were occurring in the 1990s. For the most part, these readings can be interpreted as part of a powerful backlash against feminist knowledge claims, especially the efforts by feminist criminologists to blur the boundaries between offender and victim. In what Snider (2004: 240) refers to as the "smaller meaner gaze of neo-liberalism," the sightlines were closely fixed. "'Victims' were those who suffered from crime, not those who committed it — and the higher their social class, the more traditional their sexual habits and lifestyles, and the lighter their color, the more legitimate their victim status became." Feminist criminologists would respond to this backlash on a number of fronts.

Committed to the view of criminalized women as victims in need of help rather than punishment, feminist criminologists were initially caught off guard by the Homolka case. To be sure, the woman in trouble envisioned by feminist criminologists was not a privileged young woman who engaged in sadistic sex crimes. But repeating the refrain "Homolka is an anomaly, Homolka is an anomaly" did little to prevent her from becoming the public icon for women caught up in the criminal justice system — women who are likely to be racialized, poor, and convicted of property crimes rather than of violent sex offences (see the Introduction to Part II).

With Pearson's assertions about women and violence continuing to hold sway in the popular press, feminist criminologists countered by offering up pointed critiques of her work. In her review of *When She Was Bad*, for instance, Meda Chesney-Lind (1999) took Pearson to task for her routine conflation of aggression and violence. "This is either very sloppy or very smart, since anyone familiar with the literature on aggression ... knows that when one includes verbal and indirect forms of aggression (like gossip), the gender difference largely disappears" (p. 114). Similar to those who claim merit in the women's liberation thesis, Pearson also based her argument on percentage increases in women's arrests for violence, "without any mention of the relatively small and stable proportion of violent crime accounted for by women or the fact that small base numbers make huge increases easy to achieve" (p. 115). Pearson's misuse of research findings, which Chesney-Lind saw as rampant throughout the book, included citing a study that found women's prison infractions to be higher than men's to support her claim that women in prison are "miscreants, intemperate, willful and rough" (Pearson 1997: 210). What Pearson neglected to mention was that these women were being charged with extremely trivial forms of misconduct, such as having "excessive artwork" on the walls of their cells (that is, too many family photos on display). Chesney-Lind concluded her review by acknowledging that feminist criminologists must theorize women's aggression and women's violence, but that "we need a nuanced, sophisticated, and data driven treatment — and most importantly — one that begins by placing women's aggression and violence in its social context of patriarchy" (p. 118).

Jennifer Kilty and Sylvie Frigon (2006) offer such a nuanced account in their analysis of the Homolka case. Reinterpreting the two readings of Homolka — battered wife versus competitive narcissist — as depictions of her as either "in danger" or "dangerous," they argue that these constructions are interrelated rather than mutually exclusive. While emphasizing that the abuse Homolka endured at the hands of Bernardo does not excuse her criminality, they maintain that it did constrain her choices. As such, she was *both* a "woman in danger" *and* a "dangerous woman." Kilty and Frigon (2006: 58) argue, therefore, "Rather than constructing these two concepts as dialectically opposed one must understand them as being interdependent, or more accurately, as along a continuum."

Other feminist criminologists intent on understanding the interconnections between women's experiences of violence and their own use of violence have adopted this shift away from dualistic (victim/offender) thinking and toward the use of a continuum metaphor. Introduced by Karlene Faith (1993) in her book *Unruly Women*, the "victimization-criminalization continuum" is used to signify the myriad of ways in which women's experiences of victimization — including not only violence but also social and economic marginalization — constrain or narrow their social supports and available options and leave them susceptible to criminalization. The continuum, therefore, draws on insights from intersectionality theory to showcase how systemic factors (relating to patriarchy, poverty, and colonialism) contribute to women's vulnerability to victimization, thereby restricting their agency or capacity to make choices. Unlike the more linear imagery of the pathways approach, Elspeth Kaiser-Derrick (2012: 63) suggests that the continuum can be envisioned as a web, "with many incursions and redirections from external forces (broad, structural issues like poverty and discrimination, as well as events within women's lives often stemming from those structural issues such as relationship dissolution or the removal of children by the state)."

Gillian Balfour (2008) adopts the victimization-criminalization continuum to explore the relationship between the inordinate amounts of violence experienced by Aboriginal women and the increase in their coercive punishment by the criminal justice system. Balfour argues that — despite the introduction in 1996 of sentencing reforms to encourage alternatives to incarceration (specifically, the provision for conditional sentences to be served in the community and the addition of section 718.2[e] to the Criminal Code, which encourages judges to consider alternatives to imprisonment for Aboriginal people) — women's narratives of violence and social isolation have been excluded in the practice of Canadian sentencing law, leading to spiralling rates of imprisonment for Aboriginal women. Kaiser-Derrick (2012) also utilizes the victimization-criminalization continuum to inform her analysis of cases involving Aboriginal women in light of the *Gladue* (1999) and *Ipeelee* (2012) decisions of the Supreme Court of Canada relating to how judges are to undertake a sentencing analysis when Aboriginal defendants come before the court. Focusing on cases for which conditional sentences are or were previously an available sanction, Kaiser-Derrick found that judges translate discourses about victimization and criminalization into a judicial approach that frames sentences for Aboriginal women as "healing oriented"; in essence, Aboriginal women's victimization experiences are interpreted by the courts as precipitating a need for treatment in prison (see also Williams 2009).

Feminist criminologists also responded to the backlash against feminist knowledge claims by undertaking research to evaluate the claim that women are "men's equals" in violence. To explore qualitative differences in men's and women's violence, for example, Vanessa Chopyk, Linda Wood, and I drew a random sample of 1,002 cases from police incident reports involving men and women charged with violent crime in the city of Winnipeg over a five-year period at the beginning of the 1990s. While studies that utilize the Conflict Tactics Scale have concluded that a sexual symmetry exists in intimate violence (men are as likely as women to be victims of abuse, and women are as likely as men to be perpetrators of both minor and serious acts of violence), we found a different picture in the police incident reports

(Comack, Chopyk, and Wood 2000, 2002). First, the violence tactics used by men and women differed in their seriousness. Men were more likely to use their physical strength or force against their female partners, while women were more likely to resort to throwing objects (such as TV remote controls) during the course of a violent event. Second, female partners of men accused of violence used violence themselves in only 23 percent of the cases, while male partners of women accused of violence used violence in 65 percent of the cases. This suggests that the violence that occurs between intimate partners is not "mutual combat." Third, almost one-half (48 percent) of the women accused — as opposed to only 7 percent of the men accused — in partner events were injured during the course of the event. Finally, in incidents involving partners, it was the accused woman who called the police in 35 percent of the cases involving a female accused (compared with only 7 percent in those involving a male accused). Interpreting calls to the police as "help-seeking behaviour" on the part of someone in trouble suggests that in more than one-third of the cases involving a woman accused, she was the one who perceived the need for help. Nevertheless, the woman ended up being charged with a criminal offence.

These findings are supported by data from the General Social Survey conducted by Statistics Canada, which show the scope and severity of spousal violence to be more severe for women than for men. Female victims of spousal violence were more than twice as likely to be injured as were male victims (42 percent versus 18 percent). Women were almost seven times more likely to fear for their lives (33 percent versus 5 percent), and almost three times as likely to be the targets of more than ten violent episodes (20 percent versus 7 percent) (Mahony 2011: 10). In countering the arguments made by writers like Pearson, then, the feminist agenda placed the issue of women's violence and aggression in a prominent position (see also Renzetti 1998, 1999; Marleau 1999; Chan 2001; Mann 2003; Morrisey 2003; Comack and Balfour 2004).

In the wake of the moral panic generated by media reports of a violent crime wave by girls (Schissel 1997, 2001), feminists also set out to counter the claim that girls were becoming "gun-toting robbers" (Pate 1999: 42; see also Artz 1998; Barron 2000; Chesney-Lind 2001; Bell 2002; Burman, Batchelor, and Brown 2003; Alder and Worrall 2003). In her analysis of official statistics on youth crime, Heather Schramm (1998) warned that any arguments about a dramatic increase in the rate of girls' offending should be interpreted with caution. The theme here was similar to the critique of the women's liberation thesis: because only a small number of girls are charged with violent offences, changes in the rates of girls' violent crime inflate drastically when expressed as a percentage. Marge Reitsma-Street (1999) pointed out that the majority of the increase in the rate of girls' violent crime could be accounted for by an increase in the charges of common or level-one assault (for example, for pushing, slapping, and threatening). Anthony Doob and Jane Sprott (1998: 185) concluded that the rising rate of girls (and youths in general) being charged with violent crimes did not indicate an increase in the nastiness of girls; rather, the change "relates more to the response of adult criminal justice officials to crime than it does to the behaviour of young offenders."

As well, feminist criminologists drew on postmodern insights to counter the legal and media representations of the Virk killing. Specifically, by framing the murder in terms of the "empty concept" of "girl violence" (Kadi, cited in Batacharya 2004: 77), dominant approaches rarely addressed the issues of "racism, sexism, pressures of assimilation, and the social construction of Reena Virk as an outcast," and "when they were addressed, it was always in the language of appearance" (Jiwani 2002: 441). In Yasmin Jiwani's view, the erasure of race/racism in judicial decision-making and in the media coverage of the case was "symbolic of the denial of racism as a systemic phenomenon in Canada" (p. 42; see also Batacharya 2004; Jiwani 2006).

Feminist criminologists also engaged in extensive critiques of the use of male-centred risk scales for managing women prisoners (Stanko 1997; Hannah-Moffat and Shaw 2001; Chan and Rigakos 2002). They provided critical commentaries on the apparent transformation of the original feminist vision of *Creating Choices* to fit neo-liberal and neo-conservative correctional agendas (Hannah-Moffat and Shaw 2000a), and they reflected on the lessons to be learned from efforts to refashion prison regimes (Hannah-Moffat 2002; Hayman 2006). Countering the tendency of the legal establishment and media to revert to individualized and pathologized renderings of women prisoners — an approach placing the spotlight on the personal failings of these women while keeping the political and economic factors that drive prison expansion in the shadows — some feminist criminologists began the work of connecting "the individual and personal with macroeconomic and geopolitical analyses" in the context of the global expansion of women's imprisonment (Sudbury 2005b: xvi).

## The Power and the Challenge

From invisibility and the Othering of women to the emergence of feminist criminology in the 1970s and the particular pathways that feminist criminologists have followed as they put women at the centre of their knowledge production: over the past fifty years we have slowly moved from Heidensohn's "lonely uncharted seas" to reach the point where it has become increasingly difficult to keep abreast of the research and writing on women and crime. In their own ways, the different epistemological positions of feminist empiricism, standpoint feminism, and postmodern feminism have enabled an incredible growth in knowledge about women and crime. Because of this work, we now know so much more about the lives of criminalized women — who they are, the social contexts in which they move, and the processes by which they are regulated and controlled — far more than we would have thought possible some five short decades ago. Still, feminist criminology has not developed in a vacuum. In the past fifty years feminist criminologists have drawn energy and insights from work in other arenas — particularly the violence against women movement — as well as responding to events and developments occurring within the ever-changing socio-political climate.

As Snider (2003; see also chapter 10 here) notes, it is one thing for feminists to produce particular discourses about women and crime, and it is quite another to have those discourses heard.

> Knowledge claims and expertise always work to the advantage of some and the detriment of others, strengthening some parties and interests while weakening others. Those with power to set institutional agendas, with superior economic, political, social and moral capital, are therefore able to reinforce and promote certain sets of knowledges while ignoring, ridiculing or attacking others. (Snider 2003: 355)

But the feminist engagement with criminology is by no means complete. As the chapters in this book demonstrate, it is very much a vibrant, continuing process. And in these neo-liberal times, meeting the challenge of containing — and especially countering — dominant understandings about women and crime is all the more necessary.

# Part II

# Making Connections:
# Class/Race/Gender Intersections

# Part II Introduction

*Elizabeth Comack*

In the days leading up to July 5, 2005, the Canadian media's attention was squarely fixed on the doors of the Joliette Institution in Quebec, awaiting the release of "Canada's most notorious female offender."[1] Karla Homolka had reached the end of the twelve-year sentence that she had received for her part in the deaths of Kristen French and Leslie Mahaffy, two young women who had been abducted, sexually assaulted, and killed by Homolka and her partner, Paul Bernardo.

Although Homolka may be the most notorious, she is by no means the most representative of the women who come into conflict with the law. Indeed, Homolka is very much an anomaly or exception in terms of women most likely to be criminalized. Women are most often charged with property offences such as theft and fraud rather than with serious violent crimes such as murder and sexual assault. When women are charged with a violent offence, it is most likely to be for level one or common assault. In addition, what distinguishes Karla Homolka from most criminalized women is her class position. Homolka grew up in a suburban middle-class home, while the majority of women who find themselves in conflict with the law come from marginalized economic situations. Race is another factor: Homolka's "whiteness" contrasts with the overrepresentation of Aboriginal women and women of colour in Canada's prisons.

Clearly, to place all the media attention on Canada's "most notorious female offender" into its proper context, we need a better appreciation of the nature and extent of women's involvement in crime and the ways in which class/race/gender intersect in the lives of criminalized women.

## The Nature and Extent of Women's Involvement in Crime
*A Female Crime Wave — or Penal Populism?*

Women have historically comprised a relatively small percentage of adults charged with Criminal Code offences in Canada. In 2011, for example, 21 percent of adults charged with Criminal Code offences were women (Brennan 2012: 20). This percentage, however, is larger than it was in previous decades. The total number of Criminal Code charges against women increased from just under 24,000 in 1970 to just over 95,000 in 1991, representing 8 percent and 16 percent, respectively, of adults charged with

Criminal Code offences (Johnson and Rogers 1993). Stated differently, there was an overall increase of 297 percent in women charged with Criminal Code offences between 1970 and 1991.

This large increase might suggest that a female crime wave has occurred, fuelling media and public concerns that women are becoming more violent and dangerous, more like their male counterparts. However, media reports of a so-called female crime wave typically rely on comparing percentage increases in Criminal Code charges laid against women and men, but "because of the much lower base number of charges against women for any given offence, percentage increases consistently give the false impression of much greater increases in the number of women offenders relative to men" (Johnson and Rodgers 1993: 104). For instance, Johnson and Rodgers point out that the total overall increase of 297 percent of women charged between 1970 and 1991 represents a difference in actual numbers of about 71,000. The corresponding change for men was 90 percent, representing an additional 244,700 men charged over the same period.

In more recent years, women as a percentage of all adults charged with Criminal Code offences has increased from 16 percent in 1991 to 21 percent in 2011. Nevertheless, the number of women charged actually declined over this period — from 95,057 in 1991 to 86,898 in 2011 (a 9 percent decrease). The percentage of women charged went up because the number of charges against men declined by an even greater margin; there were 517,924 men charged in 1991 and 326,902 in 2011 (a 37 percent decrease) (Johnson and Rogers 1993: 99; Brennan 2012: 20).

Crime rates provide a better sense of what is happening because they account for changes in population. Table 1 provides the charge rates for men and women in three time periods, 1968, 1996, and 2000. The patterns for women and men are generally the same. The overall charge rate for women and men increased between 1968 and 1996, and then declined between 1996 and 2000. The bulk of the increase from 1968 to 1996 for

*Table 1: Rates of Adults Charged by Sex per 100,000 Population for Selected Criminal Code Offences, Canada, 1968, 1996, 2000*

|                   | 1968 | | 1996 | | 2000 | |
|-------------------|--------|--------|--------|--------|--------|--------|
|                   | Men | Women | Men | Women | Men | Women |
| Violent Offences  | 270.5 | 15.0 | 699.3 | 97.1 | 652.7 | 112.7 |
| Property Crimes   | 639.7 | 79.2 | 870.3 | 245.3 | 636.1 | 176.7 |
| Criminal Code     | 1443.4 | 152.0 | 2334.6 | 479.2 | 2059.7 | 432.4 |

Source: Adapted from Hartnagel (2000: 104; 2004: 130)

women was accounted for by property-related offences. Women's charge rate for property-related offences then declined from 1996 to 2000, while the charge rate for violent offences increased during the same period. Men's charge rate for both property offences and violent offences decreased from 1996 to 2000. Nevertheless, the rates for women are consistently far below those for men.

More recent data suggest that the rate of men charged with a criminal offence has continued to decline, while the rate for women has shown an increase. Shannon Brennan (2012: 20) notes that this pattern is especially evident for violent crime: "Since 1991, the rate of males charged with violent crime has declined 32%, while the rate for females has increased 34%." While Brennan cautions, "Males still accounted for more than 4 in 5 people accused of violent crime in 2011," we do need to make sense of this apparent increase in women's involvement in violent crime.

Certainly, as we will examine in the proceeding chapters, media portrayals of increasing violence by women and girls have been crafted without any attention paid to the context of these offences and the life histories of the women and girls who commit them — which only makes it easier for onlookers to assume that women and girls have simply become more violent. A key consideration, on the contrary, is the question of how the lack of access to justice has resulted in higher rates of criminalization of women for serious offences. "Penal populism" — what John Pratt (2007: 3) describes as "the pursuit of a set of penal policies to win votes rather than to reduce crime or promote justice" — characterizes provincial courts that increasingly deny people bail for reasons related to unemployment, homelessness, untreated mental illness, substance abuse problems, and lack of community support. In their national study of specialized courts Kelly Hannah-Moffat and Paula Maurutto (2012: 206) found: "Bail is used instrumentally to impose onerous, therapeutically justified conditions on an offender for extended periods of time, thereby lengthening, intensifying and layering punishment in a manner that obscures penal and administrative boundaries." They found that women were particularly disadvantaged by bail conditions such as mandatory treatment orders (for example, having to complete an anger management or drug treatment program) because few programs for women exist and spaces are limited. Women charged with domestic violence offences as a result of dual charging policies (in which both intimate partners are charged in the same incident) spend more time under bail-order supervision than are men, who can gain access programming almost immediately. Women who do not successfully complete their court-ordered treatment while they are out on bail are likely to be sentenced to custody.

## Women, Offences — and the Most Likely Charges

Official statistics indicate that both women and men are most likely to be charged with property-related crimes, although property offences constitute a greater share of charges for women than they do for men. In 2012, for example, 38 percent of all Criminal Code charges against women were for property offences. The most common property offence was theft under $5,000 (making up 61.8 percent of all property charges against women and 23.5 percent of all charges against women). Some 26 percent of all Criminal Code charges against men in 2012 involved crimes against property; 41 percent of property charges against males were for theft under $5,000 (comprising 10.7 percent of all charges against men) (see Tables 2 and 3).

Women accounted for 18 percent of adults charged with violent crimes in 2012. Crimes against persons accounted for 29.8 percent of women's charges in 2012. Of these charges, 52 percent (13,903) involved the least

*Table 2: Number and Percentage of Adults Charged by Police, by Sex and Type of Crime, 2012*

| | Women | | Men | | Total Accused | Women as a % of Accused |
|---|---|---|---|---|---|---|
| **Violent Crime** | 26,664 | 29.8% | 122,744 | 37.5% | 149,408 | 18% |
| **Property Crime** | 34,026 | 38.0% | 86,134 | 26.3% | 120,160 | 28% |
| **Other Criminal Code Violations** | | | | | | |
| Prostitution | 547 | .6% | 680 | .2% | 1,227 | 45% |
| Administration of Justice | 24,827 | 27.7% | 9,8052 | 30% | 122,875 | 20% |
| Other Violations * | 3,455 | 3.9% | 19,500 | 6% | 22,955 | 15% |
| **Total Criminal Code Violations (excluding traffic)** | 89,519 | 100% | 327,110 | 100% | 416,625 | 21% |
| **Criminal Code Traffic Violations** | | | | | | |
| Impaired Driving | 10,823 | | 48,265 | | 59,088 | 18% |
| Other Traffic Violations+ | 1,931 | | 12,992 | | | |
| **Other Federal Statutes** | | | | | | |
| Drug Violations | 8,779 | | 47,058 | | 55,837 | 16% |
| Other Federal Statutes Violations | 1,858 | | 8,228 | | | |
| **Total All Violations** | 112,910 | | 443,653 | | 556,563 | 20% |

* Includes betting and gaming, indecent acts, criminal organization, obstructing a peace officer. + Includes dangerous driving, failure to stop, driving while prohibited. Source: Statistics Canada, Canadian Centre for Justice Statistics, Uniform Crime Reporting Survey.

serious form, level one or common assaults. By comparison, violent crimes accounted for 37.5 percent of the charges against men in 2012; 43.8 percent of those charges involved level one or common assaults (see Tables 2 and 4).

In this regard the case of "Canada's most notorious female offender," Karla Homolka, and her partner, Paul Bernardo, is extremely atypical. The two were charged in the deaths of two young women who were strangers to them, and stranger homicide is relatively rare in Canada. Homicide data consistently indicate that victims are far more likely to be killed by someone they know than by a stranger. For instance, among the solved homicides in 2011, 81 percent of the victims knew their assailant; almost half (48 percent) of the victims were killed by an acquaintance (friend, neighbour, business relationship) and another one-third (33 percent) by a family member (spouse, parent, sibling, child, extended family). In only 15 percent of homicides in 2011 was the victim killed by a stranger, and just over one-third (34 percent) of these homicides were related to drug trafficking or gangs (Perreault 2012: 9 and 33).[2]

Females are most likely to commit acts of violence against their spouses or intimate partners. In 2009, among those females (youth and adults) accused of a violent offence, the most common victim was a spouse or intimate partner (46 percent), followed by an acquaintance (29 percent), stranger (17 percent), and other family member (12 percent) (Mahony 2011: 21).

*Table 3: Number and Percentage of Adults Charged with Property Crime Violations by Sex, 2012*

| Crimes Against Property: | Women | | Men | | Women as a % of Total |
|---|---|---|---|---|---|
| | Number | Percentage | Number | Percentage | |
| Arson | 91 | .3% | 511 | .6% | 15% |
| Break and Enter | 1,726 | 5.1% | 13,649 | 15.9% | 11% |
| Motor Vehicle Theft | 589 | 1.7% | 3,384 | 3.9% | 15% |
| Theft over $5,000 | 347 | 1.0% | 1,079 | 1.2% | 24% |
| Theft $5,000 or under | 21,038 | 61.8% | 35,145 | 41% | 38% |
| Possession of Stolen Property | 2,017 | 6.0% | 7,267 | 8.4% | 22% |
| Fraud | 5,331 | 15.7% | 10,537 | 12.2% | 34% |
| Mischief | 2,440 | 7.1% | 12,861 | 14.9% | 16% |
| Other Property Violations + | 447 | 1.3% | 1,669 | 1.9% | 21% |
| **Total Crimes Against Property** | **34,026** | **100%** | **86,134** | **100%** | |

+ includes trafficking in stolen goods, identity theft, and identity fraud. Source: Statistics Canada, Canadian Centre for Justice Statistics, Uniform Crime Reporting Survey.

In a study of women charged with killing an intimate partner, Elizabeth Sheehy, Julie Stubbs, and Julia Tolmie (2012) found that over half of the cases involved Aboriginal women; 46 percent involved defensive violence; and 75 percent were resolved through plea-bargaining (resulting in a guilty plea to the lesser charge of manslaughter without going to trial). "Most cases appear to have had strong defensive elements on the facts. Tellingly, in only seven cases was the accused not under attack from the deceased at the time she used lethal force against him" (Sheehy, Stubbs, and Tolmie 2012: 391).

In contrast, males (youth and adults) are most likely to be charged with violence against acquaintances. In cases of homicide, for example, between 1997 and 2009 females were most likely to kill another member of their family (35 percent) or an intimate partner (33 percent) whereas males were most likely to kill an acquaintance (46 percent) followed by an intimate partner (19 percent), stranger (17 percent), or other family member (17

*Table 4: Number and Percentage of Adults Charged with Violent Crime Violations by Sex, 2012*

| | Women | | Men | | Women as a % of Total |
|---|---|---|---|---|---|
| **Crimes Against Persons:** | **Number** | **Percentage** | **Number** | **Percentage** | |
| Homicide, Attempted Murder, Other Violations Causing Death | 92 | .4% | 817 | .7% | 10% |
| Sexual Assaults—All Levels; Other Sexual Violations | 162 | .6% | 8,008 | 6.5% | 2% |
| Assault–Level 3–Aggravated | 439 | 1.6% | 2,220 | 1.8% | 17% |
| Assault–Level 2–Weapon or Bodily Harm | 5,511 | 21% | 19,605 | 16.% | 22% |
| Assault–Level 1 | 13,903 | 52% | 53,728 | 43.8% | 21% |
| Other Assaults | 1,868 | 7% | 6,138 | 5.0% | 23% |
| Forcible Confinement, Kidnapping or Abduction | 170 | .6% | 2,536 | 2.0% | 6% |
| Robbery | 995 | 3.7% | 6,344 | 5.2% | 14% |
| Extortion | 63 | .2% | 514 | .4% | 11% |
| Criminal Harassment | 885 | 3.3% | 5,939 | 4.8% | 13% |
| Threatening or Harassing Phone Calls | 207 | .8% | 564 | .5% | 27% |
| Uttering Threats | 2,145 | 8.0% | 14,433 | 11.8% | 13% |
| Other Violent Criminal Code Violations + | 224 | .8% | 1,898 | 1.5% | 11% |
| **Total Crimes against Persons** | **26,664** | **100%** | **122,744** | **100%** | |

+ Includes conspiring to commit murder, hostage-taking, intimidation, other sexual violations. Source: Statistics Canada, Canadian Centre for Justice Statistics, Uniform Crime Reporting Survey.

percent). Over this period, 88.5 percent of the accused were male; 11.5 percent were female (see Table 5).

Prostitution-related offences (keeping or being found in a bawdy house, living off the avails of prostitution, and communicating for the purposes of prostitution) comprise the only category of Criminal Code offences in which the actual number of charges involving females comes close to the number of males charged. In 2012, 1,227 adults were charged with prostitution-related offences; 547 (45 percent) of those charged were women (see Table 2). Nevertheless, these statistics can be deceptive. As John Lowman (2011: 38) notes, "Street prostitution — which is estimated to comprise between 5% and 20% of the commercial sex trade in Canada — has accounted for 93% of all prostitution law offences." Law-enforcement practices that concentrate on street prostitution as a "public nuisance" invariably result in charges being laid against women — in particular, poor and racialized women. As well, the vast majority of sex-trade workers are women, while almost all the clients are men (Cool 2004: 3). Given the nature of the trade, however, the number of men involved in the exchange of sex for money vastly outweighs the number of women. For instance, Frances Shaver (1996: 2) estimates that Montreal female street workers outnumber male street workers by a ratio of four to one. While female street workers engage with an average of twenty male clients per week, male street workers service an average of ten male clients per week, such that "only 4% of those involved (or at least potentially involved) in communicating for the purpose of prostitution are women. The remainder — a full 96% — are men, and of those, the vast majority (99%) are clients." Yet, almost half the people charged with prostitution offences are women, not men.

In 2012 women accounted for 16 percent of adults charged with drug

Table 5: *Women and Men Accused of Homicide by Relationship of the Accused to the Victim, 1997 to 2009*

| | Women Accused | | Men Accused | | Total | Women as a % of Accused |
|---|---|---|---|---|---|---|
| Intimate Relationship | 226 | 33.4% | 973 | 18.7% | 1,199 | 19% |
| Family Member | 236 | 34.9% | 880 | 16.9% | 1,116 | 21% |
| Acquaintance | 178 | 26.3% | 2,411 | 46.4% | 2,589 | 7% |
| Stranger | 36 | 5.3% | 886 | 17.1% | 922 | 4% |
| Unknown | 1 | 0.1% | 45 | 0.9% | 46 | 2% |
| Total Solved Homicides | 677 | 100% | 5,195 | 100% | 5,872 | 11.5% |

Source: Adapted from Mahony (2011: 22).

offences and 18 percent of those charged with Criminal Code traffic violations (85 percent of those charges involved impaired driving) (see Table 2). These data should be read alongside recent legislative changes with regards to compulsory criminalization of drug offences such as simple possession of marijuana for personal use and trafficking, as well as zero-tolerance for impaired driving (see, for example, Mallea 2012; Fournier-Ruggles 2011). These Criminal Code changes have had a particularly gendered impact, especially with regards to offences such as drug trafficking. A report by the Office of the Correctional Investigator (OCI 2013: 10) notes, "The number of incarcerated Black women appears to be rising quickly." Over half of these women were incarcerated for drug-related offences, especially drug trafficking charges. Interviews with Black women prisoners held at Grand Valley Institution revealed that they "willingly chose to carry drugs across international borders, primarily as an attempt to rise above poverty. There were some who reported having been forced into these activities with threats of violence to their children and/or families" (OCI 2013: 10). These data, then, suggest that not all women who enter into the drug trade are drug users. Yet a large number of incarcerated women identify as having significant drug and/or alcohol abuse problems. Mahony (2011: 35) reports that 94 percent of women in provincial custody and 74 percent of women in federal custody in 2008/2009 had substance abuse issues. Thus, it is important to distinguish among the reasons for women's criminalization and incarceration.

Finally, a significant percentage of charges involving both women and men involve the administration of justice offences (such as bail violations, breach of probation, and failure to appear in court). In 2012, 27.7 percent of the charges against women and 30 percent of charges against men were of this nature (see Table 2). Rebecca Kong and Kathy AuCoin (2008: 10) report that the rates for these offences have been climbing. The rate at which women were charged with bail violations tripled between 1986 and 2005 (from 33 to 103 per 100,000 population); the charge rate for men grew 82 percent over the same period. Individuals charged with administration of justice offences must reappear before the courts for reasons unrelated to new criminal activities. Kong and AuCoin note that convictions for these offences are high and offenders are frequently sentenced to custody (see also Taillon 2006).

While these data provide us with information about the extent and nature of women's involvement in crime, they only scratch the surface on how class/race/gender inequalities bear on which women are most likely to be criminalized.

## Women and Poverty

Gender inequality in Canada comes in a number of forms, but the most apparent manifestation is economic. Although more and more women are working for wages, and more and more women are obtaining university degrees and full-time employment, disparities between women and men in the labour market continue to prevail.

- Most employed women work in occupations in which women have traditionally been concentrated. In 2009, 67 percent of all employed women (compared with 31 percent of employed men) were working in teaching, nursing and related health occupations, clerical or other administrative positions, or sales and service occupations. In 2009 women made up 66 percent of teachers, 87 percent of nurses and health-related therapists, 76 percent of clerks and other administrators, and 57 percent of sales and service personnel (Ferrao 2010).
- Women's average earnings are still substantially lower than men's. In 2008 women had average earnings of $30,200 annually, which was only 65 percent of the average earnings ($48,000) of all men with jobs. Even when women were employed on a full-time basis, their earnings remained below that of their male counterparts. In 2008 women working full-time had average earnings that were just 71 percent of those of men working full-time (Williams 2010).
- Education does not eliminate the gender wage gap: women with university degrees employed full-year, full-time earn 30 percent less than equally educated men. Women earn less than men even if they work in the same sectors or in the same jobs. There are no occupations in which women's average earnings exceed men's, not even female-dominated areas such as clerical work and teaching (CRIAW 2005).
- Young women are considerably more likely than other women to be unemployed. In 2009, 12.4 percent of female labour participants aged 15–24 were unemployed, compared with just 6.4 percent of those aged 25–44 and 5.6 percent of those aged 45–64 (Ferrao 2010).

These disparities in the labour market translate into higher rates of poverty for women compared to men.

- Women are the majority of the poor in Canada. In 2011, 13.3 percent of Canadian women (2.3 million) were living on a low income (Silver 2014).
- It is not enough to have a job to stay out of poverty. In 2007, for example,

working-poor families accounted for 31 percent of all low-income families (Collin and Jensen 2009).

- Women, particularly immigrant and visible-minority women, make up 60 percent of minimum-wage workers. Statistics Canada figures show that a full-time minimum-wage earner living in a large city falls $6,000 below the poverty line (UFCW Canada 2013; Statistics Canada 2009).

Poverty is especially an issue for women who are single parents.

- In 2006 lone-parent families accounted for 16 percent of all families in Canada, and 18 percent of children under the age of fifteen lived with a lone parent. The vast majority of lone-parent families (80 percent or 1.1 million) are headed by women (Collin and Jensen 2009).
- Lone-parent families consistently experience higher rates of low income than do other family types. In 2007 the rate of low income among lone-parent families was 21.3 percent, over four times higher than the rate among two-parent families (5.1 percent). Female-headed lone-parent families are more likely to have low incomes than are those headed by male lone parents. In 2007, 23.6 percent of female lone-parent families had a low income, compared with 10.8 percent of male lone-parent families (Collin and Jensen 2009).
- Over one-half (52.1 percent) of lone mothers with children under the age of six live in poverty (Campaign 2000 2012).

Poverty and economic inequality are important contexts for understanding the issue of women's involvement in crime. Similar to their male counterparts, "Women who come into conflict with the criminal justice system tend to be young, poor, under-educated, and unskilled" (Johnson and Rodgers 1993: 98). A 2008/2009 snapshot survey of women in provincial and federal custody, for example, found that incarcerated women were on average younger, more likely to be single, less likely to have a high-school diploma, and more likely to be unemployed than were women in the Canadian population (Mahony 2011). More specifically, Mahony (2011) reports:

- More than half the women in provincial jails (56 percent) and in federal prisons (53 percent) were between the ages of 18 and 35 compared to 28 percent in the general population in 2009;
- 62 percent of women in provincial custody and 49 percent in federal custody were single and never married at the time of their admission, compared to 32 percent in the general population;

- 50 percent of female prisoners in provincial jails did not complete secondary school; in contrast, 2006 census data show that less than 15 percent of women over the age of 25 did not complete secondary school;
- less than one-quarter of women in provincial custody (24 percent) reported being employed full-time or part-time at the time of their admission; by comparison, 58 percent of women in the general population were employed in 2006.

Margaret Jackson (1999: 201) observes, "Over 80% of all incarcerated women in Canada are in prison for poverty related offences." In a similar fashion, Johnson and Rogers (1993: 98) locate women's participation in property offences in terms of "their traditional roles as consumers and, increasingly, as low-income, semi-skilled sole-support providers for their families. In keeping with the rapid increase in female-headed households and the stresses associated with poverty, increasing numbers of women are being charged with shoplifting, cheque forgery, and welfare fraud." More recently, Shoshana Pollack (2008: 6) connects neo-liberal policy changes to women's increasing vulnerability to criminalization and incarceration: "Drastic cuts to social assistance, the creation of a precarious low-wage job market, reduction in publicly funded daycare, and cuts to social services, addictions treatment and mental health services have eroded the social safety net. It is the already disadvantaged members of our communities who are most hard hit by neo-liberal socio-economic policies."

Nevertheless, class is not the only factor to consider in locating women's law violations. Aboriginal women and women of colour are overrepresented in crime statistics relative to their numbers in the general Canadian population.

## Racialized Women

The overrepresentation of Aboriginal peoples in the Canadian criminal justice system is a problem of historic proportions. The statistics are telling.

- While Aboriginal people comprise 3 percent of the total Canadian adult population, they made up 27 percent of admissions to provincial/ territorial institutions and 20 percent of federal custody admissions in 2010/2011 (Dauvergne 2012: 11).
- The overrepresentation of Aboriginal people in the criminal justice system has been worsening over time — a trend that is even more acute for Aboriginal women than it is for Aboriginal men. In October 1996,

Aboriginal women accounted for 23 percent of the adult female inmate population and Aboriginal men accounted for 18 percent of the adult male inmate population (Finn et al. 1999). By 2010/2011, Aboriginal women accounted for 41 percent of the female inmate population, while Aboriginal men accounted for 25 percent of the male inmate population (Dauvergne 2012).

- Within the Prairie region, the figures are even more concerning. In 2008/2009, Aboriginal women comprised more than 85 percent of women sentenced to provincial jails in Saskatchewan and Manitoba, and just over half in Alberta. In 2006 Aboriginal adults represented only 11 percent, 12 percent, and 5 percent of these provincial populations, respectively (Mahony 2011).

The intersections of race/class/gender are clearly evident in the lives of many Aboriginal women in Canada. As Carol LaPrairie (1987: 122, cited in Jackson 1999: 201) notes, Aboriginal women are "among the most severely disadvantaged of all groups in Canadian society." Statistics Canada's report *First Nations, Métis and Inuit Women* (O'Donnell and Wallace 2011) confirms this assessment:

- Aboriginal people are much less likely than their non-Aboriginal counterparts to be part of the paid workforce. The unemployment rate among Aboriginal people in 2006 was 14 percent, compared to 6 percent among non-Aboriginal people. Aboriginal women are less likely than their non-Aboriginal counterparts to be part of the paid workforce; 51 percent of Aboriginal women aged fifteen and over were employed, compared with 58 percent of non-Aboriginal women. Aboriginal women were also less likely than their male counterparts to be employed (51 percent versus 57 percent).
- Aboriginal women are more likely to be lone parents than are non-Aboriginal women. In 2006, 18 percent of Aboriginal women aged fifteen years and over were heading families on their own, compared with 8 percent of non-Aboriginal women.
- According to the 2006 Census, 38 percent of Aboriginal people aged twenty years and over had not completed high school (compared with 19 percent of the non-Aboriginal population). Some 35 percent of Aboriginal women aged twenty-five and over had not graduated from high school, compared to 20 percent among non-Aboriginal women and 39 percent among Aboriginal men.
- In 2005 Aboriginal women aged fifteen years and over had a median

income of $15,654, which is about $5,000 less than the figure for non-Aboriginal women (at $20,640), and about $3,000 less than that of Aboriginal men (at $18,714).

There is an inescapable connection between the criminalization and overincarceration of Aboriginal peoples and the historical forces that have shaped contemporary Aboriginal communities. The processes of colonization — including colonial state policies such as the Indian Act, the intergenerational effects of residential schools, and the removal of Aboriginal children from their homes through child welfare practices — have led to the economic, social, and political marginalization of Aboriginal peoples (Royal Commission on Aboriginal Peoples 1996; Hamilton and Sinclair 1991). As the Supreme Court of Canada acknowledged, "Many aboriginal people are victims of systemic and direct discrimination, many suffer the legacy of dislocation, and many are substantially affected by poor social and economic conditions" (R v Gladue 1999: 20).

For Aboriginal communities one of the legacies of colonialism is the inordinately high level of violence. While many Canadian women and children encounter violence in their lives (Statistics Canada 2011; Johnson 1996), violence against Aboriginal women and children is an even more pressing social issue. In interviews with 621 Aboriginal people living in four Canadian inner cities, LaPrairie (1994) found that 70 percent of the males and 75 percent of the females reported that family violence had occurred in their childhoods. A study by the Ontario Native Women's Association (1989) found that eight out of ten Aboriginal women had experienced violence, many of them as young children. The 2009 General Social Survey (GSS) conducted by Statistics Canada found that the proportion of Aboriginal women who reported spousal violence was more than double that of non-Aboriginal women; 15 percent of Aboriginal women reported spousal violence by a current or former intimate partner in the previous five years, compared to 6 percent of non-Aboriginal women. The GSS also reveals that Aboriginal women experienced more serious forms of intimate partner violence than their non-Aboriginal counterparts did. Almost half (48 percent) of Aboriginal women (and 32 percent of non-Aboriginal women) who had experienced intimate partner violence reported that they had been sexually assaulted, beaten, choked, or threatened with a gun or knife. Some 58 percent of Aboriginal women (and 41 percent of non-Aboriginal women) reported that they had sustained injury; 52 percent of Aboriginal women (and 31 percent of non-Aboriginal women) said they feared for their life

(O'Donnell and Wallace 2011: 40–41; see also Brzozowski, Taylor-Butts, and Johnson 2006; Brzozowski and Brazeau 2008; and Perreault 2011).

While studies on the incidence of particular types of abuse are useful in documenting the nature and extent of the violence encountered by women and children, several writers have noted the drawbacks in separating out and focusing on specific forms of abuse. Sharon McIvor and Teressa Nahanee (1998: 63) state: "Compartmentalizing 'types' of violence within Aboriginal communities into distinct categories of investigation is counter-productive. Sexual, physical, and emotional attacks are inter-related and inter-generational in our communities. Treating these acts as discrete events serves only to obscure our everyday lives." Similarly, Patricia Monture-Angus (1995: 171) tells us, "Focusing on a moment in time or incidents of violence, abuse or racism, counting them — disguises the utter totality of the experience of violence in Aboriginal women's lives." Indeed, the violence experienced by Aboriginal peoples is clearly systemic; it "has invaded whole communities and cannot be considered a problem of a particular couple or an individual household" (RCAP 1996: vol. 3 chap. 2).

One explanation often offered to account for the high levels of violence in Aboriginal communities is the use of alcohol. Sharon Moyer (1992), for instance, found that alcohol featured in 70 percent of the homicide incidents involving Aboriginal people between 1962 and 1984.[3] Accordingly, alcohol use is taken as a sign of "cultural difference" that marks Aboriginal peoples off from the rest of Canadian society. In this view, excessive drinking has become commonplace in Aboriginal communities, to the point where it leads to "drinking parties" in which violence is likely to break out (see Comack and Balfour 2004).

However, resting an explanation for violence in Aboriginal communities on the use of alcohol and, more generally, on the notion of "cultural difference," contains a number of problems. For one, it promotes an ideology of "homogeneous Indianness" (Kline 1994: 455) that denies the diversity of Aboriginal cultures. As Emma LaRocque (2002: 150–51) notes:

> Besides the problem of typecasting Aboriginal cultures into a status list of "traits," 500 years of colonial history are being whitewashed into mere "cultural differences." Social conditions arising from societal negligence and policies have been explained away as "cultural." Problems having to do with racism and sexism have been blamed on Aboriginal culture.

Many of the Aboriginal women interviewed for *Women in Trouble* (Comack 1996) indicated that they turned to alcohol and other drugs as a way of escaping their difficult pasts (see also McEvoy and Daniluk 1995). In this regard, these women are no different than many other Canadians who regularly turn to alcohol as a means of coping with deep distress in their lives. In the view of the Royal Commission on Aboriginal Peoples (RCAP 1996), alcohol abuse is not a cause of violence but a parallel means of dealing with deep distress. In a similar fashion, Aboriginal Justice Inquiry commissioners Hamilton and Sinclair (1991: 498) state: "Ultimately, it must be recognized that the presence and influence of alcohol and substance abuse in Aboriginal communities and among Aboriginal peoples are a direct reflection of the nature and level of despair which permeates that population."

Moreover, to say that violence in Aboriginal communities is the result of cultural differences raises another question: different from what? More often than not, it is the standards of the dominant white culture that are used as the measuring rod by which Aboriginal people are transformed into the "deviant Other." Such an approach only works to reproduce the racism that prevails in the mainstream society. In this regard, centring explanations for violence in Aboriginal communities on the use of alcohol can align too easily with racist stereotypes, including two of the most invidious of these, the "squaw" and the "drunken Indian" (see Sangster 2001; LaRocque 2000; Comack and Balfour 2004). As LaRocque put it so powerfully to the Royal Commission, "The portrayal of the squaw is one of the most degrading, most despised and most dehumanizing anywhere in the world. The squaw is the female counterpart of the Indian male savage and, as such, she has no human face. She is lustful, immoral, unfeeling and dirty." LaRocque draws a direct connection between "this grotesque dehumanization" and the constant vulnerability of Aboriginal girls and women to serious physical, psychological, and sexual abuse: "I believe there is a direct relationship between these horrible racist, sexist stereotypes and violence against Native women and girls" (cited in RCAP 1996 vol. 3 chap. 2).

The racist stereotype of the "drunken Indian" works in a similar fashion. Bolstered by a dominant, regularly reinforced discourse that is content to explain private troubles as being rooted in individual circumstances (as opposed to systemic processes), the common view is to see Aboriginal people as being intoxicated and "out of control." Such representations merely function to objectify and devalue Aboriginal people. Ignored are the historical processes by which alcohol was introduced into Aboriginal life and the social conditions that have fostered its continued use, as well as the general use of alcohol as a socially sanctioned resource in contemporary society.

Explanations that rest on the idea of cultural difference to account for the prevalence of violence in Aboriginal communities, then, are highly suspect. Rather than cultural difference, the prevalence of violence and alcohol use in Aboriginal communities is more accurately located as a contemporary manifestation of colonialism. As the Canadian Panel on Violence against Women (1993: 173) argued, poverty is a key factor in the perpetuation of this violence: "The impact of poverty on the Aboriginal family and community is immeasurable. Poverty, in its severest form, is a fact of life for many Aboriginal people…. It is the daily stress, financial hardship and chronic despair inflicted by poverty that contribute to the widespread abuse of Aboriginal women and children."

Aboriginal women and men are not the only racialized group to experience overrepresentation in the criminal justice system. While Black people comprise just under 3 percent of the Canadian population, they accounted for 9.3 percent of the federal prison population in 2011/2012. As Correctional Investigator Howard Sapers (2013: 8) notes, "Over the last 10 years, the number of federally incarcerated Black inmates has increased by 80% from 778 to 1,403."

Some 4 percent (fifty-five) of Black inmates in federal prisons in 2011/2012 were women, representing 9 percent of the women in federal custody. The majority of these women (78 percent) were incarcerated at Grand Valley Institution. Pollack's (2000a) interviews with Black women serving federal sentences in Ontario revealed that the women's main motivation for breaking the law was economic. Some of the women had previously been in paid employment in low-level jobs in financial institutions, corporations, and medical care facilities:

> A few participants were working at these jobs at the time of their arrest. They were also either sole providers for their children or supporting themselves through part-time work while continuing their education at college or university. However, most of the women found that the wage they received was not sufficient for providing for their families, even with subsidized child care, and sometimes turned to illegal means to supplement their income. (Pollack 2000a: 77)

Pollack suggests that Black women's conflicts with the law emanated from their concern to assert their independence and resist marginalization and state-enforced dependency (such as social assistance): "Shoplifting, fraud and drug importation were a means of releasing Black women from poverty and racist practices that reinforced their marginalization. Relying upon or supplementing their income through illegal jobs, women were able to adequately support themselves and their family" (Pollack 2000a: 78).

These patterns are not unique to Canada. Laureen Snider (2004: 213) notes, "Everywhere those most likely to be imprisoned are racial and ethnic minorities, especially people of colour." In the United States, for example, the lifetime likelihood of being sent to prison is 1 in 19 for a Black woman, 1 in 45 for a Hispanic woman, and 1 in 118 for a white woman. In 2010 Black women in the United States were incarcerated at nearly three times the rate of white women (133 versus 47 per 100,000). Hispanic women were incarcerated at 1.6 times the rate of white women (77 versus 47 per 100,000) (The Sentencing Project 2012).

While the news media continue to devote considerable attention to sensational crimes, the vast majority of offences committed by women are "poverty crimes" that reflect the systemic inequality, discrimination, and marginalization emanating from their class/race/gender locations.

## Representations of Criminalized Women

If we are looking to typecast the so-called typical criminalized woman, we might be better advised to turn our attention toward the story of Lisa Neve.

In November 1994, Lisa Neve, a twenty-one-year-old Aboriginal woman, became the second woman ever in Canada to be labelled a dangerous offender and sentenced to an indeterminate sentence.[4] Lisa's life story is one that resonates for too many young Aboriginal women in Canada. She was adopted out to a white family at three months of age. At twelve she was expelled from school for drinking with a group of friends. The police were called, and she was apprehended and put into secure custody. Lisa says that she learned early on that

> acting out meant people didn't try to shrink me, I just got attention. So I would freak out and get restrained and sent to segregation. I was always in segregation for something or other, because I was so bitter and angry. I felt robbed of my childhood, so I misbehaved. I think I was ill back then, I remember having so many issues in my mind, voices, but I didn't want to tell anybody because I thought they would send me over to the hospital. They had sex offenders there and I didn't want to go, so I just acted out, cut myself, banged my head, and scratched myself. I don't know what I was doing. (Neve and Pate 2005: 20)

Like many young women in her situation, Lisa's response was to run away to the streets, where she was introduced to prostitution, drug use (cocaine, marijuana, heroin, and Ritalin), and violence. In addition to her own experiences of victimization, Lisa too engaged in violence. She soon developed a reputation on the street as an "enforcer" because she was not afraid to protect other women involved in the sex trade from their pimps. By the age of eighteen, Lisa had some twenty-two charges against her, many of them imposed while she was in custody. As Kim Pate (2002: 466) states:

> It did not take long for the adults in authority to label Lisa as a "problem" in need of "correction." Once the labels were applied, they not only stuck, but they also attracted other labels that built upon and expanded those prior. Consequently, although Lisa had started out as "mischievous," or "a brat," she was later labelled an instigator, negative, and eventually, aggressive, sociopathic and finally, a dangerous offender.

As an adult Lisa was convicted of aggravated assault, robbery, uttering threats, and assault with a weapon. The assaults and robbery arose from disputes with other women engaged in the sex trade. In 1991, in retaliation for a previous beating that put one of her friends in hospital, Lisa forced another woman to strip, then cut up her clothes and left her on a busy highway. In 1992 she stabbed a woman with the unopened end of an exacto knife. The conviction for uttering threats came about after Lisa checked herself into a psychiatric facility in 1993 and told a psychiatrist that she wanted to kill a lawyer and his family. The lawyer in question had subjected Lisa to a brutal cross-examination during the trial of her boyfriend, who was eventually jailed for beating her. (The lawyer challenged her credibility with questions such as "Aren't you in fact a prostitute?") When the robbery charge (taking the woman's clothes) went to court in November 1994, Lisa was declared a dangerous offender and sentenced to an indeterminate sentence.

At the dangerous offender hearing, Lisa was repeatedly questioned about her sexual orientation. This issue was ostensibly relevant as a result of psychiatric evidence that she was a "sadistic homosexual." The leading Crown psychiatrist characterized her as "the equivalent of a male lust murderer." These assessments were based largely on statements that Lisa had made to psychiatrists and police officers, which she testified were fictitious and made up to shock persons in authority. Although the designation as a dangerous offender was ultimately overturned on appeal in June 1999, as a result of that designation Lisa Neve was classified as a maximum-security prisoner and spent six years in prison (including pre-trial detention), most of it in segregated, maximum-security units in two different men's prisons (Pate 2002: 466).

In overturning the dangerous offender designation, the Court of Appeal noted the typical nature of this young woman's "violent" offences, in that "every offence which Neve committed was entangled in some way with her life as a prostitute" (cited in Pate 2002: 467). The court took into account the nature of life on the street, particularly for young sex trade workers. According to Neve and Pate (2005: 26):

> For instance, they highlighted the fact that many young prostitutes are assaulted and murdered and that the majority of those murdered were female. They went on to assert that "No one should be surprised, therefore, to learn that many prostitutes arm themselves for defensive purposes.... It is not possible to evaluate moral blameworthiness without having an understanding of the context in which the criminal act occurred."

After her release Lisa continued to work hard at overcoming the impact of her imprisonment and struggled to manage her mental health issues. But as Pate (2002: 467) points out, "The biggest danger for Lisa remains, however, the reaction of others to her infamous dangerous offender label."

As Lisa Neve's story illustrates, women and girls are routinely sanctioned not only for violating legal codes, but also for violating codes of conduct that regulate and patrol the boundaries of "appropriate" female behaviour. In chapter 2, Joanne Minaker provides a historical perspective on this issue by focusing on the work of a group of affluent, white, upper-middle-class women called the Founders, who ran the Toronto Magdalen Asylum, a refuge for women and girls that operated between 1853 and 1939. Minaker shows us how the representation of the "erring female" — the term used by the Founders to refer to the women and girls they sought to help — worked as a censure or category of denunciation in a particular historical, political, and structural context. In the early twentieth century, the idea of the "erring female" reproduced and reinforced the dualism between "good girls" (those who are chaste, virtuous, and pious) and "bad girls" (those who are sexually deviant and wayward). In the process, it operated to keep female sexuality in check.

Minaker makes the point, however, that the claims justifying the institutionalization of "erring females" were not just related to their sexuality — how it is perceived and who controls it — but to their very life chances. As well, that females incarcerated under the Female Refuges Act did not have to engage in criminal activity suggests, according to Minaker, that something else was at stake; namely, reproducing a gendered, classist, and racialized social order. While the "erring female" of earlier times was constituted by her immorality, degradation, mental defect, and/or intemperance, in more recent neo-liberal times female transgression has come to be defined by inadequate parenting, promiscuity, and/or drug abuse. Although the discourse has shifted — from "incorrigible girls" to "sexually exploited children" — young women continue to be punished "for their own good" under the guise of protection. In both eras, therefore, the "erring female" is one who is censured for deviating from the dominant (class-based and racialized) standards of "appropriate" femininity. All the while, the material and social conditions that create her marginalization and social exclusion are left out of the equation.

Prostitution has historically been considered a status conferred on women who sell sexual services. Traditionally within criminology, the focus has been on the woman involved in prostitution, with very little attention devoted to the men who sought her services. The purpose of prostitution was seen to be the servicing of men's needs, which was premised on a particular understanding of male sexuality. Specifically, men had insatiable sex drives and desires that women must somehow satisfy (cf. Davis 1937). In this traditional, male-centred view, the prostitute was positioned as the quintessential bad girl, the Other, and the focus of investigation was on trying to account for the sources of her difference. Why did women enter this profession? What is it about these women that accounts for their deviance and disrepute? Answers to these questions typically singled out factors such as family dysfunction, poor socialization, bad upbringing, and individual pathology. Little effort was made to consult with the women themselves or to attend to the ways in which broader social inequalities conditioned and limited women's choices and opportunities.

To counter this male-centred view, as well as the legal and conceptual baggage associated with the term prostitution, women involved in this activity began to emphasize it as "work." Chris Bruckert and Colette Parent note in chapter 3 that "sex work" is a contentious term. For some feminists, prostitution is simply a form of patriarchal violence against women; a manifestation of the sexual, social, and economic domination of women by men. Bruckert and Parent suggest, however, that while this perspective has the benefit of calling attention to the social structures and conditions that constrain women's lives, it tends to deny women involved in the sex trade any agency, instead positioning them as victims of patriarchal oppression. Bruckert and Parent's analysis is situated, therefore, in the literature that understands sex work as a job that shares much in common with other work that women carry out in a neo-liberal, post-industrial labour market increasingly characterized by "McJobs" (Ritzer 2004).

Focusing on incall sex workers — women who provide sexual services to clients in establishments such as massage parlours, brothels, and dungeons — Bruckert and Parent draw on narratives of women involved in this sector of the sex industry to explore the labour structure and process of their work and how it is subjectively experienced by the women. Doing so enables the authors to draw parallels to the work of working-class women in other consumer services, all the while being attentive to how the social, moral, and criminal justice regulation of sex work creates particular challenges and problems for the women. Indeed, those challenges and problems were brought to the fore in the case of *Bedford v Canada (Attorney General)* (2013).

Terri Jean Bedford, Amy Lebovitch, and Valerie Scott — one current and two former sex-trade workers — challenged the constitutionality of three sections of the Criminal Code relating to prostitution: keeping or being found in a bawdy house (s. 210); living off the avails of prostitution (s. 212(1)(j)); and communicating in public for the purposes of prostitution (s. 213(1)(c)). The women argued that these provisions put their lives and safety at risk and therefore constituted an infringement of their rights under section 7 of the Charter of Rights and Freedoms, which guarantees the "right to life, liberty, and security of the person." For instance, the offence of keeping a common bawdy house prevents workers from conducting their trade in a more secure indoor location. Prohibitions against living off the avails of prostitution mean that workers cannot hire a security guard to ensure their safety. Prohibitions on communicating for the purposes of prostitution mean that workers cannot take extra measures in screening potential clients. The Supreme Court of Canada, in rendering its decision on the case in December 2013, agreed with the applicants that the three criminal prohibitions "do not merely impose conditions on how prostitutes operate. They go a critical step further, by imposing *dangerous* conditions on prostitution; they prevent people engaged in a risky — but legal — activity from taking steps to protect themselves from the risks" (*Bedford v Canada [Attorney General]* 2013: para. 60). The Court therefore ruled that the three provisions were inconsistent with the Charter and thus invalid. Noting that "the regulation of prostitution is a complex and delicate matter," the Court left it up to Parliament to devise a new approach, suspending its decision for one year to allow the time to do so (para. 165). Nonetheless, the Court also noted, "Concluding that each of the challenged provisions violates the Charter does not mean that Parliament is precluded from imposing limits on where and how prostitution may be conducted, as long as it does so in a way that does not infringe the constitutional rights of prostitutes" (p. 11).

While the Court's decision was met with relief by sex-trade workers and their advocates, many commentators expressed reservations about the decision and what lies ahead. Jennifer Koshan (2013), for one, notes that the Court failed to take a fully contextualized approach:

> In *Bedford* there is certainly some reference to the context of prostitution and its harms (see e.g., paras 64, 86–92), but there is no analysis of the gendered and racialized nature of these harms. For example, the only references to "women" in the judgment are in the Court's description of the applicant's evidence (at paras 9 to 14) and in the context of other decisions referred to by the Court.

Similarly, as Bruckert and Parent suggest (chapter 3), the prospects of a decriminalized industry are slim given the federal government's announced intentions to introduce new legislation prior to the ruling taking effect in December 2014.

Nevertheless, by analyzing incall sex work from a perspective that straddles labour theory and criminology, Bruckert and Parent offer an important corrective to traditional male-centred constructions of the prostitute as Other. When placed in the context of the data presented earlier on women's inequality and labour force participation, as well as the nature of women's "McJobs" under neo-liberal market conditions, their argument for retaining the term sex work becomes all the more compelling.

Nahanni Fontaine's chapter provides us with a different vantage point from which to explore women's and girls' involvement in the sex trade: the racialized spaces of the inner city. Fontaine begins by drawing attention to the death of Felicia Solomon Osborne, a sixteen-year-old girl from Norway House Cree Nation whose body was found along the shoreline of the Red River in Winnipeg in 2003. Felicia was one of the many Aboriginal women and girls whose lives have been abruptly ended by violence.

The violence encountered by Aboriginal women and girls came to public attention in 2004 with the release of Amnesty International's report, *Stolen Sisters*. The report, noting that Aboriginal women are five times more likely to die as a result of violence, pointed to the role that cultural and systemic discrimination played in perpetuating this violence. It also documented many of the cases of missing and murdered women — including the disappearance of women from the streets of Vancouver's Downtown Eastside. In 2005 the Native Women's Association of Canada (NWAC) launched the Sisters in Spirit initiative, which was aimed at addressing the root causes, circumstances, and trends of missing and murdered Aboriginal women and girls. By March 2010, NWAC had gathered information about the disappearance or death of more than 580 Aboriginal women and girls across Canada (NWAC 2010a). A more recent database compiled by the RCMP increased that figure to 1,181 missing or murdered Aboriginal women and girls (RCMP 2014).

Fontaine cites the few media reports on Osborne's death, all of which made a point of noting that the murdered girl had gang ties and had been working the streets. Not content to rely on such a stereotypical representation, she argues that we need to hear the standpoint of Aboriginal women and girls in order to understand their lives, including their participation in street gangs. Drawing on narratives of Aboriginal women and girls — Anishinaabe Ikwe — Fontaine explores their participation in street gangs. As she notes, most media and law enforcement representations fail to locate the phenomenon of the Aboriginal street gang in the context of settler colonialism. Fontaine, however, shows us the profound damage that colonization is wreaking on Aboriginal youth who live in inner-city spaces.

A similar analysis emerges from a study done by Elizabeth Comack, Lawrence Deane, Larry Morrissette, and Jim Silver (2013), who conducted extensive interviews with Aboriginal street gang members, women associated with the gangs, and Aboriginal Elders. Their work aligns with that of critical street gang researchers, such as John Hagedorn (2007), Philippe Bourgois (2003), and Victor Rios (2011), who argue that the proliferation of street gangs in racialized inner-city spaces can be accounted for by the sweeping changes wrought by global economic restructuring and the neo-liberal response of the state to the deepening inequality between rich and poor that these economic changes have produced. Similar to Fontaine, however, Comack and her colleagues maintain that a key factor in accounting for Aboriginal street gangs in Canada is the ongoing impact of colonialism. In this respect, Aboriginal street gangs constitute a form of resistance to colonialism, albeit one with negative consequences. Rather than being passive victims of social forces largely beyond their control, young Aboriginal men have formed "resistance identities" that involve the performance of a "hypermasculinity" centred around "being hard" and "tough." Violence — including violence against women — is a key component of this performance (Comack et al. 2013: 82–88).

According to Fontaine, colonization has not only conditioned the life chances of Aboriginal peoples, but also led to the internalization of dominant Eurocentric, patriarchal beliefs. As revealed by the women and girls that she interviewed, relations to men in the street gang are defined by a hierarchy of roles comprising "old ladies," "bitches," and "hos." Given their subordinated position both in relation to the gang and in the wider society, Anishinaabe Ikwe are left to "take it like a woman" and "be solid" in their efforts to negotiate place and space. Nevertheless, a paradox emerges in the women's accounts: despite the violence encountered in their relations with the men in the street gang, the women in Fontaine's study were provided — through that gang — with a space in which they could find solidarity and pride in their Aboriginal identities.

David Hugill's chapter takes us a step further in exploring the conditions of endangerment that women encounter in the racialized and marginalized spaces of Canada's inner cities — and the troubling representations of those women in media accounts. Between 1978 and 1992 some sixty women, many of them Aboriginal and involved in the street sex trade, were reported to have vanished from Vancouver's Downtown Eastside, known as Canada's "poorest postal code." As Hugill notes, however, Vancouver's crisis of missing and murdered women generated very little interest on the part of the media and criminal justice system prior to 1998, and it was not until 2001 that police formed a Missing Women Joint Task Force to investigate these cases. In February 2002 this new unit raided the Port Coquitlam pig farm of Robert Pickton, who was eventually charged with the murder of twenty-seven women. In December 2007 Pickton was convicted of the second-degree murder of six women and sentenced to life imprisonment.

Hugill suggests that in order to unpack the reasons behind this state inaction and media silence on the crisis of missing and murdered women, we need to attend to the spatial location of the women as residents of a stigmatized inner-city neighbourhood and the ways in which the media narratives about street-level sex workers normalize the violence they encounter. Drawing on an analysis of newspaper articles about the arrest and trial of Pickton, Hugill shows us how media discourses operate to produce an understanding of the sex worker as a source of criminal deviance and danger, and a symbol of moral corruption. At the same time, the media narratives focus on the missing and murdered women as traumatized and damaged subjects who were driven to addiction and survival sex by individualized patterns of abuse. Absent from these narratives is the broader context, the intersecting oppressions that street-involved women encounter and the role that larger structural forces play in generating the dangers that each of the women encountered in the sinister world of the inner city. Also absent is a sustained effort to draw on the standpoints of sex workers themselves — an effort that would move beyond the trope of personal tragedy as the explanation for their endangered lives.

As Cathy Fillmore and Colleen Dell (2000) found in their interviews with criminalized women, self-harm in the form of slashing is one way that the women found to cope with and survive deep emotional pain and distress. The artwork of Jackie Traverse, which concludes this section, reveals what while the resulting scars may be a source of pointed questioning from others, they are also markers of a past that is to be honoured.

## Notes

1. A search of the Internet using these keywords conducted on July 12, 2005, produced thirty-eight hits of news articles, all of them in reference to Homolka.
2. Another 4 percent of solved homicides in 2011 involved a "criminal relationship," which includes "prostitutes, drug dealers and their clients, loan sharks, and gang members" (Perreault 2012: 33).
3. Note, however, that the percentage changed over the period of study, as 78 percent of incidents involved alcohol in 1962–65 whereas 59 percent did in 1981–84 (Moyer 1992).
4. The dangerous offender legislation was passed in 1977. Between 1977 and 1999, a total of 271 people (99.3 percent of whom were male) were given that designation. Marlene Moore was the only other woman to be declared a dangerous offender during that period (in 1985). Moore committed suicide in the Kingston Prison for Women in 1988 at the age of thirty-one (see Kershaw and Lasovich 1991; Introduction to Part III here).

# 2

# Sluts and Slags
## The Censuring of the Erring Female

*Joanne C. Minaker*

> *On learning I had run off with a Chinese man my father came to Toronto.*
> *There was a loud banging at the door when my boyfriend and I were having*
> *breakfast. Two policemen came in followed by my father. I was ordered to*
> *get dressed and taken to a place where I was put in a barred cage. Shortly, I*
> *was taken into a room and interviewed by a woman. She asked if I had ever*
> *slept with anyone else. I felt I would have to damage my character to save*
> *my boyfriend from any blame. I said, "Yes." She asked, "How many?" I said,*
> *"Two." She asked me their names and I gave them. Although I wasn't sure,*
> *I told her I was pregnant, hoping that would help. I have never told anyone*
> *I was pregnant before. Almost immediately I was taken to a courtroom. I*
> *stood with my back towards the judge who sat about 10 feet away.... A po-*
> *liceman spoke.... He related the address where he found me, my boyfriend's*
> *name and that he was wearing pajamas. The judged asked me, "Are you*
> *pregnant?" I said, "Yes." He asked, "How far along?" I said, "Three months*
> *— I'll get married if you'll just let me out of here long enough." The judge*
> *said, "Remanded one week for sentence." I was taken in a black van to a*
> *jailhouse. I sat and slept on a bench in a barred enclosure and ate greasy*
> *stew at a long table with male prisoners. When I returned to court, the judge*
> *said, "You are charged with being incorrigible and I sentence you to one year*
> *in the Belmont Home [Toronto Industrial Refuge]."* (Demerson 2001: 1)[1]

It was May 30, 1939, and Velma's crime was being "incorrigible" — a code word for errant female sexuality, illegitimate motherhood, and miscegenation — essentially that she was eighteen, pregnant, unmarried, and in love with the baby's Chinese father. Deemed out of control by her father, police officers, and a magistrate, Velma was to be placed under control and punished. Paternalistically, such authorities argued that she needed punishment, not out of vengeance, but for her own good. When the Toronto Industrial Refuge closed its doors in June 1939, Velma was transferred to the Mercer Reformatory, where she stayed until March 1940.

In her eighties Velma put her experiences into a book, aptly titled *Incorrigible* (Demerson 2004). Little, however, is known about the institution she referred to in her writing as "Belmont Home." Nor do we know much about the legislation — the Female Refuges Act (FRA) — that sanctioned her incarceration, or the ways in which females like Velma were represented. My purpose here is not to tell Velma's story or re-create the lives of other women. Instead, this chapter is about the censuring practices that the women Founders of the Refuge deployed, and the discourses and representations upon which their efforts were conceived and justified. In sharp contrast to their charges like Velma, the Founders were privileged by their race and class position. Married to prominent men from Toronto's legal, medical, and business elite, these women took up the project of "reforming" or "saving" those they referred to as "erring females."

In effect, the censuring practices of the Founders of the Toronto Industrial Refuge facilitated the criminalization of thousands of girls and women between 1853 and 1939. Although Velma was not involved in the sex trade, that she — a single, white female (of English and Greek heritage) — had slept with a Chinese man and was carrying his "illegitimate" child made her deserving of the title of prostitute. The Founders were (re)producing a discourse that had tremendous social consequences for young women like Velma.[2]

Central to this process was the construction of what Carol Smart (1995) refers to as a "perpetually problematic" body, a construction that remains central to contemporary practices and processes censuring women and circumscribing their autonomy. The perpetually problematic body exists insofar as "the woman who sells what should be given away for free in the name of love (as with prostitution) merits punishment…. There is a powerful double bind here which we are still far from resolving but which constructs women's bodies as perpetually problematic" (Smart 1995: 227). Now, over a decade into the twenty-first century, being female remains bound up in contradictory expectations and dilemmas, complicated by class, race, age, (dis)ability, and sexuality.

Displaying an uneasy combination of protection and punishment as their focus, the historical records of the Refuge offer a unique venue for examining the criminalization of working-class girls and women deemed "erring." Despite immense social change and increasing tensions, the Refuge endured for eighty-six years. The records left behind reveal a great deal about how the governors viewed their charges and the discourses upon which they based their representations. A posh retirement centre in midtown Toronto called Belmont House — a legacy of the Toronto Industrial Refuge — houses largely forgotten annual reports, meeting minutes, and other documents from its previous incarnation. A small storeroom became my own personal archive, and I spent countless hours there trying to disentangle the threads of the institution's past. This chapter is based on my analysis of those records, focusing specifically on representations of, and claims made about, the inmates institutionalized at the Refuge.

A vast literature examines the moral and social regulation of women and girls (see, for example, Sangster 1999; Valverde 1991; Strange 1995). Such studies pay attention to the contradictory punitive and benevolent nature of institutional practices, but leave open much room for examining the claims that justified the institutionalization of large numbers of girls and women. I argue that the struggles of those like Velma are not just over their sexuality — how it is perceived and who controls it — but are over their very life chances, which in turn are inexorably linked to race, class, and gender inequalities. In Velma's case, for instance, white, male, and class privilege justified her confinement. For some women, however, their marginalized status kept them demonized and thus not accepted as vulnerable and in need of "protection."

While its context is historical, this all too familiar theme — the racialized, classist, and gendered punishment of female sexuality — resonates today. The sentiment and practice of punishing females in the name of protection persists in legislation such as Alberta's 2007 Protection for Sexually Exploited Children Act (PSECA) and its precursor, the heavily criticized and legally challenged Protection of Children Involved in Prostitution Act (PCHIP) of 1999.

## Theoretical Underpinnings: The Erring Female as Censure

The Founders of the Refuge referred to those they sought to help as "erring females."[3] Specific historical discourses produce particular representations — like the erring female — both explicitly and tacitly. I understand the term "erring female" as a censure. Colin Sumner (1990: 28–29) defines censures as "categories of denunciation or abuse lodged within very complex, historically loaded practical conflicts and moral debates." As Sumner's work suggests, ideological formations, social relations, and human fears of the day support and constitute censures. Pivotal in the articulation and proliferation of knowledge claims are what Laureen Snider (2002, 2003) calls "authorized knowers," those individuals and/or groups with the capacity and authority to have their claims heard and acted upon. Those occupying dominant gender, class, race, and ethnic positions have a greater capacity to assert their censures in the legal and moral discourses of the day. The Founders were people who — given their position of racial and class privilege — had managed to attain the status of authorized knowers.

This brings us to the phenomena — person, event, or identity, for example — that censures interpret or signify. In Foucauldian terms, discourses are normalizing in that they create, fuel, and sustain norms for behaviour, by dividing people into categories like good (normal) and bad (abnormal) (Foucault 1983). The concept of "erring female" as a censure was a means of keeping female sexuality in check, delineating social deviance and legitimate responses to those so classified. Rather than being used to explain behaviour (for example, socially deviant conduct) or people (criminalized girls), the censure "erring female" became a way of making knowledge claims. As a social censure, the sign "erring" signifies a problematic female, in body, mind, or character. That the inmates of the Refuge supposedly shared certain characteristics and actions — like intemperance, prostitution, or immorality — was something set completely apart from their common social-structural disadvantage and marginalization, which tended to be obscured in the process.

As Joan Sangster (1999: 34) argues, "This 'censuring process' of distinguishing the immoral from the moral woman … constituted and reproduced relations of power based on gender, race, and economic marginality." Thus, the sense of an Other is always at the heart of both the censures and the identity of authorized knowers: the term "erring female" evokes both the image of immorality, sexual deviance, and waywardness (that is, on the part of the inmates) as well as its complement — chaste, pious, and virtuous femininity (on the part of the Founders). Here we see the double bind that Smart refers to — a double standard of sexual morality that places females into either the *good girl* or *bad girl* category. In Pat Carlen's (1983) terms, the erring female is "outwith" gender norms, family norms, and other social norms, and thereby deemed a failure as wife/partner, mother, daughter, and worker.

Censures are also historically situated and tied to particular calls for action. As long as social relations are conditioned and contoured by ethnicity, race, class, and gender, these axes of power imbue their application. The concept of erring female operated as a powerful censure that facilitated the criminalization of those marginalized by gender, class, and race. Actual girls and women were targeted for reform because they were mistaken for this erring female.[4] Indeed, to some extent challenging dominant ideologies of female sexuality and gender, the Founders viewed white prostitutes, drunkards, and homeless and otherwise destitute women as objects of denigration and pity, not objects for harsh punishment (see, for example, Sangster's [2001] work on how categories of "redeemable" and "unsalvageable" were racialized). The Founders advocated various strategies in the name of protection that would bring erring females back "within" feminine restraint. They claimed that "the erring female is at once crushed by public sentiment," yet saw prostitution and sexual immorality not as causes but as consequences of their poor social position.[5] This view certainly does belie how they bought into the prevailing assumption that female prostitutes were sexually loose and in need of character reformation. They emphasized that without good moral influences, erring women would find loose company, take stimulants, and thereby slide or be induced into prostitution. Underlying their (re)production of the erring female censure was not only the desire to control or govern, but also the desire to help or protect. That they believed their work was benevolent and that they defended it in the name of protection are significant but should not overshadow their class and race privileges. They acknowledged that social structures ("abounding inequity") and poverty ("great waywardness") propelled some women onto the streets, but nevertheless stressed the women's lack of feminine virtue over their lack of economic or social opportunities. They also tied considerations to ethnicity and race to their notions of female (dis)respectability and assumptions about working-class women's failure to conform to romanticized standards of ideal femininity. By stigmatizing and targeting Irish and Italian immigrants in the early years, and by casting other racialized groups (for example, Aboriginals, Eastern Europeans) as entirely beyond the pale of their interventions, the Founders (re)produced an outcast class.

## The Socio-Political Context of Censure

The Toronto Industrial Refuge emerged during an intense period of state formation and nation-building and amid widening class and ethnic divisions, new fears of social degeneration (fed by declining birth rates among Anglo-Saxon versus non-British immigrants) and Victorian expectations of femininity, domesticity, and restrained sexuality. The Founders' claims were mediated by middle-class fears of working-class vice and tensions between middle-class sensibilities and working-class realities. These were also informed by Christian beliefs and maternalism.

During the mid-nineteenth century, immigration, urbanization, and industrialization were changing the economic, political, and cultural terrain

of a sparsely populated agrarian society (Jarvis 1979). Nearly 100,000 immigrants, primarily Irish and Catholic, had fled to Canadian shores during
the Irish potato famine of the 1840s (Duncan 1965). Difficulty finding paid
work and the meagre wage offered to women forced many Irish Catholic
women, impoverished and socially dislocated, onto the streets. During the
1850s and 1860s Irish women made up almost 90 percent of females imprisoned for crimes of vagrancy, drunkenness, and prostitution (Phillips 1986).

In Toronto an influx of immigrants, growing poverty, emigration from
rural areas, rising crime rates, and the increased visibility of prostitution
all contributed to a perceived need to deal with the excesses of vast social
change. Toronto's reform-minded citizens were quick to find a scapegoat. As
capitalism expanded and the working class grew, so too among the political,
business, religious, and social elite did the perception of a "working-class
problem." In response Toronto's police force was expanded, and by 1886
it included a morality branch with sweeping powers of arrest. Although
reformers mainly directed their claims of moral decay at the urban problem
of crime, female sexual immorality was a key reform target. While out-of-
control working-class male youth also captured the elite's ire, the "boy problem" was primarily couched in languages of aggression and masculinity, and
was widely understood as a class issue.[6] For women and girls the temptations
of the city took on a distinctly gendered character. That houses of ill fame
increasingly cropped up and more women solicited on city streets (making
prostitution more visible) did not help. Members of the clergy, politicians,
and social reformers constructed prostitution as a female problem, deflect-
ing attention away from men. In short, prostitution symbolized the growing
problems of nineteenth-century urban Canada (Strange 1995). As a group
prostitutes were outside the bounds of acceptability and largely perceived
of as being disposable.[7]

The regulation of prostitution is a classic example of how criminalization
is gendered. In the nineteenth century, prostitution was not a rigidly defined
indictable crime, but a status offence having to do with lifestyle. Legislators
passed statutes authorizing arrest and detention of prostitutes as early as
1759 in Nova Scotia, 1839 in Lower Canada, and 1858 in Upper Canada.
An early Quebec ordinance read: "All common prostitutes or night walkers
wandering in the fields, public streets or highways, not giving satisfactory
account of themselves" may be arrested.[8] In 1867 Parliament passed An
Act Respecting Vagrancy, which singled out "all common prostitutes, or
night walkers," and added that all "keepers of bawdy houses and houses of
ill-fame, or houses for the resort of prostitutes, and persons in the habit of

frequenting such houses, not giving a satisfactory account of themselves" warranted punishment.[9] Hence, practices across the country, which continue to this day, of incarcerating women involved in the sex trade were codified in law. Police, magistrates, and judges presumed that prostitution was a female vice that signalled sexual immorality, undermined the morality of a growing nation, and therefore required a punitive response.

A woman found in a public space without an "acceptable" reason for her presence could find herself under suspicion of prostitution, or it could happen simply as a result of dress, demeanour, or presumed flawed character. Police exercised considerable discretion in deciding when and against whom to apply laws. Without sufficient grounds for being in public places, working-class and impoverished women were, in Smart's terms, "perpetually problematic." Mariana Valverde (1991) argues that with sexuality constructed as belonging to the exclusively familial sphere, the notoriously public quality of prostitution makes it inherently problematic. Of course, given a woman's presumed place in the private sphere, the woman who sells sex in the marketplace is beyond the confines of heterosexual, upper-middle-class femininity. Ravaged by poverty, disease, and alcohol, and subject to unrelenting police attention, scores of nineteenth-century women found themselves detained in local jails and housed together with habitual male offenders (Backhouse 1991). By the early 1850s, some females were supervised by female officials in makeshift wings of mixed prisons.[10] Between 1867 and 1917 criminal laws delineating prostitution grew from a few regulations directed against prostitution as vagrancy, to a more complex set of provisions with wide police powers of arrest and detention (McLaren 1986). In other words, the net of social control over "perpetually problematic" females was strengthened and cast wider.[11] Within this punitive context of women's penalty we can situate the efforts of the Refuge's Founders.

## "Our Home Is for Fallen Women": The Emergence of the Toronto Industrial Refuge

At a time when women were excluded from public affairs, the Friends of the Magdalene Society, comprising a small group of Protestant, upper-middle-class British and Scottish women, proposed an alternative to the prevailing conditions. English and Scottish clergy, businessmen, and local state representatives had established separate, non-statutory institutions called "Magdalene homes," intended to divert young women away from prisons and poorhouses.[12] Linda Mahood (1990) argues that male reformers used their roles as professionals (doctors, lawyers, and ministers) to legitimate their participation in prostitution control. In Canada the Founders of the Toronto Industrial Refuge — many of whom had grown up in England and Scotland — were influenced by the Magdalene homes and refuges in Europe, and by 1853 had developed their own rescue and reform strategy on Canadian soil. To begin, a small group of Protestant, upper-middle-class British and Scottish women established the Toronto Magdalene Asylum, later called the Industrial House of Refuge for Females, or Belmont House. The institution's humble beginnings can be largely attributed to the work of Elizabeth Dunlop, who organized a group of like-situated women to construct a "Home for Fallen Women" for the purpose of providing institutional care and rehabilitation to would-be prostitutes and those likened to them (Minaker 2003). The institution opened in one of the Founder's homes, and in its first year admitted nineteen inmates. In contrast to their European counterparts, the Refuge was entirely volunteer-based, women-run, and, until the 1920s, located at a distance from the penal system.[13]

### Prostitution and the Erring Female

The dominant mid-Victorian discourse defined the female prostitute and other intemperate, homeless, or otherwise destitute women as "fallen women." The metaphor permeated art, literature, and upper-middle-class consciousness (Winnifrith 1994). The female prostitute, as the dominant culture constructed her, had fallen more deeply and required more punishment than did male customers or male prostitutes. Indeed, the legal and state authorities, prison officials, and religious male elite constituted female offenders as beyond penitence and rescue. The Founders were critical of this dominant male penal approach that criminalized women and were troubled by the plight of the women caught up in it. In their view, incarcerating women in prison was an ineffective strategy to thwart prostitution. More importantly, the Founders believed that such women deserved Christian sympathy and maternal compassion, not scorn or ridicule. Put simply, erring females required protection, not punishment. In this ethos, the Founders directed their efforts toward the moral reformation of prostitutes and other working-class women whom they saw (because of intemperance, promiscuity, or abandonment) in danger of becoming prostitutes.

The Founders were both constrained and privileged by gender. To the dominant male business, political, and social elite (many of whom were their husbands), they were subordinate. Nevertheless, they exerted considerable power in their ability to both contest and (re)produce an erring female as being someone in need of rescue and reform. In keeping with the view that the female prostitute was a prime target for intervention, the Founders advocated a different form of detention. They argued, "Vice pollutes the moral atmosphere, then, is the call for an antidote."[14] Their institution, they proposed, was a "home for fallen women," a place of safety that offered moral, religious, and domestic training.[15] Like U.S. reformatories, as Estelle Freedman (1981) and Nicole Rafter (1985a) have argued, the Refuge sought to fulfill the mutually reinforcing functions of sexual and vocational control.

The Founders did not contest the social structural conditions and ideological relations that segregated working-class women as different, as Other. Rather, they reinforced the divide between propertied and non-propertied, elite and poor, men and women, white and non-white, good girls and bad girls. The lives of the working-class women who became inmates were constrained not just by their gender, but also by their marginalized class and (for many) ethnic or race position. As Freedman (1981: 20) explains, "The line that separated the pure woman from the fallen woman demarcated privilege on one side and degradation on the other."

### Christian Stewardship and Maternalism

A Christian stewardship approach underlined the Founders' view that (prospective) inmates were more sinned against than sinning. Their model was Mary Magdalene, whom, according to the New Testament, Jesus Christ befriended and saved, curing her of evil spirits, "from whom seven demons had come out."[16] To convince a Bible-reading, churchgoing Protestant community of the worthiness of their mission, the Founders' choice of Mary Magdalene was a clever one. Insofar as they required public support and held their Christian beliefs sacred, the Founders constructed the erring female as their "fallen daughter," one warranting public sympathy, Christian compassion, and, just as significantly, pecuniary assistance.

Underlying their campaign was not only their sense of Christian duty to solve moral problems, but also their belief that being female provided them with a special expertise for intervening in such matters.[17] They relied on this "innate woman's knowledge" to justify their self-assigned status as moral reformers. In (re)producing the erring female they simultaneously constituted themselves as Christians and as respectable women, as "best suited to reform the fallen and degraded of [their] sex."[18] The image that the Founders had of themselves was dependent, then, on the women they sought to help — and so too were their careers, given that they found purpose in organizing and managing the Refuge.

## Shifting Representations and Their Implications

The category of erring female was not stable; it was a shifting representation held together by the theme of "wayward" sexuality and problematic bodies. Between 1853 and 1939, different representations of the erring female proliferated and rendered her governable. The women who found themselves inside the Refuge were marked with a variety of troublesome identities, including the "fallen woman" and the "incorrigible girl."

### Fallen Woman/Voluntary Prisoner: The Erring Female as Rescuable

The Founders preferred to view inmates as "voluntary prisoners" and declared their door open to any woman who "earnestly desire[d] reform."[19] Jane W.'s case exemplifies this representation at work. Making good on her promise to visitors at a local gaol, Jane entered the Refuge on December 14, 1859. Erring females like her, a twenty-nine-year-old prostitute, were prime candidates. The Admission Committee asked Jane her motive and country of origin, and requested information about her parents and friends. Jane, it turned out, was an Irish immigrant whose life in Canada was marked by economic and social deprivation. More importantly (to them), the Committee members asked Jane how long she had been leading "an abandoned or dissipated life."[20] She explained that she had arrived in Canada in 1856 and became involved in prostitution soon after that. Next, Jane listened to the rules of the institution and the conditions under which her entry would be granted. Like all prospective inmates, Jane had to promise to remain in the institution for twelve months (a required probation period to test the inmate's sincerity for reform), to "be obedient, industrious, clean and tidy," and to refrain from "all bad language, and improper conduct." Jane expressed her desire to reform and pledged that she would stay for one year. With a signed order from the Committee, Jane met the matron, who found her a room in an open dormitory.

Jane began a regimented routine of moral and industrial training (learning domesticity through work in the laundry) in order to "bring about a healthy state of mind and body," and she was given religious instruction and guidance (learning piety through church services).[21] This routine was augmented by a maternal discipline because, as the Founders put it, "the selfish and the violent [require] control, and our only power over them is the firm hand and tender heart."[22] The Founders argued that the routine, habits, and skills developed in the Refuge would prepare the inmates both physically and mentally for usefulness as domestic servants after they left the home. They argued: "We aim at making them good servants, and would deprecate teaching them any habit in the home that might seriously interfere with their usefulness as domestics."[23]

The Founders distanced the institution from the punitive taint of a reformatory or penitentiary, emphasizing that the Refuge was a benevolent, Christian home. They adamantly argued that "the Refuge is in no sense a prison … it is voluntary and reformatory."[24] As the Founders put it, "Recollect they are voluntary prisoners, we cannot keep them against their wills."[25] For decades, the Founders' discourse of voluntariness legitimated the institutionalization of females for their own protection.

Another inmate, Alice B., was recorded as "voluntarily" committing herself to the Refuge on March 2, 1879, at age sixteen — and did not leave until June 13, 1935. Was Alice a "voluntary prisoner?" The voluntariness of the institution was more rhetoric than practice, as Alice's case suggests.

Sarah H. entered the Refuge in the late nineteenth century of "her own free will," at age thirty-four. An English, single domestic living in Toronto, Sarah had one child. Viewed as immoral, she is typical of how the Founders saw their charges in the early years. The Founders believed that women like Sarah could be rescued if they voluntarily submitted themselves to the kindness and restraints of the Refuge. This "choice," most likely made in dire circumstances, signalled for the Founders that an inmate was an erring female in need of reformation, but also signified her consent to submit to the strategies employed to regulate, control, and otherwise govern her. Only a voluntary prisoner could be "invited, encouraged and protected" to a place of safety. Only a female in need of protection could require a probation period of twelve months to test her sincerity. Only in a Christian home could she be rescued, reformed, and restored.

By the turn of the twentieth century the Refuge had become an accepted non-penal, volunteer-run site for the governance of female sexuality. The Founders carved a niche for their institution and themselves among the Christian community, philanthropic elite, and general public of Toronto not by challenging views of the prostitute and those likened to her as Other, but by reproducing widely accepted censures. Looking beyond what the Founders claimed to what they did not say reveals that they took up the call to respond to this problematic female without disrupting, but rather by upholding, traditional race, class, and gender hierarchies. Insofar as they remained silent on several significant issues, the Founders (re)produced the erring female censure.

First, they remained silent about the role of men in prostitution. While the Founders displayed more sympathy than did male lawmakers to the plight of working-class women, they echoed the law's reading of prostitution by identifying prostitution with the women who sold their services, and they ignored male clients.

Second, they remained silent about social structures. In so doing, the Founders directed their energies only on one manifestation of poverty — namely, the presence of working-class women on the streets, in houses of prostitution, and in gaols. While women like the "good hearted, but immoral,"[26] Lizzie G. may have been responding to the stresses and strains of marginalization (rather than intentionally bumping up against middle-class sensibilities of gender and sexuality), they surely offended the standards of respectability held dear to the Founders. Whereas the Founders admitted that exposure to evil environments was the chief factor that contributed to a woman's downfall, they believed this exposure was a moral problem that could be solved by reforming individual characters. Such reformation, rather than dealing with the constraints of social structures, relied on women making "better choices," a view indicative of the responsibilization that accompanied the moral censuring of profligate young women during this era. The Founders argued, "We must never forget that many girls when 'out of place' have no homes to go to, and are driven, from want of funds to pay for respectable board, into wretched hovels, which are in most cases the haunts of vice."[27] The Founders acknowledged that social structures such as poverty compelled some women onto the streets, but refused to question the women's lack of economic and social opportunities.

Third, while the Founders inferred manifestations of poverty, crime, and destitution from women's appearance, dress, behaviour, and attitude, these conditions mattered insofar as they signified the moral character, not structural location, of each female. The Founders took such attributes as signs of individual failing rather than signals of structural circumstances. At least rhetorically, an inmate's past was deemed irrelevant once inside, as evidenced in the phrases "not a veil but a thick curtain" and "no allusion to past character" that guided the rules of management.[28] The rhetorical erasure of a woman's past history notwithstanding, censuring practices inside the Refuge were more likely rife with references to these women's "immoral" backgrounds.[29]

Finally, although the Founders emphasized that the door was open to "all fallen and degraded women," they did turn potential inmates away. In other words, there was a limited range of acceptability for potential inmates; some were found unreformable or beyond the pale of rescue. Reformability was equated with (among other criteria) degrees of whiteness, as the reformable, socially tolerable erring female was Irish or Scottish, while the *unreformable Other* was non-white or non-Anglo Celtic. Admission records show no Black or Aboriginal women (until the 1920s, when the state took over admission). The Founders did not question, but reproduced the gender, class, and racial order of the day.

### Incorrigible Girl: The Erring Female as Punishable

Eugenics discourse in the early 1910s reshaped the representation of the erring female, as someone errant not only in soul and body, but also now in mind (see, for example, Galton 1907; McLaren 1990; Dowbiggin 1997). Eugenicists argued that female sexuality was the source of race degeneracy. Indeed, eugenics discourse reinforced race, class, and gender anxieties about female sexuality, influencing the creation of the medical category "feeble-mindedness" (not medically insane or an idiot, but simple). It also led to a proliferation of techniques for diagnosing and treating venereal disease, and brought about an increased attention to sexual promiscuity among females.[30] During this period of heightened social tensions, a little-used act of 1897, amended in the Revised Statutes of the Female Refuges Act (1917), would come to have an impact on the Refuge.

In 1919 the Lieutenant-Governor of Ontario designated the Refuge as "an institution for the care of females" under the Female Refuges Act. Consequently, admission policies changed such that the Board no longer controlled who entered and how long they stayed. Clause 13 of the FRA stipulated: "No person shall be admitted to an Industrial Refuge except on warrant, signed by a Judge; or a transfer Warrant signed by the Inspector." The Refuge could no longer claim that the inmates were "voluntary prisoners." Legally committed to the institution, inmates were required by law to stay indefinitely to a maximum of two years.

To be criminalized under the FRA, girls and women did not have to commit infractions against the Criminal Code. Rather, their conduct, dress, disposition, character, and habits got them incarcerated insofar as they transgressed gender-appropriate cultural scripts. The concerns raised by child-savers, juvenile justice officials, and parents over working-class girls' wayward characters diverged from the anxieties that these same actors attached to delinquent boys. Then again, the subjection of girls to a sexual double standard was nothing new. Before the FRA, as feminist historians have observed, girls — unlike their male counterparts — were arrested and institutionalized for violations of virtuous feminine conduct and errant sexuality (Odem 1995; Myers 1999; Sangster 2000). With the FRA, girls needed only to betray their gender to warrant incarceration. The sensibilities behind specifically institutionalizing females are evident in a 1903 Annual Report: "is not always possible to win the girls by kindness. Sometimes we are forced to acknowledge that stronger measures are necessary." [31]

The Female Refuges Act was unique in the kinds of regulatory offences that it controlled — discursive constructions of errant sexuality such as "incorrigible," "unmanageable," "idle and dissolute" — and in its scope. The FRA constructed the erring female's sexuality by equating categories of idleness and dissoluteness with promiscuity and lax working-class morals (Sangster 1996). Not coincidentally, females of childbearing years were the main subjects of the Act's provisions. Under the FRA, any female between the ages of fifteen and thirty-five could be imprisoned for behaviours such as public drunkenness, promiscuity, and pregnancy out of wedlock. As Smart (1995: 55) poignantly puts it: "Women and girls who have sex outside of marriage are still regarded as promiscuous, or more colloquially as slags and sluts; unmarried women are still unable to legitimize their children without getting married." Anyone, such as a husband or parent, could swear before a magistrate as to the inappropriate behaviour of a wife or daughter. The burden rested upon the female, whose only recourse was to prove that she was not "unmanageable" or "incorrigible" — and few were successful in doing so.

The FRA appeared to invest non-state agencies and actors, such as the Refuge and the Founders, with the power to criminalize in the context of regulatory offences (Comack and Balfour 2004). Through the lens of censure, we can begin to see the expansive forms of the moral regulation of women and girls beyond the criminal justice system. Ontario's FRA, in place between 1897 and 1964, demonstrates that the power to criminalize is not restricted to criminal law. The FRA's legitimacy, in effect, gave non-criminal offences the meaning and penal consequences of crimes, thereby criminalizing those under its purview. Its authority was not questioned until the Elizabeth Fry Society called for its repeal fifty years later. In December 2002 Velma Demerson received a letter of apology from the Attorney General of Ontario. The letter stated that the FRA "had unfortunate and unjustified consequence for you and other women who were unjustifiably incarcerated under its provisions" (cited in Demerson 2004: 165).

That females incarcerated under the FRA did not have to have been engaged in criminal activity suggests that something else was at stake — namely, reproducing a gendered, classist, and racialized social order. Like the Refuge, the FRA not merely upheld upper-middle-class standards of femininity, but was also a key part of state formation and the building of a white, male-dominated Canada. The FRA did not radically restructure the practices at the Refuge, which suggests that the legislation merely replicated widespread racist, class, and gendered biases that were already at work there.

## From FRA to PCHIP and PSECA: The Neo-Liberal Guise of Protection

Today the erring female has not disappeared but rather has emerged in different forms. This is most visible in regulatory legislation, such as Alberta's Protection of Children Involved in Prostitution Act (PCHIP) and its successor, the Protection of Sexually Exploited Children Act (PSECA).

Coming into force in February 1999, PCHIP empowered police and child welfare officials to incarcerate children (in effect, young females) "whose safety is at risk, but who will not voluntarily end their involvement in prostitution" (Alberta Government 1999). The Act allowed for the youth to be held in protective confinement for a seventy-two-hour assessment, with additional provisions that allowed authorities to apply for two more periods of detainment for up to twenty-one days each if child-care workers needed more time to help the youth end their involvement in prostitution (Bittle 2006: 201). As Steven Bittle (2006) notes, PCHIP reinforced and advanced neo-liberal strategies of control through a child protection discourse. PCHIP was introduced in the wake of the release of the Badgely Commission's report, which widely condemned conventional practices of punishing young girls for their involvement in prostitution as crimes of immorality. Instead, the Commission sought to legitimize a new discourse of children as victims of sexual exploitation. Provincial governments saw the Commission's recommendations as an opportunity for helping kids "at almost any cost" (Bittle 2006: 199) through an expansive regime of policing and apprehension of at-risk children within high-crime communities. Yet beneath the discourse of children protection existed a neo-liberal ethos that made families and communities responsible for the sexual exploitation of children. In particular, families on social assistance were seen as being weakened by their dependence on welfare and lacking resiliency to respond to risk (Bittle 2006: 205). Families were therefore to be "empowered" to turn their at-risk children over to Children's Aid or the police. In this way, families were "governed at a distance" through soft-state powers of protection and control. Similarly, young girls were "empowered" to take responsibility for their choices to become street-involved and placing themselves at risk. For example, Bittle quotes from the Alberta Task Force on Children

Involved in Prostitution (known as the Forsyth Report), which led to the introduction of PCHIP:

> Although these youth are seen as victims, the Task Force believes they must still take *responsibility* for their actions and accept the consequences. Youth must be *responsible* and *accountable* for their own involvement in crime — sometimes associated with the street life — and for the decision to leave the street. (Forsyth Report, cited in Bittle 2006: 206, emphasis added)

Once in detention under PCHIP, girls were seen as suffering from low self-esteem and in need of "compassion with a hard edge" (Rose, cited in Bittle 2006: 207). By individualizing and psychologizing the problems associated with young people's involvement in the sex trade, the approach elided the material and social factors that make prostitution a "choice" for some young women.

In 2007 the Protection of Sexually Exploited Children Act replaced PCHIP (Alberta Government 2010). While the new act marked a discursive shift from "young prostitutes" to "sexually exploited children," the state's power of detention "for their own good" remained.[32] Under section 2 (1) of PSECA a police officer or director under the Child, Youth, and Family Enhancement Act has the authority to apprehend (that is, the court-approved act of taking custody of a child) "if a child's safety is at risk and is considered to be in need of protection" and to confine the child for up to five days in a protective safe house (Government of Alberta 2010). As they could with PCHIP, authorities can apply to a court for up to two additional twenty-one-day periods (forty-seven days in total). According to the legislation, "a safe and secure environment" in which the child can have access to "a number of services including drug and alcohol counselling, medical supports, counselling and psychological services, and educational and life-skills support" is intended to "assist the child in breaking the cycle of abuse" (Government of Alberta 2010). What happens during this period of apprehension and confinement would, of course, remain to be seen, but the questions around power relations, authorized knowers, and constrained choice linger on. Moreover, the individualization of the erring female — now found in contemporary neo-liberal discourse as a sexually exploited child — avoids discussion of the wider systemic and structural problems.

Just as significant, as Bittle (2006: 211) notes, "The introduction of the victim discourse and secure care has not ended the criminalization of youth involved in the sex trade; it has simply repackaged the concept of punishment under the guise of protection — it's the same foot, just a different shoe." Under the guise of protection, today young women are being detained against their will, held on non-criminal charges, and otherwise punished for conditions that are not of their own choosing, just as they were in the Refuge, before and after FRA. Their struggles (the experiences that led to their involvement with reformers and child welfare workers or conflicts with parents) are not just over their sexuality but also over their life chances; and they are inexorably connected to issues of race, class, and gender. In other words, the real problem is not incorrigibility or errant sexuality, but rather marginalization and social exclusion. Meaningful change, therefore, requires acknowledging and addressing the social inequalities and the accompanying realities that marginalized girls confront — including violence and abuse, homelessness, solo parenting, addictions, and mental health issues. Breaking these cycles involves radically changing the "risks" associated with living at the margins of society (gendered violence, poverty, and racism). In these neo-liberal times, the "risky young woman" shoulders far too great a burden.

Before the Refuge came under the FRA, race, class, and gender determined whether one was to be "kept" or a "keeper" inside the Refuge. These censures are still class-compounded and racialized. Although PCHIP, and its replacement, PSECA, emerged in the context of neo-liberalism decades after the FRA, the theme of criminalization continues. Each act is a provincial piece of regulatory legislation that had and has the power to criminalize. The erring female censure is still operating, now almost blending *punishable* and *rescuable*. Errant sexuality has been reinvented as sexual exploitation (and even socially constructed as sexual empowerment), but a similar response continues. Why? For what it sustains and replicates. The erring female incarnate represents girls and women who — by immorality, degradation, mental defect, intemperance (historically), or inadequate parenting, promiscuity, drug abuse (today), or otherwise — deviate from the dominant standards of appropriate femininity. More importantly, the erring female censure works to reinforce and reproduce dominant power relations.

Despite shifting representations, the sexual double standard remains irrefutably transfixed at the centre of the good girl/bad girl dichotomy. This condition is most disconcerting for marginalized young mothers, who, like Velma (now in her nineties), find themselves without adequate material resources and care. My research on marginalized young mothering has revealed that as social supports become more difficult to access, living conditions deteriorate and a cycle of dependency, shame, and blame continues (Minaker 2014). Still deemed "erring" for mothering outside social-cultural scripts, the young women who parent in the context of marginalization face stigma, shame, and social isolation. In the feminist quest for social justice and critique of institutions and laws aimed at controlling females, we cannot abandon the very real need for care that we all share. Dehumanizing labels like "sluts and slags" reflect a masculinist, elitist, "us versus them" mentality that prevents some people from acknowledging our collective responsibility to practise care for the Other. Historically, the underlying social-structural constraints (race, class, and gender inequalities among them) in the lives of criminalized girls and women were obscured from view under the FRA and within the Refuge. They go unchecked today because they are the very conditions that, in the great majority of cases, distinguish "good girls" from "bad girls" and work to sustain the ideological and social order.

## Notes

I want to thank Gillian Balfour, Elizabeth Comack, Bryan Hogeveen, and Bob Menzies for sharing their ideas, insights, and inquiries with me and for the enormous assistance such provided. Special gratitude goes to my daughter, Maylah Hogeveen, who reminds me to keep challenging the limiting socio-cultural scripts for women.

1. For more on Velma's case, see Dalpy 2002; Landsberg 2001; and Wong 2002.
2. For a similar point about the concentration of liminal "moral deviant" females in the anti-vice campaigns in Vancouver during the early 1940s, see Freund 2002.
3. *Annual Report*, Toronto Industrial Refuge, 1860, p. 1.
4. Carol Smart (1995: 231) makes a similar point: "I think we do need to address this Woman of legal discourse... because actual women are affected by being mistaken for her, or for failing to conform to her and so on."
5. *Annual Report*, Toronto Industrial Refuge, 1860, p.1.
6. For a discussion of the boy problem, see Hogeveen 2003. For a discussion of the girl problem, see Strange 1995 and Alexander 1995.
7. For a contemporary example we need look no further than the recent deaths of numerous women in the sex trade in Western Canada and the police treatment of those deaths.
8. An Ordinance for Establishing a System of Police for the Cities of Quebec and Montreal, 2 Vict. (1) (1839), c. 2 (Lower Canada).
9. 32 and 33 Vict. (1869) c. 28, s.1 (Dominion of Canada).
10. Following England's Elizabeth Fry, the idea of providing separate reformatory institutions for such women first materialized on North American soil in the U.S. reformatory movement, which began in 1840 and peaked between 1870 and 1920. See Freedman 1981 and Rafter 1985a.
11. In addition to harsh criminal law, nineteenth-century legislators made other types of legislation to govern female sexuality. The Contagious Diseases Act, enacted in 1865, permitted detaining women with venereal disease. Though repealed in 1870 and not fully enforced, it was the beginning of a proliferation of responses to errant female sexuality.
12. See Peter Mullan's 2002 film, *The Magdalene Sisters*.
13. While the U.S. reformatory movement influenced the role that women came to play in

the development of the Refuge, the Toronto Magdalen Asylum predated the Canadian government's establishment of the Andrew Mercer Reformatory for Females by twenty-one years. See Minaker 2003.

14. *Annual Report*, Toronto Industrial Refuge, 1870, p. 8.
15. *Annual Report*, Toronto Industrial Refuge, 1880, p. 7.
16. The Holy (Christian) Bible, New Testament, Luke 8:2.
17. Notably, they did not extend this ability to those they sought to help.
18. *Annual Report*, Toronto Industrial Refuge, 1872, p. 7.
19. *Annual Report*, Toronto Industrial Refuge, 1868, p. 7.
20. *Annual Report*, Toronto Industrial Refuge, 1868, pp. 7, 14.
21. *Annual Report*, Toronto Industrial Refuge, 1870, p. 9.
22. *Annual Report*, Toronto Industrial Refuge, 1893, p. 8.
23. *Annual Report*, Toronto Industrial Refuge, 1860.
24. *Annual Report*, Toronto Industrial Refuge, 1862, p. 7.
25. *Annual Report*, Toronto Industrial Refuge, 1877.
26. Case Records, Toronto Industrial Refuge, no date.
27. *Annual Report*, Toronto Industrial Refuge, 1864, p. 8.
28. Rules for Management, Toronto Industrial Refuge, 1876.
29. Special thanks to Bob Menzies for helping me to clarify this point.
30. *Annual Report*, Toronto Industrial Refuge, 1909.
31. *Annual Report*, Toronto Industrial Refuge, 1903, pp. 8-9
32. Alberta's central piece of legislation, the Child Youth and Family Enhancement Act, governs the legal protection of children and is the legal authority for providing child intervention services. The act supports the development and well-being of Alberta's children, youth, and families while keeping them safe and protected.

3

# The Incall Sex Industry
## Gender, Class, and Racialized Labour in the Margins

*Chris Bruckert & Colette Parent*

Prostitution has long (albeit inaccurately) been referred to as the world's oldest profession. It is striking, therefore, that the women employed in the sex industry have rarely been defined as workers — much less professionals — in either popular discourse or academic analysis. For the most part, until the 1960s, when symbolic interactionists shifted the focus (cf. Bryan 1965; Laner 1974; Velarde 1975; Heyl 1977, 1979), positivist accounts of prostitution dominated the debate (cf. Lombroso 1895 [1985]; Flexner 1920; Rolph 1955; Greenwald 1958; Glover 1969). In the 1970s new voices emerged. While radical feminists developed a gender-based analysis on the issue, sex workers in a number of countries — including Canada, the United States, England, and the Netherlands — started to organize, to speak about their work, and to defend their interests in groups such as Corp, Coyote, Pros, and the Red Thread. In opposition to the work of radical feminists, who perceived prostitution as victimization, the discourses that emerged from women within the industry emphasized the activity as work, thereby denouncing the legally defined classifications, moral subtext, and conceptual baggage encapsulated in the term "prostitution."

The term "sex work," famously coined by Scarlet Harlot (Koyama 2002: 5), represents much more than a linguistic subtlety. It is a powerful concept that undermines normative assumptions as it compels reconsideration not only of the industry but also of the relegation of sexuality to the private realm. But this reframing continues to be challenged from a number of different quarters. In Canada counter-arguments were presented in submissions to the courts in the 2013 *Bedford* case, in which one current and two former sex workers challenged the constitutionality of Criminal Code sections 213(1)(c), 210, and 212(1)(j) that de facto criminalize sex work(ers) (see: *Bedford v Canada [Attorney General]* 2013). The Women's Coalition (2011) took a prohibitionist approach rooted in radical feminism when its members argued in their factum, "Prostitution is a global practice of sexual exploitation and male violence against women" (para. 3). By contrast, the Christian Legal Fellowship, REAL Women of Canada, and the Catholic Civil

Rights League (2009) drew on the trope of the conservative right when they asserted, "Prostitution is immoral [and] it should be stigmatized" (para. 5) because it "violates the human dignity of both prostitutes and those who are witnesses to it" (para. 23).

Here we draw on qualitative research from two research projects to explore the implications, limits, and potential for conceptualizing prostitution as sex work — specifically by integrating labour theory into criminology to examine the often overlooked but long-established commercial incall sex industry.[1] The term "incall sex work" emerged from the research and speaks to the subjective importance of specific labour structures. In contrast to outcall workers (such as escorts), incall workers provide sexual services to clients in establishments such as massage parlours, brothels, and dungeons. While incall workers can be male or female and can also work as "independents" (by, for example, receiving clients in their own homes, hotel rooms, or incall locations) our examination focuses on women who labour for third parties in an employment-like relationship.

A number of theoretical and political implications emerge when we think about women's work in the sex industry as classed, raced, and gendered labour. The labour structure, labour process, and experience of women workers in this sector are all key to this discussion, and so too are links to the work of working-class women labouring in other consumer services. Indeed, numerous points of convergence speak not only to the validity of framing sex work as "work," but also to the importance of rethinking women's labour in the new economy and destabilizing the private/public and sexuality/work dichotomies.

## Theorizing Sex Work as "Work"

While feminist engagement with the question of prostitution dates back to the progressive era of the early twentieth century, it was in the 1970s, in the context of a broader rethinking of gender and patriarchy, that prostitution emerged as the symbol of the social, sexual, and economic domination of women by men.[2] Within this framework developed by radical feminists, prostitutes — and by extension pornography performers and erotic dancers — emerged as victims. Their status as victims was seen to emanate from the capitalist and patriarchal social structures and the racism inscribed in discriminatory laws and their enforcement, from mistreatment and objectification by men (pimps and customers) who experience a sense of power over all women through the purchase of one representative member, and from the circumstances of their lives — based on the presumption that they were victims of childhood sexual abuse, incest, and rape (cf. Millett 1971; Mignard 1976; James 1977; Barry 1979; Wilson 1983; Jeffreys 1985; O'Hara 1985; Wynter 1987).

This perspective continues to resonate in recent writing that asserts that sex work "itself is a form of sexualized male violence" (Day 2008: 28) existing "at the intersection of incest, rape, battery, and torture" (Holsopple 1999: 49). Indeed, in this framing sex workers are not active agents but prostituted women (cf. Raphael and Myers 2010; Raphael, Reichert, and Powers 2010; Day 2008; Carter 2004; Lakeman, Lee, and Jay 2004; Farley 2003, 2004; Poulin 2004). These sex-work-as-violence feminists also continue to link prostitution to socio-economic structures, including gender stratifications, racialization, and poverty that restrict options; colonization is identified as part of this: "[Aboriginal people] have a long, multi-generational history of colonization, marginalization, and displacement from our Homelands, and rampant abuses that has forced many of our sisters into prostitution" (AWAN nd).

Feminist conversations on sex work are, however, splintered. Some feminists have reassessed sex work (Rickart and Store 2001), listened to industry workers, and integrated sex workers' discourse into their analysis (cf. van der Meulen, Durisin, and Love 2013; O'Doherty, 2011; Bruckert and Chabot 2010; Brock 2009; van der Meulen and Durisin 2008; Parent 1994, 2001; Parent and Bruckert 2010; Jeffrey and MacDonald 2006; Mensah 2006; Ross 2006; Lewis and Shaver 2006; Shaver 2005; Bruckert, Parent, and Robitaille 2003).[3] In contrast to the sex-work-as-violence perspective this literature both assumes as a point of departure that sex work is an income-generating activity and recognizes that broader socio-economic stratifications and scripts (including gender, economic resource distribution, and racialization) condition the range of options open to sex workers — thus creating situations in which some individuals engage in sex work in the context of constrained choice alternatives (cf. Jeffrey and MacDonald 2006; Kinnell 2002; Weldon 2006; Namaste 2005; Scambler 2007). In this respect there is a recognition that restricted choice does not negate agency: "choosing" this particular work in the context of limited and often unpleasant choices does not mean that sex work is more of a survival tactic than choosing to take on other available jobs. Moreover, a diversity of factors enters into play; some women are compelled (or perceive themselves to be compelled) to engage in the sex trade by their abusive partners, their substance or drug use, their fear of deportation, or their abject poverty. For these women, prostitution is "work," although it is not necessarily as much of a job as one of a number of other income-generating activities in which they participate. In this regard the issue of substance use/abuse is key (see Parent and Bruckert 2006). While many women workers in the sex industry are not drug consumers and others maintain a professional labour relationship to the industry despite being consumers of illicit substances, for a small minority of women sex work is intertwined with drug consumption patterns. They will, unlike the women whose relationship to the industry is one of work, exchange sex for drugs.

While the literature reflects on the role of racialization and the impact of colonization on Aboriginal women, we need also to recognize that colonization plays a role in the exclusion of sex workers as women with agency. As Sarah Hunt (2013: 87) notes, "In discussions about colonial violence Indigenous sex workers are often invoked as nameless, voiceless, placeless victims, in memory of past in-justices." As Hunt explains, "The lives and voices of Indigenous sex workers are obscured by discourses of victimization that, on the surface, aim to draw attention to marginalization and colonial violence but fail to provide a space for Indigenous sex workers to speak for themselves and define their own struggles" (2013: 89). We need, in other words, to acknowledge racialized and Indigenous sex workers as women with agency and provide a space from which they can speak for themselves and define their own struggles.

Our work here, which straddles labour theory and criminology, is situated within this emerging body of literature. Labour theory not only reflects the subject position of workers in the industry, but also allows us to step outside of the traditional criminological analysis of deviance to examine these jobs as jobs. A recognition of sex work as gendered labour that occurs in a broader context of racialization immediately places the industry and its workers within a dynamic socio-economic context. In this sense we need to consider what the economic restructuring of the last three decades (intensified by the global economic downturn of 2009) means for Canadian women in general while attending in particular to how some women's choices are conditioned by intersections of gender with racialization and/or class location. In Canada not only do working-class women continue to be ghettoized in sales, service, and clerical occupations (Statistics Canada 2006), but the post-industrial labour market is also increasingly characterized by "McJobs" (Ritzer 2004: 148): low-paid, deskilled, monotonous, and highly monitored service-sector work that offers workers neither satisfaction nor stability — nor, for that matter, a living wage (Ritzer 2004: 108–15). Moreover, at the same time another parallel trend is obvious. Women increasingly inhabit a precarious labour-market location characterized by temporary and part-time work (Williams 2010). The practice exacerbates marginality: women workers in these labour situations not only experience greater gender income disparity than do their counterparts in the traditional labour market, but are also denied the security and benefits traditionally associated with employment. That said, even full-time women workers between the ages of twenty-five and fifty-four earn just 76 cents to the male dollar (Steinstra 2010: 4). Importantly the gender income gap is considerably greater for racialized women. For example, in Ontario racialized women have higher rates of unemployment, and those who are employed earn just 53.4 percent of what non-racialized men and 84.7 percent of non-racialized women earn (Block 2010: 3). It is within the context of these constraints and alternatives that women are "choosing" to work at McDonald's, in the retail sector — or in the sex industry.

The labour lens also allows us to shift our focus from structure to practices — or what workers do (Phillips 1997) — and positions us to consider the nature of the labour. It allows us to render skills and competencies visible, examine social and work relations, and reflect on how workers experience the physical, emotional, and sexual dimensions of their labour. This attention to grounded experience also speaks to specificity within the broadly defined sex industry, thereby providing an antidote to the tendency to unquestionably conflate the divergent labour practices of cam-girls,[4] peep-show attendants, phone-sex operators, street-sex workers, escorts, erotic dancers, and massage parlour/brothel employees under the rubric of "moral transgression."

While invaluable, labour theory, in and of itself, is incomplete — sex work may be work, but it is work that is marginalized, stigmatized, and criminalized. It is imperative that we integrate into the analysis the unique configuration of challenges, problems, and difficulties confronted by women working in sectors of the labour market characterized by social, moral, and criminal justice regulation. By bringing criminology into labour theory, we can attend to the ways in which social and legal discourses and practices influence the organization of labour and the labour process, increase the danger and stress negotiated by workers, and shape the relations of workers to their social and personal worlds.

It is also imperative that we integrate race and class into the analysis. Sex work, its organization, and how it is subjectively experienced are conditioned by the intersection of class, gender, and race. Race/ethnic (much like class) stratifications have "always been one of the bedrock institutions of

Canadian society embedded in the very fabric of our thinking, our personality" (Shadd 1991: 1). As numerous authors have demonstrated, Canadian society is characterized by discriminatory immigration policies, systemic racism, stereotypical media portrayals, and racist discourses that have resulted in a distribution of economic, social, and discursive resources that put racialized Canadians generally and women in particular at a disadvantage (Henry et al. 2000; Dhruvarajan 2002). Put another way, race intersects with class and gender to condition women's choices and opportunities both in the broader labour market *and* in the sex industry.

A recognition of racialization raises a number of important questions. How do racializing discourses and racialized spaces structure the incall sex industry? How do racializing practices and discourses condition the experience of racialized women labouring in the sex industry? At a more theoretical level we can ask, how can we analytically separate race and class and produce an analysis that attends to intersectionality while avoiding the pitfalls of cumulative or essentialist approaches (Joseph 2006)?[5]

## Incall Sex Work as (Criminalized) Women's Work

Incall work can be broadly defined as women providing sexual services in establishments. But the variety of these services — ranging from marginal to illegal — makes classification problematic. Some of the establishments are massage parlours that offer non-contact erotic entertainment and visual titillation only (such as vibrator and hot-tub shows); others offer erotic massage and manual (and in some cases oral) stimulation; others are brothels in which massage is rare but complete sexual services are available. Still other businesses are dungeons, devoted to domination and submission and allowing clients to self-stimulate only. In short, considerable variety exists in work that falls under the rubric of incall sex work.

That diversity is echoed in the women's perspectives. Some of the women we interviewed had jobs that did not require them to have sex, and that aspect was a precipitating factor in their decisions to work in that sector of the industry. Jacqueline, a Toronto-area dungeon worker specializing in domination, explained: *"Escort work I never really considered. I don't know, I'm just not entirely comfortable with the idea of actually having sex."* Other workers did actively engage with sexuality, and many took pleasure in the exploration of this element of the labour. As Crystal, a massage-parlour worker, told us: *"I love sex. I can really let myself go at work. I like to experience new things and try out new things."*

## The Regulatory Context

In Canada, although prostitution per se is not (and has never been) illegal, the industry and the workers are criminalized and sex workers are vulnerable to charges of communicating for the purposes of prostitution (s. 213.1(c)), procuring/living off the avails of prostitution (s. 212.1(j)), or under the common bawdy house provisions (s. 210). Women working in massage parlours, brothels, or dungeons are most frequently criminalized under the bawdy house provision 210.1(b), which stipulates that being an inmate (a resident or regular occupant) of a common bawdy house is an offence punishable by summary conviction. Sex workers can also be charged as "keepers" of a bawdy house (a much more serious offence under section 210.1(a)) if they exercise some measure of control (that is, they answer the phone or lock up at the end of the night) (Bruckert and Law 2013).[6] Notably, on December 20, 2013, the Supreme Court of Canada ruled these provisions to be unconstitutional because they infringed on sex workers' liberty interests contrary to section 7 of the Canadian Charter of Rights and Freedoms. Sex workers' hopes of a decriminalized industry are, however, unlikely to be realized because the federal government indicated that it would introduce new legislation prior to the ruling taking effect on December 20, 2014.

In addition to the criminalization of their labour (or more specifically, of their labour site), some workers in the incall sex industry (unlike their colleagues who solicit clients on the street, for example, but like erotic dancers) are also regulated in a number of municipalities through by-laws pertaining to the body-rub (and sometimes the holistic health) industry. A body-rub is defined as the "kneading, manipulating, rubbing, massaging, touching, or stimulating by any means, of a person's body or part thereof, but does not include medical or therapeutic treatment" (City of Toronto 2010) — activities that could well be defined as prostitution under Canadian jurisprudence. In effect, this means that there is a layering of regulation over criminalization — a situation that does not work in the interests of sex workers. On this point Emily van der Meulen and Mariana Valverde (2013: 321) explain, "It's rare for people working in licensed sex industry establishments to speak out against abuses as any attempt to rectify exploitative working conditions could lead to federal criminal charges, by-law fines, license cancellation, or even the closure of the business itself." Similarly, Jacqueline Lewis and Eleanor Maticka-Tyndale (2000: 445) concluded that "municipal licensing appears to increase police presence in the lives of escorts and to disempower escorts and their employers from taking action to enhance health and safety." While in principle these by-laws could create a safe and controlled space for workers, in practice they extend the regulation, impose additional levels of control, and offer few benefits (van der Meulen and Valverde 2013).

## Labour Structure

Despite the diversity of the incall sex industry, broad organizational similarities are apparent in third-party-managed establishments. In general, workers are scheduled for relatively long shifts of ten to twelve hours, although some places have eight-hour shifts and others allow women to select either long or short shifts. In many establishments, workers are expected to do receptionist duties — which can include answering the phone, booking appointments, explaining the services offered (using more or less explicit code), describing the workers, identifying and declining undesirable clients, and engaging in laundry duties. In addition to these tasks, the women are required to remain on the premises for the duration of their shifts, although they are free to fill their time according to their personal inclinations — sleeping, cooking, reading, studying, socializing.[7] They are also expected to meet the standards of grooming (such as nail policy, makeup) and appearance (such as type of attire) established by the agency. As Moxie, a brothel worker, explained: "*You were expected to have lingerie. You were expected to keep your nails done at all times. You're expected that your hair should be done. And one place I worked all of the girls wore eyelashes and white eyeliner. I don't know where that came from.*"

The establishment sets rates, with workers receiving between 40 to 60 percent of these rates, an amount that supplements the income they generate through tips and/or the provision of "extras" (although some agencies have "no-extra" rules). The workers appreciated the potential revenues — they spoke of their ability to adequately support themselves (and in some cases their children) through sex work. Workers also found that working for an agency made fiscal sense and said they benefited from the agency fees:

> They were in charge of paying the bills, cleaning, all of the day-to-day operations that I may not want to deal with. And also the legal liability for them was higher because they owned the place on paper…. It was having, like, a personal assistant — that was the concept that I was going after was having someone to deal with all the bullshit, and I just had to show up…. Being independent, you're working all of the time. Like, you're constantly answering emails, cleaning your location, shopping for new things. There's so much that goes into it that it's easier just to pay a third party sometimes. (Trina, massage parlour worker)

The women who shared this information, whose highly variable incomes ranged from $40 to $800 per day, can be understood as own-account, self-employed workers operating within a fee-for-service structure without benefit of a guaranteed income. While independent vis-à-vis income, they are nonetheless dependent contractors to the extent that they are reliant on, and required to meet the expectations of, a single operator for the physical space, equipment, supplies, advertisement, and sometimes the services of support staff. These labour sites appear, then, to be consistent with the trend toward non-standard labour arrangements. While not all non-standard workers[8] are vulnerable (Saunders 2003), for working-class women this labour-market position is, generally speaking, precarious. In many cases the jobs operate as "no more than disguised forms of casualized wage-labour, often marked by dependency on capitalist employers through some sort of sub-contracting system" (Bradley 1996: 49).

The disadvantages of the labour structure notwithstanding, workers see some positive elements in addition to the income potential. Most of the women interviewed appreciated the flexibility that allowed them to integrate and manage the many components of their lives (school, children, art, for example). Of course, the desirability of non-standard labour arrangements must be understood within the context of the steady erosion of the welfare state since the 1980s, which has expanded poor women's burdens. Women are increasingly required not only to assume extra labour but also to organize their employment in a manner that allows them to meet their myriad obligations. Women workers who need to satisfy increasing family and financial obligations as the state decreases its levels of support may therefore embrace non-standard labour arrangements, including contract and self-account work.

As dependent contractors, the women are in a paradoxical position. On the one hand, incall sex workers in commercial establishments, like erotic dancers, aestheticians, massage therapists, and hair stylists, are managed as employees — even though they are not wage labourers in the traditional sense but are exchanging a percentage of their earnings for legal protection and access to the necessary legitimizing context, physical space, equipment, and technical support. In short, these workers, like other similarly positioned workers such as hair stylists who rent a chair/booth (Gonzales 2010), are exploited in a Marxian sense of having "free" labour extracted and receiving less remuneration than the value that their labour adds to the product/service (Marx 1974 [1859]). On the other hand, as "disguised" employees, incall sex workers are denied the security and access to statutory protection and legal recourse traditionally associated with employment. The precarious labour-market situation of incall sex workers, like that of many other workers employed in non-standard labour arrangements, is at least in part a function of their exclusion from social-security protection (such as Employment Insurance, Canadian Pension Plan), non-statutory benefits (health and dental plans, disability benefits, paid sick leave), and statutory rights (minimum wage, holiday and overtime pay, job protection, notice of termination).

The issue is even more complicated when their labour-market position intersects and interacts with stigma, marginality, and criminal law. Not only are workers vulnerable to criminalization, but the illicit status of their labour site (bawdy house) also de facto excludes them from gaining access to their rights not only as workers (for instance, health and safety, labour regulations/agreements) and professionals (to form provincially authorized associations, as do realtors or massage therapists), but also as citizens (to have police protection, for instance). Their position is simultaneously hyper-regulated and unregulated, with many implications for their well-being (Gillies 2013).

### Labour Practices

Paying closer attention to labour practices and skills in commercial incall sex work does a couple of things: first, it makes the invisible visible; and second, by exploring the intersections of class, gender, and race we can highlight the role of criminalization and stigmatization in conditioning the work of women in this sector of the sex industry.

Like much service-sector employment, incall sex work is physically demanding labour that requires stamina, physical strength, and endurance. In stark contrast to the discourse suggesting that sex work is somehow "natural" and therefore not really work (and certainly not skilled work), our research found that success in this area is contingent on a particular and not uncomplicated set of skills and necessitated mastering the rules and expectations of an employer. Christina told us when she was hired she was *"emailed a list of about four pages of procedures and what's expected of you. Whether or not you should work when you're on your period — the answer was no. What to do if you got a yeast infection. Things like that."* Another worker, Crystal, explained that in her job at a massage parlour, *"You learn every day and learn new things every day."* Like waitresses, hair stylists, and other women employed in the service sector, successful incall sex workers have to be sociable, patient, courteous, and polite, and they have to be capable of dealing with a variety of people. They must present a pleasant and professional demeanour to clients.

Success also calls for a number of more specialized prerequisites, including creativity, an open attitude toward sexuality, and a positive assessment of men. In addition, workers must have basic anatomic/sexual knowledge, be able to master massage and sexual techniques, create and maintain an erotic and pleasing presentation of self, discern and respond to clients' (often non-verbalized) needs or wishes, and promote or sell their service. Crystal and Maud, another massage parlour worker, explained that their work necessitated performance skills not only to *"become the whore at work"* but also to put *"on a mask and play a certain character."* They need to be able to improvise a role play based on their reading of the expectations of clients or on the (sometimes detailed) "scripts" of clients.

Women who work in domination require additional knowledge. They must be trained to use the equipment in a safe and effective manner as well as know how to clean and care for it. They must also learn where to strike without leaving marks or doing damage. They need to know anal training techniques, recognize code words (such as yellow for caution, red for stop), and know how to instruct clients. As one of them, Anaïs, noted, providing domination services in a dungeon is a job that requires both openness and insight: *"It's more than just being aggressive and angry. It's about understanding where the bottom's [the client receiving domination services] coming from."* According to Charlotte, another dungeon worker, this specialization also requires finely tuned sensitivity so that the worker is *"able to gauge, you know, how light or heavy they [the clients] are, 'cause for a lot of them it's just visual…. They think they're very heavy into it, but they're not really."* Charlotte also spoke about the need to *"contact your anger"* when necessary. Her strategy was to recall her experience, many years earlier, of being raped by three men: *"That's how I get into the roles sometimes if I'm having trouble with it."* Some workers, like Anaïs, can, despite being bound and *"submissive,"* retain control and *"top the scene from the bottom."*

Incall sex work is not only physically demanding skilled labour, but can also be dangerous. This is, of course, characteristic of many working-class jobs that — computerization and automation notwithstanding — extract a physical toll from workers (Shostak 1980; Houtman and Kompier 1995: 221). Here, however, we see a particular cluster of risks. Workers in the incall sex industry risk exposure to infectious diseases (including, but not restricted to, sexually transmitted infections). Additionally, a number of respondents spoke of the ever-present potential for clients to be sexually and/or physically aggressive. Workers implement strategies to minimize these risks. In the case of the health risks, their tactics include the use of condoms, gloves, and lubricants, the visual inspections of clients' sexual organs, washing hands with antiseptic soap, and disinfecting equipment. Third parties can mediate the potential for physical/sexual aggression through measures such as maintaining zero-tolerance policies and bad date lists, the collection and verification of personal information (for example, name, phone number, employer of clients), requiring references, matching clients to workers, hiring on-site or oncall security persons, training workers in exit and conflict avoidance strategies, establishing emergency protocols in addition to such things as the presence of others in the location, a monitored entrance, security camera, no-locked door policies, and a two-call system and client screening. This last strategy sometimes includes profiling on the basis of race and class (Bruckert and Law 2013). Workers also endeavour to mitigate risk through their own labour practices (including the refusal to participate in submission, abstaining from alcohol or drugs at work, carrying pepper spray, and creating a "virtual" bouncer).[9]

A number of respondents evoked the language of gendered sensibility when they spoke of refusing men whom they "intuitively" perceived to be threatening — an ability based on the knowledge of experience, which allows the workers to perceive and interpret numerous minute signs of potential danger. Karen, reflecting on her own experience as a massage parlour employee, noted that workers are *"thinking all the time; you gotta be quick in case any of [the clients] try to pull something on you."* Women who offer submission services are in a particularly vulnerable position. The implications of a client's incompetence, ignorance, or maliciousness range from bruises to welts to permanent organ damage.

Sex work can also be emotionally demanding on a number of different levels. The women must cope with the valorization of youth and "lookism." Women who are older or whose appearance does not conform to narrow conventions of attractiveness may find work hard to come by. As Maxine, a massage parlour worker, commented: *"I'd have weeks without work because the parlour didn't advertise my body type or whatever. They'd just be like, 'Oh, yeah, and this is Maxine.'... 'Well, she's a larger girl.'"* As a result, Maxine told us, *"I would question myself, and I'm like, 'Should I sell out?' 'Should I get fake tits?' 'Should I go on a diet?'"* In addition to sizeism and ageism, racism also plays out in the clandestine space of the sex industry — which occurs in particular in the framing of racialized workers as the erotic/exotic Other. Trina, a massage parlour worker, explained: *"The wording that they used was always the same....Like, you know, Black girls were always referred to as choc-olate. Or ebony. And Asian was always exotic."* Incall sex workers also spoke of agency quotas on racialized workers. Lee, a Black sex worker in Toronto, spoke of *"being told by agencies because I'm Black that I may not get calls, or I'm not popular, or I'm difficult to market."*

In addition, like other direct-service employees — including waitresses (Paules 1991) and domestics (Salzinger 1991) — sex workers must retain a positive self-concept in the face of clients who, according to Jacqueline, a dungeon employee, *"don't seem to realize that you're another person."* Moreover, Angelica explained that sometimes her clients at the massage parlour *"assume I'm really stupid.... Like, I'm pretty much an object or a service."* Moreover, like women workers in other service sectors of the labour market (including bartenders and hair stylists), incall sex workers also sometimes have to deal with manipulative clients who, to procure extra services, pout, nag, flatter, or threaten to take their business elsewhere. In the sex industry the stakes are high and the process is complicated by the ever-present spectre of criminalization. Not only are some clients seeking sexual services that the woman is not prepared to offer and that may endanger her (sex without a condom, for instance), but she is also operating in a non-institutionally structured space in which the rules and expectations are difficult to enforce.

At other times workers are required to engage in emotional labour (Hochschild 1983). Some clients seek more than sexual services; they seek personal intimacy. Crystal explained that as a worker in a massage parlour, *"You got to be sweet and all that. You gotta really play the role."* Occasionally clients are seeking companionship. Jade, who works in a brothel, recalled her experience: *"There was a guy, seventy-six years old, who took two hours at a time. I took off my top but kept my bra on and we played cards... we drank wine. The guy was all alone and his kids didn't see him.... Some I've seen for five years and we did nothing."*[10] This aspect of the work requires workers to engage in "deep acting," re-creating personal experiences to "induce or suppress feel-ing in order to sustain the outward countenance that produces the proper state of mind in others" (Hochschild 1983: 7) in a commercial setting. This demanding expectation is hardly unique to sex workers; arguably, it is increasingly a job requirement of women working in numerous other areas of the service sector, including beauticians (Sharma and Black 2001), flight attendants (Hochschild 1983), and nurses (Lopez 2006; Molinier 2003).

Unlike some of those other sectors, incall sex workers are positioned to negotiate the nature and extent of their emotional labour. In a brothel, a dungeon, or, for that matter, a beauty salon, clients receive a technical service (intercourse, domination, a pedicure) and may anticipate additional intimacy and interpersonal interaction. This condition is not, however, an inherent one within the institutional confines of the service encounter. The workers are left with the choice of whether or not they will engage in emotional labour to improve the service encounter — and they might choose to do so either out of a personal inclination or to secure a regular clientele.[11]

Incall sex work thus requires workers to vigilantly guard against physical and/or sexual danger, to maintain their personal boundaries at the same time as they create an environment of intimacy, and to strive to realize the sexual (and sometimes interpersonal) fantasy of their clients. Not surprisingly, as Wendy Chapkis (1997: 79) points out, an ability to distinguish between the work domain and the personal realm is imperative for maintaining emotional equilibrium. Catherine explained that as a worker in an erotic establishment, *"You really have to be mentally strong…. You have to dissociate from your private life. You have to see it as a job."* Many sex workers are able to draw on their professionalism to mediate the emotional expectations of clients. Angelica described her work in a massage parlour: *"You can actually, like, give someone what they need emotionally but still be disconnected. It's a pretty amazing thing…. But it's not taking a lot out of me. Like, it's my work."*

The stresses of the demands of the job are further exacerbated by the illegal nature and stigmatic assumptions of outsiders. The illegality means that workers are susceptible to charges under section 210 of the Canadian Criminal Code, which necessitates continual vigilance, assessment of clients, and self-monitoring because, as Angelica pointed out, *"One day you could say the wrong thing to the wrong person."* In establishments in which owners endeavoured to circumvent the law through wilful blindness (often municipally licensed agencies that operate under the pretence that no sexual services are being offered), workers are not able to discuss challenges with colleagues or their employer. They must be vigilant in their communications with clients and discreet about their use of safer sex equipment. As Robyn, a massage parlour worker, remarked, *"You weren't allowed to have condoms in the room. Like, if they found condoms in the garbage that was a big issue because we would get inspected by the police."* Ultimately, one of the more disconcerting findings of our research was the lack of accurate legal knowledge on the part of many sex workers. As a result of misconceptions, women took ineffectual precautionary measures (such as not touching the money prior to engaging in the sex act and refraining from intercourse).

Importantly, the women's vulnerability to arrest denies workers potential resources in their negotiations with clients. Among other things, the fear of denunciation by disgruntled customers complicates workers' maintenance of their personal boundaries. Moreover, women are hesitant to turn to the police for protection or to report violent clients. Karen, a massage parlour worker, noted: *"It would feel a lot safer [with decriminalization] because you'd know that if anything happened, people would listen to you and there'd be a place to go. You wouldn't have to worry about going to jail or telling a cop. Maybe people wouldn't try stuff as much as they do."* Criminalization also denies workers the ability to negotiate labour conditions with their employers through professional organizations or organized labour action, or by evoking their statutory labour rights.

Moreover, although numerous workers — including morticians, custodians, and some sectors of the sales force — labour in stigmatized occupations, when they leave the labour site women in the incall sex industry must cope with the condemnation that accompanies the stigma of "whore" (Pheterson 1989). Annabelle, a massage parlour worker, recognized: *"It is not easy to fight against a whole population and against ideas so deeply entrenched in people's heads."* According to Karen, who also works in a massage parlour, this stigma necessitates that a woman *"not let it get you down and take your work home with you…. Don't view yourself the way society views you."* Consequently, some workers seek to isolate themselves from public censure by closeting their occupational location, creating fictitious jobs, and separating their work and private lives (including not associating with other sex workers).

Unfortunately, these tactics also mean a lack of insider support. Angelica, who had been working in a massage parlour for five months, found that her counterculture friends were carefully non-judgmental. Nonetheless, she bemoaned her lack of a network:

> It's hard to get a certain type of support. People who don't do it are always, like, "well, just stop doing it," "why are you doing it if it's hard?" It's like, "well, everything is hard!" You know? Like, if you're working, you're making six dollars an hour at a coffee shop, you're gonna have to deal with people you hate, but that's part of your job.

In practice, it appears that workers must negotiate and maintain a balance between what emerges as competing objectives of anonymity and support. While workers are, for the most part, able to find a personally suitable space on the spectrum — with anonymity/no support at one end and strong social support/vulnerability to public and private condemnation at the other — the conditions nonetheless increase the day-to-day stress, and, regardless of any compromise position adopted, the women are left in a precarious situation. Moreover, the experience of stress is intensified when the worker lacks social support in the home (Levi, Frankenhauser, and Gardell 1986: 55). As Meg Luxton and June Corman (2001) point out, a lack of support has particular relevance for women whose role and labour-force challenges may not be fully acknowledged within social and familial areas — which is certainly the case for sex workers, whose job is frequently not even acknowledged to be work.

Still, despite the myriad challenges and stressors confronted by these women workers, all of our respondents identified positive aspects of their jobs. While the financial benefits that allowed them to participate in the social sphere were foremost, they also identified a number of other benefits, including flexibility, free time, and a pleasant, relaxed work environment.[12] Moreover, they also noted a wide range of intrinsic rewards. Anaïs saw her job in a dungeon as being *"entertaining, it's fun sometimes and it's very mundane, but you know usually you don't know what to expect so it's kind of fun. It's exciting."* Some women appreciated the skills they develop. For Maud, a massage parlour worker, this included learning *"how to take control and assert limits."* Others highlighted pleasurable social and/or sexual interactions with clients. For Anaïs the work was also *"a legit way of expressing resistance against society."* Similarly, for Angelica, who had experienced sexual harassment throughout her life, the work allowed her to *"manipulate this [sexism] for my own benefit.... I feel like I'm beating the man, you know? I literally get to beat the man!"* Perhaps these features are all the more striking in contrast to the monotonous, repetitious, and unsatisfying alternatives readily available to young working-class women — the "McJobs" (Ritzer 2004).

## The Complexities of Sexualized Commerce

We are left, then, with the question of the suitability of the term "sex work" — and the critiques from radical feminists as well as from the conservative right that the sex industry does not constitute work, either because it is sexual exploitation or because the prerequisite competencies are natural and therefore do not constitute skills. Is the concept, as Sheila Jeffreys (2005) maintains, simply an attempt to make the industry more palatable through "euphemistic neutral terms"?

Stepping outside of normative assumptions, we can listen to workers such as Lea, who has a job in a massage parlour and asserted: *"It's a service that I offer."* We can make links to "reputable" jobs by applying a labour analysis. In doing this a number of commonalities emerge. On a structural level these jobs are consistent with the broader trend toward women's increased participation in service-sector employment and non-standard labour arrangements that position women workers outside of the stability and protection traditionally associated with employment. We also see how the sex industry echoes the broader social stratifications in the marginalization of and discrimination against racialized workers. When we shift to labour process, we see that like other working-class women's work in the consumer-service sector, the job of sex-trade workers requires the application of (rarely acknowledged) skills.[13] It is physically demanding and potentially dangerous and stressful, and requires workers to undertake emotional labour. It is certainly not an easy job. In the course of their workday, workers must confront and negotiate a myriad of challenges and stressors. Moreover, many workers in the commercial incall sex industry who labour for third parties are, in a Marxian sense, exploited workers.

In light of these commonalities, the pivotal question becomes: does the sexual component mark the industry as being outside the framework of labour? Despite the challenges introduced by the sex radical discourse twenty years ago (Califia 1994; Johnson 2002), the private/public and sex/labour dichotomies continue to be so firmly embedded in our consciousness that the term "sex work" is virtually an oxymoron. This approach is reproduced in labour studies in which work-site sexuality is either invisible or an inherently harmful expression of patriarchal power that renders the atmosphere oppressive (Hearn and Parkin 1995; Lobel 1993).

Arguably, this positioning is highly problematic. On the one hand, "Sexuality is a structuring process of gender" (Adkins 1992: 208), and gender and sexuality are central "to all workplace power relations" (Pringle 1988: 84). The traditional skills that women are required to bring to the labour market include the ability to assume an attractive "made-up" appearance so that "part of the job for women consists of looking good" (Adkins 1992: 216). However, more than just a good appearance is required. Increasingly, the prerequisite presentation of self is sexualized so that much of the labour that working-class women undertake has a visible sexual subtext and necessitates the negotiation of a sexualized labour terrain. On the other hand, our sexuality — in our private and professional lives — is subjectively experienced, and we must take care to acknowledge not only that class may condition the approach and meaning ascribed to sexuality (Aronowitz 1992: 62),[14] but also that there are a variety of positions vis-à-vis labour-site sexuality that speak to a spectrum of engagement.

For some working-class women, the distinction between sex work and other consumer service work may be one of degree and explicitness. This is a connection that Angelica made when she reflected on her previous labour experiences:

> *I've been a cocktail waitress and that was sex work too, but it's just over the table sex work that the government supports.... Basically, you're hired 'cuz you're pretty. Start there. Then ... the money you make is based on the shifts that you work, the shifts you get. So in order to get the good shifts you have to sell the most drinks. In order to sell the most drinks you have to be flirtatious. So, it's totally sex work.*

In short, the many points of convergence support the conceptualization of women employed in sexualized commerce as working-class women workers in the new economy, and they lend support to the linguistic shift toward the term "sex work." The illegal/illicit status of the labour not only raises the spectre of criminalization, but also facilitates an additional level of exploitation in that it inhibits workers from gaining access to both their statutory labour rights and their rights as citizens. Moreover, many of the challenges and stressors of the job do not emerge from the labour itself, but are a by-product of discourses of immorality, the lack of recognition as workers, limited social and interpersonal support, a lack of police or legal protection, criminalization, and stigma.

The sex industry's long tradition of adapting both to changing market, social, and moral conditions and to technological innovations[15] has resulted in increasingly varied industry practices and structures, which in turn have opened up the industry to new workers (Bernstein 2007). Today a sex worker may be a stay-at-home mother who responds to erotic telephone calls (Flowers 1998) or a high-school student who types erotic messages on the Internet and exchanges pictures for gifts (Robinson 2004). She may be an administrator subsidizing her wages by working as an erotic dancer two nights a week (Law 2011). She could be a woman on social assistance who makes ends meet through street-sex work (Parent and Bruckert 2006) or a full-time worker, either independent or working for or with a third party, offering sexual services in a brothel or hotel room. All of this diversity destabilizes stereotypical assumptions about sex workers; it also highlights the problems of an occupational classification that encompasses such a range of labour structures and processes.

The problem, then, lies not with the term "sex work," but with the imposed limits embedded in its application. On the one hand, the term continues to situate the industry in question outside of women's work, obscuring how the jobs inhabit a particular location on the axis of sexual labour and emotional labour characteristic of much women's work. On the other hand, it fails to capture the complexity of "sex industry" labour practices, in which sexuality is but one component. The solution may not be to abandon the particular vocabulary but to destabilize the dichotomies by inserting the private, the sexual, and the intimate into the language of labour. In this manner, we can develop a more nuanced and inclusive analytic framework of sexualized commerce to make sense of the labour of women workers — both in and outside of the industry.

## Notes

1.  In this discussion we draw on empirical data from two qualitative research projects. The first, on the incall sex industry, was undertaken in 2002 (Parent and Bruckert 2005). The research was guided by the feminist commitment to methodological approaches that centre the voices and experiences of women. Accordingly, the questions we posed were designed to illicit information regarding labour structure and process and to reveal how that work is subjectively experienced. Using snowball sampling, we conducted a series of fourteen in-depth semi-structured interviews (in French and English) lasting between one and three hours during the summer and fall of 2002. The women were all employed, or at least very recently employed, in the incall sex industry in Montreal (eight) and Toronto (six). Respondents ranged in age from twenty-one to forty, and with between four months to seven years of experience; the majority of women where white (twelve), one woman was Asian, and another Black. The second research project, which we use to "fill out" the picture, was a SSHRC-funded study on sex-industry management. We draw on a subsample of the data — twenty-four focus group interviews that took place in Toronto, Halifax, Ottawa, and Montreal during spring 2012 with sex workers who work(ed) for or with third parties in the incall sex industry. The participants, who ranged in age from twenty-one to fifty-seven (average age thirty-three), had between one-and-one-half and forty-four years of experience in the industry. As in the previous study the majority of the workers we interviewed were white (thirteen), two were Black, two Aboriginal, two identified as Aboriginal/White, and one was Aboriginal/Black (three participants did not indicate their race/ethnicity). Collectively these thirty-eight respondents from the two research projects represent a diverse cross-section of industry workers and offered rich insights.

2.  The initial analyses that situated the sex trade within questions of class, gender, and economic vulnerability were quickly displaced by concerns about the white slave trade (Walkowitz 1980; Rosen 1982; DuBois and Gordon 1983). Within this framework, these feminists started to demonize individual men as being threatening to "innocent womanhood" and campaigned for greater regulation and laws. The attempts by these earlier feminists to help prostitutes — all the while condemning prostitution — had disastrous consequences for women in the trade (Rosen 1982: 102). For an overview of later feminist positions on prostitution, see Tong 1984, Järvinen 1993, and Parent 1994.

3.  Some workers have also reasserted sexuality into the debate, challenging the appropriation of sexuality of women by men and asserting their right to control their bodies and to define their sexuality outside both traditional moral discourse and the feminist discourse that associates feminine sexuality with love and warmth. In short, these sex workers are part of a broader rethinking of sexuality as a contested terrain, the site and source of subversion (Aline 1987; CORP 1987; McClintock 1993; Chapkis 1997).

4. "Cam-girls" exchange revealing photos for "gifts" with individuals they have contacted through the Internet (Robinson 2004).

5. See Bannerji 2005 for a discussion of the pitfalls of feminist anti-race theorizing.

6. The Criminal Code defines a common bawdy house as "a place that is a) kept or occupied or b) resorted to by one or more persons, for the purposes of prostitution or the practice of acts of indecency" (s. 197). Canadian jurisprudence specifies that the definition of "prostitution" does not require actual sexual intercourse, nor need there be physical contact. This very broad definition has led to convictions under section 210 of the Criminal Code of women who worked in strip clubs where dancers gyrated on the laps of fully clothed patrons (*R v Caringi, O.J.* 2002), massage parlours that offered full body massages (including manual masturbation) but no oral, vaginal, or anal sexual intercourse (*R v Brandes, O.J.* 1997); and sado-masochism dungeons in which neither intercourse nor masturbation was offered.

7. The women working in one establishment (a dungeon) were (unless they booked off for a set period) expected to be available to be paged seven days a week, twelve hours a day, in addition to working one receptionist shift per week without pay. With the exception of this receptionist shift, they were not required to be on-site.

8. Non-standard or precarious labour arrangements are relationally understood to standard employment — which is defined as the "employment of individuals for wages and salaries by a single firm, where individuals work full time on the employer's premises, and expect (and are expected) to be employed for an indefinite period of time" (Canada 1999: 2) — and includes part-time, seasonal, short-term contracts, temporary employment, and own-account work.

9. A number of establishments did employ security personnel, but even when no such individual was on-site the women workers sometimes led clients to believe that this was the case.

10. The interview quotations from Jade, Catherine, and Annabelle have been translated by the authors.

11. By contrast, for dancers in "straight" strip clubs, where physical contact is prohibited, the technical service oftentimes is the interaction so that emotional labour becomes a job requirement (Bruckert 2002; Wood 2002).

12. Whether or not a job meets middle-class standards of "interesting" or "rewarding," it may have non-economic benefits. It may offer women social contacts and friendships (MacDonald and Connelly 1989: 66), and recognition of their labour that is not afforded full-time homemakers (Reiter 1991: 106). Greater economic contribution can also be correlated to power within the family (Feree 1984: 75), independence, status, and a sense of self-worth and self-esteem (Penney 1983: 21).

13. That skills are largely dismissed or rendered invisible is not unique to incall sex workers, but characterizes many working-class women's jobs. It does, however, affirm once again the relative and subjective nature of what are defined as skills. Class and gender continue to be associated with skills in complex ways (Gaskell 1986).

14. For example, sexual interaction may not necessarily be understood as sexual harassment (Westwood 1984). Ethnographic accounts offer a very different image of such practices as sexually explicit shop-floor banter (Barber 1992: 81). Furthermore, positioned to recognize the costs of capitalism and patriarchy, working-class women may deconstruct the advantages afforded by an asexual presentation of self (Feree 1990).

15. For example, the trajectory of strip clubs and the transformation of dancers from performers to service workers speak to the intersection of broader market forces and marginal labour. Between 1973 and 1995 the work of erotic dancers was "de-professionalized"; workers went from being salaried performance artists to service-sector employees labouring for tips (Bruckert 2002). In a similar vein, the sex industry's use of print media, telephones,

and the computer speaks to its adaptability. Certainly, Internet technology has had a major impact, transforming both existing practices (many escorts now advertise and interact with clients via the Internet) and facilitating the emergence of new practices (such as cam-girls).

4

# Surviving Colonization
## Anishinaabe Ikwe Street Gang Participation

*Nahanni Fontaine*

> *If you have come here to help me you are wasting your time. But if you have come because your liberation is connected to mine, then we can work together.* — Lilla Watson, a Murri woman who has been active in the struggle of Aboriginal peoples in Australia

In June 2003 several body parts were found along the shoreline of the Red River in Winnipeg. They were quickly identified as belonging to Felicia Solomon Osborne, a sixteen-year-old girl from the Norway House Cree Nation. Few media sources bothered to cover this story. Those that did stated that Felicia Solomon had gang ties and had been working the streets.

The murder of Felicia Solomon raises questions about the lived experiences of Aboriginal women — Anishinaabe Ikwe — and their participation in gangs. Ultimately, however, the question becomes: what do we need to learn as a community about Aboriginal women and girls and the contemporary context in which they find themselves? To address such a question, we need to hear from them.

At a gathering in the summer of 2003, several organizations — Southern Chiefs' Organization (sco), Mother of Red Nations Women's Council of Manitoba (morn), and Ka Ni Kanichihk Inc. — resolved to reach out to Anishinaabe Ikwe in order to grasp and appreciate their standpoint with respect to gangs. It was agreed that the participants in the study ought to be interviewed in a culturally appropriate, safe manner. There was also a consensus that the study should be pursued and presented from within an Aboriginal framework because there is so little indigenously driven research or analysis on the issue. As both the Manitoba Aboriginal Justice Inquiry (Hamilton and Sinclair 1991) and the Royal Commission on Aboriginal Peoples (1996) recommended, all research and program development as it relates to Aboriginal peoples must be pursued by and for Aboriginal peoples so that it is more effective, responsive, and culturally sensitive to the needs of the Aboriginal collective.

My purpose here is to report on some of the findings of this study. To be clear, this chapter is not about "Aboriginal street gangs." That is to say, I will not be discussing the creation, structure, hierarchy, and activities of the "street gang" as an Aboriginal phenomenon. No. This chapter concerns Aboriginal women's and girls' particular experiences in relation to the gang. That being said, we require a broader context in which we can situate the participants of the study, one that deconstructs the traditional discourse offered to account for the phenomenon of the "street gang." Simply put, Aboriginal street gangs are not what the dominant white settler society socially constructs them — a malignant and deviant thorn in the side of a so-called upstanding, productive, middle-class, Christian civilization. Rather, Aboriginal street gangs are the result of the settler colonial context and experience in contemporary Canada.

## Settler Colonialism and the Colonial Experience

Colonialism, in the words of John McLeod (2000: 7), involved "a lucrative commercial operation, bringing wealth and riches to Western nations through the economic exploitation of others." In the Canadian context, colonialism involved the process by which Europeans erected a settler colonial society based on the seizure of the territories of the Indigenous population. While the appropriation of land was a key element of settler colonialism, this colonization process was unquestionably racialized. As Patrick Wolfe (2006: 388) explains, "Indigenous North Americans were not killed, driven away, romanticized, assimilated, fenced in, bred White, and otherwise eliminated as the original owners of the land but *as Indians.*" European colonizers aimed to eradicate Indigenous societies — what Wolfe (2006: 403) refers to as "structural genocide" in that elimination was not a one-time occurrence but an organizing principle of settler colonial society. Settler colonization, as Wolfe points out, is "a structure rather than an event" and settler colonialism is "a specific social formation" (2006: 390, 401). As such colonialism is not simply a historical artifact that has no bearing on contemporary events. The racialization of Aboriginal people — "the process through which groups come to be designated as different and on that basis subjected to differential and unequal treatment" (Block and Galabuzi 2011: 19) — has continued to the present day. As Sherene Razack (2007: 74) notes: "As it evolves, a white settler society continues to be structured by a racial hierarchy."

Edward Said's work on post-colonialism offers important insights into representations of the colonial experience. As McLeod (2000: 21) tells us,

Said's interest was in "how the knowledge that the Western imperial powers formed about their colonies helped continually to justify their subjugation." Said observed that Western or Occidental powers spent considerable energies producing knowledge about the territories they dominated. But seldom did they endeavour to learn from and about the Indigenous inhabitants of those territories. Rather, their knowledge was founded on questionable assumptions about the "Orient" and its inhabitants that served to justify colonial domination. What Said called "Orientalism," then, "operates in the service of the West's hegemony over the East primarily by producing the East discursively as the West's inferior 'Other,' a manoeuvre which strengthens — indeed, even partially constructs — the West's self-image as a superior civilization" (cited in Moore-Gilbert 1997: 38–39). In these terms, criminal justice reports on the "Aboriginal street gang" can tell us something about how these gangs are represented in colonial discourse.

A report released by the Royal Canadian Mounted Police "D" Division, Manitoba, in 2004 stated:

> The last two decades have seen numerous street gangs rise within both urban and rural areas of Manitoba. Although there are not any strictly aboriginal street gangs, aboriginal membership in several gangs is quite dominant. Some of the major aboriginal-based street gangs in effect, per se, are the Manitoba Warriors, the Native Syndicate and the Indian Posse. Alliances and rivalries are sometimes formed between these gangs, other street gangs and even the Outlaw Motorcycle Gangs in order to control the drug trade, prostitution and other illegal activities.
>
> Recruitment of gang members is an on-going process that is done by most gangs in order to build the gang in both numbers and strength. Once focusing on the major urban centres, recruitment has now filtered into the aboriginal communities of Manitoba. A growing scenario consists of a member from the community being arrested and then later incarcerated. Upon incarceration, this person is then recruited into the gang. Some are compelled to join a gang within the correctional centre in order to ensure their protection for fear of being targeted by the gangs within the centre. Others join to belong, because they know someone in the gang or are lured by the thought of quick money and the gang lifestyle. Upon their release, they return to their communities and begin gang activity there, including recruitment of new members. (McLeod 2004)

Similarly, the 2004 *Annual Report on Organized Crime in Canada* of Criminal Intelligence Service Canada asserted:

Aboriginal-based street gangs are generally involved in opportunistic, spontaneous and disorganized street-level criminal activities, primarily low-level trafficking of marijuana, cocaine and crack cocaine and, to a lesser extent, methamphetamine. The gangs are also involved in prostitution, break-and-enters, robberies, assaults, intimidation, vehicle theft and illicit drug debt collection. Although the gangs' capability to plan and commit sophisticated or large-scale criminal activities is low, their propensity for violence is high, posing a threat to public safety. (Criminal Intelligence Service Canada 2004)

These reports share in common an interpretation of the gang as a deviant subculture centred on criminal activity, a subculture that persists because of the attraction of the gang lifestyle to its members. What many, if not all, such reports fail to recognize is the historical and contemporary colonial context that precipitated the advent of Aboriginal street gangs. Gangs did not arise owing to the "gang lifestyle," as some commentators naively argue and try to convince the general public. Aboriginal gangs surfaced, developed, and organized in response to the reality and experience of colonization and its perpetual legacy in our daily lives. Aboriginal gangs are the product of our colonized and oppressed space within Canada — a space fraught with inequity, racism, dislocation, marginalization, and cultural and spiritual alienation (Razack 2002). It is a space of physical and cultural genocide that continues to exist even at this very moment.

From first contact with Europeans, Indigenous peoples' cultures, political systems, economies, lands, and traditional social constructions and mores were systematically and methodically attacked. In this respect, there is nothing "post-colonial" about Aboriginal peoples' experience. They continue to endure dislocation, de-culturalization, ecocide, and forced assimilation. Indeed, the question often posed by outsiders is "why can't you people just leave that in the past?" Without a doubt, settler colonialism is alive and well in Canada, and remains an insidious force permeating every aspect of the lives of the original inhabitants and rightful owners of this land.

An important illustration of the lingering effects of colonialism is the altered power relations between the sexes within our Indigenous societies. Traditionally, Anishinaabe Ikwe's roles and responsibilities encompassed every aspect of community life. As life-givers and primary caregivers, women were respected and had a significant role in the decision-making processes of the community. Social relations were of an equal nature and did not involve notions that one sex was superior to the other (Gunn Allen 1992; Anderson 2000). Unfortunately, as a result of the introduction of Christianity and forced Christian marriages, incorporation into a capitalist wage economy, residential schools, and the introduction of alcohol, Aboriginal men's and women's roles changed significantly.

As Carol Devens (1992: 5) argues, "The friction between men and women is in fact the bitter fruit of colonization." This is not to imply that gendered roles and responsibilities would have remained static and unchanging, but that colonialism directed their development in ways that Indigenous peoples would not have chosen. As a consequence of colonial processes, Anishinaabe Ikwe are doubly victimized; they are disempowered and oppressed within both the Euro-Canadian mainstream and the Indigenous collective. Anishinaabe Ikwe have become what one prominent Winnipeg community member calls "collaterals of war." Leslie Spillett, the Executive Director of Ka Ni Kanichihk Inc., suggests, "In most wars women and children are collateral damage, and we can extend this concept in which 'gangs' constitute, within the Canadian colonial context, external/internal warfare whereby women and children are both victimized."

Surely, one contributing factor toward gang involvement for Anishinaabe Ikwe is the abject poverty faced by our communities. Elizabeth Comack and her colleagues (2013: 8) report on the astonishingly high poverty rates for Aboriginal peoples, particularly in inner-city Winnipeg:

> Aboriginal people are overrepresented among the ranks of Winnipeg's poor. In 2005 over four in ten (43 percent) Aboriginal people — compared to 16 percent of non-Aboriginal people — were living under the low-income-cut-off (LICO), Canada's unofficial but commonly used "poverty line." Almost six in ten (57 percent) Aboriginal children aged fourteen years and under in Winnipeg were living under the LICO, compared to 20 percent of non-Aboriginal children.... While 20 percent of Winnipeg's households were living in poverty in 2006, that figure was 40 percent for inner-city households. For Aboriginal households in the inner city, the figure was much higher — at 65 percent.

Anishinaabe Ikwe leaving poor socio-economic conditions in their home communities (First Nation reserves and Métis communities) often come to the city alone or with their families in search of equitable opportunities and a better standard of living, but instead find a dominant Euro-Canadian mainstream society that is culturally alien to and the antithesis of their own experiences. Most, if not all, Indigenous newcomers to the urban environment face myriad racist, alienating, and patronizing realities firmly entrenched within mainstream social institutions (see, for example, Silver 2006).

A second contributing factor is the loss or interruption of Indigenous cultural identity. The Royal Commission on Aboriginal Peoples (1996) noted that a fundamental component in Aboriginal youth joining gangs is the loss or dislocation of traditional Aboriginal culture. John Berry (1994), who conducted interviews with Aboriginal peoples on the notion of cultural identity for the Royal Commission on Aboriginal Peoples, argued that "behavioural expression" among the Aboriginal population was the most "concrete feature" of their sense of identity. Looking at the use of an Aboriginal language and the "daily activities related to one's culture (e.g., language, social relations, dress, food, music, arts, and crafts)" as indicators of behavioural expression, Berry (1994) found:

> Of the total adult population (aged 15 years and over), 65.4% of North American Indians on Reserve (NAI), 23.1% of NAI off Reserve, and 17.5% of Métis were able to use their Aboriginal language; 74.6% of Inuit were able to do so. There is a similar results [sic] for children (aged 5 to 14 years), but with even lower levels: 44.3%, 9.0%, 4.9% and 67.0% respectively. For participation in traditional Aboriginal activities, the pattern is repeated. For adults, the participation rates were 65.2%, 44.8%, 39.8% and 74.1%; and for children, they were 57.5%, 39.5%, 28.7% and 70.2%.

Berry interpreted these data to mean that Aboriginal peoples, particularly children, had lost a considerable degree of cultural identity since the advent of colonization.

It is under these circumstances that Anishinaabe Ikwe, some as young as eleven, are recruited by gang members and often targeted for exploitation in the sex and drug trades. According to Karen Busby and her colleagues (2002: 94), of the girls and women working in the sex trade on the streets of Prairie Canada, a higher percentage were of Aboriginal descent (58 percent) than Caucasian (42 percent). However, within the province of Manitoba, particularly in Winnipeg, that figure is likely to be much higher. Some researchers estimate that 70 percent of the youth and 50 percent of adults involved in the sex trade in Winnipeg are Aboriginal (Seshia 2005).

## Learning from Anishinaabe Ikwe

The collaborative, participatory project undertaken with Aboriginal women and girls was designed taking into consideration the expressed needs and concerns of the participants, that is to say, as the principal investigator, my main priority was to ensure that the participants felt safe and secure in sharing their narratives. I conducted a series of individual tape-recorded, life-history interviews (repeated over time) with nineteen Anishinaabe Ikwe at agreed upon times and locations. More often than not, this involved picking up the participant and going out for breakfast or lunch. As part of the exchange, each of the participants got an honorarium and a tobacco tie as recognition of the spiritual connection that occurs when two people discuss ideas, experiences, beliefs, and emotions.

The study participants ranged in age from thirteen to forty-four years and were from a variety of First Nation and Métis communities in Manitoba and Ontario. Geographically they came from both Northern and Southern regions. One woman was born in the United States but had left early on in her childhood to come back to Manitoba. The First Nations participants had lived both on and off reserve, reflecting the migratory reality of Indigenous communities. At the time of the interviews, six of the participants were housed at the Portage Correctional Institutional (a women's jail) in Portage La Prairie, and four were living at a Winnipeg inner-city girls' group home. One woman was living in Northern Ontario, and the rest of the women lived in either central Winnipeg (downtown) or the notorious "North End," an area now both physically and socially constructed as poor, decrepit, violent, gang-infested, and degenerated (see Silver 2010; Comack et al. 2013). Of the nineteen participants, all but two had parents who had attended state-regulated and mandated residential schools; seventeen of the participants had grandparents and extended family members who had attended residential schools. All of the participants reported that one or both of their parents had been involved in drugs and alcohol from early childhood. Most of the participants had experienced encounters with Child and Family Services; indeed, one nineteen-year-old participant had over 136 placements — all of them with non-Aboriginal families.

Their oral narratives[1] provided new insights into urban Aboriginal gender relations, power structures, and strategies for coping with cultural dislocation. Overall, the project provided an opportunity for *Anishinaabe Ikwe* involved in street gangs to shed light on their experience and to assert their contemporary identity to the broader community.

## Anishinaabe Ikwe in Relation to the "Street Gang"

More and more on a daily basis, in Winnipeg at least, we hear stories about Aboriginal women and girls with reference to the "increasing numbers" and "increasing violence" of female gang members or female gangs. Interestingly, however, only three of the participants in the study (the oldest ones) declared that there were Aboriginal female gang members or Aboriginal female gangs. These participants told me that at one time in Winnipeg (in the early 1980s), there was a semblance of a women's gang deriving from one of the first Aboriginal gangs in Manitoba, the Main Street Rattlers. According to Tamara, the Main Street Rattlers was born out of *"youth just hanging out, trying to survive."* Mary insisted that the formation of gangs in Winnipeg occurred as a result of youth hanging out at Rossbrook House, an inner-city neighbourhood centre for young people that, ironically, is described on its website as being established for the purpose of offering "a constant alternative to the destructive environment of the streets."[2] Tamara explained:

> From the Rattlers came the Overlords and then from the Overlords they split. They changed themselves to the Manitoba Warriors. And they started feuding, so they went and said, "Well, we are going to make our own little gang called the Indian Posse."

Lucy maintained that the gang was different back then:

> At that time, they seemed to have a code of ethics, kind of like, "do no harm" within the gang. They had a sisterhood and a brotherhood, it was a family. It was a fine line that was drawn in terms of the "do no harm" within the gang system. I remember a time when they thought it was honourable to fight with your hands, not with weapons. And that female gang members who were a part of the gang, a lot of them went into prostitution and they could not participate in the heavy use of drugs. It was frowned upon because of the "do no harm" philosophy. It was never worded that but just the way they had a reverence for each other in that way. If you got into heavier drugs, it was frowned upon from higher-ranking members in the gang.

Lucy was also of the view that relations between the sexes in these gangs were equal: *"But at that time it seemed like it was equal. Base power to both the male and female. Like, it was so closely relational. Like, you know, really cared for each other."* By the early 1990s, she said, the core of the gang had *"quickly turned to something else."* When I asked her why she thought this change had occurred, she replied:

> Because maybe not having the skill to be able to put forth their message. You know, not having the resources. Not having the support of the community because of where they come from. Because in our own community they put value on the paper, on a degree. On some kind of status that puts us in a certain type of leadership. I started seeing pieces that were start-

*ing to go on because the crime started to become more intense and more violent, like break-ins and the robberies and what not. Of course, it was fuelled by addictions.*

In opposition to these stories, most participants in the study maintained that there were now no female gang members or female gangs, only "old ladies," "bitches," and "hos," each with specific defined roles and responsibilities. Participants explained that Anishinaabe Ikwe had their connection to the gang only by virtue of their relationships with male gang members. While many participants had family relations with gang members (a father, brother, uncle, and/or cousin were in the gang), for the most part participants saw their connection to the gang as deriving from their relationship with a male gang member. This relation to male gang members defined and constructed particular aspects of women's and girls' experiences and spaces.

### Old Ladies

Throughout the interviews, many participants referred to themselves as "so and so's old lady." Old ladies are the girlfriends of male gang members. That is to say, they are women or girls with whom male gang members have some semblance of a committed and loving relationship. Tamara explained that a women's position in the gang was to further their "old man's" place and space within the gang: *"It depends who your old man is too. What his role is within the gang."* Many participants noted that some women had decision-making capacities in the gang as well, depending upon how they were perceived by male gang members. Tamara explained:

> *Her knowledge and her experience in the gang — they [male gang members] just analyze the situation with certain women. Like they think "Oh you are so fucking stupid, you don't know what the hell you are talking about" or "Hey, that's something to really think about." They categorize it like that.*

Another participant, who happened to be the boss's[3] old lady, noted that once a woman is considered and known as an old lady, everyone knows, respects, and ensures that place, particularly if her partner is incarcerated.

> *All those little men, they watch you. They follow you around or stop you for the old man ... even when he was in the Remand Centre. His little friends would come to my mom's and buzz me. I came down and he would be on the cell phone and ask why I am not answering the phone.... I went up North. No one, nobody knew I went up North. Nobody. Just me and my mom. I don't know how they knew I went up North.*

While Aboriginal gangs do not necessarily have written codes of ethics or behaviour, there are unspoken, expected, and prescribed protocols, rules, and responsibilities that everyone — including old ladies — must adhere to. Primarily, old ladies were expected to be "good." Candace explained that to be good meant, *"Don't drink or run around with guys or go to the bars. Just stay home, that's what they expect you to do. Why would you make your old lady stay at home and stay indoors? Don't go outside, talk, speak when spoken to, stuff like that."* Candace went on to explicitly note: *"Gang members and their old ladies aren't allowed to do drugs."*

Old ladies were expected to "be solid" — which implies, in the instance of physical assault, that a woman would just take the beating. To be solid means that an old lady does not seek help from social-service agencies or the police, or that she does not try to leave her partner for a women's shelter. As Tamara explained:

> *If you get out of it, the other women just say, "Okay, well then you are not solid enough." They just kind of shun you … for complaining. You don't mention it [abuse shelters] but if you mention something like that then your old man is going to get mad at you, "Why are you fucking talking that shit?"*

Tamara also maintained that Anishinaabe Ikwe stay out of the physical assaults of other Anishinaabe Ikwe by their intimate partners as a way of "being solid" with the gang: *"You just stay out of it."* Mary similarly argues that other old ladies had to stay out of each other's business:

> *We couldn't stop it because we had to take it like a woman. If your man beats you up, take it. That's your norm. That is normal. Like my ex, I got all my teeth knocked out from him and, you know, I got stabbed so many times. You just take it.*

Candace shared one incident (of many) in which she was being physically assaulted. Her story showed that not only women, but also male gang members, do not report or intervene in domestic relationships.

> *He has beaten me up a couple of times around his friends. There is, like, twenty guys there. I was twenty-six and he must have been, like, thirty.… There would be, like, twenty of them when they went to drink and he beat me up right in front of them. He just got out of remand and he said I was dogging him — fooling around on him…. They just watch. They stood back and watched. I can't believe it, a bunch of them could have stopped*

*him, pulled him away from me 'cause he had me up against the wall off my feet. Like, he had his hands around my neck and he was just yelling at me.*

The normalization of abuse and the pressures on the women to "be solid" mean that some old ladies will actually make up stories about being physically abused in order to fit in with the other old ladies. Cathy explained:

*You have to just accept it. If it is not happening to you, then you are lucky and you just keep quiet about it. I heard one girl saying things that her old man had pushed her head into the mirror while she was putting makeup on but she didn't have any marks to show for it. We'd all be showing our marks, our bruises and she didn't have any marks so we didn't believe her. So when we're alone with our old man we ask him that we heard so and so was beating up on so and so and he'll confirm that it's not like that.*

Nevertheless, many respondents emphasized that a kind of sister-hood cultivates among old ladies because they are going through the same struggles and joys and operate within the same gang context. As Candace explained it, *"We know each other and we know what we are going through and we all know what it is like."* Cathy said:

*It just seems like if you're with a man that's in a gang — like, all the women that are going out with these gang members — they are automatically friends, even if you don't like someone. You have to be polite to her when you go to their house. And your kids all hang out together too.*

Even if an Anishinaabe Ikwe is no longer with a particular gang member, according to many participants she will always have that connection through her child or children. Tamara described this connection:

*If you have a kid from a gang member you will always be involved in that gang even if it was twenty years ago, thirty years ago. You will always be connected, especially the kids, especially the kids. They are second generation. They are like blessed. They get blessed into the gang. It is like they don't have to do anything to be in a gang. It is automatically a gang member.*

While an old lady's place in the gang is determined largely by her relation with a male gang member, Cathy maintained that old ladies had some semblance of decision-making capacities and other responsibilities within the gang. For instance, some old ladies were solicited for their advice by male gang members: *"When they were selling rock, they used to ask us, 'Should we go over here tonight?' or 'What area should we do?' or 'Whose place should we go to first?' That is what they would be doing, asking us."* Cathy also explained that some old ladies were designated as "drivers," which involved chauffeuring male gang members to various locations for a variety of activities (picking up drugs, committing break and enters).

## Bitches and Hos

Most, if not all, study participants argued that at the lower rung of the hierarchy of Anishinaabe Ikwe involved in street gangs were the "bitches" and "hos." These women and girls were not looked upon favourably and were always described in pejorative ways. Sabrina noted that gang members *"always have a girl [old lady] at home that they like and stay with. But at the same time they are fucking all these other girls. Man, bringing home shit."* Sabrina went on to note that "bitches" and "hos" also get pregnant from gang members:

> But at the same time these girls run around, "like this is your baby" but meanwhile, they are fucking all these other guys, so nobody really knows what is going on. A "bitch" are the girls that dress all skanky and they run around.

Lorna maintains that *"Bitches and hos are just the girlfriends that work the streets. They call them bitches and hos. They just feed them drugs."* Candace referred to women and girls that work the streets as *"just money-makers."* The possibility of attracting such negative labels, however, was an ever-present concern for many of the women. Sabrina, for instance, commented that even by simple association, a woman or girl could be considered a "bitch" or "ho":

> You hang out with a bunch of "hos" then you are going to look like a "ho." I try to stay away from all girls because they make you look bad. They bring you down. They want to go scamming shit.

In addition to highlighting the nature of women's and girls' participation in the gang, these narratives begin to reveal the pervasive nature of violence in the lives of Anishinaabe Ikwe. The subject of violence permeated the discussions with the women and girls, who spoke of intergenerational violence, residential school physical and sexual abuse, and intra-female violence. One predominant theme was that of violence between male gang members and women. Violence in interpersonal relationships was not just an experience encountered by the older women in the study. One participant, who was turning fourteen at the time of the interview, recounted how, when she was twelve, she was assaulted by a fourteen-year-old gang member:

*I used to hang out with other gang members. I went to this one house because there was this guy that I liked. He asked me if I wanted to come over. I stayed there for a while. We usually got high, drank sometimes. This one day I said, "I want to go home." And all of a sudden, he turns out the lights. He had this white thing, it was hard. He started hitting me with it, yelling, "You're not fucking going anywhere." He was just hitting me and I was crying.... When [her friend] went in [the room], he was like, "Get the fuck out of here!" and he starts hitting her. I tried running out of the room but he just grabbed me and slammed me against the wall. I was all bruised up and beaten up.*

Of all the narratives I heard concerning interpersonal violence between male gang members and women, Candace's account of one particular incident (of the many more she was to encounter) had by far the most profound effect on me. Candace shared how, when she was around seventeen, she was pregnant with her first child and only a week away from her due date when she and her boyfriend got into an argument over another man at a party. The fight escalated to where her boyfriend *"grabbed a knife out of nowhere."*

*And he stabbed me in the stomach. It hit the baby through the baby's back and it almost came out the stomach. So after that they rushed me, everybody left that party and they phoned the ambulance. The cops took him and they don't know where the weapon was. I was in the hospital. I don't remember being in the hospital but I was there. I had a cesarean, they took it out. It was stillborn. I was due the next week.*

How can we begin to make sense of these narratives, in terms of what they tell us not only about the relations between women and men, but also about those between the women and girls involved in gang activity? Again we have to keep in mind that relations between Indigenous men and women pre-contact were of an equal, fluid nature, and that the processes of colonization have had a dramatic impact on relations between the sexes. As the Royal Commission on Aboriginal Peoples (1996) stated:

The stereotyping and devaluing of Aboriginal women, a combination of racism and sexism, are among the most damaging of attitudes that find expression in Canadian society. These attitudes are not held exclusively by non-Aboriginal people either.... Members of powerless groups who are subjected to demeaning treatment tend to internalize negative attitudes toward their own groups. They then act on these attitudes in ways that confirm the original negative judgement.

Métis scholar Emma LaRocque (2002) also discusses this process of "internalization," whereby, as a result of colonization, Aboriginal peoples have come to judge themselves against the standards of the white society. According to LaRocque (2002: 149), part of this process entails "swallowing the standards, judgements, expectations, and portrayals of the dominant white world."

In these terms, the violence encountered by Anishinaabe Ikwe in their intimate relationships with men can be interpreted as a reflection of the patriarchal ideas about women (and how they should be treated) that prevail in the wider society. Jody Miller came to a similar conclusion in her research on girls' involvement in street gangs. Miller suggests that the girls strike a "patriarchal bargain" that allows them to reconcile the negative aspects of their gang affiliation with the perceived benefits. Miller points out that "the world around gang girls is not a particularly safe place, physically or psychically" (2001: 193). When young women in that social world are seen as such ready targets of violence and victimization, association with a street gang can offer at least some semblance of protection. Nevertheless, Miller found that "many young women's means of resisting gender oppression within gangs tended to be an individualized response based on constructing gendered gang identities as separate from and 'better than' those of the girls around them in their social environments. It meant internalizing and accepting masculine constructs of gang values" (2001: 197).

To this extent, colonization has now taken on a new guise. While physical violence historically played a major role in ensuring colonial rule, violence is now taken up by our men and inflicted on our women within this new, internalized colonial regime. Given their disenfranchised and subordinate position both within the street gang and the wider society, it should not surprise us that Aboriginal women and girls would compete among themselves in an effort to negotiate their place and space. "Being solid," "taking it like a woman," and creating a distance from those women and girls who have less status therefore become important survival strategies.

## Surviving Colonialism

Throughout each of the interviews, colonization and its impact on our Indigenous culture, traditions, and existence permeated the discussions. While the study participants may not have named their lived experience using the language of colonialism, time and time again Anishinaabe Ikwe made references to *"how it was before the 'White Man.'"* It is within this colonial context that the role of the street gang as a source of support and resistance must be located.

Euro-Canadian dominant discourse would have us believe that the conditions in which Aboriginal peoples now find themselves derive primarily from the First Nations' own lack of enterprise, poor work ethic ("lazy Indians"), and overall inadequate economic, political (corrupt), social (savage), and cultural (backwards) capacities. On the contrary, Aboriginal peoples' socio-economic, political, social, and cultural conditions fundamentally derive from our collective experience of colonization. Christian missionary conversion mandates, state-regulated and executed residential school systems, the prohibition of voting, the forbidding of participation in traditional cultural and spiritual activities, and the entrenchment of the racist and sexist Indian Act are just a few of the many policies and strategies imposed upon the Indigenous collective. Each of these various activities has had — and continues to have — profound effects on generations of Aboriginal peoples in Canada.

In particular, think about the impact of the residential school system: Indigenous children as young as three were involuntarily taken away from parents, grandparents, and community and forced to live away for ten months at a time or, in some cases, years at a time. What happens to children, families, communities, and nations when our children, who, as the "Circle of Law" teaches us, are the "Fire" and "Motivation" of the Indigenous collective, are taken away and "taught" (enforced, strictly regulated, brainwashed) that everything they knew, experienced, and believed to be true about their world was "savage" and that they were "less than"? Children, families, communities, and nations slowly die physically, socially, culturally, and spiritually. The formation of Aboriginal street gangs primarily derives from this ancestral and generational colonial history and experience.

Given this context, many study participants not surprisingly relayed how their association with the gang provided them with a space in which they could be themselves and where they found solidarity and pride in being Indigenous. Tamara stated: "*What's the gang to me? Well, obviously, they have been around. They have been a support. They have been the backbone to me being alive and taking care of me.*" Cathy told me how the gang allowed her the freedom and strength to counter the dominant white society and claim her space as one of the original peoples of this land: "*It is very powerful. Like, you know, they [white society] put you really down. I find they get ignorant and racist. Like, it is almost like you're dirt. And for me, I would just stand up and say, 'No, I'm not dirt.' You know, if they want to play the part, so can I. Reverse psychology because that is how dirty they get."* Louisa asserted that the gang provided her with an environment in which she had a connection and understanding:

> *Strengths. I met a lot of friends. They took care of me and I always had money. It was someone I knew that was there for me and kind of helping me. When I was in that group home there were white, black people. It was okay but I was more happy being around my own people. And there were a couple of people from The Pas. It was nice to know somebody from The Pas. There was more understanding, like, I could understand too. I was like their little sister. That was cool.*

In these terms, Aboriginal gangs do not develop solely because of a desire or need for money and power. Aboriginal gangs develop simply because our people are not afforded the same educational, employment, political, and cultural opportunities as the rest of Canadian society. From the moment we take our first breath to the moment we take our last, we are under assault by virtue of the Indian Act. We start school only to learn that we were or are "savages" and are a burden on society. We do not see ourselves reflected positively in schools, work, or government. It is only once we start to acknowledge and recognize this factor that we can begin to move to more worthwhile approaches in dealing with Aboriginal street gangs and, in particular, Aboriginal women's place and space.

The dominant discourse surrounding gangs mostly pertains to so-called "exiting" models premised on the notion that gang members just need to either formally (request to leave) or informally (hide out and eventually be forgotten) exit the gang. Unfortunately, this is far too simplistic a solution. Gangs provide members with a sense of family, both literally and symbolically (as in "you're my homie"). Many of the study participants noted the literal family connections that many gang members have. Freda maintained that even though gang members (and their old ladies) may be from different gangs, family connections override any prescribed gang norms or codes of behaviour. She said:

> *They are all connected through their families. Some will have a cousin that is a Warrior and his cousin will be an Indian Posse and then that one's sister or stepsister will be going out with a guy that is from Native Syndicate. If you are in the same room with all of them, it's a family gathering.*

That gang members end up being family members complicates whether or not it is ever truly possible to "leave the gang."

## Street Gangs: Strength and Survival

I have been only able to offer here a portion of the various narratives and themes shared by the study participants over the span of almost two years. Nevertheless, what I have endeavoured to show is that Aboriginal street gangs — and women's particular context within the gang — did and do not develop divorced from the settler colonial context in Canada. Contrary to what most may believe, colonialism is not something that occurred in the past. The colonial experiment in Canada has never ended — European settlers did not de-colonize and go "back home." We are still under the rule of the colonizer, with all of its Western Euro-Canadian ethnocentric ideologies and institutions.

Conducting the interviews for this study was by far the most difficult research I have ever done, but I would not have traded one moment. I was so privileged to have time with these women. Far from the media portrayal of violent female equivalents of "thugs," these women represent the strength, perseverance, and beauty of the Indigenous peoples in Canada. Remembering a time when our people, our nations, and our cultures were thought to be "vanishing," I can see that these women counter that notion with their very struggle and, most importantly, survival. We were not supposed to be here. Indeed, that was the plan so methodically and strategically executed. But despite every imaginable assault, we are still here and, in some capacity or another, flourishing.

## Notes

I would like to say "meegwetch" to Elizabeth Comack for all the support and help she provided throughout the process of writing this piece, particularly her wonderful editing. Truly, this paper would not have been completed had it not been for her time, energy, and spirit.

1.  I have not edited and/or grammatically altered the participants' narratives. Specifically, I wanted to ensure respect and appreciation for participants and what they had to say and did not feel I had the right or the authority to change anything that was so freely communicated and shared.
2.  See <rossbrookhouse.ca/about/>.
3.  A "boss" is a president of one of the gangs.

5

# Dazed, Dangerous, and Dissolute
## Media Representations of Street-Level
## Sex Workers in Vancouver's Downtown Eastside

*David Hugill*

Lillian O'Dare was thirty-four years old when she vanished from the streets of Vancouver's Downtown Eastside. Her disappearance was reported in 1978. One later newspaper report revealed that she shared a birthday with Elvis Presley, had "carefully waved" blond hair, and was raised in Williams Lake, B.C. (Hawthorn 2007). Beyond these few banal details, we know almost nothing about who Lillian O'Dare was and the social or political circumstances of her disappearance.

In contrast to this biographical obscurity, O'Dare's story is freighted with an ominous historical significance. It was the first episode in a pattern of predatory violence that would claim a long list of victims in the same district. It was here — in Vancouver's oldest and poorest neighbourhood — that nearly seventy local women, many of them street-level sex workers, disappeared and/or were murdered between 1978 and 2002.

Rates of violent crime remain comparatively low in Canada. Abductions and murders tend to generate significant media attention and provoke aggressive deployments of the resources of law enforcement agencies. The 2009 disappearance of a Toronto teenager, for example, captivated local and national media for weeks and was the source of a wide-ranging investigation by police (Teotonio 2009). Events like these disrupt widely shared perceptions about what is to be expected in this country. Polling in recent decades demonstrates that Canadians have a great deal of faith in the capacity of authorities to ensure both their own personal safety and the safety of the population in general (Gannon 2005; Statistics Canada 2005). In the minds of many people violent incidents are aberrational episodes that disrupt a continuum of otherwise orderly co-existence. Canadians widely expect, moreover, that when such events do occur, they will be met with a swift and severe response by accountable public institutions.

The grisly events that happened in Vancouver's Downtown Eastside were scarcely aberrational. The disappearance of so many women — sustained over such a long period — betrays a decidedly different reality: it demonstrates that brutality and predation had become normalized in the neighbourhood. Yet even as it continued to deepen over the course of two decades, Vancouver's crisis of missing and murdered women generated little interest from local authorities or journalists.[1] It was not until a few journalists began to do some probing in 1998 that the story began to gain significant attention; and it was not until 2002, when police arrested an ex-urban farmer named Robert Pickton and charged him with the murder of more than twenty of the missing women, that the crisis developed into an important national (and international) media event. While the bulk of these crimes were unfolding, local authorities and journalists went missing in action. They failed to acknowledge that a major crisis was spiralling out of control. At best, they failed to notice. At worst, they failed to care.

What, then, was different about the events in Vancouver? Why did the disappearance of a single teenager in Toronto — a tragic but isolated incident — provoke vigorous police and media attention while for the longest time a far more expansive series of tragedies in Vancouver led only to state inaction and media silence? The answer to this question is complex and relates to an intersecting series of social and political practices that valorize certain lives while simultaneously disregarding others.[2] The social and geographical location of the women who disappeared from the Downtown Eastside operated to disqualify them from the protective assurances of authorities. As residents of a stigmatized inner-city neighborhood, as sex workers in the bottom rungs of Vancouver's street-level sex trade, as poverty-stricken members of an increasingly stratified society, and as racialized women, they were members of a social milieu that was either rendered invisible to, or cast aside from, the core constituencies served by our collective institutions. As one politician asked, citing as an example an affluent Vancouver neighbour-hood: "Do you think if 65 women went missing from Kerrisdale, we'd have ignored it for so long?" (Wood 2004).

A key part of the problem is that media narratives promote ideas about street-level sex workers that contribute to the normalization of the violence they encounter. In particular, the national print media's coverage of the arrest and trial of Robert Pickton (a moment when sex work was comprehensively discussed in media discourses) served to provide a coherent framework for understanding who street-level sex workers are and what motivates their sustained participation in the precarious market of the street. More specifically, this type of coverage produces an understanding of the sex worker as a drugged, dazed, deviant, dissolute, and corrupted "Other" whose affiliation with a notorious underworld places her (and it's always *her*) in constant threat of danger and predation. This result is accomplished through two sets of narratives: one that explicitly demonizes street-involved women and another that appears more sympathetic, describing sex workers as victims, not merely of the danger of the stroll, but also of a long history of predatory abuse, personal devastation, and all-consuming addiction. This range of media discourses operates to reinforce a dominant ideological paradigm, a tightly constricted set of boundaries through which the violence that is routinely perpetuated against street-level sex workers is rendered understandable to audiences. The narratives *produce* the sex worker as an object of popular knowledge. We need, then, to consider *how* that production is accomplished, *who* is authorized to contribute to it, and *what* some of its consequences are. My observations here are based on an analysis of more than 150 articles about the arrest and trial of Robert Pickton — articles that appeared in three of Canada's principal English-language daily newspapers (*Toronto Star, Globe and Mail,* and *National Post*) between February 2002 and December 2007.

## Producing the "Prostitute"

Over time the iconic figure of the "prostitute" has been assigned a series of divergent popular meanings. Sex workers have not only been a source of simultaneous "fear and fascination" in Western societies, but also been constituted as an affront to established morality and as "nefarious" deviant others, as Phillip Hubbard (1999: 1) shows. Despite the recurrence of certain themes, however, prevailing representations of the essential nature of the prostitute have never been static. "The boundaries separating different categories of deviance and dangerousness are not fixed and immutable, but fluid and permeable; they constantly change as a function of shifting cultural sensibilities and public concern," note Chris Greer and Yvonne Jewkes (2005: 23).

Mass media discourses have assigned a diverse range of identities to sex workers, characterizations that have resonated to varying degrees in different periods. They have defined sex workers as vectors of disease and contagion, entrapped sexual slaves, victims of the "white slave trade," endangered persons, "fallen" women, and symbols of community failure. They have also presented sex workers as unpredictable, deranged, morally depraved, and criminally culpable individuals who are "feeble-minded," a public nuisance, and an affront to public respectability, to note only a few of the most common examples (Hallgrimsdottir, Phillips, and Benoit 2006;

O'Neill et al. 2008; Sangster 2001). While many of these labels have long vanished from popular usage, contemporary media narratives continue to privilege their own set of characterizations that establish prostitutes as "distinguishable types," as particular kinds of "folk devils" (Cohen 2002). These characterizations often retain much of the fear and loathing expressed by earlier iterations.

Two stigmatizations have proven persistent. The first understands the prostitute as a source of criminal deviance and danger; the second understands her as a symbol of moral corruption. Both characterizations are central to the national print media's coverage of the arrest and trial of Robert Pickton.

### The Sex Worker as Criminal Deviant and Dangerous

Street prostitution or "kerb-crawling" has been associated with distinct forms of urban deviance since at least the nineteenth century. Judith Walkowitz's (1992: 21) survey of prostitution in late-Victorian London, for example, notes that the figure of the street prostitute operated as a "public symbol of female vice." Elements of this nineteenth-century image persist in contemporary depictions. One study of how prostitution was narrated in Canadian newspapers between 1981 and 1995 reports that sex work was routinely conflated with deviance and criminality, and that the connection between street-level sex work and narcotic dependency was often assumed to be seamless (Van Brunschot, Sydie, and Krull 1999). Another survey of prostitution-related articles that appeared in Victoria's *Times-Colonist* newspaper between 1980 and 2005 found that sex workers were routinely produced as cunning criminals believed to "take pride in circumventing the law and avoiding arrest" (Hallgrimsdottir, Phillips, and Benoit 2006: 268).

In Canada the association of prostitution with criminality has been exacerbated by a legal regime that has historically criminalized practices related to selling sex (especially sections 210 to 213 of the Criminal Code). John Lowman (2000: 1004) contends that this "outlaw status" has had devastating implications for sex workers. He suggests that by defining prostitutes as criminals the law has reproduced an ideological context in which a woman working the stroll is "particularly vulnerable to predatory misogynist violence." The illicit nature of prostitution in Canada forces the industry underground, a phenomenon that reaffirms both real and perceived connections to various forms of criminal activity.

The sex worker's status as a symbol of danger is not simply a function of her presumed connection to criminality but also a function of her presumed status as a vector of disease. This is particularly true in Vancouver, where the Downtown Eastside was assumed to be the centre of an HIV epidemic in 1997. Intravenous drug use and sex work were seen as central factors in the outbreak, a perception that marked street-level prostitutes as a decidedly dangerous population. The association of disease with danger has been particularly pronounced in the case of HIV, with the virus seen as a "quintessential sign of all that imperils a civilized future-in-the-world, an iconic social pathology," as Jean Comaroff (2007: 197) observes. The persistent conflation of sex work with the dangers of disease plays on such fears.

Symbols are central to ordering our "collective views of the world," as Richard Ericson, Patricia Baranek, and Janet Chan (1991: 5) point out. The symbol of the prostitute has long contributed to such orderings by providing an image of criminal deviance and danger that functions as an archetypal negative against which the norms of civilized citizenship can be distinguished.

## The Sex Worker as a Symbol of Moral Corruption

Sex workers have also been represented as potent symbols of moral corruption. The degree to which such characterizations have been sustained and reproduced in media narratives offers a compelling illustration of the news media's capacity to "participate in the constitution of moral boundaries of the society" in which they report (Ericson, Baranek, and Chan 1987: 60). For much of the twentieth century, sex workers were branded by press narratives as "fallen women." They were imagined, that is, as individuals who had strayed from the norms of acceptable femininity and descended into a rank world of festering immorality and licentiousness. This was particularly true of street-level workers, whose "corruption" was plainly visible to the public gaze. This "visible eroticization of the public realm," for Hubbard (1999: 77), came to represent the "most significant affront to a modern, patriarchal society in which women were considered as best confined to the sanctity of the feminized domestic space."

Even as patriarchal notions of acceptable female behaviour have been transformed, some critics argue that the exchange of sex for commercial gain has remained a potent symbol of moral degeneracy. Press narratives in the United Kingdom, for example, have consistently branded sex workers and clients as "morally degenerate" precisely because of their "willingness to reduce sex to commercial exchange" (O'Neill et al. 2008: 76). The repudiation of this commercial sexuality, for Hubbard (1999: 2), is bound up in a desire to preserve certain heterosexist norms. He argues that contemporary views of prostitution as immoral often reflect the view that "woman's sexuality should only be expressed or available within the confines of a domesticated and reproductive relationship." As such, the visible "immorality" of public prostitution has come to be seen as an affront to the enjoyment of city spaces by the mainstream public. An editorial that appeared in the *Times-Colonist* in 1981 succinctly captured this condemnatory spirit: "Whores ... not only offend ... the law, they are an embarrassment when the family goes downtown for dinner. They speak of the community's failure. They are also seen as a threat by some wives and mothers and they are bad for business" (cited in Hallgrimsdottir, Phillips, and Benoit 2006: 279). This assessment offers a striking example of how street-involved women have been contrasted against (and seen as antithetical to) conventional female subjectivities.

The assumed danger of the sex worker's immorality — her capacity to bring corruption into the sphere of morally upright men and women — both contrasts her against, and marks her as a threat to, the valorized figures of mother and daughter. Such characterizations have had important implications. Yasmin Jiwani and Mary Lynn Young (2006: 900) note in their survey of the *Vancouver Sun*'s coverage of the case of the missing and murdered women that this binary demarcates those "bodies that can and should be saved from those that are considered beyond redemption." Traditionally virtuous women (mothers, daughters, wives) are set up in sharp contrast to the "runaways" and "throwaways" mired in the corruption of street-level commercial sex. This contrast is powerfully reproduced in journalistic attempts to restore a certain dignity to the missing and murdered women by celebrating their status as family members and contrasting that role against the immoral practices of sex work and narcotic use.

## Criminality, Danger, and Moral Corruption in Media Narratives

The media narratives I studied produce a relatively coherent if uncomplicated image of the sex worker. Each of the three newspapers, with notable consistency, mobilizes a series of recurring themes to explain this figure, and offers compelling ways of understanding who it is that enters the industry and what it is that motivates *her* sustained participation. The sex workers appearing in these stories are portrayed as women who are powerfully consumed by addiction. They are constantly at risk of predation and violence, yet undeterred by (or oblivious to) the constant peril of their work. Their presence on the stroll is frequently explained by reference to previous victimization, generally a foundational personal tragedy narrative that preceded the "descent." These personal histories explain the terror of the street as only the most recent in a series of abuses. A woman's connection to the illicit drug trade and the "outlaw status" of her work, meanwhile, mark her as part of a deviant and criminal underworld, a member of that illicit class that reproduces chaos in the inner city. The conflation of illicit activity, including sex work, with particular city spaces is also a conflation of the "body of the urban outcast" with the city's "insidious" spaces, and a way of blaming street-involved people for urban decline (Sommers and Blomley 2002: 22–25). The sex worker is produced as intractably linked to the "degenerate" space in which she works (for more detail on this point, see Hugill 2010, chap. 4), and she is subjected, by virtue of this association, to the same "unremitting stigmatization" as the neighbourhood itself (Pratt 2005: 1062). These themes are reproduced in the substantive textual explanations that suffuse both the text and the visual culture of the coverage — particularly in the prominent photographs and headlines that act as "cognitive organizers" — to further embed this dominant portrayal (Jiwani and Young 2006: 904).

While prostitution itself is a constant theme in the coverage, the image of the sex worker is primarily shaped through a group of eighteen articles and profiles that attempt to provide substantive information about the people who enter the street-level industry. The majority of these articles (thirteen) are profiles of the six women whom Pickton would eventually be convicted of murdering (I call these pieces "victim profiles"); the others (five) are more general stories about women working in street-level prostitution.

The victim profiles are marked by two somewhat contradictory patterns. In one sense, they attempt to overcome the reduction of these women to the categories of "prostitute" and "addict" by highlighting the more banal aspects of their lives and personalities. Here, the women are memorialized in different ways. One is described as a poet and artist. Another is said to be a loyal friend. A third is identified as someone who loved the colour pink. These descriptions are transparent attempts to transcend stigmatization by positioning each victim as someone who was more than part of a deviant underclass. They are also attempts to invest each victim with a personal history that extends beyond her experiences in the Downtown Eastside. Accordingly, these articles are the central vehicles through which the writers relate each woman's tragic personal history; they attempt to bring her "descent" into plain view. Their central narrative function, however, is the production of each woman as a member of a family (a daughter, a mother, a sister) whose absence is mourned.

In another sense, these profiles operate to consolidate the victims' status as members of a deviant class. Themes of addiction, disease, and violence are central to these ostensibly sympathetic profiles. The attempts to memorialize respectfully, usually by highlighting each woman's proximity to common-sense notions of respectability, are tempered by persistent allusions to their deviance. In one profile, for example, Serena Abotsway is remembered as a "bubbly kindhearted woman" who was "an intravenous drug user and a prostitute." In the same article Georgina Papin is recalled as a woman who "dressed nicely and smoked crack cocaine before going to work as a prostitute" (*Globe and Mail* 2007). These paradigmatic descriptions counter evidence of conventional "decency" with blunt reminders of degeneracy.

Victim profiles like these ones, however, are far more balanced than are the five articles that describe sex workers currently working in the industry. With varying degrees of sensationalism, this second group of articles produces a strikingly narrow image of the street-involved woman. She is defined as an archetypically itinerant and irresponsible individual. Her decisions are divested of context as she is portrayed as one-dimensional in her addiction, concerned only with the pursuit of a next fix. Descriptions of women still working on the strolls are inflected by a persistent (if sometimes only suggestive) pattern of comparison that marks them as one and the same with the disappeared. In many places this conflation is unmistakable. Current workers are produced as the fortunate ones who, as one reporter puts it, "survived the era of a serial killer [only to] continue to risk it all … beatings, rape, disease" (DiManno 2007a).

This textual production does not occur in isolation; it is imbedded in a visual culture that bolsters the previous themes. Headlines and sub-headlines are central to this process; they provide key messages — "cognitive organizers" — that orient the reader's interpretation by setting the tone of the news page and establishing what information is relevant. Certain salient terms recur in these titles and reinforce themes of deviance. The terms "prostitute," "hooker," "sex worker," and "sex-trade worker," for example, appear in twelve headlines and sub-headlines while the terms "addiction," "junkies," and "drugs" appear in eight. To put these numbers in context, the words "missing" or "missing women" appear twenty-one times in the coverage. Prostitution is privileged in headlines roughly half as many times as disappearance, while narcotic dependency is emphasized in roughly one-third as many. Yet the headline culture is as interesting in what it omits as what it implies. In spite of the dire economic circumstances that many of the missing and murdered women (as well other women still selling sex in the Downtown Eastside) are said to endure, there is not a single reference to economic marginalization in any of the headlines or sub-headlines; the term "poverty," for example, does not appear in a single title. Moreover, despite the striking overrepresentation of Aboriginal women among the missing and murdered, only one reference to Aboriginality appears in the headlines — a disturbing omission that signals the coverage's prevailing unwillingness to interrogate this trend.

The cohesiveness of the image of the prostitute was further accomplished by the photographic culture of the coverage. The examined newspapers displayed twenty-nine images of street-involved women. Of these, twenty-four are photographs (or groups of photographs) of the missing and murdered women themselves, while the other five are of women who were currently street-involved. Of the images in the first group, twenty-one consisted of mug-shot style images, all of which appeared on the official missing women posters produced by civic authorities, a link that, as Jiwani and Young (2006: 904) observe, "reinforce[s] ... the women's association with criminality." These lineups saturated the coverage, appearing at least once on the front page of all three newspapers. They are unflattering and close-cropped, and conjure associations with familiar prisoner processing photographs. Clustered together as they so often are, these mug-shot collages collapse distinctions between individuals, producing the collective as a common caste, those who experienced a shared destiny born of a shared lifestyle.

While the photographs of the missing and murdered women suggest deviance largely through association, the five photographs of street-involved women establish the connection directly. These arresting images feature women injecting heroin, smoking crack, soliciting clients, sitting glassy-eyed on a dirty sidewalk, and loitering on an industrial loading bay. On their own, they have a dramatic effect, signalling the radical distance of their subjects from conventional interpretations of civilized public behaviour. They invest textual accounts of deviance with the authority of graphic proof, and their significance is further amplified by the headlines that accompany them. One image appears beneath the headline "Can't get lower than this." Another appears above the title "Always on edge" (Hutchinson 2007). A third title establishes an unmistakable link between those currently on the street and the disappeared: a lurid shot of a woman injecting narcotics into her neck appears alongside the headline "I guess I'm lucky to be alive" (Girard 2002a).

*Authoritative Sources and Sources of Authority*

The professional cultures of news production expect accounts of observed reality to be grounded in (or corroborated by) the "authoritative statements" of "accredited sources" (Hall et al. 1978: 58). Such practices are central to preserving the news organization's reputation as a disinterested and impartial observer. Articles employ outside evidence from established authorities to confer a sense of objectivity and universality on the otherwise subjective accounts of individual journalists. Such practices can be important to ensuring fairness and accuracy in reporting, but they can also have dubious consequences. In many cases, for example, a reliance on "accredited sources" has the effect of providing certain individuals and organizations with a systematic "over-accessing" to the media (Hall et al. 1978). Importantly, too, by providing access to certain people (and not others) news organizations communicate to their audiences who ought to be considered an authority on a given issue (and who should not) (Ericson, Baranek, and Chan 1987).

Coverage of the crisis of missing and murdered women provides compelling evidence of institutional overrepresentation. Authoritative claims from representatives of police departments, government bureaucracies, and various other sites of established institutional power are an important feature of the coverage and serve as a key means of advancing particular interpretations of what happened. As an indicator of how the coverage has produced particular characterizations of sex workers themselves, however, these institutional knowers are not the most relevant contributors. Information about sex workers is largely drawn from three other sources: the families and friends of the missing and murdered women, advocates and allies of street-involved women, and sex workers themselves.

The coverage produces a distinct "hierarchy of credibility" between these source groups. The family and friends of the missing and murdered women were quoted 109 times in the coverage, roughly five and a half times more than the advocates and allies of street-involved women (quoted twenty times), and roughly eleven times more than sex workers themselves (quoted ten times). The question of how sex workers are portrayed in the coverage hinges fundamentally on who is authorized to speak on their behalf. With this in mind, we need to look closely at the different ways in which journalists mobilized the information provided by these three source groups.

## The Representational Authority of Family and Friends

Statements attributed to the family and friends of missing and murdered women provide the most comprehensive source of information about sex workers working in the Downtown Eastside. These statements are central to the construction of the dominant portrayals of sex workers that emerge from the coverage. Taken together, these quotations and contributions accomplish core narrative goals. They are employed to advance the narrative of the investigation by demonstrating how personal grief intersects with each procedural development; and they are frequently invoked to explain frustration with the police handling of the case (see Hugill 2010, chap. 2).

Most significantly, here, however, this group makes two other narrative contributions: First, they are a key source of information about how each woman ended up in the Downtown Eastside's street-level sex trade; second, they provide personal and even idiosyncratic details about the individual victims, anecdotal proof that the missing and murdered women were, as one prominent headline puts it, "more than drug addicted prostitutes" (Armstrong and Matas 2007).

Family and friends, as the primary source of biographical information about the missing and murdered women, are invoked to allow journalists to explain each victim's apparent fall from grace, the circumstances that explain her involvement in the sinister world of the inner city street. While the specific content of each story shows significant variation, a discernible common denominator unites them: each story provides a personal tragedy narrative that renders the victim's presence in the Downtown Eastside understandable. A distinct pattern emerges from these narratives. Behind each of the murdered women is a history of victimization, a series of individualized abuses that both precede and are said to have caused her turn to narcotic dependency and survival sex. Biographical sketches of the victims are suffused with accounts of parental addiction, fetal alcohol syndrome, racism, sexual and physical abuse, predatory foster parents, and exploitative boyfriends. These early traumas are privileged as the decisive foundations of a life of victimization. Of the twenty articles that provide biographical sketches of the victims, twelve invoke the words of family members and friends to attest to these foundational tragedies. For example:

(i) It was a sad existence that could be traced to her early childhood. Her father died in her arms when she was 3. Separated from her mother and seven other siblings, she was put in foster homes that, according to her brother, "left a lot to be desired."

The first foster home was "a nightmare" in which she was physically abused and subjected to severe mental torture. (Armstrong and Matas 2007)

(ii) He [Sereena Abotsway's foster father] said she was severely abused before she arrived at the Draayers, adding that he couldn't elaborate because the person who inflicted the harm is still alive. "Sereena was definitely damaged," he said. She lived with the Draayers until age 17 and called them Mom and Dad. (Armstrong and Matas 2007)

(iii) Ms. Papin had a troubled life growing up in Alberta, bouncing from foster homes to group homes to residential schools. She began experimenting with drugs at age 11, her brother Rick Papin said in an interview in 2001. (*National Post* 2007)

(iv) The naïve teen ran away from a difficult childhood on Vancouver Island to Vancouver's Downtown Eastside to pursue her dream of finding a husband and having a baby.

"She found this guy and she fell in love with him," her grandfather Jack Cummer said.

"Eventually she phoned and let me know he was 15 or 20 years older than she was, so it gave her two things: A man she loved and a father figure. But she was put on the streets because he was a drug dealer." (*National Post* 2007)

(v) Sarah deVries was also troubled. Growing up as a black child in a white neighborhood in the 1970s, she was teased and subjected to racist taunts. At home, while her older siblings and parents could sympathize, they could not relate.

"It was really tough for her growing up with nobody who shared her experience on that fundamental level" said Maggie deVries, a children's book author and editor.

When Sarah was 9 her parents split up. As the youngest, she took it hard. By her teens, she was in with the wrong crowd, using drugs, running away and frequenting the streets. It's unclear whether she completed Grade 8. By age 17, she was gone for good. (Girard 2002b)

These examples are representative of a larger narrative trend that establishes the missing and murdered women as traumatized and damaged subjects, driven to addiction and survival sex by individualized patterns of abuse. Critically, these stories help to memorialize the slain. They remind audiences that the victims were not merely the haphazardly chosen prey of a deranged individual, but persons who had experienced a continuum of brutal violence. Significantly, too, by speaking out the friends and family of the disappeared provided critical energy and an impressive moral force to campaigns aimed at ensuring that what happened in the Downtown Eastside would never happen again. Yet the journalists' narrative strategy of privileging this foundational abuse is not without peril. For one, it risks individualizing each tragedy. For another, when it is divested of a broader context it can have the effect of privatizing suffering by obscuring the role of the larger structural forces in reproducing and sustaining the dangers that each woman confronted.

Statements attributed to family members and friends are also central to journalistic efforts to transcend the stigmas of prostitute and addict. They operate to reinvest the victims with a sense of conventional respectability. They demonstrate that the women were more than merely street-involved — that they were "real people with real stories" (Armstrong and Matas 2007). Each of the sources show an evident effort to restore a certain degree of normalcy to the victims. Central to this effort is an attempt to demonstrate that each of the victims cultivated conventional family relationships. Friends and family members are important here; as mourning loved ones, they provide potent proof of these conventional bonds, and as quoted sources they provide credible biographical information that illustrates their veracity. Beneath headlines such as "Sister was a prostitute but so much more" (Matas 2002), "Little sister behind the statistic" (Girard 2002a), "These are our sisters, our daughters, our mothers" (*National Post* 2007), friends and family are invoked to demonstrate, as one *Toronto Star* correspondent would have it, that the victims were "not just drug addicts and whores but daughters, wives, mothers, human beings" (DiManno 2007b). Their statements are used to juxtapose the deviant practices of narcotic use and prostitution with the "real" and "human" practices of being a distinct member of a family.

Numerous quotations attributed to Rick Frey, father of Marnie Frey, (perhaps inadvertently) establish this binary even as he attempts to restore a positive "public perception" of the victims. As Frey puts it: "The Downtown Eastside women were portrayed as being prostitutes, hookers, drug addicts. They weren't — they were our daughters, our sisters, our mothers." Elsewhere Frey is quoted as saying: "[these] are our sisters, our daughters, our mothers — all human beings" (*National Post* 2007). Similarly, Maggie deVries, sister of Sarah deVries, is repeatedly invoked, insisting that the missing and murdered women were "real people" with real family connections. The *Globe and Mail's* Robert Matas (2002) writes:

> The family of one of Vancouver's missing prostitutes is concerned that the women will be perceived as one-dimensional caricatures similar to the characters in movies about prostitution and murder.
>
> Maggie deVries said yesterday that she wants the missing women remembered as people with lives and families.
>
> "It's for real," she said in an interview. "They were real people."

Elsewhere in the coverage, Greg Garley, foster brother of Mona Wilson, memorializes his murdered sister in equally familial terms: "I remember what a great girl she was. She would have made a great mother" (*Toronto Star* 2007). In a set of victim profiles, and beneath the heading, "Tried to get clean," Brenda Wolfe is commemorated in similar tones (*Globe and Mail* 2007). A quotation attributed to a friend that Wolfe met in a substance-abuse program reads: "I will always remember her smile and the beautiful son she had while in recovery" (*Globe and Mail* 2007). In one sense these examples, and the numerous others like them, represent an important effort to restore dignity to a group of relentlessly stigmatized women. Yet in another sense they operate to entrench a binary between the presumed authenticity and innate humanness of traditional familial roles (mother, daughter, sister) on the one hand, and the implied sub-humanity of street involvement on the other. They suggest, inadvertently or not, that the normalized practices of family life are what are "real" and "human" about each victim.

### The Representational Authority of Advocates and Allies
The advocates and allies of sex workers — those who either work directly with people in the Downtown Eastside (community organization service providers, for example), and others who, in their own capacity, advocate for policy reform or institutional change that would make the practices of street-level sex work less dangerous — are uniquely positioned to provide two kinds of contributions to the coverage. Those who work with sex workers are able to offer information about the experience of street involvement. In contrast to the contributions of family members, who were primarily called upon to provide information about the life of each woman as it was before she began working in the Downtown Eastside, community workers are called upon to provide information about what is happening, or what had been happening, at the street level itself. Those who advocate for changes to

the regulatory status quo — critical academics and sympathetic politicians, for example — are primarily enlisted in the coverage to bolster criticisms of the police or the state more generally.

With these considerations in mind, we might expect the most compelling critiques of the prevailing stigmatizations of the prostitute to come from this group. As individuals who work closely with street-involved women, community workers are well positioned to challenge stereotypical characterizations. Similarly, as individuals who study prostitution or are involved in the construction of public policy, these other allies are well positioned to provide potent critiques of current conditions and may have the credentials necessary to be considered authorities in the mainstream press. Indeed, it is from this group that some of the most robust critiques of the status quo are launched. Nevertheless, they account for a very small number of quotations and contributions. In the more than 150 articles examined, only twenty statements came from this group and many of them appeared in the same articles. As such, their significance must be weighed against the much broader themes that define the coverage. The placement and context of these iterations ensured that even contributions that might be called critical were primarily employed to bolster the dominant definitions of sex workers.

As individuals with daily exposure to street-involved women, community workers and allies are in a position to provide essential context for journalistic accounts of street involvement; their institutional affiliation marks them as credible sources. Predictably, their contributions tend to appear in the articles that attempt to provide some analysis of working conditions in the Downtown Eastside. Numerous accounts invoke Elaine Allan, a co-ordinator with Women in Need of a Safe House (wish), a Downtown Eastside drop-in centre, to provide a sense of what life is like on the neighbourhood's low-track strolls. Explanations attributed to Allan offer a portrait of the sex worker as an individual whose basic judgment has been catastrophically impaired by addiction. She describes a constant physical struggle frequently misunderstood by those outside of it. As Allan puts it in one article: "These women are just so addicted. Maybe people from mainstream society think it's just a big party down there every night and these women should just pull themselves up by their bootstraps. Believe me it's no party" (DiManno 2007c).

Elsewhere, Allan is called upon to describe the experience of addiction in more detail:

Elaine Allan, who once worked at a Vancouver drop-in centre for prostitutes, knew five of the six women. Ms. Allan said drug addiction, in its final stages, robs people of their personalities.

"The reality of it is that addicted women are lonely and they're vulnerable and they're isolated and they're afraid and they get beaten up a lot. Once you're here, there's no way out." (Armstrong and Matas 2007)

Jamie Lee Hamilton, another neighbourhood advocate, is also quoted as emphasizing the power of addiction: "Everyone out there is in survival mode ... it's hard to focus on your safety when more pressing needs are getting the next fix, affording food, finding a place to stay and making sure a shameless pimp is paid off" (Girard 2002a).

Unlike other narratives about the missing women that tend to consider addiction in less contextualized ways, the explanations provided by advocates and allies offer important considerations of the multiple oppressions that street-involved women often shoulder. Taken together, they furnish compelling accounts of survival sex as an ongoing experience of victimization. Allan describes women who are not only burdened by powerful narcotic dependencies but also haunted by poverty, inadequate police protection, and an ever-present threat of violence. Her contributions disrupt, to some degree, narratives that suggest street involvement as a kind of self-selected deviance, an actively willed alternative lifestyle. As she puts it: "I know that a lot of these women come from horrific situations at home, from foster care. They've been physically and sexually abused. But there's no haven on the streets. This is where the real abuse happens" (DiManno 2007c).

This sentiment is echoed elsewhere by another WISH co-ordinator, Kate Gibson. Describing concerns that media narratives might reproduce certain stereotypical impressions, she notes:

There's a huge stigma attached to being a sex-trade worker. ... We don't want them to be further stigmatized by the media. It's hard to tell their stories fairly because there are just so many reasons why they've ended up here. It's about poverty and isolation and abuse and addiction. (DiManno 2007a)

These examples indicate the larger role that advocates and allies play in representing the experience of street involvement.

Taken together, this group's contributions provide an important disruption of the generally simplistic interpretations of prostitution that the coverage provides. Nevertheless, they are limited because, despite their relatively unique attempts to consider street-level sex work as something more than a self-selected lifestyle, they do, in many ways, contribute to a larger narrative pattern that individualizes the experience of violence on the stroll. They tend to emphasize the connection between personal histories of abuse and addiction and marginalization. While such contributions are important, and certainly not inaccurate, they have the inadvertent effect of obscuring, and in some cases even omitting, other oppressive forces that shape particular kinds of marginality. They are also limited by their location in the coverage. All of these contributions appear as anomalous disruptions in articles that profoundly emphasize deviance, criminality, licentiousness, and crazed addiction. As such, their capacity to contribute to a re-imagining of the sex worker is powerfully tempered by a more prominent textual and visual culture that aggressively inscribes simple understandings of this figure as a deviant Other and a subject with dubious morality.

Other advocates and allies do provide some of the most potent criticisms of sex workers' relationship with the police and the state more generally. Several credentialed researchers and politicians offered incisive critiques. The most significant of these "authorized knowers" is John Lowman, a renowned criminologist with a well-established history of challenging official approaches to sex work. He is invoked in five articles and in each of the newspapers. As the investigation began to unfold, Lowman provided the most scathing criticisms of the official response to the crisis. In one article, for example, he denounced the notion that sex workers are the "authors of their own misfortune" and chastised police for the selectivity of their protection (Girard 2002b). Elsewhere he argued: "If 50 women in any other category, whether housewives, women of a certain age or anyone else, went missing, believe me, the police reaction would have been entirely different" (Matas 2002).

Others made similar statements. A provincial member of the Legislative Assembly, Jenny Kwan, told the *Toronto Star*: "You have to question why the investigation wasn't taken seriously earlier. … These are real people who are somebody's daughter or granddaughter. We have to show their lives are worth something" (Girard 2002b).

To a much lesser degree, advocates and allies were able to broaden the notion of victimization by implicating the state in a critique that extended beyond a mere denunciation of police inaction. To take one sadly uncommon example, Harsha Walia, then a co-ordinator with the Downtown Eastside Women's Centre, was able to connect victimization with growing poverty, declining social assistance, and inadequate housing. In perhaps the most important critique in the entire body of coverage, Walia provided a compelling account of some of the structural forces that have reproduced the marginality of street-involved women.

> Ms. Walia says the answer to making the streets safer for women lies in addressing the root causes. She notes, for example, that under provincial regulations a single mother who has been getting social assistance will lose that support once her child turns three.
>
> "That's why a lot of single moms who can't find work and can't afford child care end up turning tricks on the street.
>
> "It's good Pickton has been convicted, but all these things — housing, poverty, child apprehension, social assistance regulations — all of those issues are making it just a lot more dangerous for women," she said. (Hume 2007)

Walia's contribution provides an unprecedented account of how structural forces have been brought to bear on street-involved women. It disrupts dominant renderings of the sex worker as a deviant addict and illuminates how structural inequality has actively contributed to the production of marginality. Unfortunately, her critique is unique in the coverage.

### The Voices of Sex Workers

Current and former sex workers play a decidedly peripheral role in the coverage and are quoted a mere ten times in its entirety. Women cast as prostitutes are only afforded a tiny role in narrating their own experiences. They are not authorized in any substantive way to construct knowledge about their lives. This process is left to others. Yet it is not merely the small number of quotations that ensure this erasure; it is also their content. Statements attributed to street-involved sex workers privilege a single and nearly univocal set of meanings. They construct and consolidate the image of the street-involved sex worker as an oblivious woman consumed by a one-dimensional drive for narcotics. For example:

> (i) Josey is a 34-year-old prostitute with scabs all over her face, the result, she said, of a bad batch of cocaine cut with Ajax. She saw the news about the [Pickton] farm on TV, but hadn't talked to anyone about it.
>
> "I just came out now," she explained, as she wandered over to a friend who supplies pipes. Crack pipes, that is, which Josey hawks on the corner for $2 a pop.
>
> Josey said she and a few girlfriends were sitting around last week,

wondering what happened to the bodies of the missing women. "Fifty girls missing and no bodies. Kind of strange."

"When I heard on the news about the farm, man, it sent a cold chill down my spine."

Josey knew many of the missing, most of them casually, one intimately. "We had just started dating," Josey, who is bisexual, said. "She went out one night and never came back." (Gill 2002)

(ii) Suarez, who uses the street name, "Brown Sugar," said she's been selling sex on Vancouver's streets since she was 14 and knew about half of the missing women.

"I guess I'm lucky to be alive," she said before wandering down the street to buy a rock of crack cocaine, which will take the edge off for half an hour. (Girard 2002a)

(iii) Toronto native Shelley Creor, who has sold her body for 11 years on the area's streets to support a four-hit-per-day heroin habit, said she has little hope that an arrest in the case would help ease the violence faced by her and other prostitutes on a daily basis.

"Nobody cares for anybody but themselves," said Creor, 38, before wandering down an alleyway for a fix, injected into her throat by using the mirror of a parked van to locate the right spot. She was soon gone in search of a $40 trick to pay for the next hit. (Girard 2002a)

(iv) "Can't get any lower than this," snorts Pauline, a crack addict whose still pretty face belies the fact that she's worked as a prostitute for 21 years, sometimes uptown, sometimes downtown, from escort agency to curbside. "When all you care about is where your next toke is coming from, you'll do the sex for just the drugs, forget the money." (DiManno 2007a)

(v) "Sure, I remember those women," says Pauline, 39.... "For years there was talk on the street of parties and pig roasts out at some farm. Some of us didn't like the idea of going so far out of the city. Or maybe I just wasn't desperate enough back then. Then the girls started disappearing.

"But the truth is, we never looked that hard at what was happening. When you're an addict, you don't care about other people's problems, you're not even aware of what's happening outside yourself. Down here, it's Independence Day, 24 hours a day." (DiManno 2007a)

There is an arresting harmony in these quotations. Taken together, they create a singular portrait. The prostitute is produced as an abject Other; a one-dimensional figure, incapable of interpersonal solidarity and concerned only with her next fix. She is never invited to comment on the conditions of her daily life, nor is she offered the opportunity to consider what might make that life less dangerous or more tolerable. It is at worst assumed, and at best implied, that narcotic dependency is the causal condition of her presence on the stroll.

Nowhere is it considered that addiction might well have emerged as a response to brutality, as a numbing agent to the horrors of marginality. Interestingly, however, the source of these quotations engenders them with a certain gravitas. Their irrefutability is established precisely because they come from sex workers themselves. Audiences tend to be compelled by personal testimony because it suggests unadulterated truth (Van Brunschot, Sydie, and Krull 1999).

## Dissecting the Dominant Paradigm

In the coverage of sex workers — and perhaps more importantly, in who has been authorized to speak — the descriptions coalesce around a relatively coherent and unified image. The accounts offer not only compelling ways of understanding who the missing and murdered women were but also a framework for understanding the lives of street-involved women more generally, including those still working the strolls of the Downtown Eastside. Other studies that have considered how the crisis has been taken up by news discourses have also observed that the figure of the sex worker was produced through a tightly limited set of categories. Jiwani and Young (2006) note that the news narratives operated to "frame" the missing and murdered women in ways that emphasized their status as addicts and prostitutes while highlighting the Aboriginal heritage of some of the women. Geraldine Pratt (2005: 1062) argues that in the "imaginative geographies" (Said 1979) of popular representations of the spaces of prostitution, sex workers "continue to be represented almost exclusively as diseased, criminalized, impoverished and degenerate bodies."

The coverage yields compelling evidence of the persistence of these same characterizations. Yet perhaps sensitive to the charge that the mass media have been complicit in caricaturizing, stigmatizing, and even demonizing street-level sex workers in the past, the coverage is also marked by efforts to both memorialize and represent street-involved women less dismissively. One of the *Toronto Star's* first reports on the case noted that "the women's loved ones are determined to attach names, faces and stories to people often ignored because they exist on society's fringe" (Girard 2002c). Importantly, coverage in each of the sources seems to reflect a similar determination. This effort takes shape in the attempts to provide background and biographical information about the women whose murders were being prosecuted. Each paper's supposed commitment to respectful coverage is enunciated by the sustained iteration of sanctimonious reminders that the slain were "real people."

Yet despite efforts to restore a degree of dignity to the murdered, in its totality the coverage perpetuates a limited set of dominant definitions. It reinscribes many of the problematic characterizations described by Jiwani and Young (2006) and Pratt (2005). By privileging narcotic dependency and foundational tragedy as the core explanations for the sex worker's presence on the low-track stroll, the coverage effectively obscures the role of structural factors in reproducing marginality and driving women into the precarious universe of survival sex. Given the limited say that sex workers are afforded in the construction of knowledge about their lives, such erasures are not entirely surprising. Deborah Brock (1998: 11) notes that at points in which prostitution has been constituted as a "social problem," sex workers themselves have frequently been excluded from suggesting solutions for the resolution of the problem. Defining sex workers as "the problem" has had the effect of keeping them "outside of the debate, silenced by groupings that can claim a more legitimate interest." Yet, as she insists, "without the contributions of those who work in prostitution, there can be no resolution."

The input of sex workers is not entirely absent from the coverage. Rather, they provide limited information, contributions that seem to be constrained by either the questions asked or the story told. These narrow contributions create the potent illusion of balanced journalism. That is, they seem to offer evidence that reporters have done the hard work of consulting all relevant parties in the construction of their narratives. One journalist, indeed, even writes with a righteous insistence of the importance of speaking to sex workers, condemning those who would try to shield street-involved women from the hazards of exploitative journalism:

> Advocates warned reporters not to exploit the sex workers on the Eastside, as if giving them the opportunity to talk about their lives was an untoward invasion of privacy. The language police scrutinize stories lest unacceptable descriptors be applied to the sad souls who lurch about Skid Row in drug induced stupor. We're all admonished about

"sensitivity" and value-neutral observations. But this isn't a morality play. It's harsh reality, the sleazy underbelly of a beautiful cosmopolitan city. It does no good to turn away or smooth out the rough, ugly details. In fact, it does harm — one more way of not looking, not seeing. (DiManno 2007b)

Reporter Rosie DiManno makes a compelling claim. She suggests that engaging street-involved women is central to a process of making them visible. Drawing on bell hooks's notion of "repositioning," David Sibley (1995: 29) observes: "Engaging with the other ... might lead to understanding, [and to] a rejection of a stereotype and a lesser concern with threats to the boundaries of the community." Yet for Sibley, any such engagement harbours an implicit danger: "Any optimism about such a move should be tempered with the thought that limited engagement, a superficial encounter, might result in the presumption of knowledge which could be more damaging than ignorance" (1995: 29). The dominant images of the sex worker that emerge from the coverage provide precisely such a "superficial encounter." Through their reliance on particular kinds of sources, their preference for particular aspects of life in the Downtown Eastside, and their profound inattention to state violence and pervasive forms of exclusion, journalistic representations of sex workers both presume and reproduce a knowledge that does more harm than good. In particular, there are problematic ramifications of contrasting sex workers with the valorized feminine roles of the conventional family, limits to the personal tragedy narrative as an explanation for street-involvement, and inherent dangers in the sustained reproduction of sex workers as a deviant and criminal population.

The persistent contrasting of sex work with conventional female domesticity has important ideological implications. In the first place, it imagines an unbridgeable gulf between the sex worker, on the one hand, and the mother, the daughter, the sister, and the wife, on the other. The role of the sex worker connotes corruption and immorality while the other group connotes a series of celebrated, morally sound modes of femininity. Accordingly, the coverage is marked by a profound effort to distance the murdered from the former category by reminding audiences of their affinity to the latter. Crucially, it is the categories of domestic value that are the primary rhetorical weapons of the journalistic attempt to restore a certain dignity to the slain.

The (perhaps inadvertent) effects of these attempts at sympathetic portrayal are profound. They position the practices of prostitution on the negative side of a good/evil dualism. The repeated reminders that, despite their presence in the Downtown Eastside, the victims were also valued members of families reinforce a perceived distance between the morality of the family space and the immorality of the spaces of prostitution. Jiwani and Young (2006: 904) argue that descriptions of the missing and murdered women as members of families make them more like "us." As they put it: "It rescues them from a place of degeneracy to a zone of normality." Yet such positioning does more than merely redeem the stigmatized. For Jiwani and Young (2006: 904):

> It conforms to the dominant hegemonic values, in that the only women who can be rescued or are worth saving are mothers, daughters, and sisters — women like us. Making them like "us" is a discursive move designed to privilege their deservedness both in terms of police intervention and social recognition.

Thus, importantly, the sex worker's degree of belonging to conventional familial structures becomes a primary determinant of her value. The implication of such constructions is that those who cannot be seen as part of the imagined "us" are irredeemable.

The coverage's privileging of personal tragedy narratives is also of central ideological importance. In one sense, it allows audiences to understand the street-involved as marginalized people, as the victims of profound personal tragedy. As Stanley Cohen (2002: 7) observes, "each society possesses a set of ideas about what causes deviation … and a set of images of who constitutes the typical deviant" — information, he contends, which arrives "already processed by the mass media." We need, then, to consider how the coverage reproduces and processes ideas about what causes deviation. Here, individualized personal tragedies are mobilized as the core explanations for the deviant turn of the sex worker, and a distinct "set of images" — predatory boyfriends, abusive parents, neglect, domestic instability — provide compelling evidence of their veracity. As such, their status as "victims" is constrained by the particular boundaries of individualized devastation. The suggestion that foundational personal tragedy explains how individuals become involved in sex work jars against compelling comparative research that contrasts media narratives about what drives women to the strolls with the actual testimony of sex workers. For example, Celia Benoit and her colleagues (2003: 276) note that media narratives tend to privilege forms of entrapment as the primary explanation for entry into prostitution; yet their research with sex workers cites a diverse "variety of circumstances" that motivated entry. They observe that just over one-third of their respondents said that they became involved in the industry because they were enticed by a presenting opportunity, such as having peers who were involved, seeing an employment ad, or having someone approach them with an offer of money for sex. For over one-quarter of respondents, however, economic duress — described as being "unable to find a job," "on welfare with small children," living "on the streets with no income," or having "bills to pay" — was a motivating factor. The authors did not consult exclusively with women working at the bottom of the street-level sex trade, but their observations are nonetheless instructive. They suggest that participation in prostitution is more complex than simply a case of personal tragedy.

The point here is not to deny or minimize the foundational atrocities suffered by many of the missing and murdered women; rather, it is to challenge the narrative closure that the coverage's privileging of these stories accomplishes. Such narrations individualize tragedy and disregard broader complicities in the reproduction of dangerous conditions and the marginalization of particular people.

There is a pronounced coherence between these simplistic individualizing narratives and the ideological core that animates the contemporary politics of neo-liberalism. Neo-liberal notions of self-reliance valorize a strident individualism and position each individual as the master of her or his own well-being. Pierre Bourdieu (1998) describes the proliferation of this logic as the "imposition everywhere ... of that sort of moral Darwinism that institutes the struggle of all against all and cynicism as the norm of all action and behaviour." Individual devastation becomes entirely more understandable in a social and political milieu in which the collective defences against such devastation have been powerfully undermined and dismantled. Thus for Zygmunt Bauman (2007: 14) the rise of a hegemonic neo-liberalism produces a context in which "it is now left to individuals to seek, find and practice individual solutions to socially produced troubles ... while being equipped with tools and resources that are blatantly inadequate to the task." Following Bauman, we can see how the narrative characterization of survival sex as the product of an individual tragedy obscures the possibility of a broader analysis of marginalization. Of course, there are peripheral disruptions of this pattern in the coverage. On their own, however, they are hardly sufficient to undermine the prevailing messages of the whole, which install personal tragedy as the decisive explanation for the sex worker's presence on the stroll.

Finally, the persistent privileging of the relationship between sex work and criminal deviance reinforces the impression of a self-imposed (or even self-selected) marginality. The sustained deployment of images that signal the interconnection of prostitution and other threatening practices naturalizes the sex worker's presence in the inner city. Narcotic dependency is installed as the first principle of her existence. Her presence in the notorious spaces of the Downtown Eastside is naturalized. The criminal space and the criminal body are represented as interlocked in a mutually constituting dialectic. Individuals are assumed to adhere to a certain set of deviant behaviours by virtue of the space they inhabit. The "association of prostitution with the drug trade as an almost natural, if not inevitable association, provides fuel for the contention that prostitution epitomizes the filth of the streets," note Erin Van Brunschot, Rosalind Sydie, and Katherine Krull (1999: 56). "Media reports do not investigate the claims that the conditions of the prostitute's life predispose them to drug use. Rather, drug use marks the prostitute as deviant." The coverage's striking emphasis on addiction and the lurid textual and visual representations of women injecting, smoking, and exchanging drugs stresses their relationship to criminality.

As Stuart Hall and his colleagues (1978: 225) observe, popular representations of deviance are frequently marked by processes of signification that imply the "convergence" of deviant practices that occurs when "two or more activities are linked in the process of signification so as to implicitly or explicitly draw parallels between them." The conflation of prostitution with illicit drug use is paradigmatic of this phenomenon. For these authors, the representation of a "convergence" of practices that breach defined "thresholds" of public acceptance escalate their unacceptability and make it easier for authorities to "mount legitimate campaigns of control against them" (Hall et al. 1978: 226). Yet, far more central to our purposes here, they observe that the representation of converging deviant practices has had the structural tendency of "translating a *political* issue into a *criminal* one." The "solution" to the problem of deviant inner-city phenomena is thus defined in terms of criminal enforcement rather than political change. The objective, they continue, is thus conceived as one of policing criminal activity rather than addressing marginalization through progressive public policies. Hall and his colleagues (1978: 229) contend that such processes simplify complex issues by "transposing" analytic frameworks that "depoliticise ... an issue by *criminalising* it."

The media coverage of the Pickton murders, then, reproduces coherent ways of understanding the street-involved woman. Through an overreliance on two well-established discourses — the prostitute as part of a dangerous underworld and the prostitute as an agent of moral corruption — it provides a distinct set of definitions that camouflage structural forms of violence. This presentation hinges crucially on representational patterns that rely on particular narrative authorities while silencing others. The relative absence of contributions from sex workers themselves necessarily limits the definitions that operate to reproduce the view that sex workers are in many ways the authors of their own misfortune.

## Notes

1.  Many residents of the Downtown Eastside were aware that something horrific was unfolding in their midst. Since 1991 local activists have been organizing an annual Valentine's Day march as a public opportunity to honour the victims of violence and demand justice for the disappeared.
2.  For a more comprehensive treatment of these questions, see Jiwani and Young (2006) and Hugill (2010).

# Scars

*Jackie Traverse*

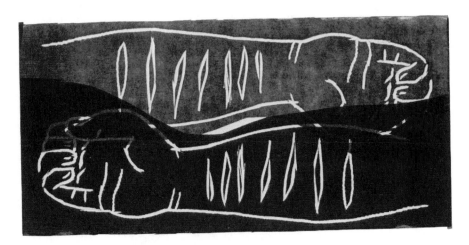

For a long time she was ashamed of her past. She had these scars, they were luggage she carried everywhere. She had explained them so many times, trapped in long sleeves, self conscious. She learned how to maneuver without ever turning her arms over. She held them tightly to her chest to save her from telling.

Why do people have to stare? Where do they get the nerve to ask me why or what? How do I respond? It's my mood, at times I tried to laugh it off, at times I've been direct. Other times I've been angry and ashamed.

Should I tell the whole story, should I say what I know now, I didn't used to like myself? I was attacked by wild cats in the jungle. Or my favourite told to me by my uncle, "that's where the hawk landed and when he flew away." I loved to believe it because I admired him so much that I could actually forget that I had the same on my arms. But I don't ever recall any hawks. I didn't want to believe my uncle would do that.

My scars. Self inflicted, self inflicted. They have held me captive for too long, held me Prisoner. Today I will wear what I want, go ahead, look, I am not ashamed any longer. I honour my Past. After all, it brought me here.

# Part III

# Regulating Women

# Part III Introduction

*Gillian Balfour*

Conditions of poverty, racism, and misogyny very much characterize the lives of criminalized women. As we have seen in Part II, the historical and contemporary narratives that construct women as errant females, prostitutes, street gang associates, and symbols of moral corruption mask their restricted choices and how the conditions of their lives have always been embedded in the socio-political context. In Part III our attention turns to how women — as prisoners, patients, mothers, and victims — have been disciplined, watched, drugged, restrained, managed, corrected, and punished.

The following chapters on the regulation of women reveal the legacy of moralizing discourses from the late nineteenth and early twentieth centuries — discourses that continue to shape contemporary regimes of control, such as the punishment and "correction" of women in prison. The more conventional view of criminalized women casts them, historically, as "correctional afterthoughts" (Ross and Fabiano 1985) or as "high need and high risk" (Laishes 2002), therefore requiring intensive management and control. The analyses presented here provide a different view. As Kelly Hannah-Moffat (2001) suggests, criminalized women have been at the centre of the state's preoccupation with punishment and public order. Indeed, a close look at the history of the regulation of women in both institutional and public spaces exposes deeply gendered, racialized, sexualized, and class-based forms of social control.

## The Imprisonment of Women

The history of women's imprisonment in Canada is "a mixture of neglect, outright barbarism, and well-meaning paternalism" (Cooper 1993: 33). Throughout the nineteenth century, criminalized women were oftentimes housed in the attics of men's prisons and treated as inconveniences or difficult to manage. These unruly women were subjected to "cruel treatment such as starvation and excessive corporal punishment" (Beattie 1977: 152–54). Recognizing the special needs of women prisoners, early prison reformers began advocating for separate prisons for women. Inspired by the work of Elizabeth Fry in England, maternal feminists sought to "domesticate" the female prisoner by relying on "maternal images (domesticity, motherhood, parental discipline, caring and nurturing) and pastoral strategies of spiritual redemption and guidance" (Hannah-Moffat 2001: 31). The infamous Prison for Women (P4W) was finally opened in 1934 adjacent to the Kingston Penitentiary for Men, and until 1995 was the only federal prison for women in Canada.

Nevertheless, numerous government commissions — one of which, the Archambault Commission, reported only four years after the prison opened — denounced P4W as "unfit for bears, much less women" (Canada 1977). The facility was repeatedly condemned for closure as government officials saw the ethos of punishment as unduly harsh and unlikely to reform the "fallen women" who were being confined within its walls. Many of those imprisoned in P4W during its first decades were young working-class white women — often unwed mothers — deemed in need of moral correction by the matrons who enforced strict regimes of domesticity framed as a maternal ethic of care. For example, one of the matrons who worked at the P4W for over two decades "recalled stories of teaching prisoners domestic skills such as knitting, sewing, cooking, and housekeeping" and relied on "benevolent maternal techniques" such as placing an angry or upset prisoner in the bathtub until she cooled off instead of administering punishment (Hannah-Moffat 2001: 88). Essentialized as wayward rather than exploited and impoverished, young women were imprisoned indefinitely for acts such as vagrancy and prostitution (Sangster 1999).

Outside the prison walls, the regulation of young women in public spaces took on a decidedly classed and racialized edge. Between 1920 and 1950 the criminalization of Aboriginal and white women for prostitution-related offences, vagrancy, and public drunkenness increased as part of a "broader web of gendered moral regulation articulated through law" (Sangster 1999: 34). By the 1950s, 72 percent of all charges against Aboriginal women were alcohol-related. Between 1940 and 1950 the Female Refuges Act was more vigorously used to incarcerate Aboriginal women than it was for white women. The FRA enabled the imprisonment of women aged sixteen to thirty-five, sentenced or even "liable to be sentenced" under any Criminal Code or by-law infractions for "idle and dissolute behaviour" (see Sangster 1996: 239–75, 2002; Minaker in this book). Joan Sangster (1999: 40) links this increase in the use of criminalization and incarceration of Aboriginal women to the migration of women in the 1950s into urban centres from reserves, leading to "spiralling economic deprivation and social dislocation." Reserve communities had been devastated by the impact of residential schools, which included physical and sexual abuse and the denigration of Aboriginal cultures and languages, compounded by the lack of economic development and education on reserves. Young women fled the isolated reserves hoping to escape extreme poverty, only to find themselves facing racism, destitution, and homelessness in the city.

Sangster suggests that policing and sentencing practices were informed by racialized and gendered images of the "drunken Indian," but were also deeply sexualized and class-based. Aboriginal women's public drinking and presumed sexual promiscuity offended middle-class sensibilities, but their sanctioning as the "degenerate Other" also retrenched the boundaries of a white middle-class femininity and hegemonic masculinity (Razack 1998: 38). Homeless and destitute Aboriginal women were viewed as "licentious wild women that symbolized sexual excess and need for conquest and control" (Sangster 1999: 44). Social workers and prison matrons described incarcerated Aboriginal women as "degenerate," "dirty," and "backward." In contrast, they responded much differently to young white women often convicted of similar types of offences of prostitution and public drunkenness (Boritch 1997: 177; Oliver 1994). White women received the "partial justice of degradation and humiliation and the positive elements of reform and discipline" (Dobash, Dobash, and Guttridge 1986). Poor white women were seen as unfortunate, childlike victims in need of protection. Nicole Rafter (1985b: 176) suggested, "Reformatories were designed to induce childlike submissiveness, and inmates were regarded as recalcitrant children."

Early twentieth-century prison reforms were shaped by the broader socio-political context of Victorian moral regulation. Alan Hunt's (2002) study of social surveys from 1902 to 1919 shows how dance halls, movie theatres, ice cream parlours, skating rinks, department stores, and city parks were all sites of systematic disciplinary supervision. State and non-state agencies attempted to regulate the heterosexual lives of young working-class women and men — focusing, in particular, on the respectability of women — through the enforcement of by-laws and curfews. As Hunt (2002: 17–18) notes, "The controls instituted by authorities did not directly regulate sex, but rather regulated the time, places and contexts in which young people could engage in heterosocial encounters. In particular these controls operated through selecting women as the primary targets of regulation in a system which functioned to responsibilize women for their sexual conduct." Interestingly, middle-class white feminists were instrumental in generating sexual purity campaigns to suppress prostitution and the spread of disease. These campaigns directly targeted young poor women and single women working as clerks in department stores (Hunt 1999a; see also Valverde 1991). The early strategies embraced by prison reformers and maternal feminist organizations such as Elizabeth Fry Societies and the Women's Christian Temperance Society was rooted in this wider context of moral regulation and of chasteness and propriety.

By the 1970s, however, explanations for the causes of women's lawbreaking, as well as strategies for prison reform, were being shaped by the liberal feminist notion of formal equality; that is, that women should have the same rights and entitlements as men. The federal government's correctional plan for the women prisoners had cycled through various configurations. Throughout the 1970s and 1980s, some women prisoners were held in provincial jails under exchange of service agreements so that they could remain close to their families and work toward their community reintegration; or they were confined in Kingston's Prison for Women and expected to participate in treatment programs inside men's prisons (Berzins and Hayes 1987). Both approaches failed to meet the needs of women prisoners for gender-appropriate addiction treatment, educational and vocational training, and support in overcoming the trauma of abuse (Clark Report 1977; MacGuigan Report 1977; Needham Report 1978; Chinnery Report 1978; Canadian Advisory Council on the Status of Women 1981; Jackson 1988). Prison reformers quickly abandoned their attempts to address women's correctional programming needs by arguing for an "equality of sameness," and instead focused on the growing crisis within P4W of prisoner suicides and incidents of self-harm.

In 1988 the tragic suicide of Marlene Moore inside P4W proved to be a profound moment in the history of the prison. Marlene had been raised in extreme poverty and was a victim of incest and rape (see Kershaw and Lasovich 1991). Institutionalized from the age of thirteen inside training schools and juvenile detention centres for status offences, such as incorrigibility and running away, she eventually became the first woman to be declared a dangerous offender in Canada — even though she had never killed anyone. Rather, she was a repeat offender who was deemed not amenable to treatment. Marlene had attempted suicide many times and was a "cutter" — someone who uses self-injury as a way of managing profound emotional crises of fear or anxiety brought on by an overwhelming sense of powerlessness (Heney 1990; Fillmore and Dell 2000). A coroner's inquest was called to determine if prison protocols for the treatment of women in crisis contributed to Marlene's death. The Canadian Association of Elizabeth Fry Societies (CAEFS) was granted unprecedented legal standing at the inquest. Their strategy was to implicate the prison regime and staff in Marlene's suicide. CAEFS believed that the security protocols at P4W had contributed to Marlene Moore's death by failing to provide her with the necessary therapeutic supports to prevent her from harming herself. Instead, prison security tended to treat women who self-injure as threats to institutional security and attempted to control women by placing them in segregation.

Following the inquest, the Correctional Service of Canada (CSC) announced the first-ever national Task Force on Federally Sentenced Women (TFFSW) to examine the conditions of women's imprisonment, their experiences in P4W, and their programming needs. The Task Force proved to be the most significant study of women's imprisonment in Canada, and served as a blueprint for what was to be unprecedented change in the treatment of criminalized women.

## The Task Force on Federally Sentenced Women

The striking of the TFFSW in 1989 was shaped by increased activism within the prison system by organizations such as CAEFS and its regional membership, Aboriginal women's organizations, and social justice groups. The socio-political context of the 1980s beyond the prison walls also reflected a broader awareness of issues affecting women's lives, an awareness underscored by the growing prevalence of feminist research in the areas of domestic violence, sexual assault, the feminization of poverty, single-parenting, and sexual harassment in the workplace. Feminist research methodologies began to reshape the analytical frameworks of activists and academics. Women's standpoint of their lived experiences of domestic violence, sexual assault, poverty, and racism began to define the agendas for change. In this way, the TFFSW was driven by a fundamentally new approach that called for the inclusion of women's experiences of criminalization and imprisonment, and emphasized the importance of community alliances in the development of a new, women-centred correctional model. A growing Aboriginal self-government political agenda also influenced the structure and aims of the TFFSW, illustrated by the inclusion of Aboriginal women (both prisoners and their advocates) on the Task Force and the commissioning of a survey of federally sentenced Aboriginal women in the community (see Sugar and Fox 1989; Hayman 2006).

The survey of federally sentenced women conducted for the Task Force (Shaw et al. 1991) was unlike most research on offenders in that it was a qualitative study that positioned federally sentenced women as experts. The women's narratives of their prison experiences provided a testament to the inadequate and damaging effects of a male model of corrections that "classified risk, prioritized needs, and fitted offenders into pre-structured programs" (Shaw et al. 1991: 55). From these narratives came the groundbreaking report *Creating Choices* (TFFSW 1990), which revealed the prevalence of physical and sexual abuse in the lives of criminalized women and how abuse intersected with other difficulties such as drinking and drugging, violence, and mental illness (Shaw 1994a, 1994b). While many of its recommendations focused on the immediate aims of address-ing the therapeutic needs of women as victims, the report acknowledged the women's experiences as being compounded by the social context of poverty and racism. The relationship between women's victimization and their own use of violence — or what Karlene Faith (1993: 106) calls the "victimization-criminalization continuum" — was instrumental in defining a new gender-responsive correctional model.

Released in April 1990, *Creating Choices* called for the closure of P4W and the construction of four new regional facilities and a healing lodge for Aboriginal women. Programming within each facility would focus on a holistic, women-centred correctional model emphasizing five fundamental principles: empowerment to raise women's self-esteem; meaningful choices involving a variety of diverse programs in the prison and the community; respect and dignity to cultivate self-respect and respect for others; a sup-portive and nurturing environment; and shared responsibility among the woman prisoners, staff, and community. A series of key recommendations in the report also called for the development of a community release strat-egy that would offer increased resources for both the accommodation and treatment of women in the community.

## The Implementation of *Creating Choices*

While the federal government accepted in principle the report's main recom-mendations, the implementation of those proposals quickly deteriorated as CSC became more interested in a hierarchal top-down model as opposed to a tripartite consensus-building model involving the community stakehold-ers, Aboriginal groups, and the government. Fears about public safety and a growing public backlash against prisoner rehabilitation also undermined the implementation process. CSC was required to enter into exchange of service agreements with the provinces in which the regional facilities were to be built, and municipal and provincial governments were under increas-ing public pressure from local people not to allow the construction of a women's prison close to their communities, especially without a perimeter wall, uniformed staff, or a traditional static security design. On one hand, the backlash from local communities was driven by a wider neo-conservative political agenda of law and order and an increasingly vocal victims' rights lobby. On the other hand, neo-liberal economics had taken hold in most provinces, calling for fiscal restraint in the spending of public dollars.

CSC further undermined the implementation of *Creating Choices* by excluding the Elizabeth Fry Societies from the National Implementation Committee, instead offering CAEFS a limited role in programming subcommittees. With this diminished status, CAEFS was quickly marginalized by the federal government, and less able to advocate for implementation of the recommendations of the Task Force report (Faith and Pate 2000). In 1992 CAEFS made the difficult decision to withdraw from the implementation process altogether to signify the organization's serious concerns over the CSC's shift in strategy in abandoning many of the principles of *Creating Choices* (see Hayman 2006).

While the implementation process was underway, conditions inside the P4W began to deteriorate. After the decision to close the P4W had been announced, the CSC's budget for P4W had been cut back to put money into the new facilities, and senior staff had begun transferring out of the prison. These changes resulted in programming reductions and increased overtime hours for junior officers who had little knowledge of or experience in dealing with women prisoners. Meanwhile, the women prisoners were becoming increasingly frustrated with inconsistencies in the prison's management and the absence of programming. They were also anxious about the lack of information related to their eventual transfer to another province. This anxiety was heightened by the amount of time it was taking to implement reforms. While the government had announced in 1990 that the P4W would be closed by September 1994, the prison actually remained in operation until July 2000.

These conditions created a tense environment that sparked a confrontation between six prisoners and front-line staff in April 1994, resulting in the all-male Institutional Emergency Response Team (IERT) being sent into the segregation unit of P4W in riot gear to conduct "cell extractions" and strip-search the women (see Faith 1995; Pate 1999a; Shaw 2000). Shortly afterward, an internal Board of Investigation quickly produced a report, which included fifteen pages focusing on the profiles of the women prisoners involved in the incident, emphasizing their violent histories and institutional records. The report described the events inside P4W as "a planned attack on staff, perpetrated by a group of violent women who were attempting to escape" (Shaw 2000: 62), thereby justifying the use of force by male officers against women prisoners. The report made no mention of the strip-searching of the women prisoners by male guards or the IERT videotape made (as per "official policy") of the cell extractions. References to the women being strip-searched by male guards and the existence of the video had been edited out of the report. In addition, the report stated that the women had been given blankets and mattresses upon their return to their cells, which was untrue. The women were left for twenty-four hours dressed only in paper gowns. Only after the CBC's *The Fifth Estate* obtained and aired a copy of the videotape were calls for a full inquiry into CSC's handling of the matter acted upon.

The report of the Commission of Inquiry into Certain Events at the Prison for Women in Kingston, headed by Madam Justice Louise Arbour (1996), described women in prison as "high needs/low risk." It also contained a critique of the CSC for what Justice Arbour termed its violations of the rule of law. Arbour described the correctional system as being "out of control" and the behaviour of the male IERT as "cruel, inhumane and degrading." The CSC's response to the incident, according to Arbour, was to "deny error, defend against criticism and to react without a proper investigation of the truth." The report made some hundred recommendations, including the creation of the position of a deputy commissioner for women, stopping the practice of using male riot squads in women's prisons, and putting an end to the long-term segregation of women prisoners.

Between 1995 and 1997 the new regional prisons in Edmonton, AB, Kitchener, ON, Joliette, QB, and Truro, NS, as well as the Okimaw Ohci Healing Lodge in Maple Creek, SK, became operational. But it soon became clear that simply building new facilities was not enough to transform women's experiences of imprisonment. The CSC's response to several incidents involving suicides, slashings, walkaways, and disturbances at the regional prisons[1] was to implement a heavily securitized approach to the management of women prisoners — one that involved the reassertion of control and punishment (Shaw 2000). In 1996 the CSC announced that all women classified as maximum-security would be moved to separate maximum-security units in three of the men's prisons, the P4W, or the Regional Psychiatric Centre in Saskatoon. While this was to be a temporary measure (lasting eighteen months to two years), it was not until some six years later — in February 2003 — that women classified as maximum-security were moved to "enhanced security units" inside four of the women's facilities.

In 1997 CSC set up a new Mental Health Strategy for Women Offenders. The strategy adopted a broad definition of "mental illness" and "mental disorder." For instance, women could be identified as having mental health needs if they had a history of relationships characterized by abuse, dependent children, low educational attainment and limited job opportunities, or significant long-term substance abuse. In short, social marginalization was being transformed into a "mental health need" (Hannah-Moffat and Shaw 2001: 47). After commissioning a series of reports on the treatment and security needs of maximum-security women and those with acute mental health needs, csc announced in 1999 the implementation of an Intensive Intervention Strategy for managing these two groups of women (see Laishes 2002).

*Creating Choices* took the position that women should not be held in the kind of secure environment that the P4W provided. It advocated cottage housing units, with an "enhanced" security unit to be used only on a temporary basis when required. Because women were seen as high need/ low risk, they required support instead of security. Rather than classification, *Creating Choices* advocated an assessment of treatment needs and the use of a holistic as opposed to hierarchical model. Following the opening of the new facilities, however, csc adopted an Offender Intake Assessment process. Initiated by cognitive psychologists for male prison populations, this scheme is based on an assessment of both risk and need, especially as these relate to rehabilitation prospects and the effectiveness of particular types of treatment. In addition to risk-based security placement and release decisions, the system assigns different levels and types of treatment based on a prisoner's "criminogenic needs." As Kelly Hannah-Moffat (2000) notes, what this approach does is redefine "need" as a "risk factor." Dependency, low self-esteem, poor educational and vocational achievement, parental death at an early age, foster care placement, constant changes in the location of foster care, residential placement, living on the streets, prostitution, suicide attempts, self-injury, substance abuse, and parental responsibilities: the system considers all of these as characteristics that give rise to criminogenic needs (Hannah-Moffat 2000: 37).

Several of csc's decisions also undermined the implementation of the healing lodge for Aboriginal women prisoners — and these decisions again violated the principles of *Creating Choices*. The initial plan for Aboriginal women at the healing lodge was to address the disconnection and dislocation experienced as a result of residential schools, child welfare apprehensions, and the Indian Act (Monture-Angus 2002). Instead, the healing lodge appeared to be governed by csc's agenda of risk management through imprisonment, rather than the approved principles of healing and meaningful choices aimed at reconnecting Aboriginal women to their land, cultures, and communities (Monture-Angus 2002: 52). For example, because the healing lodge was deemed a minimum- to medium-security-level prison, Aboriginal women classified as maximum-security — who made up 46 percent of this group of women prisoners (CAEFS 2003) — were denied access to the facility.

By 1998 it was clear that the programming for women prisoners was not going to be linked to a feminist analysis of the systemic nature of women's needs as envisioned in *Creating Choices*. Instead, CSC was implementing a system of cognitive behavioural programming, a therapeutic approach premised on the notion that "criminal offending is a result of the offender's inability to think logically, reason appropriately and to make rational decisions" (Pollack 2004: 694). Such an approach considered structural inequalities as irrelevant — it viewed any discussion of poverty, racism, or gendered experiences (such as rape) as the context of women's criminal behaviour as a denial of personal responsibility. Kathleen Kendall (2002: 183) argues that the cognitive behavioural paradigm of self-regulation "is consistent with neo-liberal strategies of individualizing social problems." Shoshana Pollack (2000b, 2004) found in her research that many Aboriginal and Black women prisoners were often confined to maximum-security units because they did not comply with the cognitive behavioural program. Women resisted program requirements of submitting to orders by security staff that were demeaning or humiliating. For women in maximum-security, non-compliance to security protocols resulted in long-term confinement in segregation, strip-searches, involuntary transfers, limited human contact — and death.

## Empowerment and Responsibilization

In 2004 CSC introduced a new correctional plan for female offenders that re-entrenched the view of criminalized women as being in need of cognitive therapy to address their criminal thinking. The plan considered women to be a greater risk because of their need for intensive treatment given the impact of severe childhood trauma of abuse and neglect upon their decision-making skills — causing them to "choose" drugs and alcohol, prostitution, and violence (see Fortin 2004a). In short, women needed to learn how to take responsibility for their choices rather than challenge the conditions under which they must make such choices. Prisoners considered "difficult to manage" or unamenable to treatment because of their criminal personalities were to be managed under Dialectical Behavioural Therapy

(DBT), which pathologizes women's experiences of victimization; women prisoners are not able to regulate their own emotions because of the impact of childhood sexual abuse.

DBT, the centrepiece of the Correctional Service of Canada's correctional planning for women prisoners, is grounded in the essentialized view of women as defined by their familial and intimate relationships. Women are psychologically damaged when these relationships are characterized by trauma (for example, sexual victimization or neglect). These experiences of trauma become "pathways" to addiction and criminal conduct (Bloom, Owen, and Covington 2003). DBT is an example of a gender-responsive correctional plan wherein women must take responsibility for their relationships through learning proper emotional regulation, anger management, and effective communication skills (ibid.). Hannah-Moffat (2010: 201) points out how gender responsive programming "inadvertently creates insidious and invasive forms of governing. Relationships, children, past victimizations, mental health, self-injury and self-esteem have all become correctional targets in the pursuit of normative femininity and gender conformity." Gender-responsive programming does not consider how women's lives are also structured by pathways of poverty and racism. Indeed, women's low self-esteem and emotional vulnerability, which can lead to abusive relationships, may stem from unstable housing or precarious employment, yet are framed as risk factors (Hannah-Moffat 2010; McKim 2008).

How can we make sense of the more regressive and punitive response of CSC toward federally sentenced women — despite the progressive recommendations of *Creating Choices* and the dramatic findings of the Arbour inquiry? In part, it would seem that CSC has become emboldened by an angry and fearful public, which was increasingly influenced by media that never seem to tire of images and stories of violent women and girls, leading to ceaseless demands for protection through a punitive criminal justice response to crime. But in addition to such neo-conservative law and order sentiments, the dismantling of the welfare state under the sway of neo-liberalism had ushered in a new model of crime control whereby offenders were to be "empowered" to take responsibility for the consequences of their choices (O'Malley 1992, 2010; Hannah-Moffat 2000). Within this new model, ideas such as empowerment — so central to the philosophy of *Creating Choices* — take on new meaning.

As Hannah-Moffat (2000, 2002, 2010) points out, feminist reformers invoked the language of empowerment as a way of recognizing women's power to make choices. The neo-liberal discourse, however, translates empowerment to mean that incarcerated women are responsible for their own self-governance and requires them to manage their own risk to themselves (Pollack 2009). In short, under neo-liberal risk-management schemes, women are now being "responsibilized." Yet this correctional discourse has also enabled the state to coercively — and in some instances to illegally — punish women (Kerr 2013). Starting in 2003 the Office of the Correctional Investigator (OCI) has reported on the overclassification of federally sentenced women, especially Aboriginal women and women with untreated mental illnesses, as maximum-security inmates. The OCI also reported that male guards held front-line positions at all regional facilities, despite continuing grievances by women prisoners of sexual harassment, abuse, and assault.

Disregarding these concerns, in 2003 CSC implemented a Management Protocol that enabled prison authorities to place women deemed "high risk to institutional security" in indefinite solitary confinement — a practice that is actually illegal under the Corrections and Conditional Release Act, the legislation that governs federal prisons in Canada. OCI has noted that almost all women inmates held on this protocol are Aboriginal. The protocol was subsequently the subject of two court cases. In *R v S.L.N.* (2010), the court commented, "The Management Protocol is a mechanism whose principal element is just that: extensive, prolonged isolation. While it is intended as an effective means of managing the most dangerous and disruptive of inmates, there seems little doubt that it is entirely capable of inflicting great damage on those to whom it is applied" (at para 63). In *Worm v Attorney General of Canada* (2011; also see the Introduction here), the B.C. Civil Liberties Association successfully argued that the Management Protocol was unconstitutional and constituted illegal conditions of confinement. In light of this legal action, CSC rescinded the Management Protocol in 2011. Troublesome practices, however, have continued. In 2014, a coroner's jury returned a finding of homicide in the death of prisoner Ashley Smith. Evidence presented throughout the inquiry revealed the systematic use of chemical restraints, such as Seroquel, in addition to relentless deprivation of human contact that served to antagonize Ashley, causing her to lash out against her captors.

In addition to the inhumane treatment of women prisoners documented in these cases, OCI has also reported a striking lack of compliance by CSC to internal procedures for reporting use of force incidents:

It is troubling to note that CSC auditors found that national and regional direction and oversight is lacking with respect to the frequency and appropriate use of physical restraint equipment in the Treatment Centres. On a number of occasions, the Office has provided its views on these matters only to be informed that revised policy directives are "under review" or "being consulted." It bears reminding that the same compliance issues, governance and accountability problems noted in the January 2011 audit have prevailed since the death of Ashley Smith in October 2007. This situation is simply untenable. (Sapers 2011: 16)

The conditions in provincial lock-ups also continue to deteriorate as provincial governments look for more ways to manage the increasing numbers of criminalized men and women struggling with drug addiction and mental illness, a situation compounded by a lack of community treatment services and affordable housing. As neo-conservative governments denounce the cost of government delivery of human services as an unfair demand on middle-class taxpayers, all the while building prisons to increase jobs in economically depressed voter-rich regions, provincial jail populations have swelled, leading to problems of overcrowding. In September 2013, for instance, all of the jails in Manitoba were overcrowded. While the total capacity of the province's institutions is 1,982 beds, 2,433 adults were being held in custody (123 percent of capacity). The Women's Correctional Centre (wcc), opened in February 2012 as a replacement to the aged Portage Correctional Institution (built in 1893 for male prisoners), has an official capacity of 168 inmates. As of September 2013 the wcc's inmate count was already at 211 — or 126 percent of its official capacity (Owen 2013).

Concerned social justice organizations and advocates have exposed the disregard for women prisoners, such as the case of Julia Bilotta, who gave birth to her first child while held in segregation in the Ottawa-Carleton Detention Centre. Bilotta was held in remand custody on fraud charges for forging cheques after being denied bail. She was eight months pregnant and requested medical attention because she was experiencing labour contractions. Bilotta was told by the prison nurse that she had indigestion and was experiencing false labour, and then was told to "shut up" because she was moaning too much. Her son's birth was breech, and as a result he experienced significant respiratory problems; Bilotta also required a blood transfusion. A formal complaint was filed with the Ontario College of Nurses, and Ontario's Corrections ministry initiated formal disciplinary proceedings against the involved staff (Pedwell 2013).

In 2013 the Ontario provincial Ombudsman released a report on his special investigation into prisoner complaints of excessive force used by staff in various provincial jails. The Ombudsman's review of inmate complaints revealed systemic disregard for the rights of prisoners and a culture of silence among correctional staff with regard to prisoner abuse. One of the cases detailed in the report involved the story of "Helen," a woman admitted to the Sarnia Jail on August 31, 2011. Suffering the effects of drug withdrawal, Helen was housed in an area containing a single cell. On being escorted to her cell the next day, she stopped to ask a manager if she could be placed in a different location. The next thing she knew a correctional officer attacked her. Helen only disclosed what had happened when she was being readied for transfer to another facility.

The Correctional Investigation and Security Unit's investigation into Helen's complaint confirmed that a correctional officer had pushed her against a wall, pinned her by the neck, and later repeatedly hit her with a closed fist while she was restrained on her bunk. The correctional staff who witnessed the incident omitted these damning details in their initial reports of the incident. It was not until much later that four officers told the truth about what they had seen. In this case, the code of silence among the prison staff was particularly powerful. The culprit was extremely influential in the jail and the local corrections community. Two officers closely connected to him had also engaged in a campaign of harassment to ensure that the witnesses kept silent and didn't "rat out" their colleague. The officer who injured Helen and his two code of silence enforcers were dismissed. But even after the Ministry removed the chief instigators from the jail, officers who had told the truth continued to face reprisals from their peers, leading one of them to resign her job (Ombudsman of Ontario 2013).

## Women in Cages

While crime rates are down in Canada, women are the fastest-growing group of prisoners, as they are throughout the world. Julia Sudbury (2005a: xvii) argues that the "global lockdown" of women inside immigration detention centres, psychiatric hospitals, and prisons is the manifestation of global capitalism's prison industrial complex, intended to "warehouse those surplus to the global economy and creating profits for private prison operators and corporations servicing prisons." Sudbury's analysis of this global lockdown reminds us of the many facets of the coercive power in Western capitalist democracies — such as the colonization (and criminalization) of Indigenous peoples, the creation of legislation to combat the "war on drugs," which has incarcerated more women than men for trafficking of drugs, and the privatization of prisons, which has created much private profit — and how these tactics aggressively affect women all over the world.

It has been over two decades since *Creating Choices* was written, rooted in the findings of the survey of federally sentenced women. Since that time, more women are federally incarcerated than ever before. In 2002–03 there were 359 federally incarcerated women (accounting for only 3 percent of all penitentiary inmates). By 2012–13, the population of women in federal prisons was at 579, an increase of just over 60 percent. One in three federally incarcerated women is Aboriginal. The number of Aboriginal women increased by over 80 percent in ten years — from 104 in 2002–03 to 191 in 2012–13 (Sapers 2013: 35–36). Does this mean that women are becoming more dangerous and engaging in serious crimes? Or, do the numbers tell us something about the criminal justice response to women and the lack of accessible services for women in our communities?

When we look at the personal histories of federally sentenced women, we come to understand that most of these women have long-standing mental health and addiction issues — which call for effective treatmen, not lengthy criminal records. In their report on federally sentenced women, Meredith Barrett, Kim Allenby, and Kelly Taylor (2010) document that approximately two-thirds of women prisoners are serving sentences of between two and five years; and "one out of every five women in the federal correctional system presents with mental health problems, a proportion that has increased by 61% since 1997" (Barrett, Allenby, and Taylor 2010: 21). The authors also report that 48 percent of women were identified at intake as having a previous or current drug addiction; over 80 percent of women self-reported histories of physical abuse and 68 percent reported sexual abuse (an increase of 10 percent since the original survey on federally sentenced women). Just under half of women report having engaged in self-harming behaviour as a means of coping with emotional pain. Moreover, almost 77 percent of women inmates have children; 64 percent of women reported supporting themselves and their children financially through paid employment, yet more than half of the women reported having less than a high-school education (Barrett, Allenby, and Taylor 2010). Clearly, criminalized women face economic disadvantage, for the most part supporting their children through poorly paid work, and are vulnerable to exploitation and abuse.

Prisoner advocate and feminist Kim Pate (2003) explains the connection between women's increased economic marginalization under neoliberal provincial governments and increased reliance by provincial and territorial governments on prisons:

We know the increasing numbers of women in prison [are] clearly linked to the evisceration of health, education, and social services. We also know that the cycle intensifies in times of economic downturn. It is very clear where we are sending the people who are experiencing the worst in the downturn in the economy and social trends. Jails are our most comprehensive homelessness initiative. In terms of the rate at which women are charged, however, there has been a 7 percent decrease overall in the number of women charged with criminal offences. In particular, we are seeing a decrease in the number of violent crimes committed by women [yet] there are increases in the number of women in prison. These increases have occurred within the context of increased cuts to expenditures for social services, health, and education throughout the country. (Personal communication, Oct. 3, 2005)

A consequence of the closure of the P4W and the construction of the healing lodge and regional prisons is that more women are being sentenced to longer periods of incarceration so that they can supposedly benefit from the treatment programs available. Prior to the closure of P4W, fewer women were receiving federal sentences because judges were loath to send women to a prison so widely condemned. Ultimately, as more women are sentenced to prison "for their own good," the public will come to view criminalized women as being more and more dangerous (Shaw 1993).

## Beyond the Prison Walls

Given the deteriorating conditions of confinement, what do women's lives look like after they are released from prison? Most women are released from federal custody on parole or conditional release, and many of them convicted of criminal offences end up "doing time on the outside" (Maidment 2006) in the form of sentences to be served in the community (typically with numerous conditions attached).[2]

In the early 1980s criminologists recognized that social-control mechanisms aimed at inducing conformity operated both inside and outside of the criminal justice system (Cohen 1985). These mechanisms are networks of professionals, such as social workers and counsellors, along with non-profit social-service agencies, such as halfway houses, detox centres, and food banks. Each agency or expert engages in the supervision and reinsertion of the non-conformist (prisoner, addict, street person) back into the social-control matrix of family and work. Over time many of these agencies — such as church-based and charitable organizations — became an extension of the criminal justice and mental health systems, competing for operational funding to house, feed, treat, and supervise ex-prisoners and patients. Although neo-liberalism seeks to make individuals responsible for solving or handling their own problems, whatever those problems might be or wherever they spring from, it also seeks to put communities into the hands of "the market" for the delivery of social services. This approach to service delivery, which is touted as being more financially prudent, is rationalized as a matter of community capacity-building and of empowering communities to take responsibility for their own problems and populations (Andersen 1999).

Critical criminologists such as Edwin Schur (1984) and Pat Carlen (2003) refer to the relocation of punishment into the community as "transcarceration," and feminist criminologists recognize that the transcarceration regimes are profoundly gendered. Through transcarceration the reach of regulatory (rather than criminalizing) agencies governs women's relationships and bodies "at a distance." Social-control networks of surveillance and observation within the community have expanded the gaze of the state through the use of halfway houses, shelters for battered women, food banks, probation officers, and community policing (Maidment 2006); and women's relationships in the community are "assessed for their criminogenic potential" (Hannah-Moffat 2010: 203). The strategies and tactics of parole supervision mirror those of the gender-responsive correctional model. Women's risk of recidivism (reoffending) is assessed according to a gendered logic. Women's risk to reoffend is determined by their relational lives with their children and partners. Relationships are "risky conditions" unless women have received proper interventions, such as anger management or cognitive behavioural therapy to take responsibility for their relationship choices. Parole board members utilize records of women's past experiences of domestic violence — especially for those who have resisted abuse — as a possible predictor for future violence (Hannah-Moffat and Yule 2011; Turnbull and Hannah-Moffat 2009; Pollack 2007).

More recently, criminologists have begun to take seriously the non-legal forms of "governmentality" — the process of social control in which the state works through civil society, not upon it (Garland 2001; O'Malley 1996). For example, low-income women on welfare are the target of moral scrutiny under the social assistance laws of Ontario. For example, if they are deemed to be living in an unreported supportive relationship with anyone (the so-called "spouse in the house" rule), they are cut off state benefits (Mosher 2014; Hillyard and Morrison 1999; Little 1998). According to governmentality theorists, the work of regulation is more diffuse across private and public domains; it involves technologies of surveillance and risk assessment that are often not administered by the criminal justice system (Ericson and Haggerty 1997).

## Investigating the Regulation of Women

The following chapters explore the historical and contemporary regulation of women. In chapter 6, Robert Menzies and Dorothy Chunn tell us the story of Charlotte — a woman who defied many of the normative sexual and gendered expectations of the early twentieth century. Charlotte, who was imprisoned for most of her life as a patient/prisoner, was forced to endure brutalizing treatments for her undisciplined independence and resistance. Menzies and Chunn map out the gendered, class-based, and sexualized regulation of women that overshadows contemporary regimes of control inside and outside of the criminal justice system.

Illustrating the historical continuity of control over women by the state, Dorothy Chunn and Shelley Gavigan (chapter 7) outline the transformation of welfare laws in Ontario since the rise of neo-conservative social politics and neo-liberal economic policies under Premier Mike Harris's government of 1995–2002. During that period, law and order rhetoric coupled with the individualism of neo-liberal economics resulted in the creation of new crime categories and a broadening of the regulatory powers of the state to properly discipline welfare recipients. Poor women with children were most vulnerable to these new policies, which ushered in a sharp reduction in welfare benefits, the ratcheting up of eligibility criteria, work-for-welfare policies, the creation of a welfare snitch line, investigations into the personal, intimate lives of welfare recipients, and the creation of welfare fraud as a criminal offence. In the end, neo-liberal governments — seemingly committed to smaller government — have increasingly relied upon the expansion of the criminal justice system to implement their policies.

The expanding reach of the state to govern women's lives through psychiatrization as criminalization, or welfare dependency as welfare fraud, is taken up by Amanda Glasbeek and Emily van der Meulen (chapter 8) in their examination of CCTV — closed circuit television installed in large urban centres under the pretence of public safety. CCTV functions as a form of security that works in complex ways across women's lives; both as crime prevention and criminalization. Racialized and poor women experience technological surveillance of urban spaces for reasons of public order and safety as a "paradox of visibility." Cameras serve to govern spaces in which women are at-risk of victimization, yet they also become a means of both state surveillance of women's street work and of private eroticized surveillance of women's washrooms.

In chapter 9 Jennifer Kilty returns us to the segregation cells of Grand Valley Institution, spaces of coercive surveillance and disciplining of women. In her analysis of the conditions leading to Ashley Smith's death in custody, Kilty argues that therapeutic regimes such as cognitive-behavioural programming operate as modes of punishment, legitimating the excessive use chemical and physical restraints to achieve compliance.

The spaces and strategies used for the regulation of women are hauntingly familiar. In the chapters that follow, historical sociologists, socio-legal scholars, and criminologists demonstrate how the state, through the criminalization or treatment of women "for their own good," responds to their resistance to social isolation due to a potent mixture of poverty, racism, maternalism, and/or heterosexism. What emerges across all the narratives of criminalized and imprisoned women's lives is the profound impact of poverty and violence — and what happens to women when they choose to resist.

## Notes

1. For instance, between January and March 1996 two suicides and a series of slashings occurred at the Edmonton Institution. In April 1996 seven women walked away from the prison; and in a media release following the "escapes," CAEFS asserted that the women who had left did so to see their families and were apprehended only a few blocks away. A disturbance occurred at the Truro prison in September 1996.

2. Conditional sentences, for example, which were implemented by Parliament in 1996 with the passage of Bill C-41, gave judges the option of imposing a community-based sentence for an offence that does not carry a mandatory minimum prison term, and if the judge would otherwise have sentenced the offender to imprisonment for less than two years (the Conservative government added further restrictions on applicable offences in 2007 and 2012; see Yalkin and Kirk 2012). A conditional sentence will have mandatory conditions attached to it (keeping the peace and being of good behaviour, appearing before the court when ordered to do so, reporting regularly to a supervisor, remaining within the jurisdiction). It can also have optional conditions attached (abstaining from drugs and/or alcohol, firearms prohibition, performing up to 240 hours of community service, attending counselling or treatment programs, abiding by a curfew). Offenders who breach their conditions serve the remainder of their sentence in custody.

# 6

# The Making of the Black Widow
## The Criminal and Psychiatric Control of Women

*Robert Menzies & Dorothy E. Chunn*

On an early autumn evening in the late 1940s, in a medium-sized city in British Columbia, thirty-three-year-old Charlotte Ross used a fourteen-inch carving knife to sever the jugular vein of her husband, Jimmy, as he sat sleeping in the living room of their fashionable duplex apartment.[1] She then turned the knife on herself, slashing her left wrist and throat, half-severing her trachea in the process. After an abortive effort to telephone the police, Charlotte slumped onto a sofa chair and gradually lost consciousness.

Hours later Jimmy Ross's son stumbled upon the macabre aftermath of the attack and called police. When officers arrived at the scene Jimmy was clearly dead. Charlotte's eyelids were fluttering and she was softly moaning. During the next two weeks, while Charlotte slowly recuperated from her wounds in the city's general hospital, police charged her with capital murder, and a string of local psychiatrists subjected her to a battery of mental assessments. When she was sufficiently recovered, Charlotte found herself in the city jail, alone in a cell, awaiting trial.

For more than two decades, as an "Order-in-Council" woman, Charlotte Ross would find herself trying to negotiate a psychiatry and law labyrinth and would experience the awesome powers of forensic justice in a more intensive and prolonged way, arguably, than has any other woman in B.C. history.[2] Her remarkable story poignantly reveals that the regulatory ideologies and practices visited upon supposedly "criminally insane" women who have transgressed the norms of womanhood far predate the neo-liberal era. Her sad journey illuminates the gendered operations of judicial and medical institutions during a key transformative era in the history of socio-legal responses to women's (and men's) madness and criminality. Her crime, mentality, intransigence, gender, and very identity combined to propel Charlotte into repeated conflict with the experts and officials who were striving to make sense of her — and to return her to what they considered a state of normalcy.

Charlotte's encounters with forensic authority shed light on the dominant cultural understandings that constitute women's normative roles in law, science, and society. Both in the context of Charlotte's time and today, medicine and law are mutually implicated in the pathologization of women in conflict with the criminal justice system. Like other feminist writing on this subject (Allen 1987; Appignanesi 2009; Chan, Chunn, and Menzies 2005; White 2008), our ongoing research on Order-in-Council women like Charlotte (Chunn and Menzies 1994, 1998; Menzies and Chunn 1999, 2013) reveals the dominant images of docile, responsible, sane womanhood that both frame the activities of psy-experts and, in turn, reflect wider understandings of gender, rationality, and order circulating globally through the public culture, then and now.

## Women, Criminality, and Madness

From its inception in the early 1870s (Scott 2011), British Columbia's mental health system was a gender-stratified and segregated enterprise (Davies 1987; Kelm 1992; Menzies 2001).[3] As in other jurisdictions (Appignanesi, 2009; Brookes 1998; Finnane 1985; Geller and Harris 1994; Ripa 1990), female patients spent their days in women-only wards and/or buildings and engaged in forms of labour, leisure, and treatment that reflected deeply entrenched gender identities and expectations.[4] But while female matrons and nursing staff may have been omnipresent in the lives of these patients, the overarching authoritative identity of medical, legal, and administrative officialdom was unremittingly male.

On various levels of experience, the institutional careers of Order-in-Council patients paralleled those of other women psychiatric inmates. They inhabited the same wards, supplied the same kinds of dreary domestic institutional service, were subjected to equivalent regimens of treatment and regulation, and endured the same long terms of confinement as did their civilly committed counterparts.[5] At the same time, their hybrid status as both criminal and insane conferred unique qualities on them, earmarking them as singular threats to an androcentric social, juridical, and scientific establishment. In contrast to "ordinary" madwomen, the "outwith" women (Carlen 1983: 155) who transgressed criminal as well as mental boundaries directly violated gender-identity standards of mind and action; in the eyes of the authorities, they required exceptional measures of domestication.

Yet, notably, the crimes of most women considered to be criminally insane were then, and remain today, relatively minor. Among the thirty-eight B.C. cases in our study, thirty involved non-violent offences.[6] Only six Order-in-Council women during the period we studied, from 1888 to 1950, were charged with or convicted of murder. All killed family members, which is typical of women who commit homicide. All except Charlotte Ross took the lives of their own children, thereby inciting cycles of pathologization and pity that typically yielded comparatively lenient responses from the courts, and often diversion out of the criminal justice system altogether (Backhouse 1996; Bernier and Cellard 1996; Kramar 2005; Menzies and Chunn 2013; White 2008; Wright 1987).

Statistically, then, Charlotte Ross was an uncommon forensic specimen. But in the wider context of gender and power relations that infused mid-twentieth-century life, it is scarcely surprising that her case became by far the most infamous of these thirty-eight criminally insane women in British Columbia. The "black widows" (Skrapec 1994) who murder their husbands or male lovers are the embodiment of intimate danger. They have always precipitated reactions that are wildly out of proportion, given their miniscule numbers and the slight risk that they actually pose to men, society, and the state (Allen 1987; Chan 2001; Chan, Chunn, and Menzies 2005; Harris 1989; Hartman 1985; Jones 1996; Knelman 1998; Myers and Wight 1996).

While reactions were by no means uniform (Harris 1989), the black widow's liminal status was her defining attribute in the eyes of the community, science, and the law. She might be mad, but her insanity also expressed itself in calculated, "cold-blooded" crimes that were not fully female or male, willed or compelled, crazy or sane. According to official renderings (MacKay 1995; Moran 1981; White 2008), many of these women knew right from wrong and were therefore legally accountable. Others, like Charlotte, seemed to inhabit a medial mental zone between culpability and blamelessness, and arguably were all the more dangerous for their marginality. The urge to punish such women seeped through the languages and practices of modern psychiatry (Knelman 1998: 87).

Like other murderous women in Canadian history (Atwood 1996; Bernier and Cellard 1996; Kendall 1999; Kilty and Frigon 2006; Kramer and Mitchell 2002; White 2008), Charlotte Ross was acting "against nature" or, rather, against the hegemonic, naturalizing images of a docile, nurturing, and subservient femininity. Moreover, in contrast to the conduct of many women who killed (Backhouse 1996; Kramar 2005; Dubinsky and Iacovetta 1991), Charlotte's actions seemed indefensible, and her inner motives opaque. Although her suicide attempt following Jimmy's murder — along with a record of prior psychiatric involvement — brought her mental capacity into question and justified the medical interventions that followed her arrest, to most observers at the time Charlotte seemed the antithesis of a prototypical victim. Her husband had never been known to physically abuse her. He was a reliable breadwinner, and had recently been diagnosed with colon cancer. Thus, Charlotte's notoriety issued mainly from her positioning as a morally questionable and recalcitrant woman whose crime could not be attributed wholly to mental disease or defect. "The most sensational murderesses," writes Judith Knelman (1998: 121), "were spirited women who were a threat to the social order. Men and women alike were fascinated by [their] audacity and aggressiveness."

Throughout her many years of entanglement with the state's medico-legal apparatus, Charlotte Ross was, for all intents and purposes, on trial for moral turpitude. Her criminal and mental status were subsumed within, and inextricably bound up with, gender-laced assumptions about the quality of her character and her worth as a woman. In these respects, however atypical her case, the arc of Charlotte Ross's forensic career retraced the all-too-familiar contours of women's experiences with the criminal justice and mental health systems.

## "Afraid of No One": The Making of a Black Widow

Charlotte Ross grew up on a farm on the Canadian prairies, the oldest daughter among fourteen children in a poor family. According to the clinical records at Essondale, the provincial mental hospital, her father was a carpenter, a "short-tempered, aggressive, independent man ... with deep religious convictions." He "could be physically violent ... and dominated his passive ineffectual wife." As Charlotte said, "*He was like me — afraid of no one.*"[7] Like many young women who came of age during the 1930s, Charlotte had an austere, arduous, and short-lived childhood. She was "*obliged and expected to terminate her schooling [at age thirteen] to help her mother look after the younger [children]*" as the family struggled to survive the onslaught of the Great Depression.

By age fifteen Charlotte had left home, but not her domestic service, finding work as a housekeeper. In the mid-1930s, while still in her teens, she met a man who was "apparently a drug addict, a dealer in narcotics, and a procurer of women." The man was said "to have seduced her," and she relocated with him to a small B.C. coastal town. He directed Charlotte to a local address that turned out to be the site of a "house of ill repute," where the proprietors seized her belongings. After some time Charlotte managed to escape from this sexual servitude, and she went on to obtain work as a waitress in what her physicians described as "one dive after another" in the Chinatown of a nearby city.[8] In the moralizing discourse of her clinical file, during that period in the later years of the Depression, "Her dealings with

men were on the basis of pick-ups and she indulged in some prostitution."
She received treatment for venereal disease, became pregnant, and obtained
an abortion.[9]

Charlotte Ross entered adulthood at an especially critical juncture in
the history of Canadian working women. Although increasingly integral to
the country's economy during the early twentieth century, young, single
women who penetrated the public realm — through either choice or necessity — inevitably confronted the gendered forces of moral regulation. For
the reigning state and civil agents and institutions of social purity, mental
hygiene, eugenics, citizenship education, and other causes, the single,
independent "working girl" of questionable repute was the embodiment
of risk to traditional values of femininity, family, homeplace, and nation
(Myers 1998; Sangster 2001; Stephen 1995; Strange 1995). Collectively,
the "occupational wanderer,"[10] the "factory girl," the "pickup girl," and their
ilk (Freund 2002; Roach Pierson 1990; Stephen 1995; Strange 1995) were
the source of innumerable evils that represented an ominous trend in gender,
race, class, and sexual relations. During World War II, when public panics
targeting the evils of female promiscuity reached a crescendo in major cities,
it was the transgressive and disreputable women like Charlotte Ross more
than the professional sex-trade workers who were the main targets of moral
enforcement sorties (Freund 2002). In these ways Charlotte's tale represents
the experience of many Canadian women who breached the frontiers of
normative family life as the twentieth century approached its midpoint.

Yet in many other respects the story of Charlotte Ross is unique. For one
thing, she managed to extricate herself from her marginal life of waitressing
and part-time prostitution and, as recounted years later by an Essondale social
worker, she improved herself "as she went along." She "worked hard, saved
her money and played the races." She took on a succession of jobs as a clothing store clerk, jeweller's assistant, and practical nurse and companion. One
of her nursing assignments, involving an elderly salesman whom Charlotte
tended through a fatal bout with cancer (authorities later described it as a
"sugar daddy" experience), gave her economic stability. In partial payment
for her services, he subsidized Charlotte's apartment and helped finance a
coffee shop that she owned and operated through the war years.

Toward the end of the war Charlotte's life course took yet another turn
when she met a prosperous local businessman, Jimmy L. Ross[11] — a seemingly sympathetic man in his late fifties. One of Charlotte's brothers would
later affectionately describe him in court as "a prince." At first Charlotte was
a hired employee, but she and Jimmy were soon cohabiting, and within two

years they had married while on vacation in the western United States. From the outset family and friends on both sides regarded the relationship with suspicion. During subsequent interviews with social workers, Charlotte's siblings depicted her as an aggressive and mercenary manhunter who had "been pursuing this wealthy man for a considerable period of time." As her sister put it, Charlotte "felt that she had made a 'good catch' in Mr. Ross and was rather inclined to look down on the rest of the family." For their part, Jimmy's business associates considered Charlotte a "gold digger" who had "taken in" their ingenuous, lovestruck friend.

Only weeks after the wedding, two shattering revelations punctured this already troubled domestic setting. First Jimmy divulged that he was suffering from cancer of the bowel and required immediate treatment. Then, while Jimmy was in hospital, Charlotte learned from her own family members that he had been leading two separate lives. Contrary to his many reassurances over the preceding three years, this "prince" had never finalized the divorce from his first wife. He also had an adult son who lived close to the Ross's home. When confronted, Jimmy claimed that he had no communication with his first wife and pleaded with Charlotte not to leave him. For a time, a conflicted Charlotte acquiesced.

It was then that Charlotte's immersion into the mental health system began. She precipitated her first psychiatric encounter by going to the city police and trying to lay an attempted murder charge against her brother. During her subsequent ten-day confinement on the psychiatric ward of the local general hospital, Charlotte accused Jimmy and her siblings of participating in a plot to poison her for her money. She threw her $1,500 diamond ring, a gift from Jimmy, down a ward toilet. During this and subsequent hospitalizations over the ensuing months, while Jimmy continued his cancer treatment, Charlotte endured insulin shock therapy and was eventually declared to be stabilized. One of her brothers advised that she be committed to Essondale, but Jimmy retorted, "I would not send a dog there."

The culmination of these events came six days after Jimmy's release from his latest hospital stay, during which doctors had performed a radical colostomy. By then Charlotte had decided to leave Jimmy because, in the later words of the Essondale social worker, "she could no longer place any trust or confidence in what he said." Moreover, after several days of nursing Jimmy and driving him to hospital daily, Charlotte's mentality was deteriorating. On the morning of Jimmy's death, Charlotte's brothers had visited the home, both later reporting (at Charlotte's preliminary hearing) that she had appeared "a wee bit sick mentally" and "seemed very strange at the time" and "she kept saying sarcastic remarks." That evening, after shepherding Jimmy through a further outpatient treatment session, Charlotte finally disclosed her intention to leave.

According to the clinical files, "an argument ensued, and she claims that she has no other recollection of what happened." When Charlotte next awoke, she was in a hospital bed. Jimmy was dead, Charlotte's slashed wrist and throat were stitched and bound, and her forensic "career" had begun.

## Unfit to Stand Trial

Following her discharge from hospital, Charlotte Ross spent nine weeks in the women's wing at Oakalla, the province's largest prison and detention centre, located in the Vancouver suburb of Burnaby (Anderson 1993). Pending her murder trial scheduled for the spring assizes, Charlotte became the object of an intensive psychiatric inquiry. With three different medical experts involved, the inquiry was aimed at judging her state of mind at the time of Jimmy's death, and her fitness to stand trial.

Charlotte Ross's legal predicament was clearly desperate. Charged with capital murder, and with all evidence pointing to her guilt, she faced very real prospects of execution by hanging (Greenwood and Boissery 2000; Kramer and Mitchell 2002; Strange 1996).[12] In theory, then, the involvement of medical experts should have been a godsend. A diagnosis of irresponsibility, incompetency, or general mental illness should have functioned to mitigate the charge or sentence, divert Charlotte out of the judicial system altogether, or — even in the worst-case scenario — support defence arguments for commuting a death sentence.[13]

Yet, as many observers (for example, Arrigo 2002; Menzies 1989; Sjostrom 1997; White 2008) caution, the presence of clinical professionals does not necessarily dilute the power of criminal law. On the contrary, by supplying a pseudo-scientific rationale for penal sanctions, the forensic clinician functions to legitimize a powerful network of medico-legal control. Far from being diverted out of law's reach, those defendants deemed "mentally disordered" find themselves channelled into hybrid realms of regulation in which their characters and mentalities are as much on trial as are their criminal deeds.

Moreover, these mental health evaluations for the courts are intensely gendered (Allen 1987; Chan, Chunn, and Menzies 2005; Chunn and Menzies 1994; Kendall 2000; Menzies, Chunn, and Webster 1992). In ostensibly being "saved from law" (Smart 1989: 47), the woman defendant collides with a malestream system of forensic judgment that imperils her freedom, her state of mind, and her identity. The "doubly deviant" female forensic patient (Lloyd 2005) encounters a level of medico-moral scrutiny that often far exceeds that experienced by her male counterparts.

The three medical men who visited Charlotte Ross in Oakalla (two were Crown appointees, the other commissioned by the defence) produced virtually identical renderings of her mind-state. Their assessments systematically replayed Charlotte's prior encounters with mental health professionals, her "paranoiac" stance toward family and authorities, and the bizarre circumstances of Jimmy's death. These themes would become indelibly inscribed in Charlotte's official files and would register recurrently through her later encounters with psychiatry. The conclusions of one assessor — an eminent local psychiatrist — were typical. After three examinations (during the first of which Charlotte remained stonily silent), he wrote: "I am of the opinion that Mrs. Ross possesses delusions of a persecutory character which unfits her to stand trial from a mental standpoint as these delusions create such a personal fear that she seemed ... duty bound to protect herself against such further occurrences."

Prior to Charlotte's assize trial for capital murder, the presiding judge held a hearing before a twelve-member jury to determine her mental competency. In their testimony, the three examining psychiatrists unanimously declared that Charlotte's delusions rendered her unfit to stand trial. Their opinion most likely gained support, in the minds of judge and jury, because Charlotte had discharged her lawyer on the very eve of the trial. On receiving this news, the judge had hastily summoned a substitute attorney from a local law firm, although the hearing was already in progress when the lawyer finally arrived. The jury deliberated for all of ten minutes before finding Charlotte unfit. Her automatic disposition under the Criminal Code was transfer to psychiatric hospital as an Order-in-Council patient, under a Lieutenant-Governor's Warrant, until she regained her fitness and could return to stand trial.

Charlotte's own memories of these events, conveyed to an Essondale physician two months following her admission, reveal much about her own experience of the trial, along with her abortive efforts to assume a measure of control over the proceedings and fend off a psychiatric commitment. She clearly wanted her day in court, but her limited knowledge of how law worked left her in an untenable position:

*I had an idea that this is what they were trying to do, to send me to this place ... so trying to stop that I used my own knowledge of what I knew of the law, if I discharged my lawyer they wouldn't go on with the trial and I would be able to get another lawyer and have a trial, but apparently they still went on with the trial…. I was waiting for the judge to nod to me and say something to me to give me an opportunity to speak, I didn't want to jump up — I didn't know just the procedures to go through, which naturally I just sat there … and several times I had the opportunity to say something if I had known the right thing to say. Anyhow the jury went out and that was that.*

Equally illuminating were Charlotte's reflections on the trial's aftermath. At a later Essondale case conference, she told the assembled hospital physicians and staff members, "*I didn't see [my lawyer] after my trial and I never saw him for seven weeks previous.*" Moreover, the evening before her trial, one of the appointed psychiatrists visited her for the first time in seven weeks. According to Charlotte, "*He said that I was looking very well and a few things and then left. He met [lawyer] in the hall and had a few words together, then [lawyer] came in to see me and proceeded to say what was going to happen.*" When one doctor asked, "Were you satisfied with that arrangement or would you have preferred to have gone to trial?" Charlotte replied emphatically, "*Well I would have preferred to have gone to trial for several reasons.*"

It is clear that Charlotte had accurately gauged the implications of her medical diversion to Essondale as an "unfit" criminal defendant. Her consignment to medico-legal limbo was an unwelcome, deeply resented intrusion. Her tireless protests against her mental confinement, her claims to be fit for trial, and her inexhaustible demands for access to justice rapidly emerged as the leitmotifs of her mental hospital experience. As Charlotte confided to her ward physician shortly after admission, commitment to Essondale was "*the very thing I didn't want to happen…. If I'm going to stand trial there is no reason why I can't stand now. Why didn't I stay in [gaol] and get my lawyer? If I was able to stay in [gaol] for nine weeks altogether, do my knitting, help the girls there, I don't know why I have to come here for treatment.*"

## "Under Close Supervision"

Charlotte Ross spent thirteen years on the wards of the Essondale Women's Chronic Building. Like other women psychiatric inpatients in British Columbia and elsewhere (Davies 1987; Kelm 1992; Geller and Harris 1994; LeFrancois, Menzies, and Reaume 2013; Reaume 2000; Ripa 1990; Ussher 2011), Charlotte found herself in a highly regulated institutional sphere in which the hierarchical doctor-patient relations were obvious and gender figured prominently in every minute detail of daily life. For many, isolation from the world beyond the walls was total and gender-segregated. Men rarely entered the East Lawn wards, particularly after the arrival of women psychiatrists at Essondale in the late 1940s. Moreover, contact between physicians and patients was sporadic at best. As Charlotte observed in a letter intended for her mother, but confiscated by staff, "*We had gotten so many Doctors in such a short time it was rather difficult to get an appointment with any of them.*"

Aggravating Charlotte's dilemma was her "criminally insane" status, which consigned her to a locked ward, restricted her comings and goings, disqualified her from grounds privileges, and inhibited her interactions with ward physicians. As Charlotte wrote in the same letter to her mother, "*I am an Order of council, and ... I can not get a Doctor that will stay long enough to get interested in my case.*" But in contrast to her tenuous and often hostile relations with staff, Charlotte clearly took pleasure in the company of other women patients and benefited from the feminine culture prevailing on the wards. "*The ladies are very nice and very considerate,*" Charlotte observed in one case conference, "*because we realize we are all in the same boat so to speak, we are all rowing for one thing, and that is to get well physically and mentally and be able to live what is considered a normal life on the outside.*"

Charlotte's experience as an Order-in-Council patient at Essondale pivoted around the continuing efforts of medical authorities to appraise her mental competency and responsibility, to chart her moral biography of pathology and violence (Allen 1987; Carlen 1983; Chunn and Menzies 1994; Menzies and Chunn 2013; White 2008), and to identify the afflictions that had allegedly propelled her into hospital. As many feminist researchers and authors have observed (Becker 1997; Caplan and Cosgrove 2004; Chan, Chunn, and Menzies 2005; Raitt and Zeedyk 2000; Stubbs and Tolmie 1999; Ussher 2011), psychiatric classification is highly gendered, as much concerned with women's moral transgressions and violations of normative femininity as it is with their supposedly defective states of mind. In Charlotte's case, she received a diagnosis of "Schizophrenic Reaction — Paranoid Type." "It is evident," physicians reasoned, "from her evasions and occasional blocking in her speech that she has systematized a delusional formation beginning at least as far back as the time of her marriage and involving ideas of jealousy, the police, and the idea that someone is after her money."

The psychiatric interviews that led to these conclusions were revealing in their own terms. Charlotte plainly took exception to the confessional, mind-probing qualities of her encounters with hospital staff. She especially resented physicians' efforts to elicit legally relevant information that, in her judgment, had no bearing on her medical status. One exchange with her first ward physician occurred shortly after her admission, and offers insight into the dynamics of these diagnostic "consults." The physician had also testified at Charlotte's fitness hearing.

Q. What do you plan? You have arrived here and now what do you think is going to happen?

A. *I just sit and wait on what you doctors say.*

Q. You are quite content to abide by the decision of the doctors outside to have you here?

A. *I certainly am not. There isn't anything I can do. I have fought and fought and fought and everything I did — what did they do on Saturday — rushed in and said you are going and here I am. I fought about coming to this place ever since they started.*

Q. The only way in which your present status can be altered is to talk to people on just [what] your future is.

A. *If it didn't help me when I was there, how is it going to help me when I'm in here?*

Q. It may not help you but it is the only possibility you have.

A. *No. I did all I could to keep from coming in here. Now I'm here anyway. I don't see any sense in my taking up your time.*

Supplementing these interviews were periodic "case conferences," in which physicians, psychologists, social workers, nurses, and other staff members congregated to conduct group inquiries into Charlotte's mentality. These exercises invariably ended in frustration. Charlotte remained resolutely silent about her criminal charges. Claiming the protections of legal process, and citing the unhappy experience of her fitness hearing, she disputed doctors' claims to be acting in her best interests. In one such encounter Charlotte showed that she was more than a match for the assembled professionals. Stymied by her continuing intransigence, an exasperated head physician finally resorted to a thinly veiled threat — an ominous expression of his ultimate power to determine Charlotte's fate:

Q. All we are interested in is your own health, your mental health and physical health. We have no interest in the legal aspect of your difficulties, it is only in your personal health we are interested so if

I ask you any question you would rather not answer you don't need to answer. I'll try to ask no question like that. In any case it is merely between ourselves from a doctor and patient angle.... Would you care to give any statements to me?

A. *I can't very well.*

Q. What transpires here is a confidence between doctors and patients and is never broken.

A. *Pardon me for saying so, Dr. [name] said that to me and he is a doctor — it isn't that I doubt any doctors it has just made me a little wary of that fact.*

Q. It makes it when you are not willing to discuss and talk freely with us very difficult for us to come to any conclusions to be of assistance to you. You can see that point?

A. *Maybe. On the other hand I don't need any assistance.*

Q. Well, you need assistance at least to get out of here.

A. *Yes, I understand that....*

Q. You tell me what you would like to do? What would you like us to do for you?

A. *Well, naturally I guess you are going to laugh at me, I would like to be left alone, let me go out and stand my trial and attend to my own affairs.... What point is my staying here? How long am I going to stay? Is there ever a chance of going out, or what is it?*

Q. You will have to stay here until we say you are ready to leave here.... And yet as you sit here not talking to me you are making it difficult for me to arrive at that conclusion are you not?

A. *Not in the way I look at it.... As I said before I talked to Dr. [name] and he said he was going to help me and I still came here. I told him then and I told Dr. [name] then. I still came here.*

Such unbending resistance could not be ignored. At Essondale, as in similar settings elsewhere, practitioners typically interpreted women's refusals of this sort as "pathologies of female protest" (Bordo 1988: 87), symptomatic of deep and dangerous mental aberrations. Following this interview, clinicians diagnosed Charlotte with paranoia and recommended insulin treatment.

Clearly, Charlotte was keenly aware of the price that she paid for refusing to assume the deferential patient role. In persistently rebuffing authorities and declining to address her charges and trial (because, in her words, "*that is legal, and that is personal*"), Charlotte confirmed the clinical impressions of her "paranoiac" personality state. Following one such encounter, the presiding psychiatrist was led to opine that she "successfully retreats behind the defense that her lawyer had instructed her not to divulge this material as it pertains to the legal and not to the medical issues involved," and that "her defenses of denial and projection are inadequate methods of dealing with her difficulties."

But Charlotte's struggles extended beyond her resistance to interviews. Over the course of many years, Charlotte's transgressions violated nearly every aspect of the mandated role for women patients. She retained a lawyer. She wrote countless letters to governmental officials and potential advocates outside the hospital. She accused staff physicians of impeding the discharge of patients through their "professional and political influence." Moreover, she was not above mobilizing her reputation as an alleged knife-wielding murderess to advantage by approaching doctors she disliked and offering to cut their throats — behaviour that confirmed their view that "she must remain under close supervision." From Charlotte's perspective, the medical men were her sole adversaries. "*It is funny,*" she confided in one conversation, "*but I have never got mad at the patients or staff in hospital — it has always been doctors.*"

In their efforts to manage Charlotte, the Essondale authorities relied mainly on the somatic therapies that were dominating institutional psychiatric practice through the postwar era. In the second summer of her detention, Charlotte endured more than two months of daily insulin injections. These treatments induced fifty-eight comas lasting several hours each morning, after which Charlotte returned daily to the ward sewing room for afternoon "occupational therapy" sessions. The effects of the insulin were immediate and profound. After a week of injections, Charlotte wrote a letter to a friend on the outside. The physicians (alarmed as much by the scarcely recognizable scrawl, no doubt, as by the contents) confiscated the letter:

> *Dear [name]. since I have been taken treatment this past week I don't believe I have had a letter from you or have I written any. I really have been too sick this past week for the first time since I have arrived here. I was doing very well on my own so to speak, and everyone has been so surprise to see me on treatment, they say they don't understand because I was the last person they expected to see taken these treatments.... And apperetly it will take untell early this fall before I am through taken them. I am taken these treatments every morning..... And feel far worse since I have been taken them. I don't mind so much if they were doing me some*

*good.... So would be pleased to see you any time you can get away. Your Loving Friend. Charlotte.*

But Charlotte's treatment had scarcely begun. Doctors introduced electroconvulsive therapy (ECT) during her fifth year in hospital, and reintroduced the shocks intermittently thereafter. During one typical course of ECT, Charlotte experienced twenty-one grand mal seizures over a seven-week period. "*All this shock,*" as Charlotte described it, was devastating. In a note conveyed to the medical superintendent, written nine years after her admission, Charlotte declared that "*the word 'Shock Treatments' or 'E.C.T.' makes me ill to my stomach.... I'm off my food can not sleep, also have lost weight.*" Some three years later, after a great many more ECTs, her ward physician speculated that Charlotte had incorporated ECT into her paranoid belief system, since she had voiced the opinion "*that electroshock was a criminal procedure and ... that it had its beginning some way that was not acceptable.*"[14] Despite her protests, the shocks continued. When antipsychotic medications became available in the mid-1950s, doctors placed Charlotte on potent doses of largactil. When her blood pressure began to plummet dangerously, they shifted to reserpine. Afterwards, they reported, "She works in the laundry and is much more amenable." For Charlotte's treatment, it seemed that patient docility was the main arbiter of a successful regimen.

If compliance was the measure of recovery for women like Charlotte, it also offered the best available means of escape from the locked hospital wards. Whether induced by electricity, chemistry, burnout, or a genuine cure, Charlotte's conduct change by the late 1950s was conspicuous. Incrementally, in response, staff began to confer previously withheld privileges, such as bimonthly "comfort" payments of $50 (supplied by the attorney general's department). Correspondingly, in perceptible gradations, the psychiatric assessments began to change. "Mrs Ross," observed one physician:

> has taken very responsible jobs in working in ... the kitchen, helping recreation to supervise grounds picnics and she had free access to the gardens and to the picking of flowers to decorate her ward and the dining room. She has talked to me about the "poor patients" and she has told me how some of the patients are confused as to whether she is a patient or a staff member.

Near decade's end, Charlotte finally earned her transfer to an open ward. Her long-awaited emancipation from Essondale was apparently within reach.

## "Not Unfit to Stand Trial"

For Charlotte Ross, as for those in similar situations elsewhere, the law was a potential redeemer, and a valued alternative to the psychiatric purgatory that had entombed her for more than a decade. Charlotte was acutely aware of the inequities that she faced in being denied access to the courts. As her hospital experience attests, Charlotte showed both ingenuity and resolve in her efforts to enlist the protections of law. From her point of view, establishing mental competency before the courts was her best chance for escape from the asylum. But as ensuing events would affirm, Charlotte had failed to gauge the full extent of psychiatry's powers over her existence.

Toward the end of the 1950s, Essondale physicians were still resisting Charlotte's return to court. According to one psychiatrist, "In her present state of health ... her personality would disintegrate in the court setting." In advising against a trial, this doctor reminded others that Charlotte faced execution if convicted on the capital murder charge. A colleague physician added that, even should Charlotte proceed to court and somehow be acquitted, she would still require further inpatient treatment under the Mental Health Act. When Charlotte protested angrily against this opinion, the doctor "told her that her response indicated that she may be ill still."

Nonetheless, as the 1960s dawned, the Essondale staff physicians, under relentless pressure from Charlotte and her lawyer — and perhaps impressed by her improved conduct on the wards — at last reported that she "had recovered sufficiently from her psychotic condition to be returned to court to stand trial." So advised, the provincial attorney general lifted Charlotte's warrant, and she returned to Oakalla pending her assize court trial in the spring.

When Charlotte Ross's day in court finally came to pass in the early 1960s, it rapidly mutated into a media circus for the local press, a field day for participating psychiatrists, and a topic of titillation for a captivated public. In the tradition of Victorian murderesses, about whom much has been written (Knelman 1998), Charlotte came to be portrayed as the quintessence of the crazed and lethal black-widow temptress whose warped mentality and morals had exploded into untold mayhem (Shipley and Arrigo 2004; Skrapec 1994). With all context and nuance purged from her story, Charlotte found herself reduced to a cipher for the objectifying, cautionary tales that issued forth in the courtroom, medical science, media discourse, and public culture about the dangers and disorders of femininity gone wrong.

After the jury's double-negative declaration that Charlotte was "not unfit to stand trial" (despite her diagnosis by three prosecution psychiatrists as a "paranoiac schizophrenic"), the trial proper began. Under the headline "Hidden Fears Beset Once-Happy Woman," one journalist's account described "a comely brunette on trial for her life." She looked "haggard and drawn after nearly three days in the prisoner's box, the last two listening to testimony surrounding the ... knife-slaying of city car dealer Jimmy L. Ross." According to this rendering, "Mrs. Ross sat with downcast eyes as one of her brothers described her sudden change of character ... how she suddenly became transformed from a cheerful, happy, normal person to an individual beset by nameless fears and suspicions — an individual who secreted a gun in her bedroom and who obtained cartridges to fit it." Charlotte's union with Jimmy devolved, in her brother's testimony, into a "supposed marriage" to a "common law husband" — an invalidating theme subsequently reinforced by both prosecution and state-appointed psychiatrists. Then medical witnesses for both defence and Crown offered a litany of evidence attesting to Charlotte's mental state at the time of the killing, and her resulting incapacity to distinguish right from wrong under the Canadian Criminal Code's version of the McNaughton rules.[15] One expert testified, "She was ... upset by the prospect her common law husband was jilting her, or about to jilt her." Another, who had treated her two months before the murder, revealed that Charlotte had "thought her food was poisoned by Jimmy Ross. She had said 'they wanted to kill me because I was not good enough for the social position.'"

On the fourth and final day of the trial, Charlotte herself took the stand. "Dressed in black, with black and white gloves," as one newspaper reporter recounted, "she hesitated before answering questions from counsel, and gave her replies quietly. During her testimony, the spectators in the public gallery were so quiet the rustle of counsel's gowns sounded unnaturally loud. She denied any recollection of events leading up to the death of Jimmy Ross." Unsurprisingly, Charlotte's version of events did not go unchallenged. "Crown prosecutor," the reporter continued, "submitted Mrs Ross to a searching cross-examination of her life leading up to the time she met Jimmy Ross and went through a form of marriage with him."

When the trial ended, the assize court jury deliberated for all of thirty-four minutes before rendering a verdict of "not guilty by reason of insanity."[16] Initially Charlotte was relieved to hear the presiding judge order her returned to Oakalla. In a subsequent visiting-room conversation (surreptitiously recorded by the prison matron) with her brother-in-law, a protestant minister, Charlotte confided that "she had asked to be sent back here, as she felt that she just could not face Essondale again, and her lawyer had told her that she would only be here for about a week." It was with shock and disbelief, then, that Charlotte learned about the provincial attorney general's decision to issue a second Order-in-Council, which called for her return to Essondale for another indeterminate term of confinement. For Charlotte, this double jeopardy outcome was the worst-case scenario. The Oakalla prison matron reported that when she broke the news, Charlotte "raved" about the attorney general, "said she came her[e] at the Lieutenant Governor's pleasure and Mr. [Attorney General Robert] Bonner had stepped in and taken over and he was doing everything to suit himself."

## Aftermath: Still Afraid of No One

In the wake of her insanity acquittal, Charlotte, now forty-eight years old, incredibly found herself back on the closed wards of Essondale. At first defiant, Charlotte "refused physical examination" at readmission "on the grounds that she no longer came under the jurisdiction of the hospital authorities." But she quickly realized the grim realities of her plight. And while even the physicians acknowledged the folly of her continuing detention, they stopped short of conceding that her protests might be entirely rational under these surreal circumstances. "She presents a most difficult problem," wrote her presiding psychiatrist, "in that her very real and justified resentment at being detained in hospital indefinitely is difficult to distinguish from her morbid state of paranoid schizophrenia." Ambivalently, he and his colleagues petitioned the provincial attorney general, Robert Bonner, to vacate this new Order-in-Council, but he refused. Meanwhile Charlotte began to deteriorate and, during the following winter, doctors subjected her to two months of sleep therapy[17] followed by another course of chlorpromazine.

A year later, authorities at last deemed Charlotte Ross sufficiently sane to exit Essondale on leaves of absence. On the outside Charlotte reverted to working variously as a housekeeper, waitress, and domestic under the long arm of an indeterminate Order-in-Council that placed strict conditions on her freedom. But, true to form, Charlotte resisted supervision. As her caseworker complained, "After Care appointments and visiting as a part of hospital service were dismissed scornfully as she has 'never received any treatment or service'.... She repeatedly said she would not be 'snooped upon'.... and that I must not show my face around the motel again." Charlotte continued to evade social workers and miss appointments until the Essondale administrators finally placed her on AWOL and notified police. By the mid-1960s, Charlotte was again back in Essondale, now called Riverview,[18] where physicians reaffirmed her diagnosis of "schizophrenic reaction paranoid type." She spent another three months on the wards, still *"Waiting to get my final release from the Attorney General."*

Release came the following autumn when Attorney General Bonner grudgingly lifted Charlotte's Lieutenant-Governor's Warrant. Three days later, Riverview Hospital medical staff discharged her. There was no follow-up, for, in the words of the discharging physician, "Mrs. Ross is so evasive that it is almost a physical impossibility to keep in touch with her. Her employment has been sporadic and the hours irregular and she will not make an effort to arrange appointments. She has not once given a change of address. We know of no community agency who would give service to so unreasonable and paranoid a client."

Charlotte Ross had one further encounter with medico-legal authority — a voluntary admission toward the end of the 1960s after her employer, for whom she was working as a domestic, reported to police that she was voicing delusions. Now considered a hopeless case, Charlotte received short shrift from hospital staff: "Despite an attempt to dissimulate and play the role of a normal person," doctors wrote, "she betrayed her basic condition and personality on several occasions evidencing extreme verbal hostility with slight provocation." Charlotte's continuing truculence also earned her a new label as a "Personality Pattern Disturbance — Paranoid Personality." Physicians also made several references to the pathological condition of her entire family. Yet, ironically, they discharged her into the arms of these same relatives.

Sadly, Charlotte's life continued to spiral downward after this last official encounter with the provincial mental health system. In the early 1970s a public health officer in another region of British Columbia contacted Riverview Hospital for information about a new patient, Charlotte Ross. She was living alone in a farmhouse eking out a marginal existence on unemployment insurance and was afflicted with "many problems, both physical and mental." After that, the files tell us nothing more about her.

Some might argue that Charlotte Ross was the architect of her own fate. As medico-legal officialdom would have it, Charlotte's downfall was best understood as a cautionary tale about the ravages of a disordered mind, the perils of a woman's promiscuity, and the end that awaits those misguided or diseased female mental patients who fail to yield to the reasoned ministrations of therapeutic science. But such an account — replicated again and again throughout the historical clinical files of female mental patients in British Columbia, as elsewhere — represents at best a partial and refracted rendering of women's experiences with the state's psychiatric apparatus.

Charlotte Ross's melancholy tale reveals just how tenuous and open to challenge were the psychiatric lines of demarcation between defect and reason, madness and sanity, good and evil. If Charlotte did leave a legacy, it lingers in the fallacies, hypocrisies, and contradictions that she managed to expose in the state's relentless efforts, through its public mental health enterprise, to domesticate "criminally insane" women.

Her ultimate decline and fall in no way detract from Charlotte Ross's exceptional capacity — despite her status as a reputed madwoman and murderess — to contest the androcentric, normalizing practices of constituted medico-legal authority. However high the cost, Charlotte had arguably wrested back her right *"to be left alone,"* and after so many lost years she was still *"afraid of no one."*

## Notes

For a longer version of this chapter, see Menzies and Chunn 2005. We are grateful to Elizabeth Comack and Gillian Balfour for their valued editorial input and support, and to Wendy Chan and the two chapter authors who reviewed a draft of our original chapter published in the first edition of *Criminalizing Women*. All errors and omissions are, of course, our own.

1. To safeguard confidentiality, we withhold and/or alter dates and place names throughout the chapter. Charlotte Ross, like all other names mentioned, is a pseudonym.
2. Order-in-Council women included those considered unfit to stand trial, or not guilty by reason of insanity, or transferred from prison because of mental disorder. Charlotte Ross was one of thirty-eight Order-in-Council women whose clinical files we surveyed in a project on the experience of gender, crime, and "insanity" in British Columbia's mental health system between 1888 and 1950 (Chunn and Menzies 1998; Menzies and Chunn 1999, 2013).
3. The main institutions were the Victoria Lunatic Asylum (1872–78) and its successors — the Public Hospital for the Insane opened in 1878 and the Provincial Mental Hospital, Essondale, in 1913. The percentage of women in mental hospital admission registries and provincial census statistics were, respectively: 23 percent and 25.6 percent in 1881; 22.6 percent and 29.1 percent in 1901; 30.7 percent and 41.5 percent in 1921; 42.2 percent and 46.0 percent in 1941; and 45.7 percent and 48.6 percent in 1951 (Menzies and Chunn 1999: fn 17; see also Labrum 2005).
4. During the early twentieth century, the facilities of the Public Hospital for the Insane were reserved exclusively for women. The gendered deployment of patients shifted again in 1930, with the opening of the Women's Chronic Building (later East Lawn) at Essondale.
5. Through the first century of British Columbia's public mental health operations, the vast majority of individuals entered hospital as involuntary civil commitment patients, under the province's Mental Hospitals Act, following an application by a family member, other citizen or authority, with certification by two physicians and ratification by a magistrate or justice of the peace (Davies 1987; Kelm 1992).
6. These non-violent offences included vagrancy (nine in total), public intoxication, incorrigibility, defamatory libel, public nudity, and causing a disturbance. One case involved self-injury, bringing an attempted suicide charge.
7. Unless otherwise indicated, the passages quoted in the chapter are taken from Charlotte

Ross's Essondale clinical record. We reproduce all excerpts from letters and other documents verbatim, with no corrections of spelling or grammar errors.

8.  On racialized images of white women living and working in Chinese communities, and efforts to regulate them, see Anderson 1991 and Backhouse 1994. On the events and aftermath of the 1924 Janet Smith case, which involved a Chinese "houseboy" falsely accused of murdering his white female co-worker, see Kerwin 1999, and Macdonald and O'Keefe 2000.

9.  See Chunn and Menzies 1994, Sangster 2002, Stephen 1995, and Strange 1995 on the moral regulation of young Canadian women during this era; Freund 2002 and McLaren 1987 on campaigns against prostitution; Cassel 1987, Chunn 1997, and Mawani 2002 on venereal disease control; and McLaren 1993 and McLaren and McLaren 1997 on abortion.

10. This term originates with the prominent Ontario psychiatrist, medical professor, and mental hygienist C.K. Clarke (Stephen 1995).

11. By coincidence, Charlotte and Jimmy shared surnames.

12. While a short-lived unofficial moratorium on the capital punishment of women had prevailed earlier in the century, by the 1940s Canadian women murderers were again, albeit infrequently, being condemned to the scaffold (Dubinsky and Iacovetta 1991; Greenwood and Boissery 2000; Kramer and Mitchell 2002).

13. From Canadian Confederation in 1867 through to the abolition of capital punishment in 1976, the federal cabinet in Ottawa undertook an automatic review of all capital sentences, commuting about half of these cases to life imprisonment (Strange 1996; Swainger 1995; White 2008).

14. Charlotte had a point. Ugo Cerletti pioneered ECT after witnessing how electrical shocks had a calming effect on pigs in an Italian slaughterhouse. On the origins of ECT see Breggin 1993, Frank 1978, and Funk 1999.

15. On adaptations of the cognitive "knowing right from wrong" test yielded from the 1843 McNaughton case and still enshrined in s.16 of the Canadian Criminal Code, see Bloom and Schneider 2006. On the "negotiation" of the responsibility concept in historical capital murder cases, see White 2008.

16. Possibly the jury decision was influenced by the knowledge that a guilty verdict might lead to a capital sentence.

17. Historical accounts of prolonged sleep therapy and other somatic "treatments" include, in Canada, Collins 1988, Funk 1999, and Perreault 2012; and elsewhere, Breggin 1993 and Whitaker 2010.

18. In 1964, in the wake of revisions to the British Columbia Mental Hospitals (thereafter Mental Health) Act, the Provincial Mental Hospital, Essondale, became Riverview Hospital.

# 7

# From Welfare Fraud to Welfare as Fraud
## The Criminalization of Poverty

*Dorothy E. Chunn & Shelley A.M. Gavigan*

In Canada and elsewhere, attacks on the policies and practices of the Keynesian welfare state since the late twentieth century have led to the dismantling and massive restructuring of social security programs for the poor. These sweeping welfare reforms, which intensified through the 1990s — aptly characterized by some as a war on the poor — have a disproportionate impact on poor women (see, for example, *Falkiner v Ontario* 2002; Klein and Long 2003; Little 2001; McMullan, Davies, and Cassidy 2002; Mosher et al. 2004; Savraese and Morton 2005, Swan et al. 2008). As Lynne Segal (1999: 206–7) argues: "The continuing offensive against welfare provides, perhaps, the single most general threat to Western women's interests at present — at least for those many women who are not wealthy, and who still take the major responsibility for caring work in the home." Indeed, it is no exaggeration to say that welfare law is primarily (and ideologically) concerned with the lives and issues of poor women, especially lone-parent mothers.

Welfare "fraud" occupies a central place in this attack on the poor. "Fraudsters" have always been a state concern in most liberal democracies, but the preoccupation with welfare "cheats" in the late 1990s and early 2000s was unprecedented. Although the preoccupation with welfare fraud is now less pronounced than it was a decade ago, the threat of it is still a weapon used against the poor. Moreover, it is only the most visible form of assault. In Ontario, for instance, the attack on welfare in the late 1990s also included deep cuts to the level of benefits (*Masse v Ontario* 1996; see also Moscovitch 1997: 85), an expanded definition of "spouse" (*Falkiner v Ontario* 2002), restructuring of the legislation from "welfare" to "work,"[1] mandatory drug testing, the introduction of a "quit/fire" regulation (which requires the cancellation or suspension of assistance to a recipient who resigns employment without just cause or is dismissed with cause),[2] the implementation of biometric finger-scanning (Little 2001: 26), anonymous snitch lines designed to encourage individuals to report suspected welfare abuse by their neighbours (see Morrison 1998; Morrison and Pearce 1995), and "zero-tolerance" in the form of permanent ineligibility imposed upon anyone convicted of welfare fraud (see *Rogers v Sudbury* 2001: 5; *Broomer v Ontario* 2002). In the past decade in Ontario, "welfare fraud" seems to have garnered less political and social attention than in the heyday of the attack on social assistance. However, the welfare system continues to operate within an ideological framework that shows welfare recipients as inherently "defrauding" the system.

This restructuring of welfare has shifted and been shifted by public discourse and social images (see Evans and Swift 2000; Golding and Middleton 1982; Misra, Moller, and Karides 2003; Mosher 2000; Mirchandani and Chan 2007). Few people, it seems, qualify as "deserving" poor anymore. Welfare fraud is welfare *as* fraud. Thus poverty, welfare, and crime are linked.[3] Simply to be poor is to be culpable, or at least vulnerable to culpability.

Two Ontario women convicted of welfare fraud offer case studies of the culpable poor in the early period of neo-liberal welfare reform. In 1994 Donna Bond, a single mother of two teenage children, was charged with welfare fraud in the amount of $16,477.84 over a sixteen-month period — she had not disclosed a bank account in her annual update report.[4] At trial, Bond testified that she had saved, and deposited, all the money she had ever received from her part-time employment, baby bonus, child tax credits, and income tax refunds (all of which she had disclosed in her annual reports to welfare). Initially she had planned to buy a car with this money, but then realized that her children would "require financial assistance to deal with [their serious health] problems in the years ahead" (*R v Bond* 1994: para.8). So she decided to set the money aside as a trust fund for them. Bond said she had "honestly believed that she did not have to report the savings because they were for the children" (*R v Bond* 1994: para.13).

The trial judge admitted to a dilemma:

> I was very impressed by the sincerity and achievement of the accused and troubled by the paradox of criminalizing the actions of this woman who scrimped as a hedge against the future financial health needs of her children. If she had spent this money on drinking, or drugs, or in any other irresponsible way, there would be no basis for any criminal charge. A conviction seems to send the message it was wrong to be conscientious about the welfare of her children and foolish to be frugal. (*R v Bond* 1994: para. 14)

Convict he did, however. And he was neither the first nor the last "sympathetic" judge to enter a conviction for fraud against a welfare mother (see Martin 1992; Carruthers 1995). Arguably, this case is one in which reasonable doubt as to guilt ought to have existed. Had she not been convicted of welfare fraud, this normatively perfect mother might well have been a candidate for "Mother and Homemaker of the Year." Yet the trial judge found Bond culpable: "Her commendable frugality and her selfless motives for committing the offence [were only] matters for consideration on sentencing" (*R v Bond* 1994: para. 14).

Some seven years later, in the spring of 2001, Kimberly Rogers pleaded guilty to welfare fraud that involved receiving a student loan and welfare assistance at the same time (previously but no longer permitted by Ontario's legislation).[5] Because she was pregnant, and had no prior criminal record, the judge sentenced her to six months of house arrest. However, as a result of the Ontario government's zero-tolerance policy, which then stipulated three months, and later permanent, ineligibility of people convicted of welfare fraud, Rogers had no source of income (Keck 2002; MacKinnon and Lacey 2001: F1, F8). Seeking reinstatement of her benefits, she wrote in an affidavit to the court: "I ran out of food this weekend. I am unable to sleep and I cry all the time" (cited in Keck 2002). Through a court order, she did receive interim assistance pending the hearing of a challenge to the constitutionality of the new ineligibility rules (*Rogers v Sudbury* 2001), but her rent ($450.00 per month) consumed the bulk of her monthly cheque ($468.00 per month). As a friend later observed, "No one can stretch $18.00 for a whole month" (MacKinnon and Lacey 2001: F8).

Isolated, in her eighth month of pregnancy, and confined to her tiny apartment, Kimberly Rogers died of a prescription drug overdose during a sweltering heat wave in August 2001. The circumstances of her death gave rise to a coroner's inquest in the fall of 2002. The coroner's jury made fourteen recommendations for changes in government policies and practices, including the repeal of the zero-tolerance lifetime ineligibility for social assistance as a result of welfare fraud (Ontario 2002; see also Eden 2003). Following their defeat of the ruling Conservatives in October 2003, the newly elected Ontario Liberal government did repeal the lifetime ban.[6] Although this was a welcome reform, Kimberly Rogers would still be liable to a welfare fraud conviction today and, if living under house arrest, she would still have only a pittance to live on after her rent was paid.

The *Bond* and *Rogers* cases raise many theoretical and empirical questions related to regulation, law, and morality, and the relationship between them at particular historical moments. We draw on these cases to analyze the intensified criminalization of poverty signified by the shift from welfare fraud to welfare *as* fraud. We argue that the shift reflected a reformed mode of moral regulation in neo-liberal states. In contemporary society, neo-liberal ideologies and the conceptualization of welfare as fraud continue to harm the lives of the poor.

The concept of moral regulation was developed initially during the 1980s by Marxist-influenced theorists (see Corrigan and Sayer 1981, 1985; Hall 1980) who linked it to processes of state formation. Through the 1990s a number of Canadian scholars pointed to the importance of non-state forces and discourses in moral regulation, arguing that the state does not hold a monopoly on "social" and "moral" initiatives (Valverde and Weir 1988: 31–34; Strange and Loo 1997; Little 1998; Valverde 1991, 1998; see also Dean 1994, 1999; Hunt 1997, 1999b). In our view, however, the state never ceases to be a player, even when benched, ignored by some, or outmanoeuvred by others. Thus, it remains important to identify the links, forms, and sites of state action and inaction.

We draw on a large body of socio-legal scholarship that has advanced this form of inquiry and analysis and illustrate our examination of shifting modes of moral regulation with reference to the historical treatment of poor women on welfare (see Little 1998; Gavigan and Chunn 2007).[7] We focus in particular on the always precarious position of such women within the overarching (apparently anachronistic) category of the "deserving poor" through the example of welfare legislation and policy.[8] The welfare law reform of the late 1990s and early 2000s and the continuing preoccupation with welfare fraud — the redefinition, restructuring, harassment, and disentitlement, coupled with the ever-present threat of criminal prosecution — suggest that the state and its coercive apparatus continue to play an important role that requires close analysis.

## The Double Taxonomy of Moral Regulation: Compulsion and Self-Regulation

Moral regulation has no agreed upon meaning, but most scholarship in the area begins with the collaborative work of Philip Corrigan and Derek Sayer. In *The Great Arch: English State Formation as Cultural Revolution*, they linked moral regulation to the "cultural" project of English state formation:

> Moral regulation: a project of normalizing, rendering natural, taking for granted, in a word "obvious," what are in fact ontological and epistemological premises of a particular and historical form of social order. Moral regulation is coextensive with state formation, and state

forms are always animated and legitimated by a particular moral ethos. (Corrigan and Sayer 1985: 4)

While Corrigan and Sayer placed the moral regulation project squarely within the realm of state actions and legal relations, other scholars theorizing regulation and control through the 1990s maintained that the state must be decentred (Valverde 1991), or its relationship with non-state agencies better appreciated (Valverde 1995), or erased as a significant player altogether (Valverde 1998). For Mariana Valverde, the heart of moral regulation or moral reform in a "moral capitalist setting ... is not so much to change behaviour as to generate certain ethical subjectivities that appear as inherently moral" (Valverde 1994: 216; see also Weir 1986). The focus is less on the material consequences of regulation or reform than it is on the discursive context.

Although sympathetic to this "decentring" emphasis, we want to argue for a renewed focus on social and state forces, and in particular on the contradictions and contributions of forms of law and state to gendered and anti-racist class struggles in the realm of moral regulation. Moral regulation must be situated expressly within the context of capitalist class relations and struggles — not least of which is capital's globalized attack on the "straw house" of the Keynesian welfare state. In developing our position, we draw on Stuart Hall's early work on law, state, and moral regulation; specifically, his analysis of the reformist sixties era of the "legislation of consent" in Britain, when laws relating to divorce, homosexuality, abortion, and prostitution were liberalized (Hall 1980).

Hall's (1980: 2) organizing question is: "What was it about the shifts in the modality of moral regulation which enabled this legislation, plausibly, to be described as 'permissive'?" He notes that "the legislation of consent" contained "no single uncontradictory tendency" (p. 7). By way of illustration, he looks at the influential Report of the Wolfenden Committee on prostitution and homosexuality and argues that it "identified and separated more sharply two areas of legal and moral practice — those of sin and crime, of immorality and illegality" (p. 11). As a result, Wolfenden created "a firmer opposition between these two domains" and "clearly staked out a new relation between the *two modes of moral regulation — the modalities of legal compulsion and of self-regulation*" (Hall 1980: 11–12; emphasis added).

Wolfenden recommended decriminalization and "privatisation of selective aspects of sexual conduct" (Hall 1980: 13), notably off-street prostitution and homosexual relations between consenting adults in private, and increased regulation of visible sexual activities such as "street-walking" and "male importuning" that were "offences against [the] public sector" (pp. 10–11). Hall identifies the "double taxonomy" of the Wolfenden recommendations: toward stricter penalty and control, toward greater freedom and leniency (p. 14). Here, then, was the core tendency of the permissive legislation of the 1960s: "*increased regulation* coupled with *selective privatisation* through contract or consent, both in a new disposition," a "more privatised and person-focused regulation, tacit rather than explicit, invisible rather than visible" (p. 21; emphasis added). In short, a clearer distinction was made between "public" and "private," state and civil society (p. 13).

In identifying the double taxonomy of control and penalty and freedom and leniency, or simultaneous deregulation and increased regulation, Hall reminds us of the complexity of the unity of the 1960s reforms. The state was pulled back and reinserted in different ways in the same pieces of legislation; its invisibility in one area was reinforced by its visibility in the other. Thus, "self-regulation" was inextricably related to increased "public" regulation. The lines between unacceptable public and permissible private conduct were more sharply drawn. In this way, two modalities of moral regulation, legal compulsion and self-regulation, one neither displacing nor transcending the other, co-existed in a complex unity.

Before applying this conceptualization of moral regulation to our exemplar of welfare fraud, we first examine welfare reform during the 1990s in order to consider the increased interest and legal shifts in the area of welfare fraud.

## Reforming Welfare in the 1990s

Although concern about welfare fraud is not a new phenomenon, the unrelenting punitiveness of the crackdowns under neo-liberalism is. Anti-fraud campaigns during the 1970s and early 1980s (see Golding and Middleton 1982; Rachert 1990) led to the review and total restructuring of welfare policies in Canada and other Western countries through the 1990s (see Bashevkin 2002; Moscovitch 1997; Gustafson 2009). Here we focus primarily on Ontario reforms to illustrate the shift from welfare fraud to welfare *as* fraud.

A pivotal moment in the welfare history of Ontario occurred in 1988, when the Social Assistance Review Committee (SARC) released *Transitions*, a six-hundred-page report with 274 recommendations on Ontario's social assistance system (Ontario 1988). The report devoted only seven pages to issues of "system integrity" and "welfare fraud" and yielded but two recommendations, which were motivated not out of any belief on the part of the Committee that fraud was rampant, but because they wanted to address and instil "public confidence" in the system (Ontario 1988: 384–86):

> We have no evidence to suggest that fraud in the social assistance system is greater than it is in the tax system or the unemployment insurance system. Nevertheless, because public confidence in the social assistance system depends in large part on the belief that the funds are being well spent and that abuse is being kept to a minimum, we accept that some of the measures adopted to control social assistance fraud may need to be more extensive than they are in other systems. (Ontario 1988: 384)

Notably, however, the report identified adequacy of benefits as the "*single most important weapon in the fight against fraud in the system*" (p. 384).

Responding to the recommendations concerning "system integrity," Dianne Martin (1992) criticized the Committee for abandoning its own guiding principles, in particular its commitment to the creation of a welfare regime based on the dignity and autonomy of social assistance recipients. Martin (1992: 93) pointed out that the most reliable indicator (conviction rate) placed the incidence rate of welfare fraud in Ontario at less than 1 percent. She was particularly concerned about the disproportional criminalization and punitive treatment of women on welfare (p. 91). The guiding sentencing principles stressed deterrence as "the paramount consideration" even where the case was "pitiful" (p. 66; see also *R v Thurrott* 1971; Carruthers 1995). Deterrence continues to be "the paramount consideration" a judge should take into account when determining the appropriate sentence for welfare fraud (See *R v Collins* 2011; *R v Allan* 2008).

From an almost insignificant place in *Transitions*, the fight against welfare fraud emerged as a centrepiece of provincial welfare policy in Ontario during the 1990s, irrespective of governing political party (see Moscovitch 1997; Little 1998: 139–63; Morrison 1995). However, in the implementation of their election platform, "The Common Sense Revolution," the Conservatives under Premier Mike Harris introduced changes that were more neo-liberal than conservative (see Cossman 2002; Coulter 2009; Maki 2011: 50), including the most draconian welfare reforms of any Canadian province.[9] Taking their cue from the Klein administration in Alberta (see Denis 1995; Kline 1997), the Harris government made welfare — and in particular a vow to "crack down" on "fraud" — the core of its welfare policy (Ontario 2000a, 1999).

Almost immediately after its election in 1995, the Harris government implemented a 22 percent cut to welfare rates and redefined (that is, expanded) the definition of spouse in welfare law in order to disentitle a range of previously entitled recipients (see Gavigan 1999; Mosher 2000). All of Canada's welfare poor live on incomes that are thousands of dollars below the poverty line, but in post-1995 Ontario the welfare-rate cut widened the "poverty gap" even further (NCW 2005: 87, Figure 5.2; see also Little 2001; McMullin, Davies, and Cassidy 2002). Between 1995 and 2004, the household income of a single employable recipient of social assistance in Ontario fell from 48 to 34 percent of the federal government's low-income cut-off measure; the income of a single parent with one child dropped from 76 to 56 percent of the poverty line; and the income of a couple with two children on welfare fell from 67 to 50 percent of the poverty line (NCW 2005: 66, Table 5.1; see also Gavigan 1999: 212–13). Between 2004 and 2009, the household income of a single employable individual on social assistance in Ontario remained at 41 percent of the after-tax low-income cut-off. During this same time period, the income of a single parent with a child in Ontario rose from 69 to 77 percent of the low-income cut-off and the income of a couple with two children also rose from 59 to 65 percent of the low-income cut-off (NCW 2010: Table 13). Between 1990 and 2009, inflation increased by 45.9 per cent. However, most welfare incomes in Canada did not increase at a similar rate. This left many people on welfare in Canada in worse positions than those who had received welfare decades earlier (NCW 2010: 8). Likewise, the impact of the expanded definition of spouse on single mothers was "devastating" (Little 2001: 27). In the eight months immediately following this reform, "more than 10,000 recipients were deemed ineligible under the new definition and cut off social assistance" (Little 2001: 26). Some 89 percent of those were women.

Further to these measures, the Harris government proudly announced its stance on welfare fraud: "The new zero tolerance policy is the first of its kind in Canada, and a key step in Ontario's welfare reforms."[10] Zero-tolerance meant permanent ineligibility for anyone convicted of welfare fraud, an exceptionally severe consequence given that the discourse and politics of welfare fraud have obscured the imprecision of what is considered to be fraud, and by whom. In Harris neo-liberal discourse, "fraud" came to encompass all forms of overpayments, whether resulting from administrative errors or not, including people in jail whose welfare should have been terminated upon incarceration, as well as formal fraud convictions. The government's own "Welfare Fraud Control Reports" tended to collapse categories, frequently failing to distinguish between benefit "reduction" and "termination," and the reasons therefore (see, for example, Ontario 2003). Yet, as the coroner who presided at the Kimberly Rogers inquest observed of the evidence that had been presented during the two months of hearings: "While overpayments are common, overpayments due to fraud are very uncommon" (Eden 2003). Indeed, research into abused women's experience of welfare within this discursive practice of welfare fraud (Mosher et al. 2004) as well as research into the nature and extent of welfare fraud (Mosher and Hermer 2005) reconfirms both the problem with definition and the sharp drop between "allegations" and actual convictions:

> The number of convictions [in Ontario] for 2001–02 (393 convictions) is roughly equivalent to 0.1 percent of the combined social assistance caseload and one percent of the total number of allegations. Statistics from the Municipality of Toronto for 2001 provide a similar picture: *80 percent of 11,800 allegations made against recipients were found to be untrue, in 19 percent of the remaining allegations there was no intent to defraud,* 117 cases were referred to the Fraud Review unit, of these 116 were reviewed by a special review committee, 95 were referred on to the police and charges were laid or pending in 91 (less than one percent of the total allegations). (Mosher and Hermer 2005: 34; emphasis added)

One reason that 99 percent of the allegations of welfare fraud were unfounded may be that the "overwhelming majority of the $49 million [trumpeted in the Ontario Welfare Fraud Report for 2001–02 as going to undeserving recipients] can be attributed to errors, mistakes, oversights of one form or another, made by applicants and by administrators and not to fraud" (Mosher et al. 2004: 51).

The complexity of the rules and the reporting requirements facing welfare recipients have also become more difficult and intrusive in the time since the *Transitions* report was released (Morrison 1995: A12–A14; Mosher et al. 2004; Sossin 2004; Herd, Mitchell, and Lightman 2005), thereby increasing the likelihood that a recipient may unintentionally commit "fraud." As Lorne Sossin (2004) noted, the social assistance bureaucracy is so complex that it leads to a process of "bureaucratic disentitlement," whereby would-be recipients are denied benefits. For instance, the previous legislation permitted a welfare recipient to receive social assistance as well as an income-based student loan in order to attend college or university. However, as Kimberly Rogers learned, a change in the regulations ensured that a full-time student doing that runs the risk of a welfare fraud conviction (Keck 2002; MacKinnon and Lacey 2001; Ontario 2009).

Far from addressing a residual concern triggered by a few "cheats" (McKeever 1999: 261–70), policies of "enhanced verification," zero-tolerance, and permanent ineligibility illustrated a significant shift in the conceptualization of welfare. Along with ever more intrusive measures to ensure recipients' eligibility (Little 2001; Mosher 2014; Herd, Mitchell, and Lightman 2005), the Harris government created a snitch hotline to encourage the anonymous reporting of suspected fraud and abuse by neighbours. Rather than instilling public confidence in the social security system (Ontario 1988), these initiatives, which continue to the present day, encourage and maintain a lack of public confidence by conveying the impression that fraud was and is rampant, and that every person on welfare needs to be watched and reported on and tested.

The shift in the direction of increased surveillance and criminalization of welfare recipients — notably women on welfare — illustrates too that the coercive form of criminal law and the regulatory form of welfare law are inseparable. The Criminal Code continues to be used to prosecute welfare recipients when fraud is suspected, and even "sincere, devoted mothers" like Donna Bond find themselves at risk of prosecution and conviction. Yet for all the heightened intensity and investigation of welfare fraud, the convictions boasted by the Ontario government in its own statistics have amounted to no more than 1.36 percent of the total number of welfare recipients in the province and less than 1 percent based on statistics from the National Council of Welfare (2005).[11]

## Women, Welfare, and the "Never Deserving" Poor

Despite the contemporary shift in the prevailing mode of moral regulation, the welfare reforms of the 1990s did not mark a complete departure from past practices. On the contrary, Canadian welfare legislation and policy show important historical continuities (Abramovitz 1996; Little 1998; Mosher 2000). First, welfare policy has always been premised on the separation of the "deserving" from the "undeserving" poor. Second, the social support accorded to the deserving was, and continues to be, based on "the principle of less eligibility" — or the assumption that welfare recipients should not receive more money than the worst-paid worker in the labour force. Third, the "deserving" have always been at risk of falling into the ranks of the "undeserving." Single mothers on social assistance have been and are subjected to intrusive and "moral" surveillance of their homes, their cleanliness, their child-rearing abilities, and their personal lives (Little 1998; see also Buchanan 1995: 33, 40; Mosher and Hermer 2005: 44; Kiran and

Mirchandani 2007: 52–53; Herd, Mitchell, and Lightman 2005). Fourth, there have long been criminal prosecutions for welfare fraud (Rachert 1990; Martin 1992: 52–97; Evans and Swift 2000).

What made the 1990s different from earlier times, then, was the ideological shift from welfare liberalism to neo-liberalism (see Stenson and Watt 1999; Clarke 2000). It was a shift that, however, still required a major state presence and resources. On one hand, the state was ideologically de-centred but no less present (Denis 1995). The form of the state and its social policy shifted at the turn of the millennium; social programs designed to ameliorate or redistribute were eroded, laying bare a heightened state presence that continues to condemn and punish the poor. On the other hand, the effect of this ideological shift was a huge expansion in the category of "undeserving" poor. Virtually everyone is considered as "never deserving"; even those who do receive social assistance are viewed as temporary recipients who must demonstrate their willingness to work for welfare and who ultimately will be employed as a result of skills and experience gained through workfare and other government-subsidized programs.

Thus, lone-parent mothers who historically were more likely to be deemed "deserving" than were childless men and women are now no longer so "privileged" (Buchanan 1995; Moscovitch 1997; Little 1998; Mortenson 1999; Mosher 2000; Swift and Birmingham 2000; Bashevkin 2002; Benshalom 2008; Crookshanks 2012), as even Canadian courts have begun to acknowledge that, as in *Falkiner v Ontario* (2002: 504, para. 77), "the statistics unequivocally demonstrate that both women and single mothers are disproportionately adversely affected by the definition of spouse" in welfare law. As that case found, "Although women accounted for only 54% of those receiving social assistance and only 60% of single persons receiving social assistance, they accounted for nearly 90% whose benefits were terminated by the [new] definition of spouse" (p. 504, para. 77).

Similarly, Janet Mosher and her colleagues (2004: 56–59) found that welfare reforms have made women more vulnerable than ever to abusive men (see also NCW 2007; Brush 2011). Deep cuts to benefits increase women's dependence on material assistance from others to supplement their welfare cheques, and that assistance most often goes unreported. The expanded definition of spouse also makes it more likely that women will violate the "spouse in the house" rule. Abusive men take advantage of women's heightened vulnerability by reporting or threatening to report their current or past partners to welfare authorities, alleging fraud. As a result, women are trapped in abusive relationships. As one such woman said:

*It was all to do with welfare. I just got into an abusive relationship that I could no longer get out of because now someone could accuse me of fraud.*

*Um, it's like … if he gave me some money and we had an argument, he'd say something like, "I'm sure you didn't tell your worker that I gave you two hundred dollars the other day. You know, you could get in trouble for that."* (Cited in Mosher et al. 2004: 58)

Women face contradictory messages from "welfare-to-work" policies. Such policies simultaneously demand independence and self-sufficiency while at the same time requiring unquestioning obedience to welfare rules that preclude opportunities for long-term advancement (Crookshanks 2012; see also Gazso and Waldron 2009).

The contemporary expansion of the "undeserving poor" has required a massive redeployment but, arguably, not a reduction in the allocation of state resources to welfare. The downsizing of social assistance payments is accompanied by a concomitant increase in state-subsidized make-work and workfare programs that will ostensibly return participants to the labour force. There has also been a dramatic increase in the state-implemented technologies and programs aimed at ferreting out and punishing the "undeserving" poor (Mosher 2000; Swift and Birmingham 2000; Mosher et al. 2004; Savarese and Morton 2005; Gustafson 2009). For instance, the Harris Tories' lifetime ban following a conviction for welfare fraud ensured both a lifetime of (secondary) punishment (without parole) and unameliorated poverty.

The past and the present contexts in which welfare and welfare fraud are being framed, then, show important differences. We have witnessed a profound attack on the "social" — indeed, the erosion of social responsibility — and the "authoritarian" neo-liberal state is a key player in this attack. Despite the apparent transcendence of social relations and state forms (in favour of dispersed pluralities of power), moral regulation must be understood in relation to state and social policy.

## Moral Regulation Revisited

The increased emphasis on welfare and welfare fraud is tightly linked to the process of state re-formation in liberal democracies. We concur with (moral regulation) scholars who argue that the success of the "new right" in Ontario and elsewhere cannot be reduced to economics and globalization. Rather, restructuring and the decline of the "social" must be understood in the context of a vast cultural offensive to transform society [in which] the ability to wield state power is essential.... Far from losing its sovereignty, the state reasserts its power over the lives of citizens.... It turns itself into the "authoritarian state," one of whose main characteristics is to usher in a new, more intense regime of moral regulation. (Denis 1995: 373; see also Hall 1988)

Again, as Hall (1980: 7) argued, the "legislation of consent" was shot through with contradictory tendencies, which made the "unity" of the various statutes involved "a necessarily complex one." Those contradictory tendencies are apparent in the welfare reform in Ontario and elsewhere during the 1980s and 1990s, a reform that restructured the relation between the two modes of moral regulation — self-regulation and compulsion. Specifically, the welfare reforms show a "double taxonomy" in the movement toward both expanded privatization and increased regulation. For one thing, they show the intensified individualization of poverty through the emphasis on personal responsibility, the imposition of self-reliance, and the relegation of former welfare recipients to the market (see also Cossman 2002; Benshalom 2008). The slight and grudging acknowledgement of social responsibility for the poor that marked the Keynesian state was rescinded. Now, as in the nineteenth century, poverty is a problem of individuals in civil society, and the solution to poverty is an individualized matter to be found principally in the labour market and/or marriage.[12]

This intensified individualization of poverty has major implications for lone-parent women. Historically, the "deserving" mother on welfare may have been "hapless" (Evans and Swift 2000) and "pitied, but not entitled" (Gordon 1994), but she was also a public servant of sorts so long as she was considered to be (morally) fit. The entry of both married and single women into the labour market altered the prevalent norm about the legitimacy of women's unemployment. After the welfare reforms of the 1990s, the necessity of the functions performed by mothers and housewives was no longer considered a reason for women to fail to attain economic self-sufficiency (Benshalom 2008). During the 1990s, Ontario and other governments began divesting themselves of public servants, including "welfare moms," and placed the emphasis on creating choices to work and become self-sufficient. Now work is strictly confined to the (private) market, and mother work no longer receives even the tacit recognition that it was accorded by Keynesian states. The promotion of individual responsibility and self-reliance and the equation of work with paid, private-sector employment are very clear in the statement of key principles underpinning Ontario's reformed welfare system: "Doing nothing on welfare is no longer an option.... Participation [in Ontario Works] is mandatory for all able-bodied people, including sole-support parents with school-aged children" (Ontario 2000b; see also Lalonde 1997).

Defining work as paid employment means that women who do unpaid work can no longer be dependent on the state, but they can work for welfare or be dependent on an individually responsible, self-reliant, employed spouse. The Harris government underscored this point by refining and expanding the "spouse in the house" rule on the ground that "no one deserves higher benefits just because they are not married."[13] In the decade or more after Mike Harris left power, the Liberal government refused to narrow the definition of spouse that was legislated by the previous government. Thus, while "welfare dependency" became a form of personality disorder signifying inadequacy, and was "diagnosed more frequently in females" (Fraser and Gordon 1994: 326), the "approved" alternative, or perhaps supplement, to the market for lone-parent women is marriage and the family (Murray 1990). As Segal points out: "This is why single mothers can be demonized if they *don't* work, even while married women with young children can be demonized if they *do*" (Segal 1999: 206). The "spouse in the house" rule also implicitly suggests that if a mother appears to be partnered with a male outside of legal marriage, she is not perceived as conforming with the moral code of the mother as caretaker (Gazso 2012).

Concomitant with the emphasis on an intensified individualization of poverty is the intensified state regulation and surveillance of dwindling numbers of public welfare recipients, now redefined as individuals who need "temporary financial assistance ... while they satisfy obligations to becoming and staying employed" (Ontario Works Act 1997, s. 1). Since welfare "is temporary, not permanent," according to the Ontario Works Act (s. 1), the state must ensure that public money is not being wasted on "fraudsters." The Ontario legislation invokes the neo-liberal language of self-reliance through employment, temporary financial assistance, efficient delivery, and accountability to taxpayers.[14] While pouring extensive resources into the establishment of an elaborate and constantly expanding system of surveillance aimed at detecting and preventing fraud and misuse of the social assistance system, and concomitant with massive cuts to welfare rates, the government allocated considerable money for special staff with expanded powers to investigate welfare fraud: three hundred such investigators were hired in 1998–99 and the government later provided "additional funding for up to 100 more staff to do this work" (Ontario 2000b). Similarly, government resources were needed to create and maintain the Welfare Fraud Hotline and a province-wide Welfare Fraud Control Database, to implement biometric finger-scanning (Little 2001: 26) and to prosecute alleged "fraudsters." Clearly, the state will spend considerable public money to police welfare recipients — but not to provide for them.

If we move beyond what government authorities themselves say, it becomes evident that the moralization and criminalization of the poor in general and "welfare moms" in particular are far from seamless. Contradictions are evident both among those who apply welfare law and policy and among those who are the targets of moralization. Judicial decision-making, for instance, is not uniformly punitive in cases involving mothers charged with welfare fraud. Some criminal cases in which women were convicted of welfare fraud for "spouse in the house," and hence of not living as a single person, do illustrate the neo-liberal ideological shift from bad mothers to bad choices (see *R v Plemel* 1995; *R v Jantunen* 1994; *R v Slaght* 1995; and *R v Sim* 1980)

But not every woman charged with welfare fraud is convicted, or if convicted, sent to jail. Some judges go to lengths to ensure this. Donna Bond received a conditional discharge, fifty hours of community service, and six months' probation, all of which left her without a criminal record upon successful completion of the conditions.[15] In another Ontario case, Trainor J. refused to convict a battered woman for welfare fraud (*R v Lalonde* 1995; see also Carruthers 1995). Finally, the coroner's jury at the inquest into the house-arrest death of Kimberly Rogers made fourteen recommendations aimed at eliminating or softening the harsh welfare reforms that were implemented in Ontario during the 1990s.[16]

Recent case law suggests that some judges continue to be sympathetic to some individuals who are charged with welfare fraud. In *R v Wilson* (2005), Michelle Wilson received a conditional discharge and eighteen months' probation after she was charged with welfare fraud. Wilson had falsely reported that she was living with her parents and had also not disclosed the existence of student loans. Wilson was a single mother who had been able to obtain two Bachelor of Arts degrees and was working toward a Master's degree. Conditional discharges have been given to those who used welfare money to improve their current situation or if a conviction would undermine a person's current situation (*R v Ahmed* 2005; *R v Bjorn* 2004). Those who engage in blatantly fraudulent behaviour or who have used the welfare funds solely to augment their financial status usually face incarceration (*R v Collins* 2011; *R v McCloy* 2008; *R v Allan* 2008). In a similar trend in the United States, among persons charged with welfare fraud those who succeed in becoming independent of state assistance are praised by judges and receive more lenient sentences (Kimmel 2007).

Accounts of "welfare mothers" also reveal diversity in practices among financial aid and front-line workers (Mortenson 1999). Some workers are empathetic and supportive; in *Lalonde*, for instance, welfare authorities had acquiesced to the man's presence in the home and only charged the woman after her partner "self-reported" his presence (*R v Lalonde* 1995). Others are punitive and controlling of their "clients" (Little 2001; Mosher et al. 2004; Powers 2005). Likewise, the poor, including "welfare mothers," are far from constituting a homogeneous category (Swift and Birmingham 2000; see also Gavigan 1999: 213–18). While welfare recipients arguably have a common class position, the ways in which they acquire that class position are diverse and mediated by other social relations of gender, race, sexual orientation, and ability or disability that in turn influence how and the extent to which mothers on welfare, for instance, are active agents in shaping these relations.

In 2006 the overall poverty rate in Canada was 11 percent; for racialized persons the poverty rate was 22 percent (NCW 2006). With regard to labour-market participation, racialized Ontarians are far more likely to live in poverty, to face workplace barriers, and, when they have found employment, to earn less than the rest of Ontarians (Block 2010: 3). Furthermore, the disparate experiences of different racialized groups and poverty are missing in both academic literature and society at large (Gazso and Waldron 2009; Quadagno 2000). Indeed, the ways in which race and ethnicity influence a person's susceptibility to, and experience of, poverty call for examination — with a need also to question how factors such as race influence attitudes toward redistributive policies such as welfare. For example, research suggests that support for redistribution is lower when recipients are portrayed as Aboriginals (Harell, Soroka, and Ladner 2013).

Many women live in constant fear of scrutiny that may result in the loss of welfare assistance for not reporting income, having partners stay overnight, or being reported for child abuse and losing their children (Mortenson 1999: 122–23; Little 1998, 2001; *Falkiner v Ontario* 2002: 515, paras. 103, 104). As a result, they engage in continual "self-censorship" of their activities (Little 1998: 180). Others resist or challenge welfare law and policy through the establishment of and participation in informal support networks of "welfare moms" and/or anti-poverty agencies and organizations

(Buchanan 1995; Little 1998; Mortenson 1999). A significant component of neo-liberal welfare reform in Ontario was the overhauling of the social assistance administrative regime. Since the late 1990s, the social assistance administrative regime has been heavily, often intrusively, involved in the day-to-day lives of welfare recipients. The experience of welfare in Ontario is described by welfare recipients as dehumanizing, degrading, and demoralizing (Herd, Mitchell, and Lightman 2005: 73).

Interview studies also reveal ideological contradictions among "welfare mothers." A few espouse the social Darwinism of neo-liberal law and policy. They see themselves as short-term, "deserving" welfare recipients who through workfare programs and/or their own hard work will become "contributing" members of society again (Mortenson 1999; see also Seccombe, James, and Walters 1998). Some also feel resentful of and more "deserving" than other mothers on welfare, who they believe are "faring better in the distribution of scarce resources, including jobs" (Swift and Birmingham 2000: 94–95). In contrast, others strongly reject the neo-liberal thrust of welfare legislation and policy, equating workfare programs and the rationales for them as government propaganda. One woman interviewed by Melanie Mortenson said she went to a workplace orientation and found that "it was unbelievably stupid." She added: "You have to be gung ho about making nothing and not getting any benefits or security, is basically what they're telling you in so many words.... It's a cheap labour strategy" (cited in Mortenson 1999: 66).

The regulation/deregulation contradiction in the area of welfare legislation and policy reforms aimed at the poor should also be viewed in the context of government actions related to the welfare of the affluent and the regulation of capital. Increased criminalization and punishment of welfare fraud have occurred simultaneously with the deregulation and "disappearance" of corporate crime (Snider 1999; see also Pearce and Tombs 1998: 567–75; Tombs 2002; Glasbeek 2002). Massive welfare cuts targeting poor people are implemented at the same time as huge corporate tax cuts, which, together with direct fiscal subsidies, arguably are forms of social welfare for the rich (see, for example, Young 2000; Abramovitz 2001; Klein and Long 2003). The deregulation and de facto decriminalization of corporate wrongdoing benefit a minority of (primarily) affluent white men, while the criminalization of poverty and the intensified prosecution of welfare fraud punish the poor disproportionately (see Beckett and Western 2001).

As Laureen Snider (2006: 205) points out, the disappearance of corporate crime does matter:

Abandoning state sanctions has far-reaching symbolic and practical consequences. State laws are public statements that convey important public messages about the obligations of the employer classes.... The situation is paradoxical indeed: while crimes of the powerful were never effectively sanctioned by state law, such laws are nonetheless essential to the operation of democratic societies.

The concomitant deregulation of corporate crime and increased punitiveness toward welfare fraud (and "street crime" more generally) suggest that in an authoritarian form of liberal-democratic state, government interventionism is redirected, not eliminated (Denis 1995: 368; see also Hall 1988). State withdrawal from Keynesian social programs and the economy occurs in tandem with government activism around issues such as youth crime and "terrorism" (Denis 1995: 369; see also Hermer and Mosher 2002). This shift in the focus of state interventionism has important implications for the regulation of the poor, and in particular, of lone-parent women.

## "A Bad Time to Be Poor"

The reformed mode of moral regulation in Canada and elsewhere during the late twentieth century typified the reformed relationship between public and private under neo-liberalism. In Keynesian states a prevailing ideology of welfare liberalism provided a rationale for at least limited (public) state intervention to assist the "deserving" poor. In "authoritarian" neo-liberal states, a discursive shift to an emphasis on formal equality (sameness) has informed a new rationale for valorizing the (private) market as the only solution to poverty. As a result, to protect the public purse anyone who asks for state assistance must be scrutinized carefully, and welfare can only be a stopgap measure prior to the recipients' entry into paid employment. Therefore, while non-state practices play a role in moral regulation, the state clearly continues to be a major player as well.

The ideological and discursive shifts from welfare liberalism to neo-liberalism have also had a drastic material impact. They have exacerbated the poverty of all welfare recipients, but particularly lone-parent women who historically were among the most "deserving." In some contemporary moral regulation scholarship, "poverty" is a discursive construct displacing the class analysis that characterized the Marxian-informed literature of the early 1980s (Corrigan and Sayer 1981, 1985; Hall 1980). Our analysis of the shift from welfare fraud to welfare *as* fraud supports those who continue to argue for the interconnectedness of the material, social, and cultural and the need to look at the political and economic issues of redistribution as well as identity/self-formation (Fraser 1997; see also Roberts 1997; Segal 1999).

In the first decade of the twenty-first century, welfare law and policy shifted again, away from the excesses of the 1990s toward arguably more "humane" treatment of the poor. The moral regulation of the poor under neo-liberalism is not uniformly oppressive: courts sometimes refuse to convict, and some welfare workers are empathetic. In the decade following the neo-liberal welfare reforms, some governments even proclaimed a "kinder, gentler" approach to the poor. Following the election of the Ontario Liberals in 2003, for instance, Sandra Pupatello, the new minister of community and social services, said that the Harris Tories had treated people on welfare as "a typical punching bag," and she expressed the new government's commitment to a "series of reforms" so that "the system actually works for people."[17] The Liberal government subsequently eliminated the lifetime ban, increased welfare rates by 3 percent, and implemented several of the forty-nine recommendations contained in a government-commissioned report on ways of improving the province's welfare system (Matthews 2004).

After 2003, under a Liberal government, social assistance rates rose by 15 percent (Ontario 2013). However, these welcome changes did not substantially ameliorate the effects of the harsh welfare reforms of the late 1990s and early 2000s. The new Ontario government failed to heed calls for meaningful policy change to social assistance and obfuscated the severity and existence of gender and economic inequality (Coulter 2009).

Following the Liberal party's re-election in 2011, a commission was struck to investigate the social assistance system in Ontario. In 2012 the Commission for the Review of Social Assistance released its report, *Brighter Prospects: Transforming Social Assistance in Ontario*, recommending that the bureaucratic structure be simplified. Specifically, it recommended the elimination of half the rules and directives in the system (Ontario 2012: 17). The Commission also called for changes to the definition of spouse, stating that the spousal relationship definition should be altered to include two people who have lived together for at least one year (and not three months) (Ontario 2012: 22). By 2014, the Liberal government had failed to heed these two recommendations, which, if put into action, would enable women who need social assistance to navigate the system without unnecessary stress or indignity.

In the 2013 budget the Liberal government introduced a number of changes to social assistance, which it said were made to remove barriers and increase opportunities for workplace participation (Ontario 2013).

Some of the changes would be beneficial for recipients of Ontario Works and the Ontario Disability Support Program (ODSP). Recipients would be able to keep the first $200 of employment earnings each month before their social assistance benefits were reduced (Ontario 2013). However, the 2013 Ontario budget changes were insufficient to address the severity of the problems that continue to plague welfare recipients (Income Security Advocacy Centre 2013 ).

Despite attempts to improve the state of the social assistance regime — and although the Matthews Report (Matthews 2004) incorporated the views of some low-income people and their advocates[18] — the Liberals did not follow up immediately with measures that would fundamentally alter the legacy of the Harris Tories. While the Liberal government was much less focused on criminalizing welfare than was its predecessor in power, it did not make changes that would improve a welfare scheme that consistently fails those who need it. The new mode of moral regulation exemplified by the conceptualization of welfare *as* fraud remains in place. Early on, the Liberal government stated its commitment to "no tolerance" for welfare fraud (see Galloway 2004: A9).

Likewise, the Liberal government retained the conviction of successive governments that "employment provides an escape out of poverty," an especially problematic assertion "in the context of a labour market that is characterized by precarious, low-waged work" (Income Security Advocacy Centre 2005: 6). The "Great Recession" of 2008 further intensified pre-existing labour market problems with regard to employment prospects for welfare recipients. There have been less employment prospects for *all* Canadians. In times of declining economic growth, as there is less economic surplus to be distributed and lower levels of well-being, there is an increased risk that families at the lower end of the income distribution will fall into poverty (Quadagno 2000). The assertion that "employment provides an escape out of poverty" is also questionable given that additional factors such as gender or race can act as barriers to employment. For example, systemic discrimination in our society and institutions creates barriers of access, limited mobility, and disproportionate concentrations of racialized labour in part-time and temporary employment (Pruegger, Cook, and Richter-Salomons 2009).

The overweening focus on paid employment militates against any significant increase in what the Liberal government has acknowledged are "unacceptably low" rates of assistance (Income Security Advocacy Centre 2005: 8). In 2013 Minister of Community and Social Services

Ted McMeekin stated at a community consultation: "If it were up to me, I would raise social assistance rates by a lot more than $100. But it's not up to me" (Addison-Webster 2013). The benefits are so low that those on social assistance live below the poverty line "in a constant state of economic precariousness" (Income Security Advocacy Centre 2008). It is still "a bad time to be poor" (Klein and Long 2003), especially for the many lone-parent women and their children who have been relegated to the ranks of the "never-deserving."

## Notes

This chapter is a revised, edited version of Chunn and Gavigan 2004. We are indebted to and acknowledge with thanks Elizabeth Mullock (Osgoode JD 2013) for her excellent research assistance for the revisions. We also thank Elizabeth Comack, Gillian Balfour, and Steve Bittle for their comments, and Laura Lunansky and Yui Funayama for research assistance, on the earlier version of this chapter.

1. General Welfare Assistance Act, R.S.O. 1990, c. G.6, as rep. by Social Assistance Reform Act, 1997, S.O. 1997, c. 25 enacting Ontario Works Act, 1997, S.O. 1997, c. 25, s. 1 [OWA] and Ontario Disability Support Program Act, 1997, S.O. c. 25, s. 2 [ODSPA]. The purpose of the Ontario Works legislation is to establish a program that, as expressed in s. 1:
    (a) recognizes individual responsibility and promotes self-reliance through employ-ment;
    (b) provides temporary financial assistance to those most in need while they satisfy obligations to become and stay employed;
    (c) effectively serves people needing assistance; and
    (d) is accountable to the taxpayers of Ontario.

2. Ontario Works Act, 1997, O.Reg. 134/98, Reg. 33.

3. See Hermer and Mosher 2002 for commentary on Ontario's Safe Streets Act 1999, S.O. 1999, c. 8. This legislation renders illegal the street activity of "squeegee kids" and panhandlers.

4. Welfare recipients were then required to report annually on their circumstances, in order to ascertain continued eligibility for assistance. In Ontario financial eligibility is now "reverified" on at least an annual basis, and ongoing "verification" and reporting requirements have intensified. A recipient is obliged to self-report any change in circumstances immediately.

5. Ontario Works Act, 1997, O.Reg. 134/98, Reg. 9 (a) and (b), provide that no single person who is in full-time attendance at a post-secondary educational institution is eligible for assistance if the person is in receipt of a student loan or is ineligible for a student loan because of parental income.

6. The permanent ineligibility sections of the Regulations were repealed by O. Reg 456/03 made under the Ontario Works Act, 1997.

7. For a political economy approach to these issues, see Fudge and Cossman 2002.

8. The racist dimensions of welfare law should be emphasized. Historically, welfare legislation excluded (implicitly or explicitly) lone-parent, racialized, and ethnic minority women. More recently, they have been disproportionately represented among the "undeserving" poor (see Roberts 1997; Chunn and Gavigan 2005).

9. See *Masse v Ontario* (1996); *Rogers v Sudbury* (2001); *Broomer v Ontario* (2002).

10. Ontario Progressive Conservative government policy statement, Jan. 18, 2000, Ontario PC News and Headlines (mikeharrispc.com).

11. The statistics available from the Ontario Ministry of Community, Family and Children's Services reveal a steady decline in criminal convictions for welfare fraud: 1,123 in 1997–98; 747 in 1998–99; 547 in 1999–00; and 393 in 2001–02 (Ontario 1999, 2000a, 2000b, 2002, 2003: Table 1). With respect to the zero-tolerance lifetime ban, the Income Security Advocacy Centre reported that a total of 106 individuals became permanently ineligible to receive financial assistance due to welfare fraud offences committed between April 1, 2000 (when the ban took effect) and November 27, 2002 <www.incomesecurity.org>. See also Mirchandani and Chan (2007: 32), who note that there is a lack of reliable statistics both federally and provincially on the actual rates of welfare fraud.

12. This is illustrated clearly by the repeal of the General Welfare Act in Ontario, and the introduction in its place of Ontario Works legislation.

13. The Ontario Court of Appeal struck down this expanded definition of spouse for "its differential treatment of sole support mothers on the combined grounds of sex, marital status and receipt of social assistance, which discriminates against them contrary to s. 15 of the Charter" (Falkiner v Ontario [2002]: 515 para. 105). Significantly, a person is deemed to be a spouse after three months' cohabitation; this is a much shorter time period of cohabitation (about two years and nine months shorter) than is required under Ontario's provincial family law legislation before spousal support obligations and entitlements are triggered.

14. See Ontario Works Act, 1997, s. 1 (a), (b), (c) and (d).

15. Sentencing took place on Sept. 19, 1994. R v Bond (1994) certificate of conviction (on file with the authors).

16. See "Verdict of Coroner's Jury into the Death of Kimberly Ann Rogers," released on Dec. 19, 2002. The coroner's inquest, which lasted two months, involved eight parties with standing, all represented by counsel, and forty-one witnesses. The jury heard that of the five thousand or so welfare recipients in Kimberly Rogers's home community of Sudbury, there were at most one or two convictions for welfare fraud annually. Evidence before the jury showed that "the Crown and the Courts were unaware that upon conviction the accused would be subject to a suspension of benefits." Recommendation 14 called for ongoing professional training of criminal justice personnel in this regard. The fourteen recommendations form part of a letter dated Jan. 17, 2003, sent by the presiding coroner, Dr. David S. Eden, to the chief coroner of Ontario (on file with the authors).

17. Ontario, Legislative Assembly, First Session, 38th Parliament, Official Debates (Hansard), no. 17A Wednesday Dec. 17, 2003, at 868.

18. Significantly, Aboriginal Peoples were not consulted about their social-service needs (Income Security Advocacy Centre 2005: 8).

8

# The Paradox of Visibility
## Women, CCTV, and Crime

*Amanda Glasbeek & Emily van der Meulen*

We live in a "maximum surveillance society" — so it is said (Norris and Armstrong 1999) — in which "virtually all significant social, institutional, or business activities ... now involve the systemic monitoring, gathering, and analysis of information in order to make decisions, minimize risk, sort populations, and exercise power" (Gilliom and Monahan 2013: 2). As surveillance becomes increasingly sophisticated, and as the reach of surveillance extends further into the fabric of our everyday lives, so too has a rich literature developed alongside it. Defined as the "dominant organizing practice of late modernity" (Haggerty 2009: ix), surveillance, or the ability to both see and know — that is, to engage in "social sorting" (Lyon 2003) — is now understood by social scientists to be key to neo-liberal governance (Haggerty and Samatas 2010; Doyle, Lippert, and Lyon 2012; Lyon 2007, 2006; Hier and Greenberg 2009).

While surveillance can take many forms, including dataveillance, border control, monitoring of health records and welfare administration, traffic logics, and more, our focus here is on camera or video surveillance in public space. Video surveillance technologies, and especially closed circuit television cameras (CCTV),[1] have become an increasingly normalized and ubiquitous aspect of the urban landscape, whether they are deployed by state functionaries (such as the police), by the owners of mass private property (such as shopping malls), or by local merchants and business improvement associations (Hier 2010). As Clive Norris (2012: 29) notes:

> Public space CCTV is now a truly global phenomenon. In less than two decades it has expanded from a local initiative in a few small towns in the U.K. to become the international crime prevention "success" story of the new millennium, set to penetrate every major city, in every country, on every continent. Like electricity, it appears that video surveillance will become a central part of the global urban infrastructure across the planet.

The proliferation and popularity of CCTV rest on a logic of crime prevention assuming that criminal activity is deterred by virtue of being seen. In addition to supposedly preventing crime, CCTV also offers the "seductive" promise of acting as a "perfect witness" should a crime occur (Norris 2012). Through these broad goals, and in the context of heightened public anxieties about crime, CCTV is intended to make people *feel* more secure in their everyday lives. In other words, the "legitimating rhetoric" (Lett, Hier, and Walby 2012) of CCTV is that areas monitored by camera or video surveillance are safer spaces.

Given these logics, it is surprising that CCTV has not been systematically analyzed through a feminist lens. As a policing technology intended to address fear of crime, CCTV might well be thought to be specifically relevant for women, who report higher levels of fear of crime than do men, and who are more likely than men are to modify their behaviours in light of such fears. For example, the 2008 Canadian General Social Survey records that while women and men tend to believe that crime is increasing in their neighbourhood in roughly equal proportions (34 percent and 32 percent, respectively) they do not have the same relationship to that perception of crime. Nearly one in four women (24 percent) reports feeling somewhat or very unsafe walking alone in her neighbourhood after dark, compared to only 7 percent of men. Accordingly, nearly 60 percent of women, compared to 34 percent of men, plan their daily activities with safety in mind. Perhaps most startlingly, this gendered fear of crime means that while only 3 percent of men report that they would stay at home at night because they are afraid to go out alone after dark, a full 17 percent — or nearly one in five women — do engage in this kind of avoidance strategy as a direct result of their fear of becoming a victim of crime (Brennan 2011). In other words, fear of crime acts as a form of social control for women, who in order to minimize their risk of victimization do not exercise their full citizenship rights of mobility and public participation (Caiazza 2005; Pain 2001; Valentine 1989). In light of these general trends, one might reasonably assume that women would be considered a key source of information about both the implications of being watched as well as about how best to create safer cities. To date, however, little work has been done to elicit women's relationship to the monitoring and policing work of urban surveillance.

Here we seek to address this gap by returning women to the analysis – by placing their concerns about crime, crime prevention, and urban surveillance at the very centre of the issue. Drawing on a small but encouraging body of feminist literature on urban surveillance and its significance as a policing mechanism, combined with empirical data from a pilot study carried out in 2011 and 2013 with women in Toronto, we set out to explore women's relationships to and experiences with CCTV in public space. In particular we consider their fears of becoming victims of crime and CCTV's impact as a policing and, sometimes, criminalizing technology. What this study reveals is that CCTV, measured against its claims of deterrence and evidence-production, not only fails to make women feel safer but also contributes to the unequal social relations that produce women's feelings of insecurity in the first place. Indeed, the ways in which women spoke about CCTV as an "embodying" technology (Ball 2006: 312) challenge many assumptions about what surveillance does as a regulatory or policing mechanism.

This gendered analysis of the day-to-day effects of CCTV on women's relationship to crime and public safety significantly alters how we see sur-veillance as a crime-prevention technology. The reasons for CCTV's failure as a solution to issues of urban safety are gender-specific and have not been fully discussed in the literature. At its core CCTV does not offer itself as a solution to the problems that women identify as their priority. At the same time women are disciplined by, and sometimes even criminalized by, CCTV, leaving them more vulnerable, more subject to policing, and, ultimately, less safe.

## CCTV: A Disciplinary Overview

The promise of CCTV is two-fold. Installing cameras in different urban spaces — from malls to sidewalks to public transit to convenience stores and beyond — is meant to be a tool of crime management by virtue of deter-rence or quick detection. Consequently, cameras are heralded for enhancing citizens' sense of safety more generally. CCTV's popularity tends to spike, and the presence of cameras tends to proliferate, in the immediate aftermath of traumatic criminal events (Hier 2010). Yet, despite these promises, and a few select success stories that are sensationalized in the media and by police (Norris 2012), empirical studies of the effectiveness of CCTV demonstrate that the technology is not effective at either deterring or resolving crime (Welsh and Farrington 2003; 2007). Grounded empirical studies of CCTV's limited crime-prevention abilities, however, have done little to stem its rapid expansion. This seeming paradox has led social scientists to ask what it is that CCTV does do.

Early analyses of CCTV suggested that it acted as a modern-day equiva-lent of the Panopticon, the architectural prison design imagined by Jeremy Bentham in the seventeenth century and used as the central metaphor for discipline in Michel Foucault's *Discipline and Punish* (which, in the original French, was entitled *Surveiller et punir*). According to Foucault (1977), the Panopticon operated as a central technology of power through which the watched learned to discipline themselves because they were always subject to the gaze, although they could not see their watchers or verify that they were being watched in any given moment. Foucault's key insight on the Panopticon was that it functioned in such a way as to make the inmates themselves the bearers of the power relations being exercised through surveillance. Certainly, in their one-way vision (the watchers can see us, but we cannot see the watchers), the unverifiability of the gaze (we never know if and when we are being watched), the anonymity of the gaze (we do not know who is watching), and the privileging of the visual image of conformity over other forms of discipline, urban surveillance cameras seem to replicate many of Foucault's central insights on the powers of the surveillant gaze (Koskela 2002a).

Yet many scholars have either abandoned the Panopticon metaphor or are cautious about overextending its relevance for urban surveillance cameras (Haggerty 2006; Haggerty and Ericson 2000; Mathiesen 1997). Cities and prisons do have important differences: in cities, a person is not confined and isolated or compelled to be there. To the contrary, cities are sites of unpredictable mobility and (at least in most cases) are geographic spaces used on a voluntary basis. In addition, while the prison Panopticon has a central line of authority, urban surveillance cameras are used for a variety of purposes and by a wide number of actors, most of whom are not connected and many of whom have narrow intentions (such as the convenience-store owner who wants only to minimize shoplifting). Thus, rather than being a mechanism of top-down control or discipline, CCTV is diverse and used in a range of different sites, with differing governance intentions and effects (Koskela 2002a). Finally, the panoptic model cannot capture the reality that in a maximum-surveillance society, we are all implicated in the act of surveillance, even as we are subject to it. Through the use of our own hand-held personal devices, such as smart phones, our participation in social networking, and our often enthusiastic use of programs such as loyalty cards, most of us (often willingly) submit to surveillance and are agents of surveillance in complex ways (Albrechtslund 2008; Andrejevic 2005). These considerations do not necessarily mean that all surveillance is equal or does not exist in webs of power and inequality; nor does this insight minimize the connection of surveillance to regulation, policing, and discipline. However, these factors have forced scholars to think about urban surveillance in more complex ways. As Clive Norris (2012: 38) notes, CCTV "may have all sorts of effects and utilities that are not captured by the simplistic notion of crime prevention and detection" or by the single metaphor of the Panopticon.

Instead, CCTV has been best conceptualized as a largely symbolic device that advertises an effort at crime control in the context of fear of crime in public space; simultaneously, if tacitly, it affirms particular bodies as having legitimate access to that space while others do not. Thus the rapid expansion of CCTV has been ascribed not to its technological and crime-fighting capacities per se, but to fear of crime and the endless, if paradoxical, search for "security" (Zedner 2003). This search for security is often understood by scholars as having a class (and sometimes racialized) basis: that is, the "security" on offer through the implementation of cameras that watch public spaces (or spaces where the public may reasonably expect to go or be) is a moralized and middle-class sense of "order" (Norris 2012; Coleman 2005, 2003; Coleman and Sim 2000; Fyfe and Bannister 1996). Even more specifically, CCTV in urban centres, often implemented as part of urban revitalization initiatives, works less as an encompassing panoptic vision in which all are subject to the gaze than, more particularly, to monitor "risky spaces and dangerous faces" (Hier 2004) as part of a larger project of taming urban space and enabling the policing of "suspect identities" (Norris and Armstrong 1999). In this sense, CCTV works insofar as it is harnessed to a larger neo-liberal project of transforming urban spaces from sites of heterogeneity and, therefore, risk into predictable, ordered, and homogeneous spaces of consumerism (Ruppert 2006; Huey, Ericson, and Haggerty 2005; Ruddick 1996).

Yet, despite the increasingly sophisticated theoretical, technological, and empirical analyses of urban surveillance (see, for example, Doyle, Lippert, and Lyon 2012), the issue of gender has remained a footnote. Indeed, at best, in the literature to date, women tend to appear (if they appear at all) in an ambiguous relationship to surveillance mechanisms. On the one hand, if CCTV is understood as part of the neo-liberal project of "the malling of public space" (Williams and Johnstone 2000: 192), women are most likely to appear as already-consumers and as already-anxious urban citizens and, thus, as those for whom CCTV might matter most. This kind of account places women at the wrong end of claims about the disciplining order of surveillance, and especially its role in disproportionately policing Black men, the poor, and marginalized youth. On the other hand, women are also understood to have much more direct concerns about intimate intrusions, especially bodily intrusions, and thus are potentially those with the most to fear from an unchecked gaze. This uncomfortable duality is evident in some of the literature on public perceptions of CCTV. For example, Stéphane Leman-Langlois (2009: 45) observes that "women are significantly more likely to approve of camera surveillance and to dismiss concerns of privacy loss and unnecessary surveillance and control. However, women are also more likely to raise concerns when cameras are installed in more private areas (changing rooms, toilets, etc.)." This kind of claim tends to envision women as a homogenized group, an assumption that stands in stark contrast to other literature on CCTV and urban policing, which concludes that CCTV has fracturing effects on forms of urban citizenship by specifically targeting those who do not seem to belong to the newly sanitized city (see, for example, Norris and Armstrong 1999). In addition, these assumptions reproduce "a tendency in traditional sociology to over-corporealize women" (Ball 2006: 303) while simultaneously reifying a public/private distinction in which women's bodies are imagined as markers of a boundary space between these spheres.

## Capturing Women's Experiences: The Paradox of Visibility

To the extent that we know what we do about women's relationships to CCTV, that knowledge has been derived mostly from large-scale surveys of public opinion about camera surveillance that include demographic information about gender. Generally, these surveys find little gender difference in the high acceptance rate and overall public legitimacy of CCTV (Dawson 2012; Ditton 2000; Bennet and Gelsthorpe 1996). And yet, as Danielle Dawson (2012: 285) notes:

> Surveys fail to capture the various nuances of public opinion. No matter how cleverly the questions are asked, they do little to provide answers to *why* publics hold the opinions they do. The inability to account for the varying subjective experiences which emerge in the process of engaging with camera surveillance calls for a qualitative approach to data-gathering.

Our research interest was to get at just such subjective experiences by speaking to women about their complex feelings about CCTV.

We thus turned to a mixed-method and participatory research approach called Concept Mapping (Burke et al. 2005; Trochim 1989; Kane and Trochim, 2007). Methodologically stronger than focus groups or in-depth interviews alone because of its inseparable qualitative and quantitative components, Concept Mapping allowed us to engage in a structured yet inherently participatory process whereby study participants brainstormed, organized, and prioritized their own experiences with video surveillance. The research took place over three study phases, each of which included a diversity of Toronto women (transgender women inclusive) recruited primarily from local community groups and organizations. The first phase involved five structured brainstorming sessions involving five socio-demographic groups: sex-working women; low-income women; racial-ized women: women over the age of sixty-five; and women who frequent Toronto's entertainment or club district. The women who participated in the research were all over the age of eighteen and self-identified as belong-ing to one of these groupings. Each brainstorming session hosted between nine and fourteen participants for a total of fifty-one women involved in this first phase.

In typical brainstorming fashion, the sessions revolved around a focal statement to which participants filled in the blank: "One way that video surveillance in Toronto makes me feel is...." The audio-recorded sessions were facilitated by a member of the research team and continued until a saturation of ideas and experiences was reached (typically two hours). Participant responses ranged from a single word or phrase to in-depth stories of police abuse and violence. Upon completion of the brainstorming groups, the research team reviewed the complete list of responses generated across all groups and compiled them into a discrete set of unique statements for use in phases two and three. In these final two phases participants rated and sorted the various statements for intersectional, quantitative analysis and provided group feedback on the preliminary results (see van der Meulen and Glasbeek 2013).

To help situate participants' responses, we turned to some of the few scholarly analyses of CCTV to focus explicitly on women. Hille Koskela (2000, 2002b) has argued that because video surveillance is most often controlled by men it tends to deploy and extend a masculine gaze, which can be experienced by women as a form of voyeurism or an "electronic Peeping Tom." This insight was substantiated in our brainstorming ses-sions with Toronto women. Many of them similarly identified cameras as "creepy" and intrusive:

> Like, I am thinking maybe there is a man watching — they have a ten-dency, like, women's bodies. Private parts. You know what I mean? [It makes me] uneasy and uncomfortable.

*Exactly which bodies are in charge of surveillance cameras? What exactly is their agenda?... And exactly how is that going to then affect [different] types of people, of women?... [It makes me feel] paranoid. Worried. Especially I think as a person of colour and a woman, it would just make me feel paranoid and scared.*

Given arguments that cameras make spaces safer, such anxieties are significant. As Sheila Browne (1998: 218) has also argued, "More men sitting in front of cameras adds visibility. It does not necessarily add security." Koskela (2000) notes that the masculine qualities of video surveillance tend to produce contradictory emotional relationships in women: they feel both safe and insecure. In other words, for women, video surveillance engenders a "paradox of visibility" — a term borrowed and adapted from Helen Jones (2006), who examines the nexus of human rights, surveillance, and privacy in Afghanistan. She conceptualizes women's efforts to subvert patriarchal violence and oppression, such as through wearing the burka, as an example of the "paradox of ... women's *invisibility* in the face of systemic surveillance and abuse" (p. 506; emphasis added). Drawing from our own data, we adapt this concept to argue that there exists a paradox of *visibility* for women in Toronto. Specifically, the male gaze of cameras designed to make spaces safer also serves to "reproduce and reinforce male power" (Koskela 2000: 256), the very thing that makes women fearful of public space in the first place. This is a paradox that women navigate in multiple ways.

## Women, Crime, and Victimization: The Failure of CCTV

Perhaps the most obvious place to begin an inquiry into the relationship between gender and surveillance is in the realm of violence against women. As Corrine Mason and Shoshana Magnet (2012: 106) argue, "Placing violence against women at the centre of [the] analysis [works to] complicate concerns related to surveillance technologies." Our brainstorming sessions with Toronto women made it clear that sexual violence is what concerns women most, that they do want to feel safe from violence, and that they would welcome cameras if the instruments performed this function. In itself, this conclusion goes a long way toward explaining why, when asked to complete the statement "one way video surveillance makes me feel is ...," many participants initially answered by saying that cameras make them feel "safe." When we asked for clarification on what they meant by "safe," the conversation frequently came around to a discussion of sexual assault and violence. The following conversation from our brainstorming session with racialized women offers but one example of this common concern:

> Facilitator: *Okay. So sometimes [*CCTV*] can be good and important. Can someone help me then —what are we thinking of here? Anyone?*
> Participant 1: *I think — I don't know. Like, sexual assault and stuff. Like, catching people.*
> Participant 2: *Yeah, like that. Especially for sex workers and vulnerable women, I think it can be good. To protect us in that way.*
> Participant 1: *And catch rapes or, you know, any sort of acts of violence against women and girls.*

It was also clear from our sessions that women wanted cameras to work in this fashion. Accordingly, the potential role of CCTV as an initiative in the effort to address violence against women was more important to the participants than its usual justifications in national security or sanitized consumerism, as the following excerpts demonstrate:

> *I feel like surveillancing is important especially for things like sexual assault and things like that, but for some reason I don't understand why they are in stores or why they are in the airport…. Why do you need it in the airport? I don't know.*

> *It's kind of weird sometimes when you go to a grocery store … where people go with their families to buy groceries. What's the purpose of putting them in grocery stores? It's supposed to be a pleasant experience and then you look up and there's that huge dome. They are in every single aisle.*

These types of imaginings differ markedly from how CCTV is usually talked about, by both surveillance practitioners and scholars. In these participant quotes, we see women prioritizing a function of CCTV that is importantly different from that which is assumed in much of the literature. Rather than seeing themselves as implicated in the projects of secure consumerism or national security, these women identified themselves as outside such discourses and yearned for something notably different.

At the same time, women were not naïve about surveillance cameras: no woman expected that cameras would act as a deterrent to sexual assault, much as they might want it to. As one woman put it, "*I think it would be a beautiful, beautiful thing if video cameras could prevent women from being raped* [but] *I don't believe that they have any impact on that at all.*" While women clearly identified safety from male violence as their priority, and while many women wanted to believe that cameras could — and indeed should — play such a role, this desire co-existed with a more pragmatic understanding of cameras in their everyday lives:

> *Yeah, I just don't want to start second guessing that because then I won't — I believe, and everyone is supposed to believe, that they are there to keep us safe … I know sometimes they don't work … But that's what we're supposed to think and I hope that's true. I want to feel safe when I go out, you know? It can't always happen. Just because there is a camera doesn't mean someone is going to super-hero fly out and — [Everyone laughs]. Okay, I do hope for that.*

For the women we spoke to, deterrence was not a realistic expectation. From these women's perspectives, CCTV fails as a crime-prevention technology.

Yet this did not mean that women necessarily concluded that cameras are not helpful. Rather, women hoped that cameras could offer them protection by acting to witness instances of sexual assault, as this conversation among women who frequent the club district indicates:

> *Participant 1: I was talking about crime, too. Fights. Assaults. Rape. You know, being sexually assaulted. I feel that there are some times — we all know or hear of cases, you know, if you were sexually assaulted or raped or whatever you want to call it and there's always this — it's really hard to go through the system and actually —*
> *Participant 2: They don't take you seriously.*
> *Participant 1: Yeah. So with that extra surveillance there, I feel a little bit better than that. Did it actually happen? There's always those that say, "Oh, did the rape actually happen or did you provoke it or something?" and with that kind of surveillance around — especially in the club district. We're all dressing extra nice and there are people who are extra drunk. I do feel safer being in the club areas with surveillance around.*

As this conversation reveals, to the extent that women see cameras as helpful, it is because they know that, when it comes to reporting instances of sexual assault, women do not tend to be seen as credible in their own right. In this belief, they are not wrong. Studies show that sexual assault has a low "founding" rate: that is, reports to police of sexual assault are determined by police to be "unfounded" at a higher rate than any other reported crime (DuBois 2012). Cameras, women hope, will provide evidence that they are telling the truth about sexual assault, especially when their behaviour strays from a performance of themselves as ideal victims or of respectable femininity (because they dress "extra nice," or consume alcohol, for instance).

Thus, CCTV joins other masculine technologies (such as the Sexual Assault Evidence Kit) that act to "witness" women's stories of being assaulted and as a form of corroborative evidence of sexual assault, even though these conditions have not been an evidentiary requirement since 1976 (Feldberg 1997; Doe 2013).

It should not be surprising, then, that this narrowed conceptualization of the protective functions of CCTV — that is, as a technology that may attest to women's truthfulness in sexual-assault cases — does not work equally well for all women. Some women appear to be less credible than others. For women whose very existence challenges white, heteronormative, and middle-class definitions of femininity, who live at the economic and social margins of the normative order, and/or who experience very high rates of violence (such as sex workers and women who live much of their lives on the streets), the presence of open-street cameras tends to generate ambivalent feelings, as revealed in the remarks of one sex worker:

> The reason I said I was confused [about CCTV] was because I had ... about a year and a half ago I went into a certain laneway that has cameras, and I did it purposefully because I was under the influence of crack cocaine and ... I was getting bad vibes about this guy but I wasn't quite sure and the money was good so I thought "Why not," right? And then he essentially assaulted me and I called the police and everything and when the police come and they try to check the cameras, they weren't working.... What are the cameras there for if they are not working?

Significantly, this woman actively sought out a space where she knew there were cameras even though the camera would, or should, also be recording the criminalized activity in which she was engaging. Her acceptance of cameras and, indeed, her hopefulness about them accord with research into marginalized populations' relationships to cameras, which similarly testifies to a complexity of feelings and experiences not typically captured in broader analyses of CCTV as a technology of governance. That is, if cameras are generally understood as part of the cleansing of urban spaces and as a policing technology that broadly functions to target the homeless, the visibly poor, and others who are seen as disruptive to public order, one might reasonably expect that those same populations would understand cameras as oppressive and as something to be avoided at all costs. Yet, as Laura Huey's (2010: 64) work with homeless populations in Toronto, Vancouver, and Edinburgh found, these groups do not see CCTV only as a tool of repression. Rather, they see it as giving voice to a "significantly more complex landscape of thoughts and beliefs as to the meaning and uses of CCTV" that included its potential as something that could be used for their protection and security. In the case of the sex worker going into the laneway, the participant similarly incorporated video surveillance into her own strategy of safekeeping, even though she was well aware that she might become the target, rather than the beneficiary, of the camera's vision. In this light, it is not surprising that she was frustrated, to say the least, when she discovered that the cameras she had relied upon for her protection did not work.

The sense that cameras do not work and, perhaps even more profoundly, do not "see" what the women hope they will see, was also commonly expressed and led many women to develop a deep distrust of the equipment. This distrust had two dimensions — with the first being women found that cameras did not capture the events that they thought were significant. Generally, cameras were understood to be "myopic" (Leman-Langlois 2002) and selective, as exemplified by this woman's experience in her own housing complex:

> I live in a place [with] cameras…. We paid rent but it was a harm reduction building, so it was legal to use. It was legal to own. So we had cameras everywhere. I got assaulted and robbed and I went to the office and they told me to get out of the office. The only reason they use those cameras is selectively. To use it to find … someone they think is a drug dealer in the building.

This example also draws out the second dimension of distrust, which is that many women did not believe that the camera operators were actually interested in their safety. To the contrary, for many women, the cameras' ability to catch a perpetrator was cold comfort, at best, and had very little to do with their own well-being, as these chilling examples indicate:

> At the same time, you know, you guys can look at it — everybody can look at it differently…. If I go around the corner and I know there's a camera there and I don't come out, I want somebody to know who did it.

> Even though the cameras, you know — I guess for me the fact that they might catch some dude — I suppose it could be a woman but probably a dude who is going to try to kill me on a date — that's going to be later. That's going to be after it already happened and that after-it-already-happened kind of evidence isn't worth it to me…. The after stuff is just to make it easier for them to close their case and DNA me or whatever. It's not really about me not getting raped or killed.

Distrust, distance, and a profound sense of a disconnection between themselves and the architects of camera security permeate these accounts. As a crime prevention and detection device, CCTV falls short, at best, and indeed, fails miserably for most women who are primarily concerned with their sexual and bodily integrity in public spaces.

## CCTV, Criminalization, and Policing

Visibility, however myopic that vision, is not just a problem for women in terms of their efforts to stay safe from (predominantly) male violence. Cameras also function to render women's indiscretions, including criminality, visible. Some of the women we spoke to were engaged in criminal activities, which, not surprisingly, also structured their experiences of CCTV. One woman, for example, told us of how cameras had been used to catch her after she had shoplifted from a grocery store:

*Another time when my son was a baby ... in the [grocery] store. I was going in there and a guy stopped me and said, "Do you mind coming upstairs" and I go upstairs in the office and they have, like, five different pictures of me, like on video, of stealing. I used to stick it in the baby carriage and stuff. But they didn't catch me at the time I was doing it.... I used to steal all the time but they didn't catch me at the time so they must have been looking at them after. But they had them all there.*

One might argue that incidents like these offer evidence that cameras work as intended — that is, as a detection (although clearly not a deterrent) device aimed at specific criminal activity. Yet, even this rationale is not as straightforward as it might appear. This kind of CCTV work is profoundly gendered — and yet relatively unexplored within the surveillance literature.

Although studies of CCTV tend to imagine women as consumers — there is a general assumption that women will be supportive of CCTV, in part because it helps to secure spaces of consumerism — many of the women we spoke to clearly did not see this as a priority; and in any case women's relationship to consumption is complex. Not all women identify as consumers and, indeed, for women, theft, typically shoplifting, is the single largest crime category that brings them into conflict with the criminal justice system (Mahony 2011). Not surprisingly, then, women who do not meet normative expectations of the ideal consumer, principally because of their visible class and/or racial markers, had some of the most negative relationships to CCTV.

In a conversation with a facilitator, a low-income woman expressed her reservations about shopping in malls:

> Facilitator: [*Cameras*] *make you feel like you don't want to go out in these public places [like malls]?*
> Participant: *Why would you want to? Being watched everywhere you go. If I want to be a thief, I'll be a thief. Cameras are not — I hate it. I hate it. They are already assuming you're going to take something. Go for it.*

A racialized woman admitted:

> *There's so much humiliation and shame that I personally can't handle it. I just can't go into [retail] space [where cameras are installed] anymore. For me, there's only so much I can take. I feel like I'm a pretty assertive person but if you always enter certain spaces and they are always like, "What are you doing here?"... You know, you are not trying to help me. You just want to see if I'm going to take anything. Right?*

These angry sentiments show important differences. In the first case the participant was not opposed, in principle, to the criminal act of theft. In the second case the participant made clear that she did not, and would not, steal. Yet both women, and many others, identified cameras as a technology that "saw" them as criminal, no matter their actions, their intentions, or their personal stories. They were made to feel guilty and suspicious by virtue of being the targets of surveillance. They were being surveilled because of who they were, and yet were highly cognizant of their class and/or race precisely because they were surveilled.

Just as notably, the production of some women as suspect identities did not flow from their behaviour in public streets, although most of the critical literature on the implementation of urban surveillance has focused on their effects in such sites. Once again, a disconnection exists between how CCTV is understood as a neo-liberal policing technology and the experiences that women described in our brainstorming sessions. Although scholars of CCTV have focused on the disciplining gaze of cameras in urban spaces, analyzing them as mechanisms of class-based and racialized order maintenance that target disorder as embodied by the homeless, youth, and/or racialized populations, arguably these populations are imagined as male — that is, as homeless men, young men, and racialized men. Women do not tend to loom large as public crime figures; nor do women's bodies typically figure into public imaginings of urban disorder, unless as victims of masculine disruptions (Glasbeek 2006b). For that reason women are absent from a great deal of scholarship on urban surveillance as a policing and disciplining technology.

The notable exception to this general rule is sex work. If women are generally invisible as criminals in public crime talk, they have a heightened visibility as prostitutes: sex workers embody female public disorder (Brock 2009). Yet cameras have a limited, at best, utility as crime prevention or detection tools for sex-working women who are victims of violence. On the contrary, some sex workers identified surveillance cameras as an intervention that enhanced the dangers they face:

> *It makes our work harder. It makes us more unsafe because ... you have to find a place — people are already having to work farther and farther out and in darker and darker corners or, you know, more at risk with clients or whatever in their spaces, and so you have to find more corner-y places that don't have a camera. So, how does that make us safer?*

> *I feel like I am going to get into trouble, just when I am working and especially if I am doing in-calls because I think this stuff — like me coming and going is being recorded and I feel like it's going to be used against me somehow.*

In response, women who work in the sex trade self-consciously worked to produce themselves as "normal" so as not to attract the attention of cameras:

> *I will try to look more innocuous.... I will try to blend in and not be as noticed especially when I am working. Like, I am going to work in jeans and stuff like that. Still dressed up but not too dressed up, or otherwise I will dress really, really good and try to do... like, the Bay Street kind of look. So I look like some person who has a legitimate job.*

> *Well, I work in-call in the hotels.... And because technically it's supposed to be a higher-end hotel, I feel safer because I've been to the other extreme. But at the same time, I know when I first started I was twenty-five. I'm much older now. Back then it was ... high, high shoes and now today I go to an in-call and ... I will literally go dressed in jeans and my earphones on, because I just don't want to be, to have people looking at me.*

The efforts of these women to minimize their visibility are telling. However, such efforts to "fit in" may miss the mark.

Most women experienced the sense of being watched for specifically feminized signs of unruliness regardless of their profession, as a disciplining gaze that worked to police their broader conduct. In addition to rendering (some) women's criminality visible, CCTV has an even more pervasive, indeed pernicious, effect — namely, to police women's illicit behaviours more generally, as these examples show:

> I was doing something really bad one day [laughs]. In the club district. In an alley. I stopped myself ... I said ... "Oh my God. I don't want to end up in a magazine or a newspaper article [entitled] 'This is what your kids are doing'" and I did stop myself.

> Participant: For me, camera here [in the seniors' residence] doesn't help. Doesn't give me protection. Doesn't do anything except that I feel like a suspicious person.
> Facilitator: You feel like a suspicious person?
> Participant: They want to know what I am doing. What I drink. When I came. When I left. This isn't what I need. Camera cannot give me protection.... This is a little bit helpful for information. Not protection.

> [Cameras make me feel] watched. Slightly horrified. It actually never occurred to me that they would be in nightclubs themselves or observing us inside of nightclubs. That's usually a lot of times where you do drugs or alcohol or making out with somebody and that feels like a real invasion of privacy.

Importantly, it is not just criminality that is the focus of the camera's reach, but women's behaviours, demeanours, and mobility more generally. These contemporary experiences of urban surveillance substantiate Koskela's argument (2012: 49) that "the histories of (controlling) gender/sexualities and of surveillance are very much connected." Surveillance cameras not only dissolve the lines between illicit and illegal activities; they do so in a profoundly gendered way that has implications for women engaged in a variety of activities.

## Gender Matters

Our work with Toronto women demonstrates, above all, that gender matters to any analysis of surveillance, and especially to the ways in which CCTV does, or does not, work. In many ways CCTV offers an increasingly technologized example of a longer historical pattern whereby women's public presence has been subject to a male gaze that acts to discipline them and police the boundaries of a normative femininity (Gardner 1995). For this reason alone, CCTV should attract the attention of feminist scholars interested in how women are policed and monitored more generally. But, as our brainstorming sessions with Toronto women show, there may be more to the story. Specifically, as an increasingly ubiquitous feature of the urban landscape and a technology designed exclusively around the act of looking, CCTV poses real dilemmas for women — dilemmas that are not easily resolved. If the work of camera surveillance is to increase visibility in order to either decrease crime or, at the very least, to increase public confidence in the safety of urban spaces, then paying attention to how visibility has gendered effects is significant. While it is evident that women do want some things to be visible — and especially for sexual assault to be "seen" — it is also evident that CCTV cannot be counted on to see the things that women want it to. Indeed, for many women, seeing is *not* believing, an experience that challenges CCTV at its ontological base (Norris 2012).

If we think about CCTV as part of the urban landscape, a now-embedded part of the design of the city, and as a material and structural feature of daily urban life, we must also consider its role in shaping the ways in which women come to understand their own relationship to practices of surveillance that make broad promises of producing safety. Specifically, our study with women in Toronto offers support for the argument that women have contradictory feelings toward CCTV; that it can make women feel both safe and insecure, sometimes simultaneously, although this is not equally true for all women. Our findings also suggest that it is in the space between the fear of crime and being policed that women find that CCTV offers them untenable choices. In the end, CCTV reproduces the very conditions that make gender important. From their embodied experiences of CCTV, women offer important lessons on why CCTV fails and, just as important, on why gender matters to an analysis of urban surveillance.

## Note

1. We recognize that the term "CCTV" is becoming anachronistic, as newer technology is transforming camera surveillance from analog to digital form and, thus, is no longer closed-circuit and resembles television less and less. Nonetheless, we use the term as a recognizable shorthand for what others have also termed "open street surveillance cameras." For discussion of technological change, see Ferenbok and Clement (2012).

# 9

# Examining the "Psy-Carceral Complex" in the Death of Ashley Smith

*Jennifer M. Kilty*

Over the past two decades the governance of federal prisons for women in Canada has changed significantly with the adoption of "gender-responsive" programming (Bloom 1999). Still, despite the Correctional Service of Canada's self-lauding as "a world leader in women's corrections" (csc 2006: 4), feminist criminologists have been critical of the incorporation of this "women-centred" approach into traditional penal structures and practices that are punitive in nature. One aspect of this critique pertains to the discourses, practices, and effects of the "psy-carceral complex."

This "psy-carceral complex" operates not only via discourses of medicalization but also through the punishing embodied practices of isolation and sedation. The tragic case of Ashley Smith is a prime example of these tendencies. It showcases how therapeutic interventions can operate as instruments of punishment—and how the effects of these interventions harm rather than heal, rehabilitate, or transform criminalized women. Here, drawing on Alison Liebling's (1992, 2004, 2001) work, in which she examines the daily practices of penality as possessing a certain emotional tone that adds to the "depth and weight of imprisonment" upon the prisoner, I examine how, as in Smith's case, the moral aspects of the rhetoric of therapeutic discipline contribute to prisoner distress, suicidal ideation, and self-harm.

## The "Psy-Carceral Complex": Medicalization Discourses and Associated Practices

Medicalization is a sociological term used to describe the process of identifying, labelling, defining, and describing a condition or collection of "symptoms" in and through medical language, terms, and discourse (Conrad 2007; Conrad and Schneider 1992; Kilty 2012a; Moynihan, Heath, and Henry 2002). As Peter Conrad (2007: 5) notes, the process of medicalization — or "to make medical" — can be applied to conditions that most people would agree are "medical" issues (such as epilepsy) as well as a host of conditions and behaviours that are more controversial (alcoholism,

ADHD, menopause, or erectile dysfunction). For Conrad, "The main point in considering medicalization is that an entity that is regarded as an illness or disease is not ipso facto a medical problem; rather, it needs to become defined as one" (p. 5–6).

Early literature in the field focused on the medicalization of sexuality and the discursive efforts to remove homosexuality from the purview of theological discourses that constitute it as a sin in order to remake it as a treatable mental illness (Conrad and Schneider 1992). Similarly, feminist scholars have examined the myriad ways in which women's bodies (notably, through cosmetic surgery, pregnancy and childbirth, menstruation, and menopause) are medicalized through advancements in Western medicine, the growth of medical psychiatry, and the burgeoning field of psycho-pharmacological interventions (Ehrenreich and English 1973; Kilty 2008, 2012a; Offman and Kleinplatz 2004; Ussher 1991, 2010). In the carceral context, medicalization discourses are evident in two central practices — the overuse of prescription psychotropic medications and (typically cognitive-behavioural) therapeutic programming.

## Governing through Sedation:
## Psychotropic Medication Use as a Technology of Power

The everyday effects of medicalization are arguably most evident in the rapid market expansion of and growing reliance on the pharmaceutical industry to treat or cure all manners of symptoms (Healy 2004; Moynihan, Heath, and Henry 2002). For example, Alia Offman and Peggy Kleinplatz (2004) draw attention to the repackaging of the antidepressant Prozac as Serafem to treat Premenstrual Dysphoric Disorder in a corporate effort to maintain and expand the Prozac monopoly in the treatment of depression, itself a psychiatric diagnosis that is widely contested as a gendered construction.

Emphasizing "breakthrough medications," pharmaceutical corporations imply that a potential quick fix exists in the form of a daily pill that will solve complications that arise from the broader social ills of poverty, criminal disenfranchisement, and the structural disadvantages that flow from racial-ized, class-based, and gendered discrimination. Medicalization obscures socio-political and structural explanations of certain behaviours in favour of those that primarily root differences in the pathological individual. Just as the medical establishment "has always functioned as an agent of social control" (Conrad and Schneider 1992: 34), the correctional system has long embraced the medical model's location of criminal behaviour within the damaged minds and flawed cognitive processes of individual women. This medicalization discourse complements the risk logic that structures correctional management practices in ways that focus only on individual responsibility for criminal actions and rehabilitative transformation, to the complete neglect of other social and structural factors (Kendall 2000; Kilty 2008, 2012a; Pollack 2006; Pollack and Kendall 2005).

Contemporary researchers suggest that with the growing social distrust of medical authority amid neo-liberal political agendas that emphasize self-governance and reduced state social responsibility, Western citizens have become increasingly knowledgeable about and even active participants in their own medicalization, taking up its language, discourses, and associated practices to the point of seeking out specific medications that they are often exposed to through direct-to-consumer advertisements. Despite these tendencies, inappropriate medicalization engenders a number of questionable consequences, including: stigma, poor and often incomplete treatment decisions, iatrogenic illness, wasteful financial burden, and the diversion of resources to unnecessary forms of care (Conrad 2007; Healy 2004; Kilty 2012c; Moynihan, Heath, and Henry 2002). These dangers are only aggravated in correctional settings, in which individual and social problems — such as poor educational success, addiction, and histories of victimization — are often initially conceptualized in medical terms only to be then reconstructed as institutional security risks (Dell, Fillmore, and Kilty 2009; Hannah-Moffat 2000, 2001, 2004, 2006; Kilty 2006, 2012a, 2012c). The personal and social welfare needs of prisoners collide with the paramilitary ethos of institutional security, thus ensuring that treatment in the forms of psychotropic medications and cognitive-behavioural programming can function punitively rather than therapeutically in prison settings (Kendall 2000, 2002; Kilty 2008; 2012a, 2012b; Pollack 2006; Pollack and Kendall 2005).

Given the easy congruence between treatment and punishment, it is not surprising that growing numbers of criminalized women are diagnosed with mental disorders (Laishes 2002; Langner et al. 2002). In fact, 42 percent of all prescription medication orders are for psychotropics, and 51 percent of the incarcerated women taking psychotropics are taking two or more different types of these medications (Langner et al. 2002). Not only is the rate of medication orders for women prisoners significantly higher than it is for women in the community, prescription patterns are also regionalized and racialized, with the highest rates of psychotropic medication use found in the Prairies, where there is a disproportionate number of Aboriginal women in prison (Langner et al. 2002). These extraordinarily high psychotropic prescription rates correspond with the regular prescription by prison psy-experts and physicians of potent antipsychotic medications as sleep aids to criminalized women. This practice reflects not only the misuse of these types of medications (Caniato et al. 2009; Coe and Hong 2012; Tcheremissine 2008), but also an abuse of power that may contribute to ongoing drug dependence given that so many prisoners suffer from problematic substance use.

The atypical antipsychotic[1] drug Quetiapine, branded on the market as Seroquel, is one of the most popular sedatives used in carceral settings. It is frequently prescribed to newly arrived prisoners before the requisite psychiatric and observational assessment has been conducted. While marketed as being useful in the treatment of schizophrenia and bipolar disorder, and in conjunction with an antidepressant for major depressive disorder, it has a number of mild and potentially severe side effects, including: weight gain, frightening hallucinations, involuntary, repetitive body movements (tardive dyskinesia), dependence, somnolence, sluggishness, fatigue, dry mouth, sore throat, dizziness (orthostatic hypotension), abdominal pain, constipation, upset stomach, inflammation or swelling of the sinuses or pharynx, blurred vision, and hypothyroidism. Moreover, recent research evidences possible psy-dependency on Seroquel, as well as withdrawal symptoms characteristic of discontinuation syndrome (Caniato et al. 2009; Coe and Hong 2012; Kilty 2008, 2012a; Tcheremissine 2008).

In addition to high levels of psychotropic medication prescription, the psy-carceral complex also consists of cognitive-behavioural therapeutic programming used to motivate criminalized women to be compliant prisoners who choose to self-govern in socially responsible ways within a highly controlling prison environment (Pollack 2006).

## Therapeutic Programming: Disciplining the Criminal Mind

Feminist scholars have conceptualized correctional therapeutic programs as technologies of government that in the context of rehabilitative efforts designed for criminalized women are implemented to "tame the shrew" (Pollack and Kendall 2005) and "remake women into respectable ladies" (Carlen 2002b). The correctional premise behind these programs is to reform "the criminal mind" so that the individual is better equipped to make pro-social decisions. Inherent in this discourse is the presumption that "crime is a result of criminal personalities that transcend gender, class, ethnicity and race" (Andrews and Bonta 1998, cited in Pollack and Kendall 2005: 84).

Therapeutic programming for women is underpinned by the gendered, class-based, and racialized assumptions of relational theory: that women, more so than men, are primarily motivated and influenced by the establishment and maintenance of interpersonal relationships with others; these connections are also thought to have a direct impact on women's sense of self-worth and self-esteem. A cornerstone of correctional programming is to encourage the prisoner to develop healthy "pro-social" relationships, which are understood as helping to reduce the individual's likelihood of reoffending. This assumption ignores structural relations of power and the material effects of colonization and slavery that lead racialized men and women to be so vastly overrepresented in prison populations worldwide (Comack 2006; Comack and Balfour 2004; Sudbury 2005a).

The stated goal of therapeutic programming in the correctional environment is to foster responsible self-government; the expectation is that women will internalize correctional discourses and thereby actively participate in their own regulation. While Correctional Service of Canada (csc) has long acknowledged the victimization-criminalization continuum (Pollack 2006), paradoxically, in practice, correctional programs effectively deny this logic. Shoshanna Pollack and Kathleen Kendall (2005: 75) note, "If program facilitators acknowledge external factors, such as violence or poverty, they are thought to be feeding in to the offenders' denial and rationalizations of their offense." The authors cite research that shows "how cognitive-behavioral programming encourages participants to adopt the criminal personality story line to the exclusion of all other constructions of self and experience."

By emphasizing the "criminal personality story" and denying that women's experiences of trauma, victimization, substance use, and structural disadvantage contribute to their pathways into crime, correctional programming initiatives treat women's criminality only as a defect of the individual mind. This practice contributes to the construction of criminalized women as both "disordered and disorderly" (Pollack and Kendall 2005: 76), which then tautologically supports the use of psychotropic medications. Situating criminalized women's histories of victimization as an excuse or inappropriate rationalization for their offending behaviour demonstrates that while csc acknowledges the importance of considering gender, the institution has yet to generate a gender-responsive approach to therapeutic programming (Hannah-Moffat 2008).

Indeed, prison is scarcely the setting or environment to foster equitable and trusting therapeutic relationships deemed necessary in gender-responsive treatments (Bloom 2003b; Bloom, Owen, and Covington 2005; Hannah-Moffat 2008). As Kelly Hannah-Moffat (2008: 213) so eloquently argues:

Feminist-inspired approaches seek to incorporate safety into the structure, content and location of the programme (community where possible) and the choice of treatment provider. These issues are all salient to treatment "successes." The RNR [risk-need-responsivity] and gender responsive approaches continue to understate the fact that prisons are not necessarily warm, caring, safe places in which women can be empowered to create meaningful connections. In fact, quite the opposite is typically the case. This is not to suggest that meaningful intervention cannot, or should not, occur in prison but rather to suggest new lines of inquiry into the importance of the treatment context. For women in particular it may allow for a revisiting of the community as a more appropriate and under used space for treatment.

These are important words to consider in examining how, in the particular case of Ashley Smith, the psy-carceral complex operated not as a therapeutic support and impetus for rehabilitation, but rather as an instrument of punishment.

## Ashley Smith and the Psy-Carceral Complex

Women's criminality has long been essentialized as being inherently rooted in their damaged biological and psychological makeup. Correctional practices such as rehabilitation treatment as well as the security protocols of segregation, shackling, and searching effectively pinpoint the individual as being entirely responsible for her criminality; that is, excluding all other possible factors. While this is not a new phenomenon, depending on the individual and her circumstances the results of this logic and its associated practices can be tragic. Such was the case for Ashley Smith.

During the early morning hours of October 19, 2007, while on a formal suicide watch in a segregation cell at the Grand Valley Institution for Women in Kitchener, ON, nineteen-year-old Ashley Smith stood on her cell toilet and did her best to blur the image on the closed-circuit video camera in her cell with a tube of lip balm. She then stepped down, tied a hand-fashioned ligature around her neck, and lay down on the floor between her cot and the cement wall in order to better hide from the view of staff. Guards, who were bureaucratically instructed from on high *not* to intervene until Smith passed out, followed their orders. Indeed, staff did not enter her cell to intervene for upwards of fifteen minutes, by which point Smith had died. In accordance with the law, the entire event was video-recorded for posterity.

Smith's untimely death immediately evoked national and international attention and correctional scrutiny similar to the events that followed the 1994 unlawful cell extractions and strip searches of eight women at the Kingston Prison for Women (Arbour 1996). Following an investigation into her death in custody, Canada's federal Correctional Investigator, Howard Sapers, declared Smith's death "preventable" (2008). Despite motions filed by the Correctional Service of Canada to seal video materials and documents related to Smith's forced restraint, involuntary chemical injections, and medication prescriptions during the time when she was incarcerated in Quebec, the Ontario Court refused the motions and demanded that the evidence be made available. While the first coroner's inquest was formally terminated, after eleven months of testimony and seventeen days of deliberation, the coroner's jury for the second inquest[2] returned a verdict of homicide on December 19, 2013. While the jury concluded that the actions and inactions of correctional staff contributed to Smith's death, it made no finding of criminal or civil liability for individual actors. The jury also provided 104 recommendations to the presiding coroner, identifying a number of ways in which CSC could better serve criminalized women, particularly those suffering from mental illness. Among the most important recommendations were those to abolish indefinite solitary confinement and to prohibit women's segregation for a period of more than fifteen days. The jury also noted that the conditions of segregation should be the least restrictive possible.

By all accounts, Smith was a difficult prisoner to manage. Her resistance to authority began as a young teenager growing up in Moncton, N.B. Ashley had been suspended from school at age fourteen for her disruptive behaviour, and by fifteen she had been before juvenile court for various minor offences such as trespassing and causing a disturbance (Sapers 2008; Richard 2008). A community psychologist assessed Smith in March 2002 at her parents' request, finding no evidence of mental illness. Her behavioural problems continued, and she was suspended from school multiple times in the fall of 2002. By the age of fifteen, Ashley was facing multiple charges, including common assault, trespassing, causing a disturbance, and breach of probation. In March 2003 she was admitted to the Pierre Caissie Centre for psychiatric assessment, where she was diagnosed with ADHD, learning disorder, borderline personality disorder, and narcissistic personality traits (Richard 2008: 16). She was discharged early for unruly and disruptive behaviour and sent to the New Brunswick Youth Centre (NBYC), where she was released and readmitted multiple times over the next three years for incidents such as throwing crabapples at a postal worker, pulling fire alarms, and breaching probation (Richard 2008: 18). While in custody at NBYC, she accumulated additional charges for her misconduct, which resulted in most of her time being spent in the "Therapeutic Quiet Unit" or segregation. She was also pepper-sprayed and subjected to physical restraints such as the "WRAP":

> The "WRAP" consists of applying restraint belts beginning at the inmate's feet, all the way up to his or her shoulders, ceasing all possibility of bodily movement. Then a hockey helmet is place on the head which would prevent one from injury themselves in the event that they topple over, and also preventing the subject from biting anyone. After the "WRAP" was applied, Ashley had to be picked up by staff in order, to move her to another location, as all movements, including walking, are impossible. (Richard 2008: 22)

In July 2006, six months after Smith turned eighteen years of age, a motion was made under the Youth Criminal Justice Act to transfer her to an adult facility. She unsuccessfully fought the transfer. On October 5, 2006 Smith was transferred to the Saint John Regional Correctional Centre, where she spent most of her time in segregation due to behaviour deemed so unruly by the institution that she was tasered and pepper-sprayed, and placed in shackles and restraints (Sapers 2008; Richard 2008). Her unruly behaviour resulted in further criminal charges, which, when merged with her youth charges, amounted to a federal term of imprisonment. On October 31, 2006, Smith was transferred to an adult federal prison, the Nova Institution for Women in Truro, N.S. This transfer marked the start of the eleven and one-half months she spent in federal custody, which ended in her preventable death.

## The Psy-Carceral Complex as an Instrument of Punishment

The Correctional Investigator (Sapers 2008) identified a lengthy list of individual and systemic failures that contributed to Smith's preventable death, many of which are an integral part of the psy-carceral complex. Most obvious is that prison authorities failed to ensure that Smith received a full and complete psychological or psychiatric assessment, which in turn prevented the generation of a comprehensive treatment and correctional plan. While most parties generically acknowledged that Smith was suffering from "mental health issues," a vague phrase repeated throughout inquest testimony, without a complete assessment her case file lacked any clear identification of what those issues and her subsequent needs were.

Despite the lack of a concrete diagnosis, Smith was prescribed psychotropic medications, including Seroquel, to sedate and control her resistant behaviour. Sapers (2008) acknowledges that Smith's recalcitrant behaviour (spitting, biting, kicking, punching) occurred in response to the provocation of staff members using force and restraints against her. Smith refused to take psychotropic medication orally, and videotaped evidence shows multiple staff members physically restraining her as they subjected her to involuntary chemical injections. Forced or coercive medicalization is antithetical to gender-responsive ideals that call for calm, caring, and supportive therapeutic environments (Bloom 2003b; Bloom, Owen, and Covington 2005; Hannah-Moffat 2008; Liebling 2004, 2011; Tartaro and Lester 2009). For Smith, psychotropic medication became an instrument of punishment that diminished her ability to resist carceral control and exhibit corporeal autonomy (LeBlanc and Kilty 2013).

One of the major points of conflict was Smith's self-injurious behaviour, and in particular the act of tying ligatures around her neck, which staff identified as attention-seeking and manipulative (Sapers 2008; LeBlanc and Kilty 2013). The carceral context is bound by institutional hierarchies that lead to power imbalances, unease, tension, and even fear among staff members and prisoners (Liebling 2004, 2011; Pollack and Kendall 2005; Sudbury 2005a). The recognition of self-injury as attention-seeking and manipulative leads to the correctional response of strip-searching the prisoner and placing her in a segregation cell on suicide watch to better monitor and manage her behaviour. Given the abuse histories of many criminalized women (Comack 1996), strip-searching is a form of revictimization that is amplified by the isolation experienced in segregation — which is in turn commonly conceptualized as being a prison within a prison (Arbour 1996; King 1999; Sykes 1958). This practice is hardly a therapeutic response considering that when prisoners are in isolation their self-injurious behaviour is known to increase in frequency and severity (Liebling 1992; Liebling and Ward 1994; Liebling et al. 2005; Kilty 2012b, 2012c), which was the case for Smith.

Correctional policy also prevents women housed in segregation from gaining access to therapeutic programming, which in Smith's case meant that her permanent segregation status — itself a contravention of section 22 of the Corrections and Conditional Release Act and paragraphs 29–32 of the Commissioner's Directive 709 on Administrative Segregation (Sapers 2008) — barred her from participating in programming interventions. This practice inadvertently lengthens the time served in prison, an extrapunitive consequence. Segregation is the official response used when a prisoner behaves violently or breaks institutional rules; therefore, placing women who self-injure in segregation sends a mixed message that it is acceptable to punish a woman who is experiencing mental health distress (Arbour 1996; Kilty 2006, 2012b, 2012c; LeBlanc and Kilty 2013). The psy-carceral complex's use of segregation for distressed prisoners is thus an instrument of punishment rather than a therapeutic endeavour for self-harming prisoners, like Smith.

As the conditions of Smith's confinement deepened and hardened, she became increasingly distressed. Her main forms of human contact remained either violent (for example, when guards would enter her cell to physically subdue her) or emotionally distant (for example, when guards would pass trays of finger foods[3] through the small slot in her cell door). Psychologists have since described Smith's self-injurious behaviour, while maladaptive, as an attempt to draw staff into her cell to combat the constant isolation to which she was subject (Sapers 2008). Despite the considerable literature that demonstrates the harmful emotional and psychological effects of isolation in solitary confinement (Arrigo and Bullock 2007; Haney 2003; King 1999; Liebling 1992, 2004, 2011; Liebling and Ward 1994; Liebling et al. 2005; Sykes 1958; Tartaro and Lester 2009 — among countless others), CSC continues to rely on one in-house study (Zinger, Wichmann, and Andrews 2001) that maintains there is no ill effect to justify what critics see as an extrapunitive practice. Solitary isolation may be conceptualized as extrapunitive because it adds an additional layer of punishment to what is already the punitive nature of incarceration; it ensures that the individual prisoner is not only separated from the community and her children, family, and friends, but also segregated from other prisoners and most of the prison staff. To remain alone for up to twenty-three hours a day is highly retributive and offers nothing by way of gender-responsive correctional rehabilitation.

## The (Im)Moral Performance of Canadian Prisons for Women

Alison Liebling's extensive research on suicide and self-harm, long-term confinement, and the moral performance of the prison provides an analytic lens for understanding the Smith case. In much of her recent scholarship, Liebling (2004, 2011) examines the ethos of prison life and management — something she identifies as being absent in state evaluations of prison performance. In the United Kingdom, the push to examine the moral performance of prisons grew as a result of the twenty-five-day riot that occurred in April 1990 in Strangeways prison in Manchester. The investigation into the riot was documented in the Woolf Report (1991), which, like *Creating Choices* in Canada (TFFSW 1990), condemned prison-regime brutality and outlined a series of progressive reform recommendations that aimed to foster procedural fairness, professional ethics, moral and legal account-ability, and general decency in prisoner treatment. Despite these progressive reforms, feminist criminologists have documented that the reformed prison environment remains fertile ground for repressive politics in both Canada and the United Kingdom.

In their theoretical examination of this paradox as it occurs in Canadian penality Dawn Moore and Kelly Hannah-Moffat (2005: 97–98) argue that CSC's gender-responsive correctional regime for women operates as a kind of a liberal veil that cloaks punitive correctional practices within therapeutic ideals:

> It is dangerous to fall into the juxtaposition of punitiveness and thera-peutic initiatives. The endurance of the project of change in Canada offers a different kind of punitiveness to those incarcerated here, one in which the object of punishment mandates that individuals with vary-ing histories of trauma, violence and marginalization must attempt to heal themselves while in prison, a space which offers the antithesis of the support and empowerment the Canadian penal systems imagine they provide.

Liebling's empirical research identifies a similar pattern occurring throughout the institutional arrangements in U.K. penality. As she points out, prisons "have become more inhuman and degrading (in England and Wales, in conditions of high security) than they once were" (Liebling 2011: 532). These findings communicate that despite the well-meaning and progressive reforms outlined in *Creating Choices* and the Woolf Report, the oppressive nature of the prison has not dissipated — as demonstrated by the continued instances of self-harm and suicide seen in both penal systems. Pat Carlen (2005) describes this phenomenon as "the layering of penal disciplinarities," whereby new penal discourses and practices fail to supplant already established routines and instead work to reinforce them.

While the penal reforms described in both *Creating Choices* and the Woolf Report note the importance of strengthening prisoner-staff rela-tionships and improving the general conditions of confinement, Liebling's examination of the moral performance of the prison focuses on the material realities of prison life in a way that remains largely absent in state research.

By moral performance we mean those aspects of a prisoner's mainly *interpersonal* and material treatment that render a term of imprisonment more or less dehumanizing and/or painful.... There is a significant empirical link between aspects of a prison's moral performance and (a) levels of psychological distress, anxiety, and depression found among prisoners; and (b) its suicide rate. Poor treatment leads to negative emotions. (Liebling 2004: 469)

Liebling's research identifies a series of conceptual dimensions "that matter" in any consideration of prison legitimacy and moral performance: (a) relationship (respect, humanity, relationships, trust, support); (b) regime (fairness, order, safety, well-being, personal development, family contact, decency); (c) social structure (power, social life); and (d) individual (meaning, quality of life) (2004: 154–55). These dimensions are not mutually exclusive; they overlap conceptually. Liebling found that their key aspects are values relating to interpersonal treatment: respect, humanity, fairness, order, safety, and staff–prisoner relationships (2004, 2011: 534). She points out how the ways in which "trust and power flow through the institution" profoundly influence the prison's moral performance: "Prisons were more punishing and painful where staff were indifferent, punitive or lazy in the use of authority" (2011: 534). Perceptions of regime fairness and trust subsequently lead to lower levels of prisoner distress (Liebling 2004, 2011). Liebling argues: "These dimensions work via safety — so that what makes a prison feel safe — the most important determinant of distress — is responsive, approachable and respectful staff" (2011: 535).

If we peel back the liberal veil that shrouds Canadian correctional mandates and programs as primarily rehabilitative (Moore and Hannah-Moffat 2005), we uncover a system that appears to be incapable of providing adequate mental health care. Instead, Canadian prisons for women sacrifice the values of meaningful choice, empowerment, dignity, respect, and shared responsibility (as originally outlined in *Creating Choices*) in favour of punitive institutional security-management protocols — such as the use of segregation for prisoners that self-injure — that foster animosity between and can problematically pit staff against prisoners. As for the question of regime fairness in the Ashley Smith case, her correctional management clearly operated through discourses and practices built upon an ethos of security and punishment that left her feeling unsafe and increasingly distressed. This punitive management style severely damaged Smith's relationships with staff.

*Immoral Performance Based on Relationship Dimensions*
On the level of individual prisoner-staff relations, the militaristic style of training for correctional officers arguably creates a system in which front-line staff members follow orders regardless of any moral objections they might have to the procedures. Testimony at the coroner's inquest into Smith's death provides evidence of this pattern; front-line staff were uncomfortable with the order to "wait and see" before intervening to remove ligatures from the prisoner's neck. In a way that is similar to Liebling's findings (2004, 2011), based on the treatment to which she was subject, Smith clearly understood her construction as dangerous and risky and she responded in kind by re-sisting institutional orders that she believed were unfair and disrespectful, or that made her feel unsafe. By starting from the premise that Smith was "disordered and disorderly" (Pollack and Kendall 2005) and must be man-aged by the strictest forms of security and physical and chemical restraints, the correctional authorities dissolved any manner of trust between prison officials and Smith as a moral subject/agent.

In line with this social distancing, and despite the prisoner's regular contact with institutional psychologists, the system had no formal multi-disciplinary mental health team in place to manage Smith's case; indeed, some of the staff members charged with monitoring Smith while she was in segregation lacked mental health training (Sapers 2008). Rather than being a case of building relationships based on trust and respect, Smith's connections to prison staff reflected vast and irreconcilable imbalances of power that left her feeling powerless, unsupported, unsafe, and dehuman-ized — with the term "dehumanized" being used not only in reference to Liebling's (2004, 2011) finding that humanity is one of the key values of the relationship dimension, but also to characterize the videotaped evidence of Smith bound and gagged in her cell and hooded and duct-taped to her airplane seat while she was in transport between institutions. The lack of adequate training and instruction for prison staff members — enabling them to think critically and morally about the tense situations that arise on the front lines, including the ways in which they are instructed to engage with distressed prisoners housed in segregation — ensures the construction and maintenance of an environment in which tragedies such as Smith's death will continue to occur.

The staff responses to Smith's self-injurious behaviour reveal an overlap between the values that Liebling (2004, 2011) identifies as making up the relationship and regime dimensions. Initially, staff responded immediately upon learning that Smith possessed tools for self-harm, negotiating with her to hand over pieces of glass, screws, and ligatures (Sapers 2008). When they failed to coax these items from Smith, staff entered her cell and used physical force to remove them. During her eleven and one-half months in federal custody, staff used force against Smith in well over 150 incidents; she was repeatedly tasered, pepper-sprayed, and strip-searched. The Institutional Emergency Response Team was deployed on several occasions to subdue her and to prevent her from harming herself. These chronic abuses of power clearly devastated Smith's quality of life, which she described in one of her journal entries: "Most people are scared to die. It can't be any worse than living a life like mine" (cited in Richard 2008: 23).

Staff fatigue escalated after senior managers disciplined front-line staff, on at least one occasion, for intervening too early in an attempt to aid an asphyxiating Smith (Sapers 2008). Front-line staff members were confused by the mixed messages of policies demanding that they remove harmful contraband and of bureaucratic instructions to "wait and see," which eventually led them to permit Smith to retain ligatures in her possession for extended periods of time. Inquest testimony suggested that these exhibitions of power created a culture of fear among front-line staff, which led to a mistrust both for their employer and for Smith. Inconsistency in staff responses to Smith's self-injurious behaviour may be read as "indifferent, punitive, or lazy in the use of authority" — reactions that Liebling (2011: 534) found caused distress among prisoners and undermined the prison's moral performance.

Sapers (2008: 16) also cites the overreliance on largely security-focused intervention approaches and the misinterpretation of the Situation Management Model (SMM), which states that "all interventions employed by CSC staff must be reflective of a prisoner's behaviour at the point of intervention" and "physical force cannot be applied unless a particular situation truly warrants it at a particular moment in time." Using force against a distressed Smith repeatedly failed to curb her self-harming behaviour, and served only to further erode trust and damage staff-prisoner relations. With lines of communication devolving into stressful antagonism and resentment, opportunities for the relational therapeutic connection required of gender-responsive programming (Bloom 2003b; Bloom, Owen, and Covington 2005; Hannah-Moffat 2008) evaporated. Without trust or humane care, Smith's distress increased while her feelings of safety and perceptions of regime fairness decreased — all of which points to the prison's failed moral performance.

## Immoral Performance based on Regime Dimensions

Videotaped evidence indicates that prison staff — rather than working to build and strengthen interpersonal connections with Smith — invoked the "wait and see" approach in the extreme, intervening only after the prisoner turned blue, had significant trouble breathing, and broke blood vessels in her face from ligature use. The coroner's jury acknowledged this troubling fact, recommending that front-line staff not be required to seek authorization if they determine that immediate intervention is needed to save a prisoner's life; and that all staff members who provide mental health care report and be accountable to health-care professionals rather than to security protocols.

In a practice that was administratively flawed in documenting the use of force, neither health care and psychology agents nor the institutional security officers provided commentary on these abuses of power (Sapers 2008). The Correctional Investigator, Sapers, concluded that Smith's management plans were "highly security-focused and devoid of their most important element: how to safely address Smith's increasingly dangerous self-harming behaviours. Front-line staff were simply referred to the Situation Management Model, despite the increased frequency and intensity of Smith's extremely dangerous behaviours" (Sapers 2008: 17).

Health-care staff, who probably had the most expertise and experience in dealing with self-harming prisoners in a therapeutic manner, were resigned to conducting post-use of force assessments and facilitating Smith's transfer to the regional psychiatric treatment institutions (Sapers 2008). The staff did not officially comment on the nature or severity of Smith's self-injurious behaviour, failed to document that the continuing misinterpretation of the smm was placing her at high risk of permanent injury or even death, and were not called upon to conduct follow-up medical examinations after any of these incidents (Sapers 2008). In the same vein, the team of institutional psychologists did not seek outside assistance or request help from regional health-care managers or psychologists to ensure better treatment for Smith (Sapers 2008).

Breakdowns occurred, then, in the lines of communication at every level of correctional management. For example, csc generates daily Situation Reports that document significant incidents involving prisoners across the country. The reports, distributed throughout the organization, are supposed to be reviewed closely by senior executives at national and regional headquarters. Incidents involving Smith were noted weekly, and often daily, throughout her incarceration — so that, according to Sapers, even the most senior staff within csc, "including the Commissioner of Corrections, the

Senior Deputy Commissioner, the Deputy Commissioner for Women, and the Regional Deputy Commissioners" must have been alerted to the challenges of Smith's behaviour. "Yet there is little evidence that anyone beyond the institutional level effectively intervened before Smith died" (Sapers 2008: 18).

The staff, institutional, and bureaucratic failures to communicate culminated at Grand Valley Institution when Smith's high risk for committing suicide was not formally recorded or communicated to all staff on duty the night before she committed suicide (Sapers 2008). Ironically, since Smith's death in 2007, csc has produced a number of in-house research reports on self-injurious behaviour that continue to deny that segregation and maximum-security status are not therapeutic and actually exacerbate the behaviour (see Gordon 2010; Power, Beaudette, and Usher 2012; Power and Brown 2010; Power and Riley 2010; Power and Usher 2010, 2011a, 2011b, 2011c, 2011d; Usher, Power, and Wilton 2010). These reports suggest a collective refusal to acknowledge that the strict security focus used to manage Smith (and other self-injuring prisoners) aggravated rather than prevented her self-injurious behaviour. Subsequently, csc continues to adhere to principles of security and punishment that do not encourage respectful or trusting staff-prisoner relationships or fair regime practices. The result, as Liebling (2004, 2011) demonstrates, leads to prisoners feeling unsafe and distressed — the key markers of immoral prison performance.

The erosion of trust between Smith and prison authorities had its roots in two related and unlawful administrative regime practices: permanent segregation status and frequent institutional transfers. Throughout her eleven and one-half months in adult federal custody, Smith was transferred a total of seventeen times involving eight institutions and across five provinces (Sapers 2008). The majority of these institutional transfers had little or nothing to do with her needs. They were instead carried out to address administrative issues such as cell availability, incompatible prisoner populations, and staff fatigue. Each transfer further weakened Smith's trust in her captors' ability to keep her safe or to prioritize her well-being. The transfers escalated her resistant behaviours and made it increasingly more difficult for the Correctional Service to manage her (Sapers 2008; LeBlanc and Kilty 2013). The Correctional Service used these repeated transfers to keep Smith housed in maximum-security segregation cells, as each transfer, court appearance, or short stay in a regional psychiatric treatment facility — where she remained in maximum-security isolation — erroneously lifted her segregation status and reset the "segregation clock." This is nothing more than political manoeuvring aimed at avoiding the legal and policy directives to conduct five-, thirty-, and sixty-day mental health reviews for segregated prisoners (Sapers 2008; LeBlanc and Kilty 2013). Smith's perpetual rotation through different institutions in part thwarted attempts to obtain a comprehensive psychological assessment (Sapers 2008).

Liebling's (2004, 2011: 534) premise that prisoners experience greater distress in prisons in which staff are unsympathetic or punitive helps to explain Smith's ordeal, and the outcome. A young woman spends nearly a year in segregation in an adult federal penitentiary for an index offence of throwing crabapples at a postal worker as a youth. She experiences this treatment as being unfair and unjust. Moreover, she not surprisingly comes to see the prison setting as unsafe and her keepers as iniquitous. Smith's repeated transfers and permanent segregation status, and the broken lines of communication and damaged staff-prisoner interpersonal relations, are tangible evidence of the hegemonic power relations of the psy-carceral complex that contribute to the immoral performance of Canadian prisons for women.

## An (Im)Moral Place and a Preventable Death

Ashley Smith clearly understood her psy-carceral treatment to be extrapunitive: she filed multiple grievances about the highly disciplinary conditions of her confinement. In their restrictive efforts to try to prevent her from harming herself, and also as a display of hegemonic carceral power relations, prison authorities refused to permit Smith access to writing materials, making it exceptionally difficult for her to formally document her mistreatment. Of the seven grievances she did file, csc accepted none and again violated their own laws and policies by failing to open the final grievance on time — reviewing it two months after her death (Sapers 2008). Smith grieved a number of different things, including: being subject to excessive uses of force; csc's refusal to accept a grievance complaint that was written by another prisoner on her behalf when she was refused writing utensils; being unable to leave her cell for physical exercise for a four-day period; having insufficient personal supplies (including toilet paper, soap, deodorant, underwear, and sanitary products for menstruation); and failing to receive a copy of the decisions made in her segregation status reviews (Sapers 2008).

csc's ignorance and dismissal of Smith's grievances align too easily with their "women-centered" programming initiatives that endorse teaching already vulnerable and structurally marginalized women "distress tolerance." As Pollack and Kendall (2005: 79) succinctly explain:

Not only may it [distress tolerance] encourage women to accept and internalize their oppression, it could furthermore serve to thwart their legitimate protest against the prison regime. By encouraging a simple acceptance of the oppositions, tensions, and incongruities embedded within prisons, critical analysis and understanding is discouraged. Fundamentally, the failings of the prison regime are framed as rooted within prisoners' pathology. This way, the institution becomes legitimized while prisoners are discredited.

In addition to the extraordinarily high rates of psychotropic medication used to govern a population typically constructed as unruly, risky, and mentally unstable, therapeutic programming initiatives further reinforce criminality as a result of individual psychosocial failures that do not account for the structural disadvantages that incarcerated women face.

Correctional rehabilitative efforts have long relied on medicalization discourses and associated practices to add a sense of benevolence to the prison's moral performance. As a result of its "gender-responsive" agenda, in which psy-interventions are firmly entrenched, Correctional Service Canada (2006) now boasts that it is a world leader in the development, implementation, and delivery of evidence-based programs designed to make offenders accountable, change their behaviours, and reduce risks to the Canadian public. This is part of CSC's self-proclaimed moral performance. The Ashley Smith case threatens the credibility and believability of these claims and peels back the liberal veil that cloaks Canadian correctional discourses and practices (Moore and Hannah-Moffat 2005). The tragedy of Smith's preventable death reveals that an institution based on a system of rewards and punishments, hegemonic power relations, and dehumanizing practices such as segregation, strip- and body-cavity searching, mandatory psychotropic medication prescriptions that may result in involuntary chemical injections, and regime strategies that actively work to legitimize institutional practices while discrediting prisoner complaints and grievances can hardly be said to perform morally. This condition was fully acknowledged by the coroner's jury, which noted in its list of recommendations that Smith's experiences of carceral mistreatment and confinement should be used as a case study in training all levels of Correctional Service management and staff.

Indeed, in its poignant recommendations the coroner's jury reflected many of the criticisms outlined here. For example, recognizing the inherent inability of the correctional system to address mental distress, the jury recommended that women with mental health issues and those who self-injure should serve their sentences in a treatment facility rather than a security-focused prison. The jury also recommended that CSC work to become a restraint-free environment and that prisoners who experience mental health issues be involved in the training, planning, research, and policy development for prisoner mental health care. Given CSC's refusal to support some of the same recommendations when proposed by the Office of the Correctional Investigator (see CSC 2011), it remains to be seen whether, and if so how, the Correctional Service of Canada will implement the jury's recommendations.

## Notes

1. Atypical antipsychotics (also known as second-generation antipsychotics) are a group of tranquilizing drugs used to treat psychiatric conditions. Both generations of medication block dopamine receptors, but atypicals were initially thought to cause fewer motor control disabilities in patients, such as unsteadiness, body rigidity and involuntary tremors. Recent research shows the side effect profile of atypicals to be similar to first-generation drugs, causing *The Lancet* to conclude, "The time has come to abandon the terms first-generation and second-generation antipsychotics, as they do not merit this distinction" (Tyrer and Kendall 2009).

2. The first coroner's inquest began in May 2011, but was delayed when Smith's family filed a formal legal challenge to include evidence of their daughter's treatment throughout the entire eleven months of her federal confinement. The inquest was delayed again in June 2011 to allow for the proceedings to be webcast. When the presiding coroner was replaced due to her pending retirement, the Smith family challenged the right of the new coroner to continue the inquest and called for a mistrial. On September 30, 2011, the Ontario Coroner's Office formally terminated the inquest and dismissed the jury. The second coroner's inquest began on September 30, 2012. With Dr. John Carlisle acting as the presiding coroner, the scope of the inquest was widened to include the effects of long-term solitary confinement, repeated institutional transfers across different regions and provinces in the country, the role of mental health care and management, and the complications arising from housing youth who come of age in custody and are transferred to adult institutions.

3. Smith was not allowed utensils for fear that she would use them to harm herself; she was subsequently given only finger foods to eat for months at a time (Sapers 2008).

# Part IV

# Making Change

# Part IV Introduction

*Gillian Balfour*

Today most Canadian university undergraduate criminology programs include courses with titles such as "Women, Crime, and Social Justice," "Women and the Criminal Justice System," or "Women, Law, and the State." These courses are offered either as special topics courses or as a part of the established curriculum. As well, more women are teaching in university classrooms, and more women are attending universities and colleges than ever before. Chances are that many of the young women students sitting in criminology courses are interested in the various careers that were once male bastions, such as policing and lawyering.

All of this raises the question of whether feminist writers have overstated their concern for the invisibility of women in criminology. Hasn't academia been transformed by the work of feminist criminologists and socio-legal scholars?

In short, the answer is yes ... and no. While these significant transformations should not be minimized, considerable work remains to be done — inside and outside of academia. Poor women, racialized women, and women with mental health needs continue to face demoralizing and brutalizing conditions that place them at risk of being criminalized or disciplined by the state. Over the last two decades, we have seen an international "incarceration binge" of locking women up (Snider 2003: 354), most evident in the spiralling numbers of Aboriginal women admitted to Canadian prisons and jails. In addition to the increasing use of imprisonment by the state, the tactics of control have become more security-focused and, in some cases, deadly. The Office of the Correctional Investigator continues to document the degrading conditions of confinement for women prisoners, especially those with severe mental health needs.

Discussions of how to engage in making change with the aim of realizing social justice for criminalized and incarcerated women are critical. Over the past three decades in Canada, feminists intent on making change have engaged in various strategies to address the conditions inside women's prisons, such as launching human rights complaints to seek redress for illegal conditions of confinement, and advocating for greater correctional accountability and oversight. Making change to realize social justice also requires going outside of the criminal justice system to address the conditions of exploitation and oppression that foreground women's criminalization, such as the prevalence of gendered violence, the continuing impact of settler colonialism, and the widening gap between rich and poor. Under the grip of neo-liberal austerity that seeks to restrict mandates of government-funded agencies to deliver core services rather than rights-based advocacy, feminist organizations find themselves increasingly challenged in their efforts to realize social justice. As well, feminists struggle to reconcile the tensions between a politics of abolition that questions the very existence of prisons, and working inside jails and prisons as volunteers, teachers, and legal advocates providing support, programs, and services to prisoners.

How, then, do we move forward? Do we continue to deploy law against the state to demand accountability and oversight? Do we engage in crafting policies and promoting practices that better serve the needs of women? Do we participate in and support the strategies of social justice groups as they endeavour to bring about significant change? While there is certainly room for cautious optimism on all of these fronts, there are lessons to be learned from the past that can frame how we move forward in our efforts at making change to realize social justice for women — both inside and outside the prison walls.

## Holding the Correctional Service of Canada to Account

Throughout the 1980s feminist activists attempted to challenge the criminal justice response to women, especially the treatment of women prisoners, in a number of ways. Some of these strategies included a human rights complaint against the Correctional Service of Canada and participation in a coroner's inquest into the death of Marlene Moore. But little substantive change was achieved. The establishment of the Task Force on Federally Sentenced Women in 1989, however, held the promise of a transformative moment in the struggle for prison reform in Canada. The problems involved in implementing the principles of *Creating Choices* revealed not only the barriers that feminists face in achieving full participation in the change-making process, but also the tightening grip of neo-liberalism on the management of prisoners. As Shoshana Pollack (2004, 2006) and Kelly Hannah-Moffat (2010) show, well-meaning feminist research and advocacy for women as victims of male violence have resulted in a gender-responsive program inside women's prisons that has absorbed the victimization discourse — but not in the way envisioned by feminists. Far from examining and taking into account the impact of socio-economic and racialized conditions that frame women's choices (such as where they live, if they are able to work, food security, and parenting resources), gender-responsive programming imposes a psychological frame on women's needs that retrenches an essentialist view of all women as defined by their relational lives. An understanding of women's coping strategies, such as substance use or defensive violence, needs to include an intersectional analysis of how these women's lives are structured by conditions of social exclusion.

Despite the earlier findings of the 1996 Arbour Commission report (see Part III Introduction here) that denounced the CSC for its illegal strip-searching of female prisoners inside the Prison for Women, conditions of confinement continued to deteriorate. In response, prisoner advocates turned again to law, seeking legal recognition of and remedy for the discriminatory treatment of women prisoners. In March 2001 the Canadian Association of Elizabeth Fry Societies and the Native Women's Association of Canada — along with twenty-five other social justice groups — wrote to the Canadian Human Rights Commission (CHRC) urging that a "broad-based systemic review be conducted pursuant to section 61(2) of the Canadian Human Rights Act, regarding the discriminatory treatment of marginalized, victimized, criminalized and institutionalized women in Canada" (CAEFS 2003). The coalition asserted in its letter that discrimination existed on three main grounds: sex (especially those women held in maximum-security units in men's prison); race (the treatment of Aboriginal and other racialized women); and disability (the treatment of women with cognitive and mental disabilities).

In its written submission to the Human Rights Commission, CAEFS (2003) argued that the security classification system used by CSC is determined by an assessment tool that is fundamentally gender-biased and class-based. On the one hand, a woman is assessed according to criteria such as whether she has been a victim of spousal abuse, has "inappropriate sexual preferences," or has "sexual attitudes that are problematic" (CAEFS 2003: 24–25). On the other hand, middle-class norms infuse criteria such as whether a woman has a bank account, collateral, or hobbies, has used social assistance, lacks a skill or trade or profession, resides in a criminogenic area, or lives in a poorly maintained residence. CAEFS was also highly critical of the practice of confining those women classified as maximum security in segregated units inside men's prisons. As well, the Association pointed to the disproportionate classification of Aboriginal women as maximum-security prisoners — which happens in large part due to the inappropriateness of the risk-assessment tool that translates social marginalization into individualized risk. Aboriginal women were also granted conditional release at slower rates and later stages in their sentences, despite section 84 of the Corrections and Conditional Release Act, which is aimed at the reintegration of Aboriginal women into their communities. Similarly, CAEFS pointed out that the discrimination against women with mental and cognitive disabilities is built into the security classification scheme: those disabilities are one of the factors to be taken into account in assigning a prisoner's security classification. Associating security concerns with disability de facto constructs persons with a mental illness or disorder as "dangerous" (CAEFS 2003).

After extensive consultation and investigation, the CHRC released its report, *Protecting Their Rights*, in January 2003. In its profile of federally sentenced women, the report maintained, "The reasons why women offend, their life experiences and their needs are unique." Some two-thirds of federally sentenced women are mothers, and they are more likely than male prisoners to be the primary caregivers to their children. Federally sentenced women experience much lower employment rates than do their male counterparts. They have less education than the general Canadian population, and experience significant poverty. An "overwhelming" number — 80 percent — of federally sentenced women report histories of abuse. One of the "most disturbing" statistics cited by the Commission concerned the overrepresentation of Aboriginal women in maximum security: "Although Aboriginal women account for only 3% of the female population of Canada, they represent 29% of the women incarcerated in federal prisons and account for fully 46% of the women classified as maximum security" (CHRC 2004: 6). As well, the report noted that federally sentenced women "are three times more likely than their male counterparts to suffer from depression. They also experience higher rates of mental illness, self-destructive behaviour such as slashing and cutting, and suicide attempts" (p. 8). Women with mental health issues are also disproportionately classified as maximum security.

The Commission identified systemic human rights problems in the CSC's treatment of federally sentenced women, and made nineteen recommendations for immediate action to be taken on the part of the service. In February 2005 CSC announced its response to the CHRC report — a multi-year action plan to implement the recommendations. The CSC acknowledged that the plan was not one that would "fundamentally challenge the concept of incarceration as applied to women offenders" because it only addressed "those suggestions which can be implemented within the legislative frame ... of the *Corrections and Conditional Release Act*" (CSC 2005b: 2). Nevertheless, while some of the CHRC recommendations were accepted in principle or in part, others — like the recommendation to change the blanket policy of not allowing maximum-security women at the healing lodge to one based on individual assessment — were not. In a press release issued a month following the report, CAEFS, NWAC, and other advocacy groups expressed their alarm over what they considered to be "the tacit acceptance by the Canadian Human Rights Commission of the relative inaction of the Correctional Service of Canada" on the issue of the systemic discrimination against federally sentenced women (CAEFS 2005c).

Confronted with a disappointing response by the CHRC to the inaction of CSC to address the discriminatory treatment of women prisoners, CAEFS and its coalition partners were not dissuaded from the importance of holding CSC accountable. To this end, the coalition made a formal submission to the United Nations Human Rights Committee to examine the federal government's claim that its treatment of women prisoners does not violate the United Nations Convention Against Torture and Other Cruel, Inhumane, or Degrading Treatment or Punishment (CAEFS 2005b). Utilizing the exhaustive research collected for the CHRC complaint, CAEFS and its partners argued that the CSC was in violation of U.N. Article 2 (prevention of acts of torture) in its classification and maximum-security units, its continued use of cross-gender monitoring and searching practices, its treatment of Aboriginal prisoners, its use of segregation, and the lack of gender-specific training, educational, and therapeutic programs (CAEFS 2005b). Sadly, as we have learned through the death of Ashley Smith and the Criminal Investigator's reports of a troubling lack of compliance by CSC to ongoing demands for appropriate treatment of women prisoners, human rights law appears to have done little to hold the Correctional Service to account.

## Using Law to Address Violence Against Women

As prisoners' advocates utilized legal strategies such as human rights legislation to bring into view the discriminatory — and indeed abusive — treatment of prisoners inside the Prison for Women, feminists mobilized outside the prison to bring about meaningful change in the area of violence against women. Far-reaching feminist-inspired reforms to sexual assault laws throughout the 1980s and 1990s were intended to increase women's willingness to report sexual assault to the police, to protect women from withering cross-examinations by defence lawyers, and to set out the conditions of consent to sex. Each of these reforms and successful legal challenges was met with entrenched opposition by criminal defence bar lawyers and an increasingly vocal men's rights movement (see Minaker and Snider 2006; Gotell 2007; Comack and Balfour 2004).

Another important field of legal reform was the decision by the Supreme Court of Canada that gave legal recognition to the Battered Woman Syndrome in cases of women who kill their abusive partners. In *R v Lavallee* (1990) the Court accepted the expert witness testimony of a psychiatrist who maintained that Angelique Lavallee killed her abusive common-law spouse in self-defence because she suffered from learned helplessness as a result of living under the constant threat of violence. In the end, Lavallee was acquitted — a feminist victory of sorts. As feminist socio-legal scholars have argued, however, this Supreme Court decision did little to condemn male violence as a systemic problem, and it failed to recognize women's violence as a "rational" and "reasonable" action when located within the social context in which it occurs (Martinson et al. 1991; Comack 1993; Noonan 1993).

Following the *Lavallee* decision, pressure mounted from advocacy groups — the Canadian Association of Elizabeth Fry Societies in particular — for the government to conduct a review of cases involving women who were convicted of murder or manslaughter but had been unable to use their history of abuse to prove that they were acting in self-defence. Consequently, Ontario Court Judge Lynn Ratushny was appointed in 1995 to conduct a review of ninety-eight cases. The *Self-Defence Review* (Ratushny 1997) recommended law reform in the areas of self defence and sentencing. Although that proposal itself seemingly represented another feminist victory, only seven of the ninety-eight cases were recommended to be granted relief, and the government agreed to this in only five of those cases. No women were released from prison as a result of the review.[1]

Since the Ratushny review was undertaken, researchers have noted that women are increasingly vulnerable to criminalization when they use violence in self-defence (Pollack, Battaglia, and Allspach 2005) and, under rigorous zero-tolerance policies, women continued to be countercharged for domestic assault — even when they call the police for help (Comack, Chopyk, and Wood 2000). More recently, law professor Elizabeth Sheehy has examined the criminal justice response to eleven women accused of killing the men who have beaten them, revealing that in some cases women were acquitted or charges were dropped; however, in most instances women who killed their abusers pleaded guilty to a lesser charge and were not afforded the legal defence of self-defence or Battered Women's Syndrome (Sheehy 2014). Now, as then, men's rights groups have attacked feminist legal scholars as "morally depraved" and inciting murder.[2]

It would seem that changing law alone is not sufficient to produce a sea change in how society addresses the issue of violence against women, given widely accepted views of women who use violence against men as "monsters" and their advocates as "liars." A case in point is the Supreme Court of Canada's decision to acquit Nicole Ryan of charges of conspiracy to commit murder when she attempted to hire someone to kill her abusive husband. The court found that Ryan's actions were reasonable in the context of fifteen years of domestic violence (*R v Ryan* 2013). Public backlash was swift in this case, alleging that the "abuse excuse" was being used to exonerate a woman with a penchant for revenge against a husband who had left her for another woman (Hutchinson 2013).

## Addressing Violence Against Aboriginal Women

Nowhere has violence against women been more pervasive and deadly than for Aboriginal women. Statistics Canada reported in 2008 that Aboriginal women are five times more likely than non-Aboriginal women to die of violence (Statistics Canada 2009b). In response to the lack of action by federal and provincial governments to address violence against Aboriginal women, and the number of Aboriginal women reported missing, the Native Women's Association of Canada (with the support of Amnesty International) joined forces in 2004 to launch its Sisters in Spirit campaign across Canada to document the cases of Aboriginal women who had disappeared or died a violent death. NWAC estimated that almost six hundred Aboriginal women had gone missing over a period of two decades (NWAC 2010a); more than 30 percent of those women had gone missing since 2000. Amnesty International provided funding for the research and writing of a report presented at the United Nations Forum on Aboriginal Peoples. In May 2005, NWAC received $5 million over five years from the federal government to assist in a number of projects, including the creation of a toll-free hotline for families to report their missing women; the creation of a national registry of missing Aboriginal women; and the implementation of a public awareness and education campaign. NWAC would also provide the government with a policy analysis and recommendations to address violence against Aboriginal women (NWAC 2010a).

The most troubling finding of the Sisters in Spirit campaign is the failure of the criminal justice system to adequately protect Aboriginal women and girls from violence (Amnesty International 2004). NWAC draws parallels between the rape and murder of Helen Betty Osborne by four white men in The Pas, MB, in 1971, and the unsolved murder of sixteen-year-old Felicia Solomon in Winnipeg in 2003. As Nahanni Fontaine (chapter 4) points out, it is only through the experiences of young women like Felicia that the connections between the legacy of colonialism and gendered violence can be made. Despite the importance of NWAC's work in developing a national database on missing and murdered Aboriginal women that will contribute to a policing framework for conducting investigations, in 2010 Sisters in Spirit funding was cut, replaced with a $10 million fund to provide services to families of victims of violent crimes. In its public statement opposing the reallocation of funding, NWAC challenged the federal government for dismissing the need for dedicated resources for investigating cases of murdered Aboriginal women (NWAC 2010b).

Numerous reports have documented escalating violence against Aboriginal women. In 2010, following the conviction of Robert Pickton for the murders of six women of the Downtown Eastside of Vancouver, the B.C. government announced the Missing Women Commission of Inquiry. The commission was mandated to investigate critical police failures to properly investigate the reports of missing women, many of whom were Aboriginal. As Commissioner Oppal noted in his report:

> A disproportionate number of the missing and murdered women were Aboriginal: while three per cent of BC's population consists of Aboriginal women, they comprise approximately 33 per cent of the missing and murdered women. Of the 33 women whose DNA was found on Pickton's farm, 12 were Aboriginal. Aboriginal women experience higher levels of violence, both in terms of incidence and severity, and are disproportionately represented in the number of missing and murdered women across Canada. (Oppal 2012:15)

The Commission was told of the conditions of women's lives in the Downtown Eastside: extreme poverty leading to prostitution, grossly inadequate housing, food insecurity, barriers to health services, drug dependency and painful drug withdrawal, and entrenchment in the community (Oppal 2012: 14). Yet critics noted that almost all of the recommendations made by the Inquiry only addressed the technical and bureaucratic inefficiencies of the criminal justice system that led to the critical failure in the police response. Moreover, while funding was provided for the Vancouver city police and RCMP members to be represented by legal counsel, no funding was provided for legal representation of Aboriginal women's organizations to speak before the Inquiry. As NWAC and the Canadian Feminist Alliance for International Action stated in a press release following the release of the Inquiry's 1,400-page report:

The Native Women's Association of Canada was shut out of the B.C. Missing Women Commission of Inquiry…. The Inquiry proceeded without Aboriginal women's organizations, without any Aboriginal organizations, and without women's organizations who know about the lives of vulnerable women…. This process was discriminatory and a betrayal of Aboriginal women and girls. Because the Government of British Columbia refused to provide funding for legal counsel for parties granted standing at the Inquiry, the Inquiry itself violated the rights of the most vulnerable women. It excluded them; it did not listen to them. (NWAC 2012)

Also in British Columbia, in 2012 Human Rights Watch International — an organization that typically provides oversight to protect human rights in conflict zones in developing countries — was asked by the Tachie First Nation in Prince George to conduct an investigation of the prevalence of police-perpetrated violence against women in their community. The report, *Those Who Take Us Away*, documented accounts of girls and women who were bitten by police dogs, punched while handcuffed, and strip-searched by male RCMP officers. One woman reported being sexually assaulted by RCMP officers who threatened to kill her if she told anyone (Human Rights Watch International 2013: 6). The women of the community were unwilling to be named or to name the officers who assaulted them for fear of reprisal. Since the release of the report, the Commissioner of the RCMP and the Prime Minister's Office have denied all allegations made by the women.

By documenting human rights abuses, litigating human rights complaints, engaging in public commissions of inquiry and launching national education campaigns, feminist, anti-violence, and decolonizing groups such as NWAC, Amnesty International, and CAEFS have endeavoured to make change that would realize social justice through recognition and redress of the conditions of endangerment that underpin women's criminalization, as well as the conditions of their incarceration. But the struggle continues.

## Moving Forward?

How, then, should we address the conditions of social exclusion (poverty, and racialized and sexualized violence) that appear to enable the regulation of women inside and outside of the criminal justice system?

Laureen Snider (chapter 10) calls on us to fully appreciate the devastating impacts of neo-liberal economics on women — and how neo-liberal policies were put in place despite feminist claims-making through raising public awareness and conducting research. Snider raises two vital questions for feminists in their pursuit of social justice: first, is it even possible to make change in neo-liberal times; and second, are there ways of bringing the symbolic value of criminalization to bear while containing its harmful effects? In Snider's view, if substantive social change is to take place, feminist knowledge claims need to become a part of the "knowledge-power-change nexus." Snider reminds us that under neo-liberal and neo-conservative governments, some feminist criminologists have drifted toward a carceral feminism — a politics of punishment and retribution — that has forged problematic alliances with law and order regimes to achieve formal recognition of women's victimization. For example, some feminists have proclaimed that the compulsory criminalization of domestic violence, zero-tolerance crime control policies, and mandatory minimum sentences are all necessary to denounce gendered violence and exploitation. Yet, as Chris Bruckert and Colette Parent argue in chapter 3, the criminalization of sex work as sexual exploitation has not only failed to achieve the safety of women but also enabled their endangerment on the streets. In similar fashion, as Dorothy Chunn and Shelley Gavigan, and Amanda Glasbeek and Emily van der Meulen also point out in their chapter, law and order politics have devastating impacts on low-income women and street-involved women who become targets of state surveillance and control.

Working toward social justice requires that we confront the realities and tensions of working with women in prison — as volunteers, teachers, advocates, nurses, or lawyers. For some, the challenge of working within the prison system is justified by the great need of women prisoners for support and resources. For others, working outside of the prison system — documenting violations of correctional policy, meeting with politicians, and using the media to demand accountability — is also vital to the struggle to challenge and improve the treatment of women inside.

In the wake of Ashley Smith's death in the Grand Valley Institution for Women in Kitchener, feminist social worker and prisoner advocate Shoshana Pollack introduced a prison education program, Inside/Outside. As she explains in chapter 11, Inside/Outside is an opportunity for university students to come to prison to learn with prisoners, with both groups earning university credits. The impact of the educational opportunity upon the women prisoners who have participated is profound, as the narratives of Monica Freitas, Bonnie McAuley, and Nyki Kish confirm.

The spiralling rates of incarceration of Aboriginal women and the destructive impacts of Western correctional practices that isolate women from their traditional identity are another critical challenge to feminist engagement with the correctional system. In chapter 13, Colleen Dell and her colleagues explore how Aboriginal women in prison have internalized the colonized image of the "dirty squaw." Through oral traditions of storytelling and songwriting, correctional practices can be decolonized to develop a space for Aboriginal women to reclaim their authentic traditional lives.

Not all feminists agree on the necessary strategies for addressing the brutalization of women in their communities and inside prisons. In the United States, a strong prison abolitionist movement spurred on by the mass incarceration of over seven million people has grown to include the abolition of criminal justice responses to gendered violence. Vikki Law (2010: 85) explores "the different methods women have employed to protect themselves, their loved ones, and communities" and how women "promote safety and accountability without resorting to state-based policing and prisons." Other academics believe that in the face of a global lockdown — despite attempts to intervene on behalf of prisoners — prison abolition and decarceration are necessary responses to the expansiveness of carceral power (Piche and Larsen 2010).

Most feminists would agree that there remains a troubling disregard for feminist research in terms of political and public discourse about "what to do about crime." U.S. feminist criminologist Meda Chesney-Lind (2004) points to the importance of the conditions of change-making and activism as key strategic pieces in the struggle for significant change:

> Clearly, as professionals who study of the problem of crime, we should be able to claim a certain degree of credibility when it comes to public discussions of crime policy. Yet, when many critical decisions are made about these issues, we are almost never on the guest list. Why? It has been my experience that most academics, particularly in the United States, are wholly unplugged from the world of politics, particularly in their local communities, and are often completely unaware of what it takes to engage in pragmatic political activism. This situation is no accident, of course. Rather, it is the consequence of decades of political domination by conservative political leadership which, among other things, sought to shift the social sciences away from the activism that had characterized our fields in earlier decades.

What, then, are the challenges that now confront feminist criminologists? Throughout this book we suggest that women are more likely to be criminalized today — labelled, processed, and punished — because of the ravages of a neo-liberal form of governance. How do we make sense of the trends toward a more punitive regulation of poor and racialized women? What are the sites and conditions of change-making? How can we best imagine our work to advocate on behalf of these women? These are the kinds of perplexing questions that feminist criminologists will continue to grapple with in the near future.

## Notes

1. For a synopsis and commentary on the *Self-Defence Review*, see CAEFS 1997.
2. See, for example: <avoiceformen.com/feminism/elizabeth-sheehy-cant-even-justify-herself-blamefeminism/>.
3. The Native Women's Association of Canada is a national organization that represents the political, economic, and cultural interests of First Nations and Métis women. See <http://www.nwac.ca/>.

# 10

# Making Change in Neo-Liberal Times

*Laureen Snider*

Making change in neo-liberal societies is not difficult. The air fairly bristles with "reform chatter" as entrepreneurs keen on privatizing chunks of criminal justice jostle with experts from ever-widening groups of disciplines, subdisciplines, and specialties eager to offer themselves as consultants and reap lucrative fees. What *is* difficult is making change that matters to disempowered, marginalized people, change that provides tools they can use to lessen oppression, challenge repression, and change the relations of power.

Critics have argued for decades now that the reliance by some feminists on criminal law and institutions of criminal justice is misguided — bad policy, bad praxis, a theoretical and intellectual dead end (Chesney-Lind and Pasko 2013; Girard 2009; Bumiller 2008; Mosher 2006; Little 2005; Snider 1994). Criminal law individualizes and disempowers those it is supposed to help — as illustrated by the continued use of countercharges and contempt of court charges against women, the continued marginalization of women who do not fit a hegemonic female ideal, the backlog of cases in "specialized" courts, and the lack of "teeth" behind protection orders (Koshan and Wiegers 2007; Women's Court Watch 2006). Widespread zero-tolerance provisions, specialized courts, and police units, inserted into domestic violence statutes to stop state officials from ignoring women's pleas for help (or so we thought), have also served to intensify state surveillance over women already victimized by violence, racism, and poverty. In some instances, state officials forced progressive feminist movements into uneasy alliances with neo-conservative groups lobbying for increased punitiveness and state coercion (Girard 2009; Collier 2005). In others, feminist groups actively promoted intensified criminalization — for example, against those demonized as "sex traffickers" (Bernstein 2012). The result is that criminalization policies have aligned with neo-liberal governments to incarcerate ever increasing numbers of (primarily) poor, young Aboriginal and Black men (Johnson and Dawson 2011; Mosher 2006; Comack and Balfour 2004; McDermott and Garofalo 2004), a process that has been labelled "the carceral turn" (Garland 2001; Wacquant 2009a, 2009b).

There are numerous other problems in a reliance on criminal justice "remedies." Despite a few well-intentioned efforts to move beyond "traditional" criminal justice approaches (Malloch and McIvor 2011; Fortune et al. 2010), the criminal justice system in the modern democratic state remains structurally and ideologically ill-equipped to deliver empowerment or amelioration (Chesney-Lind and Pasko 2013; Fortune et al. 2010; McDermott and Garofalo 2004). In practice, even explicit ameliorative agendas such as restorative justice take second place to the priorities of security, and are thus restricted to offenders classified as low risk. Criminal justice does not have a Janus-like quality, a legitimating, positive, or life-affirming mission to balance its repressive side. Institutions of criminal justice become visible to media and governments when they fail to contain and control inmates (hence the primacy of security), not when they fail to empower. Quite the opposite: officials who follow the stated mission of the Correctional Service of Canada (2010) — to "actively encourage and assist offenders to become law-abiding citizens" — expose themselves to media accusations of "coddling criminals" (Bruser 2011; Platt 2012). Thus, unlike schools, which can be called to account for failing to educate, or hospitals, which can be embarrassed for failing to heal, calling prisons to account for failing to rehabilitate or empower is likely to backfire, as it has so many times in the past (Garland 1990, 2001).

Lobbying for equal-opportunity repression, not a progressive goal under any circumstances, is particularly problematic when evidence indicates that when *some* differences between male and female punishment were gender-sensitive, they actually worked to the advantage of (some) women and girls (Chesney-Lind and Pasko 2013; Baskin 2006; Mosher 2006; McMahon and Pence 2003; Hannah-Moffat 2002; Rafter 1985a; Zedner 1998).[1] Moreover, in a neo-liberal, punishment-obsessed culture, any evidence showing "leniency" in the criminal justice system will instantly be seized by sensationalistic media voices eager both to foment and to capitalize on anti-feminist backlash. And the policy lesson taken from studies showing male-female differences in treatment will unfailingly be interpreted as a call to punish women more, not to equalize by punishing men *less*. This and similar iatrogenic consequences of feminist-inspired initiatives have led many of us to argue that, instead of focusing on obtaining punishment and revenge for the very real injuries that women suffer at the hands of men, feminists should move back to a focus on changing the social conditions that make women and children easy and legitimate targets for male rage. This means spending more time and effort on struggles to attain equal resources for women and children, working for more community-based public services, for universal state-subsidized child care, and for income equality. The ultimate goal must be to establish social and cultural conditions that create and sustain less desperate populations — of men, women, and children — for only by doing this can we build less violent societies (Snider 1998).

The purpose of this chapter is to advance that goal by using the lessons of the past as guidelines for the knowledge work, resistance, and praxis of the future. The discussion is organized around two broad questions. First, is it possible to make significant ameliorative change in neo-liberal times? At the present moment progressive groups are forced to spend inordinate amounts of energy and money on defensive battles to forestall draconian budget cutbacks and prevent powerful neo-liberal and neo-conservative forces from reversing feminist victories won decades earlier on everything from abortion rights to equal pay for work of equal value. Second, what about institutions of criminal justice? Should strategies using criminal law be completely abandoned, or are there ways of maximizing the symbolic impact of criminalization while minimizing its inhuman consequences? The chapter begins by exploring the pivotal role of knowledge claims. Understanding how change is forged requires, first and foremost, dissecting the role of experts, of expertise, and of authorized knowers and knowledge claims. It is essential to examine the impact and results of feminist and non-feminist claims that have constituted woman as victim and as offender. Only by analyzing how feminist knowledge claims and expertise become part of the knowledge-power-change nexus is there any hope (there is never any guarantee) of fashioning research and praxis with truly counterhegemonic potential.

## Gaining Ground:
## Reconstituting Woman as Offender and Victim

The first and most obvious lesson of the reform efforts of the past is that making change is a complex and complicated activity. The belief that we can either control or predict the future is a modernist dream.[2] Trying to control change is an impossible task because we are describing in static terms an ever-moving, constantly reconstituted social reality (Foucault 1977, 1978b). Our knowledge claims transform the objects we are writing about. This does not happen in ways that we can predict, or have consequences we neces-sarily desire. Feminist and non-feminist research, evaluations, and critiques continuously inspire new belief systems, policy initiatives, and procedural reforms, which constitute new and different social and cultural situations out of which come the next set of evaluations and changes, simultaneously responding to and constituting yet another distinct set of conditions. Ad infinitum.

To interrogate the knowledge/power equation, then, we must ask how feminist knowledge has been fed back into Canadian society. This means treating knowledge produced by feminist and non-feminist criminologies as productive and constitutive, as an essential component of changes in the conception of woman as victim and as offender, and in the policies devised to simultaneously control and assist her. Our claims as authorized knowers and our actions as reformers have become integral parts of a complex process that has transformed the entire landscape of criminal justice, from the belief systems of police officers to black letter law. Most crucially, they have transformed and reconstituted the subject of feminist reform efforts: the battered wife, the rape victim, the prostitute, the criminalized and incarcerated woman. Thanks to feminist "discoveries" about her, she has become a different kind of subject than she was in 1955 (Heidensohn 1994; Snider 2003).

However, to say that feminist knowledge claims are an important part of the power/knowledge nexus, and that we cannot understand the process of change without looking at "our" part in it, is not to say that feminist claims have automatically been integrated into state policy. Far from it. To understand the reception of knowledge claims, how they are interpreted, received, and publicized, we must shift analytical focus from knowledge produced to knowledge heard. Knowledge claims are bids to power, bids that work to the benefit of some parties and the detriment of others. Those with power to set institutional agendas — players with superior economic, political, social, and moral capital — are therefore able to influence which/whose claims are heard and listened to. There are two essential differences between claims that get written up in the *Globe and Mail* editorials and inserted into the briefing notes of cabinet ministers, and those than languish on life-support in intensive-care units (a.k.a. Sociology and Women's Studies departments). Knowledge claims with "legs" are those that resonate with dominant cultural agendas (see Girard 2009; Collier 2008, 2012; Mann 2012; Garland 2001), and those that promise economic and/or political rewards to groups that matter. Most critical feminist claims demand a redistribution of income, power, prestige, and benefits from the most powerful groups in the society to the least. It is hardly surprising that much more work — more research, more activism, more time — is required to get these claims heard. And if getting an audience for critical claims is difficult, getting them translated into workable and ameliorative policies is tougher still.

As Elizabeth Comack suggests in chapter 1, the goals of second-wave feminist criminology were to study the forces that maintained female inequality, and to change them. The defective, inferior woman constituted by nineteenth-century criminologists was revealed as a product of the patriarchal lenses of the "scientists" who "discovered" her (Lombroso and Ferrero 1890 [1985]; Goring 1913; Pollak 1950; Hooton 1939). Early feminist studies replaced these gender-biased views and knowledge claims with ones that acknowledged women's inequality (Smart 1976; Morris 1987; Bertrand 1969). Gender bias and misogyny were not restricted to positivist criminology, or to the nineteenth century: 1970s labelling and "new criminology" perspectives depicted rebellious boys as heroes resisting the yoke of capitalism and conformity while rebellious girls, if mentioned at all, were either promiscuous copycats or victims of their hormones and pathologies (Becker 1963; Taylor, Walton, and Young 1973).

The resulting feminist criminologies — liberal, radical, and socialist — were critiqued by the next generation of feminist knowers (Daly and Chesney-Lind 1988), and in many cases by the original authors as well. Feminist knowledge claims of the 1980s were castigated for failing to take differences between women into account. By attempting to speak "truth" in the name of *all* women, researchers inadvertently privileged the perspectives of the white, upper-middle-class, educated woman. Poststructuralist/postmodern perspectives today incorporate race, class, sexual orientation, and other differences between women and men into their accounts (Chesney-Lind and Pasko 2013; Comack 2006; Smart 1995; Bosworth 1999; Worrall 1990, 2002).

In the 1970s and 1980s, feminist work attracted considerable public attention. Patriarchal and discriminatory practices in every profession and occupation were unearthed and publicized. Components of feminist arguments migrated from position papers and articles in obscure journals into people's belief systems and institutions. Overt gender bias gradually became unfashionable. In this process, science and scientific expertise came under attack. Feminists (and environmentalists and other critics) deconstructed the expert by revealing that "objective" scientific studies in a number of arenas were fatally flawed by the (unacknowledged) gender, race, and class biases of the authors. The cumulative effect of these studies was to destabilize expertise in the public mind. Outsiders (that is, the great majority who are not credentialed as scientific "experts") saw that expertise is fallible. Scientists see the world and interpret their experiments through culturally formed prejudices and biases, which often include male-gendered glasses.

Equally credible experts disagree. "Scientific knowledge," once considered unchallengeable, was revealed as a human — and largely male — creation. Through destabilizing expertise, the *fallible expert* was constituted. In criminology, questioning the mainly male "experts" of the past meant showing that the emperors of science had no clothes. One important effect was to open the door for those seen as victims and offenders, equipping them with evidence and language to resist scientific knowledge/power claims about their lives, their motivation, their realities (Snider 2003).

A second and more direct result of feminist research was the constitution of *woman as victim*. Quantitative and qualitative research in the 1970s and 1980s revealed that women were regularly beaten and abused by their male partners, and harassed or assaulted by males in positions of power over them, by employers, brothers, and fathers (MacKinnon 1987; Marsh, Geist, and Caplan 1982; Matthews 1994; Stanko 1990). Police were unlikely to respond when called for help because they classified such calls as domestic disputes, private issues best settled between the couple — which meant, by the male partner. In police subcultures husbands were seen as having the right and duty to control their wives. "Everyone knew" a wife was emotional, often unreasonable, nagging her man until he (understandably) lost control. As long as male discipline did not go "too far," such practices were tacitly accepted (Dobash and Dobash 1979). This research evidence persuaded many feminists that zero-tolerance provisions were the only way to make police and courts take "wife-battering" (as it was then called) seriously.[3]

Feminist research on sexual assault followed a similar trajectory. It showed that rape was much more common than was previously thought, and that women who reported rape were either not believed or blamed for failing to prevent it (Brownmiller 1975). If charges were laid, victims were forced to endure nothing less than a second assault in court — and beyond it in the court of media-driven public opinion. As Carol Smart (1989) pointed out, the rape trial became a "pornographic vignette" in which victims were forced to relive the attack to establish their own credibility. Feminist researchers interpreted sexual assault as an important mechanism of patriarchal dominance. Well-founded fears of rape kept women docile, "in their place," under male control. Women ultimately, always, bore the blame, the shame, and the baby. To change this situation, feminist claims-makers lobbied for laws that replaced rape statutes with "sexual assault" laws emphasizing the violent nature of the act, and for new laws of evidence aimed at lessening victim trauma on the stand and increasing chances of convictions (Ruebsaat 1985; Snider 1985; Mohr and Roberts 1994).

Women serving time in reformatories, jails, and prisons — formerly depicted by Lombroso as "worse than any man," as defective and therefore in need of treatment and/or containment (Adelberg and Currie 1993) — were reconstituted as needy and victimized. Second-wave feminist research highlighted differences between male and female prisoners. The female prisoner became "the woman in trouble" (Comack 1996), less violent, less dangerous, a woman deserving "help" rather than punishment. The violence that women did commit was more likely to be familial and defensive, not aggressive and stranger-oriented. Female prisoners had different demographic characteristics: they were more likely to have suffered physical and sexual abuse (especially the latter), to be custodial parents, and to come from an ethnic/racial minority — Aboriginal in Canada, Australia, and New Zealand, Black or Hispanic in the United States, Caribbean/Black or Asian in Britain (Carcach and Grant 2000, 1999; Finn et al. 1999; Canadian Centre for Justice Statistics 1997, 2000; Bureau of Justice Statistics 2000; British Home Office 1999). Despite this, fewer programs were offered to female prisoners, who were incarcerated for acts overlooked or celebrated in males, such as sexual "promiscuity," and kept inside longer and at higher security levels than their offender profile would dictate (Chesney-Lind and Pasko 2013; Carlen 1983, 1988; Chesney-Lind 1981, 1987, 1988b; Hannah-Moffat 2002).

The most significant and important result of such feminist claims has been the constitution of a new subject, a female offender who "knows" at some level of her identity that women are often victimized by men, and that this is socially and legally censured. She also "knows" that experts who diagnose and proclaim the "truth" of female prisoners make mistakes. Thus, we see the emergence of the prisoner "with attitude," the woman who enters prison equipped with new tools of resistance. This subject draws from this culturally available knowledge store to develop strategies of resistance and to maintain less censured individual selves and identities (Chesney-Lind and Pasko 2013; Bosworth 1999; Worrall 1990).

The woman victimized by physical or sexual assault occupies a different discursive space than the criminalized woman, though she may be the same person.[4] Knowledge claims have constituted her, at least in the Western world, as the Believable Victim. In the larger culture today, the female victim of domestic or sexual assault is officially recognized as deserving assistance from the state, action from the police, and accountability and revenge from the criminal justice system — which does not mean that she receives such assistance (Girard 2009). The raped woman has become "the paradigmatic victim subject" in neo-liberal (North) America (Bernstein 2012). Expectations about what criminal law can accomplish have been raised, as has consciousness. Middle-class and working-class women are more likely to have the resources — psychological, political, and economic — to escape violent partners and to both demand and expect redress for their victimization. Here as elsewhere upper-middle-class white women have benefited most from feminist efforts to compel the state to take attacks on women seriously; Aboriginal, marginalized poor women the least (Comack 2012; Chesney-Lind and Pasko 2013).

If the criminal justice system is called in, however, *all* women lose control of the process. Decisions about how the attack should be treated and what should happen to the offender are out of a woman's hands. She becomes "the complainant," and is henceforth a legal category, a statistic, a good or bad witness, a "case" to be processed in the most "efficient" manner (see Spohn and Tellis 2012; Comack and Peter 2005). For the institutions and actors of law and criminal justice, only certain victims are deserving; they distinguish between the good victim and all others. The faithful wife, the good mother, the gainfully employed, and the teenager living with parents — in general, women who are acting out conventional patriarchal scripts — fall into the "good victim" category. Even for her, the ideal legal subject, the "justice" experience is corrosive. However the single mother on welfare, the Aboriginal woman on a reserve, the runaway street kid, the prostitute — women without the moral, social, and economic capital to force criminal justice to take them seriously — are relegated to the "other" category. This woman becomes the subject who is, literally and figuratively, hard to believe.

One caveat: it is ontologically and epistemologically impossible to find linear cause and effect links between knowledge claims, feminist or otherwise, and changes in cultural climate, law, and policy. Cause and effect are complex and overdetermined,[5] an intricate and massive series of feedback spirals and loops as factors constitute each other. Nor is this process conspiratorial, directed by all-knowing, all-powerful classes, ethnicities or genders. Knowledge claims and dominant discourse seep into individual consciousness and personalities to different degrees and in different ways. The argument here is that the "common-sense" beliefs of Canadian society about victimized and criminalized women have changed over time. Female offenders and victims increasingly make their own claims, adapting cultural resources (knowledge claims and morality tales) to their individual or collective advantage.

Overall, the knowledge that women in the past have been victimized by men in every dominant institution — family, school, church, and workplace — is now widespread. The very success of the feminist movement in getting women's complaints taken seriously is a major factor generating resistance, in the form of counterclaims, countercharges, and backlash. This "push-back" has also become part of the feedback loop.

## Losing Ground: Neo-Liberal Realities

Many women today are worse off materially than their counterparts were forty years ago. Welfare and (un)employment benefits are harder to obtain and retain; education and day care are more expensive and increasingly unavailable. Those in the bottom third of the income pyramid face more intrusive surveillance and greater demonization if they are perceived as stepping out of line. In neo-liberal societies, those unable or unwilling to meet the stepped-up demands of neo-liberal societies, the "flawed consumers" (Bauman 1997), are constituted as "risky subjects," feckless inadequates who must be forcibly "responsibilized" or punished, preferably both. The failures of feminist change-making efforts must be located in the context of the dismantling of the Keynesian welfare state and the allied rise of an anti-feminist backlash.

### The Gendered Impact of Dismantling the Welfare State

Canada, with its export and resource-based economy, has always been particularly vulnerable to global economic conditions (Fudge and Cossman 2002: 13). In the 1970s mounting inflation, government deficits, and intensified global competition, spurred by new technologies that freed capital from the geographic constraints of the nation-state, undermined the economic, political, and intellectual viability of the Canadian welfare state. The transformation in government personnel, thought, policy, and rhetoric was quick and profound (Cohen 1997) — these knowledge claims were easy to "hear." Priorities such as fighting unemployment, inflation, and poverty disappeared. Cutting government deficits, freeing business from the "yoke" of government, tax cuts, and privatization became the new priorities. With the acceptance of doctrines proclaiming markets as the only legitimate regulatory mechanism, policies aimed at protecting citizens from the harsh realities of profit maximization weakened and disappeared. "Labour-market flexibility" became the new mantra, and policies were tailored to meet that goal (Fudge and Cossman 2002: 14). Responsibility for individual welfare became "less a matter of collective, social or public obligation" (Fudge and

Cossman 2002: 3–4); producing the self-reliant citizen became the ultimate goal of government and the ultimate achievement of the responsible citizen.

The gendered impact of this shift has been documented by a host of scholars (see Collier 2005, 2008, 2012; Mosher 2006; Little 2005; Brodie 1995; Bakker 1996; Bashevkin 1998). Judy Fudge (2002) traced the history of federal civil servants in Canada, 60 percent of whom are women in low-level clerical positions. The rise and subsequent decline of the women's movement can be traced from its nadir in 1944, when all married female civil service employees, seventeen thousand of them, were fired to provide jobs for returning World War II veterans, to its peak in the late 1970s. Several things came together for the women's movement during that time. The Liberal government created the Royal Commission on the Status of Women (1967), accepted its major recommendations, and set up the Office of Equal Opportunity (1971) and the National Commission on the Status of Women (1972). All three government-funded bodies pushed hard to secure equality, in areas from divorce law to pension reform. Liberal feminism — predominantly middle-class, educated, and white — became a force to reckon with. In the federal civil service, with studies showing that formal equality had not produced substantive equality, the principle of equal pay for work of equal value was adopted (Fudge 2002), and a fifteen-year battle for compensation and back wages ensued. In the late 1980s and 1990s, with the media fanning the flames and conditions in the private sector deteriorating, public servants were demonized as overpaid, underworked fat cats. This massive resentment meant that gender equality could not be achieved by paying women more; equity would have to be achieved by paying men less. Thus the wages and working conditions of both sexes deteriorated. Ironically, on October 29, 1999, the Treasury Board agreed to pay compensation to women for past injustices. But the wages and working conditions of both sexes continued to deteriorate. According to the Canadian Labour Congress (2009) approximately 33 percent of men and 40 percent of women in the federal public service today hold some sort of precarious form of employment, a lose-lose solution that the Conservative government of Stephen Harper promised to make even worse.

Other components of the welfare state were refashioned with similar effects, from the late 1980s on. Fudge (2002: 110) sees the free-trade election of 1988 as pivotal, arguing that it signalled "the loss of national sovereignty and dismantling of the Canadian welfare state." Working conditions in the public and private sectors deteriorated; job and wage cuts were common as out-sourcing and "just in time" management took hold. Increased levels of exploitation, increased income inequality, massive unemployment, and a general lowering of wages resulted. Tax law (Philips 2002), retirement income (Orenstein 2011), immigration (Macklin 2002), and health care (Gilmore 2002) were all subjected to the rigors of the free market. Services that delivered profits to the private sector were expanded; unprofitable services atrophied. Thus by the late 1980s feminist discourse morphed into gender neutrality, and social justice was replaced by market discourse. While these policy shifts had an impact on men, women, and children, they hit certain groups much harder than others. The virtues of neo-liberalism — self-reliance, commodification, and market dependence — are harder to achieve if you are poor, uneducated, disabled, or marginalized by race or ethnicity. When governments turn their responsibilities for day care, elder care, and health care over to the private sector, those who cannot pay for services are punished. When retirement income is privatized, those who have been excluded from the labour market (traditionally mothers), and those who never earned much (also more likely to be women), suffer most.

The neo-liberal revolution, then, has altered the quality of life and life chances of all women. From the 1990s on — and continuing today — those at the top of the income distribution hierarchy would see their incomes grow exponentially; those in the bottom quintile would suffer declines (Collier 2008; Morrow, Hankivsky, and Varcoe 2004; Schrecker 2001). For middle-class and working-class families, it now takes the combined wages of two breadwinners to provide the equivalent in purchasing power to the wage of one full-time, unionized breadwinner (usually male) in 1975 (Fudge and Cossman 2002). Although government programs in Canada have thus far prevented total destitution for those on the bottom, inequality has risen sharply, within categories as well as between them (McInturff 2013; Yalnizyan 2013). Wage distribution for women has become much more unequal. Women of the baby boom generation have, by and large, benefited from feminist struggles for access, wage, and pension equality. Younger women, particularly those with less social or racial/ethnic capital, face highly competitive labour markets that deliver few good jobs for anyone. Those dependent on the state and those unable or unwilling to take on "responsible," profit-maximizing roles are worst off, suffering not only loss of income and entitlement, but also intensified censure, surveillance, and incarceration.

Many of these changes, particularly in Canada, happened despite feminist struggle, knowledge claims, and lobbying.[6] The elite-sponsored forces that "caused" neo-liberal reform were largely economic and political.

Foreseeing the spectre of declining profitability and defining this as a crisis of capitalism, captains of industry, political leaders, and state officials used Chicago-school economics ("science") to legitimize, publicize, and celebrate knowledge claims consonant with elite views of the world and elite priorities. Their actions as agents on all cultural and social fronts persuaded state elites to institute policy reforms that reduced the "burdens" — of employees, regulations, and taxes — on business. Their private troubles became national and international problems because they had the structural and ideological power to make their claims into self-fulfilling prophecies. The 2007–08 fiscal crisis exacerbated the situation: government deficits (incurred in part by bailing out the investment banks that caused the crisis in the first place) became an excuse to intensify cutbacks in public and social services. Most neo-liberal reforms were sold to the populace — the bulk of these changes were voted in — with promises of prosperity and wealth on the one hand and threat of economic disaster on the other. Entrepreneurial citizens, it was promised, will get rich (the rest will get intensified social, legal, and moral control). Not coincidentally, and notwithstanding the 2008 crash, the resulting society has delivered disproportionately large benefits to the elites that sponsored these changes (Williams 2012).

### Anti-Feminist Backlash and Punitiveness

Both backlash and accelerated punitiveness are intricately related, though not directly or through linear cause and effect, to the material and ideological changes introduced by neo-liberal policies. The consequences are particularly dire for the most marginalized women. Some of the most dramatic and far-reaching effects have been on the lives of "woman as offender" and "woman as victim."

While rates of incarceration for both women and men have increased (MacCharles 2012), women have experienced the most dramatic growth. This is glaringly obvious in the most neo-liberal Anglo-American democracy, the United States, where the number of male and female prisoners rose from under five hundred thousand in 1980 to over two million in 2009 and still it grows. As one study concluded, "Approximately one-third of all Black males will experience state prison in their lifetime" (Austin et al. 2001: 14). Not only that, the combined effects of zero tolerance, "three strikes" laws, and draconian anti-drug legislation have narrowed the long-standing gender gap: since 1995 women's rate of growth in incarceration has outpaced that of men (Austin et al. 2001). As always, the female offender is highly racialized. From 1986 to 1991 rates for African-American women for drug offences rose by 828 percent; for Hispanics, 328 percent, for white women, 241 percent (Chesney-Lind and Pasko 2013; Chesney-Lind and Faith 2000). In Canada Aboriginal women make up almost 33 percent of the female population incarcerated in federal prisons, yet only about 4 percent of the Canadian population (Wesley 2012). There is no comparable increase in female crime rates to explain or justify this mania for incarceration (Belknap 2001).

With the alpha power adopting intensified incarceration, other societies susceptible to its rhetoric and example have copied and (more rarely) resisted U.S. penal policies. In England and Wales the number of prisoners increased by 41,800 (to over 86,000) from 1993 to 2012 (Ministry of Justice 2013). In Australia the prison population increased by 31 percent from 2002 to 2012 (Australian Bureau of Statistics). Although 93 percent of inmates are male, women in these countries have also increased their market share. Until a majority Conservative government took power in 2009, Canada's federal government tried to bring rates of incarceration under control, instituting restorative justice alternatives for juveniles and Aboriginal people and issuing directives advising judges to use non-custodial sentences wherever possible (R v Gladue 1999; Finn et al. 1999). Many provincial governments resisted their lead. Although the provinces only handle adult prisoners on remand and those serving sentences of less than two years, Alberta and Ontario[7] have made incarceration more certain and more punitive, setting up boot camps, cutting inmate pay, charging federal prisoners room and board (30 percent of daily wages, which range from $1 to $4 a day for women inmates),and banning smoking. Given that most inmates smoke, tobacco is an important currency of exchange inside the prison, and inmates do not have the option of stepping outside to light up.

For woman as victim, the consequences of feminist-inspired reforms reshaping domestic and sexual assault have been, to say the least, mixed. Zero-tolerance policies on spousal assault produced more female offenders, with women getting charged with contempt of court for their unwillingness to testify. Or they faced criminal charges when their abuser claimed, "She hit me too" (Snider 1994, 1998; Comack, Chopyk, and Wood 2000). Here too punishment is racialized and class-specific — most prisoners are young, poor, and from minority groups — with sharp increases in the incarceration rates of impoverished Aboriginal men accompanying zero-tolerance provisions (Comack and Balfour 2004). Since the 1990s, however, under feminist pressure, specialized police services and domestic violence courts have been created in some provinces to address the unique experiences of women experiencing violence, create safer environments for abused women, lessen the emotional and financial burden on victims, and address the backlog of domestic violence cases caused by zero-tolerance policies. Progress has been slow: the specialized courts are still backlogged, marginalized women are still treated unfairly, and many victims are still blamed for their abuse (see Women's Court Watch Project 2006).

Sexual assault laws have accomplished some of the goals that feminists had hoped for, namely more charges laid and higher conviction rates (Roberts 1991; Ursel 1991). But as Lise Gotell (2009) suggests, such outcomes are seldom found in cases involving the most vulnerable of women: Indigenous women, homeless women, and drug-dependent women. Similarly, disabled women are more likely to be sexually assaulted because of their dependency upon those who are likely to harm them, such as caregivers, yet they are also easily discredited and infantilized at trial for their lack of competency (Benedet and Grant 2007, 2013). Indeed, feminist-inspired victories of affirmative consent laws have not resulted in a decentring of rape myths. Nor is there evidence that women feel safe or are safer. Despite extensive changes in laws of evidence, testifying in court is still an ordeal for the victim. While more attention is shifting to the culpability of judges (see Women's Court Watch Project 2006), recent comments by a judge in Manitoba who claimed that "sex was in the air" given the victim's "suggestive attire and flirtatious conduct" (Busby 2014; McIntyre 2011) suggest that there is still a long way to go. As Elizabeth Comack and Gillian Balfour (2004) illustrate, the old defence practice of "whacking the complainant" — that is, destroying her credibility in every legal way — is alive and well in Canadian courts.

These results are not surprising. They are a natural consequence of seeking change through the criminal justice system and the adversarial imperatives employed there. Moreover, it is hard to envisage an alternative within criminal justice institutions that would improve the process for the victim without assuming that every accused is guilty. Within institutions of criminal justice, then, neo-liberal governance has fashioned a new "common-sense." Despite hard empirical evidence to the contrary (Johnson 2006; Carlen 2002a; Comack, Chopyk, and Wood 2000), conceptualizations of domestic assault today portray men and women as equally aggressive, as equally likely to bully and inflict damage on their partners (see Collier 2012; Mann 2012). Gender-neutral policies and programs in institutions threaten gender-sensitive regimes; feminist claims about gender and female equality have been muted.

Outside criminal justice, the anti-feminist backlash has invaded every institution, from education (where boys are now seen as victims of discrimination) to workplace harassment. The word "feminist" has been transformed from a badge of honour to a stigma (Masuch 2004). Canada's federal government, in 1998, cut subsidies to the National Action Committee on the Status of Women and awarded subsidies to the anti-feminist group Real Women (Fudge 2002). Fathers' rights groups, one component of the powerful men's movement, claim that family law discriminates against fathers and demand their "right" to sole custody of children (Mann 2012; Girard 2009; Minaker and Snider 2006). Intolerance of feminist positions and policy reversals are widespread — in many U.S. states the right to abortion is threatened, pregnant cocaine addicts are charged with felonies against the unborn child (Tong 1996), and equal rights amendments are seldom seriously discussed. Moral panics about violent girls, female stalkers, and homicidal mothers fill newspapers and magazines, videos, and the Internet. Stories that reflect unfavourably on "feminists" receive prime time. Selected interviews with shelter clients often highlight those (few?) who claimed that anti-male doctrines were being forced upon them (Mann 2000). By the late 1990s there was an increased emphasis on collaborations between services for abused women and the state. During the same period, however, funding for services for assaulted women decreased in most provinces (Strega 2006), and services to protect women fleeing abuse were eroded. What remains is a focus on crime, punishment, and increased surveillance of women. Cuts in funding for services for abused women increase tension between community agencies, forcing them to compete against each other (see Durazo 2007). If organizations are to work collaboratively, funding and support need to increase and remain stable for all services.

Neo-liberal governance has required the constitution of a new subject, the responsibilized individual. The goal of government became not to deliver social justice or full employment, or guarantee minimum standards of living to those on the bottom, but to enable citizens to become consumers who can fend for themselves. Everyone is to make prudent investments and put their faith in the private sector and in markets — outcomes delivered by the market are just and fair by definition. You get what you deserve. Consumers have been "set free" from the yoke of government — free to turn themselves into commodities, marketing their skills, wombs, genes, and identities. These measures were sold to the electorate, through knowledge claims, in three basic ways: they were argued as necessary (to cut government deficits), as beneficial (to ensure that citizens take responsibility for themselves), and as forms of freedom (delivering tax cuts and less intrusive government).

The result has been extensive privatization, the fraying of the social safety net, and sharply heightened levels of inequality (Cossman and Fudge 2002; Schrecker 2001). Increased inequality and more desperate, fearful populations have always gone hand in hand with greater punitiveness and higher levels of state coercion (Martin 2002: 355). As people on the bottom become more desperate, the privileged become more fearful. Both segments feel resentful, fearful, more victimized, and less well served by government. Insecure people in unequal societies consent to more state control over the people supposedly beneath them — the people with less income, power, and prestige. As long as "criminals," "welfare cheats," "violent girls," and "squeegee kids" are the object of repression, and as long as the controls are directed against Them and not Us, coercion is legitimate and politically popular.

## Making Change in Neo-Liberal Times

Clearly, attempting to change societies is a complex undertaking. In the process of change-making, feminist knowledge claims, like all others, become part and parcel of the reality they attempt to alter, thereby constituting a new reality. Once knowledge claims get published and known, the social environment is changed. One useful analogy might be to picture "society" as a complicated, humungous sweater made up of many different types and colours of yarn. Each new knowledge claim represents a stitch, a contribution to the shape and pattern of the whole, which changes the overall pattern, however slightly. Critical, barely heard counterhegemonic arguments may be represented by light-coloured, weak, or dead-end strands; hegemonic arguments from dominant groups, those picked up and celebrated, are fashioned in bold, bright colours, of tough sturdy yarn. Hegemonic claims are the most numerous, and basically determine the shape of the sweater. However, feminist knowledge claims are now part of the whole, and their presence therefore alters that whole.

While the first part of this chapter has shown where and how feminist claims were heard, the second part has illustrated where they were not heard, and why. To return to the sweater analogy, we have seen how dominant economic and political forces tore the Keynesian sweater apart, refashioning it to fit not the entitled or victimized woman, but the genderless — or male? — neo-liberal subject. Some feminist and some critical claims — those legitimating increased punitiveness and incarceration — were reworked and incorporated in this new design, and now strengthen neo-liberal motifs. The combined forces of capitalism in perceived crisis, acting in concert with the state, are sometimes too powerful for oppositional groups to overcome. In the last twenty-five years, agents who embodied capitalist interests, speaking in the name of prosperity and progress, proved figuratively and literally irresistible.

Thus policy shifted in directions that left women more equal before law in theory, but materially poorer. The picture is not all gloom and doom. Some women, primarily white, educated, and middle-class or above, reaped enormous benefits from feminist change-making initiatives. They (we) now enjoy legal rights to education and access into professions, top jobs in important institutions, and marriage to equally successful partners. Their children have the best of the public services that remain, in addition to gaining access to the best of the private sector. Even the double shift facing all employed mothers, where child care and household maintenance chores must be done on top of wage labour, has been lessened for these women because they can hire nannies and housecleaners (usually less privileged women). Many of the benefits of feminist change-making have been similarly class and race/ethnic specific. For women in the bottom 50 percent of the income pyramid and for racialized women, the consequences of some feminist claims, when joined with neo-liberal mentalities, sensibilities, and policies, have been dire.

What can we learn from this? Is it possible to make significant human-enhancing change in neo-liberal societies, or institute policies that are less likely to backfire? Yes. While we cannot control how our arguments are heard, or predict their consequences, we can make our messages harder to "mishear." This approach requires walking a fine line because messages deemed "too radical" will never make it into political arenas, while those labelled "reasonable" may be incorporated and co-opted, sometimes with disastrous effects (see Collier 2012; Mann 2012; Girard 2009; McMahon and Pence 2003).

Women facing criminal charges, or incarcerated women, are a case in point. The consequences of feminist change-making efforts around women in prison have proved problematic because of how women's needs have been translated by politicians and correctional officials. Prison activists and feminist researchers (often the same people) argued for change in women's prisons that would empower inmates, helping them overcome the multiple victimizations most prisoners have endured (Chesney-Lind and Pasko 2013; Task Force on Federally Sentenced Women 1990; Bertrand 1999; Hayman 2000; Gelsthorpe 1989; Hannah-Moffat and Shaw 2000a; Shaw 1993). The subject they constituted was the capable woman who needs more choices, better alternatives, and more humane, self-enhancing counsel. If it is now accepted that prisons cannot be abolished, at least not yet, this criminalized woman needs gender- and ethnicity-sensitive prisons. Instead, these claims were heard through discourses of risk and the language of risk assessment, in which women with multiple needs — the most traumatized, those with the least education and the worst backgrounds — become high-risk offenders (Hannah-Moffat 2001). With risk assessments unmistakeably "proving" that these women are the most likely to reoffend, the neediest and most dispossessed inmates get herded into maximum-security facilities, where they are deprived of programs that inmates in the "normal" population receive. How, then, can messages of empowerment be made harder to "mishear"?

First and foremost, the dialogue with criminalized women and with those paid to keep them inside is of paramount importance. There will always be "better" and "worse" prisons; and with punitive neo-conservative and neo-liberal forces now in the ascendance, struggles for ameliorative change may, at the very least, stave off further regression. Going silent means that the only voices governments and correctional authorities hear are vindictive and fear-obsessed, which provides a certain recipe for longer sentences and meaner prisons. Moreover, though arguments for humanitarian treatment of the incarcerated cut no political ice today, working with inmates and officials to humanize prison environments and empower those inside is the only possible option for people who care about prisoners.

Second, critique and policy are separate but equally necessary discussions. As Pat Carlen (2002b: 19) points out, misheard messages may occur not because one party is sadistic or malicious, but because "different parties hear differently." Feminist objectives must be seen through the lens of prison managers, because these people have to translate them into operating procedures. They will therefore have different priorities, points of view, and ways of seeing the female prisoner. They must negotiate change through a myriad of complex and contradictory government regulations, keep unionized staff (who also see differently) onside, and prevent security lapses. Security trumps all other objectives in today's prisons, given vengeance-obsessed media and politicians constantly on the lookout for sensational items. It is essential to hear, respect, and understand the differences that parties bring to policy discussions without silencing any of the voices. As Carlen points out, unlike academics, senior administrators and prison staff have to act. They do not have the luxury of "talking off the top of their critiques" (Carlen 2002b: 18).

From a praxis perspective, social action always starts with the obvious, which in this case is the uncontroversial, "common-sense" reality that punishment involves gendered bodies. Experience teaches us that seeking gender-sensitive regimes is less likely to backfire than is arguing for equality between male and female institutions. Women still make up a tiny percentage of prison populations (less than 5 percent in most countries), and the last thing that progressive forces want to do is increase those numbers. As we have seen, arguing for equal punishment in a punitive culture will be heard as wanting more women to be punished more, not as a call to punish men less. Seeking parity rather than formal legal equality is less likely to deliver "punishment in disguise" (Hannah-Moffat 2002; Carlen 2002b: 13). Courtroom strategies that aim to widen law's understanding of "free choice" and of "rational behaviour" may decrease convictions because they require law to formally recognize the realities facing the abused wife or Aboriginal street prostitute. What is rational for the white, middle-class, middle-aged man is not necessarily rational for the woman escaping a man she thinks will kill her, or the runaway whose alternatives are turning tricks or going hungry (or going "cold turkey" from addictions, which many see as much worse). Specialized courts and police services cannot erase the deep seeded beliefs that many officials hold regarding these women, nor have they served to make women feel safer.

Thus, progressives might fight for judicial instructions that ask courts to consider not what the classic "reasonable man" would have done, but "what was reasonable for this defendant under these circumstances?" (Hudson 2002). Interrogating the meaning of "real" choices is also essential: to choose the law-abiding options endorsed by corrections, people must be able to acquire the essential goods and services of life through legitimate means. Poverty and racism, sexism, and other "isms" prevent most marginalized people from doing this. Arguments pointing out such basic facts (repeated again and again — which, again, makes it hard for policy-makers to "hear") highlight the crucially important link between inequality and criminality, a linkage obliterated by the now dominant "science" of risk assessment.

Looking at sexual and domestic assault, how can we lessen the chances of mishearing here? First, we must recognize the very real victories that feminist activists have achieved. Definitions of domestic and sexual assault have been clarified and extended, and there has been real and significant progress at the all-important level of *habitus*. In all Anglo-America democracies, males who beat up or sexually assault women are more likely to be named, blamed, and shamed. Their behaviour is no longer seen as normative or legitimate. "Common-sense" beliefs in mainstream culture have changed; offenders are now more likely to be shamed by peers; some, if they define their offences as violent (which many do not — but that too requires long-term ideological work on our part) will even shame themselves. The symbolic stigma of criminal law accounts for an unknowable proportion of this cultural shift, which is why criminal law "solutions" must remain in the policy mix at some level.

However, experience should teach us not to look to institutions of criminal law to improve the life of the female who is victimized. We need to devise ways of combating the iatrogenic consequences of zero-tolerance and similar "reforms" while retaining their symbolic impact. To prevent the widespread phenomenon of countercharging victims of domestic assault, police officers have been trained to use "equivalence of violence" directives (Comack and Balfour 2004). They are explicitly directed to consider, before laying countercharges, whether the complainant's violence was equivalent to that of the defendant. They are also told to consider whether the aggression was offensive or defensive, aimed at self-preservation or at injuring the other party (Comack and Balfour 2004).

Seemingly intractable problems with change-making through criminal law remain. Institutions of criminal justice cannot deal with the material and social realities of offenders or victims; they can only offer equal punishment. Some knowledge claims heard in the past delivered increased punishment for the putative offender without producing empowerment for the putative victim. In most criminal events, "victim" and "offender" are one and the same; among the troubled populations that fill Canadian courts and jails, most have been both victim and victimized (Chesney-Lind and Pasko 2013). However, law, in statutes ranging from youth prostitution to break and enter, sees the two categories as binary opposites — an approach that ignores the material and social conditions of most criminalized populations and takes the spotlight off inequality and puts it onto punishment (Phoenix 2002: 69). Change-making efforts should therefore concentrate less on improving criminal law and more on altering the material and social conditions of the most marginalized.

One promising step, for instance, is Ontario's Bill 168: Occupational Health and Safety Act Amendment (2010), which covers violence and harassment in the workplace. The hope is to force employers to take harassment on the job seriously and remedy or ameliorate its root causes rather than ignoring or firing complainants, the "solution" too often adopted in the past. This initiative is based on decades of feminist research and advocacy pointing out that women are stalked, harassed, and sometimes killed by partners while at work. Another promising initiative, also produced by feminist advocacy, is Toronto's new integrated domestic violence court system (Baluja 2011). Initiated on June 10, 2011, as a pilot project, this court system recognizes that women in crisis often have to negotiate both criminal and family court systems. This integrated court, in which one judge will preside over both cases sequentially, has the potential to avoid some of the confusions and revictimizations that occurred in the past. Both of these initiatives attempt to reduce reliance on criminal law. We are taking baby steps, perhaps, toward recognizing the truth enunciated by Diane Martin, a distinguished criminal lawyer and law professor, who concluded, "Regardless of the motives of those seeking new crime control methods, the end result is similar: status quo power relations and distinctions based on race, class, age and gender are preserved and reinforced" (Martin 2002: 356).[8]

Outside the criminal justice system, institutions designed to nourish, educate, or heal have considerable counterhegemonic potential. No social order is static. Neo-liberal knowledge claims constitute new realities, and their consequences provoke resistance. Fudge (2002) argues that women's workloads, in both productive and reproductive spheres, have been dramatically increased by privatization, thereby creating an unstable gender order that is ripe for change. Researchers can take advantage of the world's forty-year experiment with neo-liberal governance by designing research that highlights the often-tragic results of privatization and commodification. Cultural products — videos, personal documentaries, blogs, books — make such messages come alive far better than do articles in academic journals (though both are necessary). However, such initiatives must take account of the cultural environment that they will inhabit, and particularly its eagerness to find individual scapegoats rather than structural causes. The neo-liberal subject constructing blame will always gaze down, seeking out the proverbial bad apple, the incompetent Crown attorney, the careless employee, the neglectful mother. Revealing the structural sources of the social conflicts shaping individual circumstances does not make for easy sound bites, but it is essential nevertheless.

Finally, knowing the class and race-biased consequences of past change-making efforts, progressives must propose solutions with the potential to benefit all women, not just the most privileged — and the only way this can be done is by working with and incorporating the knowledge, perspectives, and experience of marginalized women.

# Notes

The author wants to acknowledge with thanks and gratitude the superb research assistance of April Girard-Brown, Ph.D.

1. This advantage was never universal. Historically, young, white working-class women were the main beneficiaries of institutions such as the reformatory movement (Rafter 1985a; Freedman 1981; Dobash, Dobash, and Guttridge 1986; Zedner 1998). Similarly, today it is primarily "good mothers," faithful wives, the chaste, young, white, and working class or above who are believable as victims or merit "less culpable" designations as offenders.

2. That dream is rapidly becoming a nightmare, with governments adopting proposals from right-realist criminology promising that the safety of the privileged can be ensured by surveillance and incarceration of the desperate; and with "scientific research" depicting "criminals" as morally flawed individuals unable or unwilling to defer gratification (Gottfredson and Hirschi 1990).

3. While zero-tolerance policies are still being implemented across the country with a focus on the "primary aggressor," they are in addition to specialized police units, specialized courts, and legislation in some provinces — all of which have at times been supported and criticized by feminists.

4. Actual female bodies are often both victim and victimized; but formal law rigidly categorizes them as binary opposites.

5. Cause and effect are still impossible to determine; however, some recent research has worked to demonstrate links between knowledge claims and policy change (or lack thereof) (see Collier 2005, 2008; Girard 2009).

6. Elizabeth Bernstein (2012) argues that neo-liberalism and what she labels "carceral feminism" reinforce each other; that is, this particular feminist practice has enabled the carceral turn. However, the punishment-pushing alliance of radical feminism and right-wing Christian evangelical movements has been more powerful in the United States than in Canada, where liberal feminism has dominated many major institutions (such as the Supreme Court and Status of Women Canada). In 2006, however, the Conservative federal government drastically cut its funding to Status of Women Canada and changed the organization's mandate to exclude gender equality and political justice.

7. Quebec is the dramatic exception to this wave of punitiveness; a distinct society indeed.

8. This is one of the problems with strategies of restorative justice and decarceration. The other is the monumental public opposition, from those who have accepted neo-liberal ideology, to any policy that appears to be "soft" on "criminals."

11

# Rattling Assumptions and Building Bridges
## Community-Engaged Education and Action in a Women's Prison

*Shoshana Pollack*

As I was being "processed" into the women's prison, the guard at the front desk asked, "What are you doing here tonight?" I responded, "I am meeting with my students for the first day of class." Looking perplexed, she said, "Students?" "Yes," I said, "I am a university professor and am meeting with the students in my Social Work class." Still seeming confused, she said "Students?" "Yes," I repeated, this time adding, "I am teaching the Inside-Out Prison Exchange Program." "Oh," she said, "You mean the *inmates*!"

The power of a construct such as "inmates" serves to solidify an image of certain people in our minds. Dominant discourses — the language and ideologies that structure how we "know" something to be true and the evaluative assumptions embedded within them — can be difficult to disrupt. People have a tendency to see them as given, normal, and/or "the Truth." In the arena of crime and punishment, particularly within correctional frameworks and in the media, certain ideas about inmates, punishment, risk, and recidivism are generally quite fixed and rarely contested. The tendency is compounded by how the experiences and narratives of incarcerated people are rarely publicly disseminated or given credibility; prisons are closed institutions, and the general public has very little knowledge of what goes on within them. Even when academics writing from critical perspectives challenge dominant criminal justice discourses, the impact of these critiques "on the ground" is questionable; and when university and college professors teach courses in criminology and law that encourage students to engage critically with theories of crime, punishment, and correctional practice, the teaching is generally done "from a distance" — lacking sustained engagement with those experiencing the very processes and systems being taught and studied.

Opportunities do exist in various forums for incarcerated people to "share their stories" — conferences and/or workshops, for instance. Yet how these stories are shared and structured are typically shaped by the agenda of those who are organizing the events. The stories thus often take a predictable shape. For example, many conferences focus on "what works" to reduce the recidivism rate for criminalized women (and men), and therefore presentations, including those by individuals with lived experience, tend to reflect the contours of the "what works" frame. That frame is saturated with deficit-based discourses about the mental health and substance abuse issues of criminalized women and the assumption that prison programming empowers women to think differently and make better "choices" (see, for example, Pollack 2012). The dominance of this narrative frame means that alternative ways of constructing self and experience are rendered unthinkable and thus unspeakable.

How can we speak about these issues and hear perspectives that emerge from outside the boundaries of the acceptable criminalization and punishment frameworks? My focus here is on dialogue and, in particular, on how we speak, listen, and hear the "unspeakable" so as to make known perspectives that are otherwise silenced and rendered illegitimate by dominant discursive frames. Focusing on dialogue points not only to the importance of speaking but also to how we listen. Rather than being a one-dimensional act, listening is relational. The listener hears with a particular set of assumptions, values, agendas, and frameworks through which the speaker's words are interpreted. Our motivations for wanting to hear the stories of the Other are multiple and influence the interpretive frameworks that we bring to bear as we listen. Listening, therefore, requires active self-work and awareness of personal motivations and assumptions; it requires a deliberate strategy for engaging in dialogue that is aimed to disrupt rather than reproduce the stale, damaging, and always partial knowledge about the Other. Programs that address these issues do exist, and I have personal experience with one of them: the use of circle pedagogy in a university class modelled on the U.S.-based Inside-Out Prison Exchange Program.

## The Inside-Out Prison Exchange Program Model

The Inside-Out programming—a prison exchange program founded and developed in the United States by Lori Pompa—was introduced in Canada in 2011 through the efforts of Dr. Simone Weil Davis, a professor of English and gender studies. Inside-Out courses are university-run classes that take place in a prison and include both students who are incarcerated and those who are not. The courses, a semester long, can be offered in any academic discipline, and in Canada all students (whether they are incarcerated or not) are granted university credits for successfully completing a course. In my own work, as a full-time professor in the Faculty of Social Work at Wilfrid Laurier University in Kitchener, I co-ordinate the Inside-Out program with our correctional partner, the Grand Valley Institution for Women. One of the social work classes I teach as an Inside-Out course is called "Diversity, Marginalization, and Oppression." My classes, with twenty to twenty-two students (and equal numbers of incarcerated and non-incarcerated students), meet weekly for a semester in a prison classroom to examine issues of power, diversity, crime, and social justice.

Inside-Out classes have some similarities to what is termed "critical service learning" (CSL), an approach to education that involves community members learning together and working toward some sort of social justice goal. CSL emerged as a response to a paternalistic "helping" model embedded in many service learning approaches, which maintain the status quo and view change or transformation as predominantly individual and personal rather than as collective social change. In contrast, a CSL pedagogical approach has at its core the notion that social problems are caused by systemic inequalities, and it therefore works to understand personal and collective transformation within this context of structural disadvantage (Mitchell 2008). One of the concrete ways in which this can occur in Inside-Out classes is through a collaborative class project that the entire class works together to define, develop, and complete. Built into the process of this endeavour is an awareness that all people have different skills and resources and that the process of doing social justice work should reflect these principles.

The pedagogical philosophy of the Inside-Out program is also different from most university-based teaching. Importantly, the professor does not lecture but rather facilitates activities and dialogue designed to explore the course content collectively and build relationships between participants. These classes are based on an assumption and expectation that all class participants are peers; all of us are considered "knowers" and we embrace an understanding that knowledge comes from various sources, including and going beyond scholarly texts and research. For example, we consider experiential knowledge — including that which emerges individually and collectively from the knowledge co-created in Inside-Out classrooms — to provide important insights into theoretical concepts (such as power, justice, punishment, social change, and accountability) that we study together. Emotions, perspectives, texts, intuition, and experience are all considered valid and important sources of information that, through dialogue and a collaborative process of examining a wide variety of perspectives, lead to a particular kind of community-building, beyond and within the prison walls.

Each instructor who teaches Inside-Out courses is required to take a week-long training in its pedagogy and philosophy. However, individual instructors bring their own preferences, politics, ideologies, skills, and styles to the class, just as they do in conventional university teaching. I usually teach social work courses that engage with critical social theory and examine the process and impact of personal, collective, and systemic inequalities such as those related to gender, race/culture, class, and sexual orientation. Inside-Out is an experiential learning model, which means that students are simultaneously experiencing the concepts that they are studying. In my classes, the course content related to racialization, gendering, and other forms of marginalization and "othering" are experienced by the very nature of being in a women's prison. For example, the reality that the majority of outside students from my university are white skinned while many of the inside students are racialized is experienced viscerally and provides a platform for thinking about how criminalization processes are enacted differentially. Additionally, as part of the experiential learning process, I ask students to be reflective and deliberate about how they engage, to consider what emotions and thoughts are motivating their responses, and to examine where their own ideas and perspectives came from. Students are also encouraged to be constantly aware of their communication styles (verbal and non-verbal). Together we take responsibility for creating a classroom setting that is conducive to an open sharing of perspectives and also allows us to bring our whole selves to the encounter.

## The Problematics of Hearing the Stories of the Other

All students (both inside and outside) are required to apply to take an Inside-Out course and are interviewed by the instructor. Part of the interview process involves a discussion about what motivates the student's interest in this course. In my experience, many outside students indicate a concern about how the Canadian criminal justice system has become increasingly punitive (based on U.S.-style penality) and state that they want to study with incarcerated women in order to get a better sense of the lived realities of criminalization and imprisonment. They often say that they want to "hear women's stories" and work toward developing better solutions to the issues confronting this group of women.

While "hearing women's stories" has become a catch phrase within feminist and social work spheres over the past few decades, it is not without its problems. Allison Jones (1999: 314), for example, suggests that "cross-cultural" classroom dialogue is not necessarily a "liberatory practice," particularly for marginalized students. Her concern is with the tendency for racialized or otherwise marginalized students to be called upon to tell their stories in ways that are actually experienced as silencing and harmful. She suggests that problematic dynamics can occur when the "dominant group's wish for knowledge and mutual understanding is expressed through the desire: 'I want you to teach me!'" (p. 312). Underneath this desire, Jones argues, is not a search for understanding about how we are all complicit (in different ways) in the reproduction of inequalities or a collaborative invitation to work toward change; rather, the desire is often reflective of a search for "redemption" or "exoneration" from being implicated in colonial processes. The search for redemption may come in subtle forms, as illustrated by Kayla Follett (2012), a former outside student in one of my Inside-Out classes. In a conference presentation, Follett (2012) stated that her experiences of courses that engaged with analyses and critiques about how various groups of people are marginalized enabled students to remain detached from these issues in insidious ways. She noted that in her experience of undergraduate classes about equity issues, "We seem to convince ourselves that we are not part of the problem and we appropriate someone else's pain, story, experience."

Both Jones (1999) and Follett (2012) illuminate a process of "distancing" that allows the listener to extract one's own self, history, actions, and ideas out of the story being told. There are very likely complicated reasons for this, but the end result can be a furthering of the othering process and a paralysis in regard to moving toward personal and collective change. In an Inside-Out classroom, it may be easy to slip into the notion that the main source of difference is between incarcerated and non-incarcerated students, but a preoccupation with this dichotomy can lead to the reproduction of certain divisions rather than dislodging or disrupting them. Students may experience commonalities and differences between all participants, irrespective of the incarceration status.

In my Inside-Out classes I try to establish an environment that allows for students to share and analyze the complexities and intersections related to power, marginalization, and oppression rather than to only "hear the stories" of one group of people. This can be challenging for some outside students who may be self-conscious or concerned that their own personal perspectives are not valid sources of knowledge because they have been formed through their experiences of being privileged (for example, by whiteness or class privilege). This stance, however, can also lead to a distancing or othering and hold students back from authentic engagement through which they may openly reflect on the complexities of power and privilege. In an effort to create a classroom space that is conducive to authentic self-reflection and dialogue, I draw upon Parker Palmer's pedagogical concept of a "circle of trust," a dialogical process that has resonances with both Aboriginal talking circles and Paulo Freire's (2003) "culture circle."

## Circle Pedagogy: Engaging the Whole Self

The format and ethos of most university classrooms do not foster a holistic learning approach; students are rarely encouraged to bring their whole selves to the educational process. In fact, many disciplines actively discourage students from doing so, with admonitions for using the first-person voice in papers, classroom dialogue centred solely on intellect and argumentation, and the implicit rule that the only valid sources of knowledge come from academic theories and academicians. In contrast, circle pedagogy supports a learning process premised upon notions of equality, interconnectedness, shared exploration, and the acceptance of multiple viewpoints (Graveline 1998; Cowan and Beard Adams 2008). This approach to dialogue is somewhat antithetical to conventional university teaching and classrooms, in which the professor is typically considered the expert charged with "depositing" knowledge into the minds of students (Freire 2003).

Circle pedagogy refers to more than how classroom furniture is arranged. It is a deliberate means of reflective communication that takes place while all participants are sitting in a circle, and it involves participants taking turns speaking and listening. It entails an active reflective process about how they feel and think while listening, with a sharing of authentic responses to the conversation. The circle symbolizes interconnectedness within diversity, equality, and shared responsibility for the dialogue. The purpose of this type of discussion is not to be "right" or to convince other group members that your perspective is the correct one; rather, the purpose is to bring a diversity of perspectives into the room in order to collectively examine a topic of concern from multiple perspectives and viewpoints. Further, Freire's concept of a "culture circle" highlights the political dimensions of knowledge construction and discourses. The culture circle pedagogy is premised upon the idea that knowledge about disadvantaged groups tends to be created by those with power and privilege rather than emanating from the lived experiences of marginalization and oppression. Freire believed that shared exploration with and between marginalized people leads to a more equitable type of education and social change — one that has at its core the lived realities of disadvantaged people.

The notions of holism, engaged education, or "learning with the whole self" are embedded in many approaches to circle work. Aboriginal talking circles, for example, reflect the four directions, signifying the bringing together of the whole self — body, mind, emotions, and spirit — and the interconnectedness of all things (Graveline 1998). Bell hooks (1994: 14), drawing upon the work of Buddhist monk Thich Nhat Hanh, emphasizes "wholeness, a union of body and mind, and spirit" in engaged pedagogy. Parker Palmer's circle of trust encourages connection with inner wisdom, the sources of which may be multifaceted, not exclusively intellectual. Jean Graveline (1998: 141) states that in an Aboriginal talking circle "participants from diverse backgrounds can gain insight as they 'speak heartfully' and 'listen respectfully' together reflecting on experiences of racism and cultural difference." What these various approaches to circle work have in common is a dialogical pedagogy that honours individual and collective wisdom and that is founded upon a holistic and collaborative learning process.

To initiate this learning process I begin my classes by having students read a chapter from Palmer's *A Hidden Wholeness*. In the chapter, "Deep Speaks to Deep," Palmer provides basic principles for developing a circle of trust, including "no fixing, no saving, no advising, no setting each other straight" (2008: 115). For many people, especially if they have been social-ized in Western educational institutions that emphasize competition and "being right," these are challenging strictures. Furthermore, for those of us in the helping professions and in particular for students in professional education programs such as social work, this approach is an ironic juxtapo-sition to their reason for seeking a degree that trains them to do precisely that: help and advise. Like the argument that Jones advances concerning the hearing of stories of those deemed Other, and Follett's contention that diversity education leads to a distancing, Palmer suggests that the desire to help or advise may be (unconsciously) motivated by a desire to feel virtuous or exonerated from responsibility for the problem.

> Instead of keeping the space between us open for you to hear your soul, I fill it up with advice, not so much to meet your needs as to assuage my anxiety and get on with my life. Then I can disengage from you ... while saying to myself, "I tried to help." I walk away feeling virtuous. You are left feeling unseen and unheard. (Palmer 2008: 118)

Palmer's approach involves "receptive listening." One aspect of that method is to allow brief silences to occur during which participants can privately reflect on what has been said, and another is to respond to the commentator with questions to help speakers reflect more deeply on their own words. The concept of an "inner teacher" underpins this pedagogy. Participants connect with their inner teacher or their own internal wisdom when they are given the space and safety to do so. Receptive listening and authentic speech can allow participants to gain access to their own truths unfettered by a need to convince or persuade or influence others in any particular way. Palmer refers to this type of speech as "expressive speech" and contrasts it with "instrumental speech," which is aimed at achieving a goal, to teach or "help" or convince (p. 119). When we are given permission to speak in ways that are not about showing how much we know or an attempt to influence other people's thinking, spaces are created that facilitate the speakers' abilities to "hear" their own words and to reflect on what these words mean to them and why they have said them.

How do students experience the circle pedagogy? To explore if and how circle work has an impact on students' learning in our Inside-Out program, I initiated a research study with the support of the Walls to Bridges Collective, a group of outside and inside alumni and instructors of Inside-Out courses. We interviewed thirty-eight students about their experiences of the class process and content. Students highlighted how circle work helped to shift the power imbalances in the classroom, not only between instructor and students, but also among the students themselves.

The feeling of being equal permeated their responses and reflected the often unspoken awareness that many people hold biases, judgments, and assumptions about incarcerated women. The circle format both allowed students to reflect openly on these biases — sometimes internally and occasionally publicly — and provided a space in which new formulations and new experiences could reconfigure dominant understandings of gender, crime, and imprisonment. Students identified the feelings of equality among participants that the circle format invoked as allowing a non-judgmental space to emerge.

> We all sit around in a circle, so we're all facing each other. There is no judgment. There is no right or wrong answer. It's like a safe haven. You're able to voice your opinion about the topic. You're able to ask questions, elaborate on somebody else's ideas or thoughts, and there's no backlash. It's like a ... You're just embracing the whole room and everybody's developing together. ("Frances," Inside Student)

Another comment reflected the sense that "everybody's developing together":

> *There wasn't ... No one's better than anybody else. I mean, they were learning from us, we were learning. I know that sounds awful — "they" and "us" and "other." We were all learning from each other. There was no one person that was like, "okay I'm the boss." Nothing like that. It was all equal. It was, everyone had their chance to speak and say their opinion on how they felt about the readings or what they had learned or if they had researched something.* ("Jessica," Inside Student)

Jessica stressed her feeling that the learning was not unidirectional — all students were learning from each other. Interestingly, she also reflected on how her own language revealed the dichotomy of "us" and "them," thereby signalling the power of categories to structure our thoughts, expectations, and approaches to relationships. Despite the primacy of these categories, Jessica experienced the classroom dialogue as being equal — no one "was better than anyone else."

Jose, an outside student, also expressed an awareness that everyone carries biases and assumptions about "us and them," but suggested that the circle pedagogy disrupted the hold that these ideas have on how we think and engage:

> *The most important thing was the enthusiasm, the courage, the zeal, and maybe all the students, they knew this class was going to be different, so we have to leave all our preconceived notions, all our biases in the home. But in the classroom, we had to present ourselves with a certain level of honesty and integrity. The classroom environment was particularly different and it explored how we could be more human while presenting our ideas.* ("Jose," Outside Student)

Power differences and biases do not disappear simply because we want them to. They also do not disappear when someone tries to make us ashamed of them. The students' comments point to a method of being mindful to both the existence and power of dichotomies while simultaneously engaging in a collective examination of them. Circle work can facilitate a consciousness about how dichotomies such as prisoner/student and criminal/law-abiding, and other means of categorical separation, keep our minds and hearts closed to one another, allowing us to feel secure in what we think we know. These dichotomies and assumptions, even while framed in seemingly benign discourses about "voice" and "storytelling," at worst reify and at best create slightly different divisions. Everyone in an Inside-Out class has a "voice" and a "story." Everyone is a listener and a learner.

## Disrupting the Discourse

> *They take people and they lock them away from society, and they expect them to change and get better.... And then the people in society pay thousands and thousands and thousands of dollars to do this. So, there's such a disconnect. So, I believe that everybody needs to work together to solve the problem. The public are spending their money whether they want to or not. So, it's pretty awesome when we can get to transcend the walls and come together with the community a little bit and try and make things better and bring light to what's happening inside, and give people hope inside that they have a different future. But we couldn't do it without the community. Because otherwise, you're isolated in these walls in this clandestine, scary, mysterious place. So you really need to break down those walls for any change to happen. It involves both community and inside.* ("Hannah," Inside Student)

It was an incarcerated student named Nyki (see her contribution in chapter 12 here) who prompted me to think more deeply about how models such as Inside-Out may trouble and disrupt what can be known about incarcerated women at a discursive level. At the closing ceremony of one of her Inside-Out classes Nyki stated: *"Pre-conceived notions. We are all guilty of harbouring them. Notions of what we think things are supposed to be. Things like prison and education. Of what and who the student is, and what and who the convict is."*

In her work on calling subjects into being, Judith Butler provides a helpful way of understanding the productive and limited disruptions of engaging with carceral institutions and discourses. In thinking about what it means to be considered fully human, Butler asks: "Who can I become in such a world where the meanings and limits of the subject are set out in advance for me? And what happens when I begin to become that for which there is no place within the given regime of truth?" (Butler 2004: 58). For Butler, engaging these types of questions is a matter of justice — not only in regard to how one is treated by social structures and how societies are constituted but also in regard to how one is (un)recognized as fully human and how one is (un)able to articulate versions of one's self when the discursive limits constrain what is possible or knowable. Drawing upon Foucault, she states that there are certain bodies that are deemed illegitimate, unreal, impossible. To intervene in the name of transformation, she writes, "means precisely to disrupt what has become settled knowledge and knowable reality." In the process, "norms themselves can become rattled, display their instability" (p. 28) and can therefore be redefined. Remember the officer who was challenged to rethink her notion of "inmate" in order to understand why I, a professor, was requesting entry into the prison? Her conception of what is knowable about the women behind the walls was, as Butler suggests, "rattled," and she was forced to grapple with the disruption of how she thought about women prisoners.

How people become "known" through the discourses of those who have the power to define and regulate and how they come to know their own selves within these discourses are concerns related to self-definition. In a study I conducted a few years ago, women who were interviewed about their post-prison experiences wrestled with the ways in which their experiences and behaviours — their very selves — were enacted through correctional discourses and relationships with parole officers. Specifically, participants spoke of how narratives about "riskiness" discounted their own understandings and usurped alternative renditions of self, needs, and experiences. Julie stated, for example, that even when correctional workers "come face-to-face with somebody, *really* face-to-face — they can't even see you" (Pollack 2010: 1270). The challenges of "being seen" through powerful dominant narratives are reflected in this woman's decision to no longer take part in the discursive construction of "who" she is. Julie stated that her previous attempts to narrate a self-story were eclipsed and transformed by the assessments and documentation of mental health professionals, in particular. Consequently, in an attempt to contest discursive correctional constructions of her "self" she no longer participates in the storying process, telling people instead to "open my file, read it. I don't have anything else to say. That's it" (Pollack 2010: 1271). The process that Julie describes is reflective of what Gayatri Spivak (1988) refers to as "epistemic violence" — criminalized women are (un)known through dominant discourses that circumscribe their experiences and which they themselves must reproduce either by letting the files speak for them or by narrating the same self-story that lies within the file pages.

Butler's idea of "rattling" is resonant of a political dimension of programs such as Inside-Out: the reconstitution of incarcerated women (and men) as knowers, as university students rather than "offenders" and "inmates." Some of the student responses relayed earlier suggest that dominant norms, categories, and assumptions are shaken and thereby opening up possibilities for alternatives.

## The Walls to Bridges Collective: Community-Building and Social Change

The Walls to Bridges Collective also works to disrupt and rattle assumptions about criminalized women, education, and imprisonment. Our group has been meeting biweekly since 2011 at Grand Valley Institution for Women. Our mission states: "Through collaboration with people living inside and outside prison walls, we will strive to connect and build bridges by educating, informing and advocating about social justice and education for criminalized women and transpeople" (see Walls to Bridges Collective, Wilfrid Laurier University website).

As part of our commitment to community-building both within the prison and in the outside community, we conduct workshops utilizing circle pedagogy and experiential activities aimed at challenging people's presuppositions, and we engage in collective dialogue about topics such as women and crime, criminalization, punishment, education and employment, and social change and advocacy. We have hosted events in the prison and have been invited guests to community groups and university classrooms. Additionally, some of our members from the inside have been granted passes to do public speaking at community events. Given that we work as a collective, there are very few visible signifiers of who is incarcerated and who is not (incarcerated women at this prison do not wear uniforms), and some of the most powerful learning occurs when participants in our workshops realize they are trying to figure this out — how to categorize us, in essence, how to "think about" or "know" us. Disruptions occur almost immediately as people are thrown off balance when they realize the extent to which they are preoccupied with who is a prisoner and who is a "normal" university student, especially when their preconceptions are inevitably revealed to be incorrect.

Michelle Brown (2009) argues that most of us are "penal spectators" of the violence of incarceration. A penal spectator is "a bystander and outsider as opposed to an engaged participant or witness. She may stare curiously or reflectively, peer sideways from her peripheral vision, or gape and gawk directly, but the object of her gaze is inevitably other people's pain" (p. 21). Many of us are not only scholars, students, and researchers but are also practitioners, advocates, and/or activists. While often positioned as a duality — you are either a scholar who critiques from outside the system or you are a practitioner in the system that reproduces correctional norms — such a construction ignores the reality that we are all, as Brown says, complicit onlookers of various kinds. There is no redemption or exoneration because we are all integral parts of colonial, racist, sexist, and exploitative systems. I think both the Inside-Out classes and the work carried out through the Walls to Bridges Collective engage directly with the issue of distance and spectatorship and grapple with the complex and uncomfortable reality of doing work about and within penal spaces with its multiple contradictions, messiness, and disruptions. Those disruptions — like the ones I have touched on in this chapter — have the potential to "rattle" subjectivities and trouble notions about who can and cannot be a "knower" and an agent of change.

# 12

# Experiencing the Inside-Out Program in a Maximum-Security Prison

*Monica Freitas, Bonnie McAuley & Nyki Kish*

## Inside-Out and Its Effect on My Imprisonment: Monica Freitas

Sitting in my cell, I reflect on the past two years of my life and the intense emotions I have experienced within the Canadian judicial system. Many women experience very low self-confidence and quite frankly do not see any way out of the crime cycle that most are accustomed to in order to survive life's hardships. Having harmful thoughts, negative self-talk, and experiencing marginalization, oppression, and constant judgment at the hands of the people that are supposed to assist us with rehabilitation and reintegration into our communities prove to be very challenging. Due to the numerous challenges that I have been facing — having a criminal record, being away from my supports and loved ones, and experiencing extreme emotions of guilt, shame, and loneliness — my efforts and focus during my incarceration have been on obtaining higher education, advocating for and empowering female inmates, and educating our communities about the criminalization of women and its long-term effects on society as a whole. I attribute my passion and fervour for these important causes to the Inside-Out program.

Inside-Out completely changed my perspective on learning and encouraged me both through the class dialogue/activities and essays to challenge myself and others. The course facilitator and her assistant were there to encourage healthy dialogue and a positive environment, where each participant could explore their personal boundaries and perhaps challenge society's perceptions of prisons, punishment, and incarcerated women. There was no evidence of anyone exercising power or privilege over one another, as the class had mutually and democratically agreed upon guidelines of conduct at the beginning of the program. By doing this, the facilitator empowered each person to become not only students, but teachers in their own right.

I have concluded during my time behind "the walls" that we all have a plan, whether we chose it or it was chosen for us. We cannot help who, what, and where we are, but it is what we do with our lives that differentiates us from becoming oppressed, oppressors, and the liberated. I believe that education is necessary from the grassroots level in order to ensure that society creates an environment where all individuals feel respected and equal and have fair access to the basic necessities of life.

## "Inside the Walls": Bonnie McAuley

My name is Bonnie and I am doing a life/twenty-five sentence for the murder of my husband. I completed year eighteen on August 22, 2013. I began my sentence at the Prison for Women in Kingston, Ontario, in 1995 and at that time I also began taking courses from Queen's University by correspondence. I have three adult children and two grandchildren. I was a registered nurse outside and when I obtain this second degree I may be eligible to teach nursing in a college setting. Unfortunately, as the years have passed my chances at bursaries and outside funds for education have decreased considerably. I am now in a financial position where I'm not able to continue my education without financial help from others.

Three years ago the opportunity arose where I was able to apply for a degree course through Wilfrid Laurier University in a program referred to as Inside-Out. My hopes were increased immediately. The course would be compensated entirely by the Lyle S. Hallman Foundation, which awarded Wilfrid Laurier with a substantial amount of money. The course would be funded through Wilfrid Laurier and paid for me in its entirety. Unfortunately, I did not get into the first course. I was devastated. In December 2011, I applied to a social work course called "What is Family?" and I was accepted into the program. Since then I have applied to and completed three courses — with outstanding marks.

When I started the class in the first Inside-Out course I glanced around at the students and I have to admit that what I saw was mostly upper-class, privileged, educated females who I thought I would never fit in with. But the circle and the icebreakers helped me to get to know and like each person on an equal level. They also made me realize that for the most part these women were just the same as me. The circle also enhanced our learning in the Inside-Out program. It brought university outside to the inside. These wonderful circles became "circles of trust" and it definitely removed that upper-class feeling that I had developed at the beginning. The circle also encouraged dialogue among two very different classes of students.

I am privileged enough to be starting a fourth Inside-Out course on social literature. These courses have helped increase both my self-esteem and self-confidence. I am truly blessed to be part of this wonderful program.

## Jail the Body, Free the Mind: Nyki Kish

I spent two years and nearly four months imprisoned within a maximum-security unit at the Grand Valley Institution for Women (GVIW), a multi-security-level women's federal penitentiary in Ontario. In what follows I share the hurdles, rewards, and general experiences I encountered in studying at a post-secondary level from inside a maximum-security prison. I explore issues around participating in a prison educational program during Canada's shift into a "tough on crime" penal policy, and I also attempt to express, through my own experience, how Inside-Out pedagogy and the prison environment interact, and how the two are entirely contradictory in effect.

### Being Held in a Maximum-Security Prison

At the time I was introduced to the Inside-Out program, I was being held in a maximum-security wing of the Grand Valley Institution for Women for a mandatory twenty-seven-month period, a sentence stipulation anyone with a life sentence, like myself, must endure. The maximum-security unit, which the Correctional Service of Canada calls the secure unit and which everyone else refers to as "max," is a fifteen-cell, twenty-seven-bed "supermax"-inspired wing, containing three isolated five-cell corridors where women are kept. The small, narrow, fluorescent-lit, self-contained corridors are known as "pods." We spent the majority of our time on the pods; we were allowed out of the unit only to ask for a maximum of one hour outside in the evenings and for visits and programs. On pod, we were locked in the cells for 14.5 hours daily. We were often double-bunked. When I first arrived, I remember clearly my first impression being: How could anyone exist for two years in such a small, uncomforting space? My second impression quickly followed: What meaningful experience could one even craft from such an existence?

All pursuits that interest me, from volunteering, to making art, to connecting to the natural world, were cauterized from my life upon my being put into Grand Valley's max, and I quickly hoped that education could be that time's saving grace. But from a resource and opportunity standpoint, the max offers less than little. An option to privately purchase correspondence courses exists, should an imprisoned woman have access to the $500 to $800 course fees; however, a switch to online learning increasingly limits choices for the select few who can afford this option, as imprisoned people in Canada have no access to the Internet. Further, what available government assistance for post-secondary courses to inmates used to exist in Ontario was also cut from the federal budget in 2012. Indeed, post-secondary pursuits in the Grand Valley Institution's maximum-security unit have always been rare and are increasingly becoming rarer. Further, they are pursuits that, by my experience, are warned against by most of the max staff because of the limitations of the unit.

There are four dated computers installed between two program rooms near the pods that are prioritized for women working through secondary school, not all of which ever steadily work. Accessing them is *always* a challenge. Movement in max is authorized by guard discretion in conjunction with room scheduling, and the two rooms are also used as the library, chapel, gym, court, intervention, psychology, and institutional program room, and even the women enrolled in secondary school are denied access regularly. Being able to type, research, or even work safely in a calm or quiet environment presented daily hurdles, most of which we never satisfied. As mentioned, the majority of our time was spent on pod and in cell where there are no computers, no working space, and only what study supplies we purchase through the canteen, which are limited to lined paper, pens, and erasers.

Access barriers, though significant, were not enough to stop us from wanting to pursue schooling. Beyond structural limitations, however, regular violent disruptions and emotional upheaval occurring between women and staff and among the women make the max one of the most hostile, unstable places a person could study in. In Grand Valley, the secure unit is used to hold not just people with life sentences, but also women with violent histories and women who experience varying mental illnesses and who do not function in the general population. The max offers little for us to do and is not a treatment unit to which those with mental illnesses should be surrendered. The conditions culminate to make max the perfect environment for violence. Moreover, aside from chemically restraining women, discipline and isolation are the utilized responses to any emotion or incident in max, which only perpetuate incidents and chaos on the unit, as emotional responses were, generally, our natural reactions to the intensely regulated, regimented institutional environment. Finally, because of the small size of the pods, when incidents occur, they generally shut down at least the involved pod, if not the entire unit, affecting us all. Such was the daily reality of being kept in the max. Still, as Inside-Out was being introduced into Canada and into GVIW, organizers were quite careful in pushing for the inclusion of max women, and included we were.

I completed the first four Inside-Out courses that were offered at GVIW while imprisoned in the max; it was Canada's very first Inside-Out class that I shared as my first experience with the program. "Diversity, Marginalization, and Oppression" was the course title, and with this course began the most meaningful experience I had during my imprisonment in max.

## The Inside-Out Program's Pedagogy and Format

Inside -Out pedagogy promotes a collective, dialogue-based experiential learning. Every class takes place with university students who are both imprisoned and not imprisoned. A supportive rather than competitive tone is encouraged and equality in voice is promoted. Assigned readings are discussed, usually in one large class circle, followed by dialogue-based activities that are carried out within smaller class groups to deepen our analyses. The large circle is generally re-formed to end each class with personal reflection on the session. The opening, dispersing, regrouping ritual of the large and small circles in Inside-Out created something of a sacredness to the classes for me. Inside-Out as a whole does not follow conventional education mechanics, but presents instead as a transformative life and academic experience.

Toward the end of each course, a final project is developed by the entire class. Final projects are usually action-oriented and are often produced with themes of social justice and advocacy. By the end of the courses strong bonds tend to form between the imprisoned and outside students, both because of the starkly unconventional nature of the program that we students mutually experience, and because syllabi tend to be tailored to be relevant to issues of imprisonment (for example, the courses I participated in studied prisons, punishment, human rights, and oppression, which always gave us amply solid grounds upon which we became united and galvanized).

## My Experiences with the Inside-Out Program

The courses are held in the medium-security compound of the prison, meaning that in order to attend I had to be taken off pod by guards, frisk-searched, and escorted to and from the classroom, while during class being under constant supervision of prison staff. During class I sat among all the students, both the women in this prison and as well, the outside students. In that setting and *only* in that setting there was no way to identify me as a maximum-security prisoner. At the time of our very first class, I had been in a max pod for eight months, and I remember feeling instantly more human than I had since being convicted. It was not long after that first Inside-Out class when I realized how compromised my social skills had become as a result of my living conditions. I was no longer, by that time, accustomed to being spoken to with respect, or having any atmosphere where my thoughts were valued or where I could express my opinions unpenalized. The allowance of my being able to have the limited periods of free expression that came through Inside-Out ultimately became invaluable to my surviving the max, and I stress that this aspect of the program will continue to be invaluable to any imprisoned women being held in the max who engages in Inside-Out.

The supermax style of imprisonment that Canada has embraced within several aspects of the country's prison industry is, in my opinion, inherently dehumanizing. Supermax-style units are not built with anything but containment, control, and minimized maintenance in mind, and this led to atrocious effects on the hearts and minds of those of us who were subjected to exist within their walls. Very rarely did I ever get the opportunity to connect with others in any way that was not superficial or quite guarded in nature. And while no prison guards are stationed on pod with us, women in the max are watched all day through multiple cameras; as well, all of our conversations can be listened to by staff through a speaker system. What we said and did on the pods was constantly monitored, scrutinized, and used to determine our "institutional progress." Such control over ideas and casual conversation left me wary to engage at all, and I spent the majority of my first twenty months in the prison in the cells to which I was assigned. Even when I did interact with the other women on pod, because the pods only typically imprison three to five other women, the environment was always extremely isolating and socially strenuous.

Contrary to the max environment, it has consistently been my experience that there is a healing quality to the circle setting that Inside-Out embraces. In class circles there was no hierarchy and there were not the power struggles that dominated my experience with both guards and other imprisoned women in max. In class circles I felt safe to think and share and interact, and especially as our class read texts and poetry relevant to oppression, criminalization, and issues of imprisonment, I began to find something I had lost in the trauma of experiencing the penal system: my voice. Even the simplest activities that occur within the Inside-Out setting, such as reading aloud, listening and being listened to within a group of people, and being encouraged to disagree and challenge ideas, counteracted the negative impacts of imprisonment in max. Being allowed to be this way during classes reminded me of the self I developed before my imprisonment and class after class, slowly but surely, I regained confidence, vitality, and drive that I was not aware I had lost. I finished my first Inside-Out class feeling like I had found liberation from within prison walls. It has been echoed to me by other participants that such is the case for many Inside-Out students, both imprisoned and not.

## Public Perception, Deservingness, and Stigma

The trend of labelling criminalized people as "undeserving" of education and other opportunities is neither new nor undocumented, and with our having access to the limited, however meaningful, post-secondary education that the Inside-Out program offers comes a great degree of carefulness and public relations management on the part of the prison administration and involved universities. While forces within both institutions vocally proclaim the program internally, frequent were our class conversations which navigated toning down, tailoring to "public perception," and properly presenting the products our classes produced through the final project of the Inside-Out course. Within CSC, almost every change that is implemented is announced to the prison population with a clause about how said change interacts with Canada's public perception of this prison system. Indeed, public perception is most often the guise under which we as an imprisoned population are denied even the most basic human rights and dignities. It is the excuse given to keep computers from being purchased and from allowing the ranges to be air-conditioned (though we endure soaring temperatures regularly), and it is the most common reason we are given when we are told what a gift it is that a few of us are able to learn. I do not dispute that under our current system, programs like Inside-Out are indeed a privilege; I dispute that they ought to be.

The acceptance on the part of imprisoned participants that we were receiving a privilege in our ability to study university courses comes about in relation to the arguments that we are imprisoned and learning while many non-imprisoned Canadians are never able to engage in university, and that the costs of these courses for imprisoned students are largely carried by the program. It is said to us that much of the public does not believe imprisoned people should have meaningful opportunity. This argument against meaningful opportunity for imprisoned people generally stands upon the logic that imprisoned people should be experiencing punishment in a setting undesirable enough and reduced enough from the average quality of existence in Canada to deter the next citizen from partaking in crime, rather than being able to develop oneself in any positive, significant manner. This logic of course rests upon the notion of individualized responsibility within a reactionary approach to the social issue of crime; it does not consider that imprisoned people might experience imprisonment as a result of lack of opportunity and marginalization. Nor does this logic consider the ripple social effects of an institution that would return educated people into communities rather than people who have only experienced trauma, isolation, and deprivation for extended periods of time.

In this prison we often listen to mainstream media expressing support-ive narratives about Canada's turn away from an alternative, non-punitive penal system toward the neo-liberal, reactionary, "tough on crime" prison industrial phenomenon that has spread globally. I have been imprisoned through the implementation of the Stephen Harper government's 2012 Omnibus Crime Bill C-10; I have experienced, since my conviction, the in-creasing social aggression being imposed upon the marginal and most often impoverished identities that comprise the majority of Canada's women's prison population. I have felt the devastation, and I do not use the word lightly, of existing within a cage within a society that is accepting a drastic policy overhaul of one of its dominant institutions, its prison system, without understanding the changes or their immediate or long-term effects. It has felt inexpressibly awful. We were told in the max that the public essentially wants us to suffer, that suffering is what we deserve, and that this is why max is so structurally suppressive. Even though the Inside-Out program began in Canada in the fall of 2011, just as the Conservative "tough on crime" agenda was producing its effects, the program can only ever reach a small portion of the women in this prison, even fewer of the max popu-lation. For those few of us who are eligible and allowed to participate from max, maintaining the security clearance to attend in the medium-security compound presented itself as a constant hurdle, one which I always found to be nearly too stressful to maintain.

## No Security: The Constant Threat of the Max Unit's Level System

Because there is a constant surveillance of us in max, even our most menial actions and interactions are documented, assessed, and used by staff to guide decisions about how our time is spent. Decisions impact all of us — from long-term realities, such as parole, to our immediate quality of life. Most significantly, the max unit operates with every prisoner being represented by a level, in a four-level system, with level one offering the most restrictions and level four offering the most privilege. Level one prisoners may not leave the unit without being shackled and handcuffed and without being escorted by several guards. Level four prisoners can leave the unit without any hand-cuffs or shackles and with only one CSC staff, who does not necessarily have to be a guard (for example, a teacher or prison psychologist may escort a level four maximum-security prisoner throughout the medium-security compound). Levels are assessed weekly at staff meetings and provide the max staff an enormous, immediate, and generally arbitrary form of control over our realities. Only at level four may one participate in most programs institutionally, including Inside-Out, and throughout my participation in four separate Inside-Out courses I was not able to maintain a level four status.

I did maintain the required level four for three courses; it was during the fourth course my level four was reduced. There had been several prior occasions when staff had threatened to reduce my level. Levels could be reduced on grounds as generic as "deteriorating behaviour," and the standard of our behaviour was determined largely by the opinions of our jailers. The jeopardy of Inside-Out always being taken from me created a permanent tension in my prison life; Inside-Out was the only meaningful activity I had access to during the two-year-plus period I was imprisoned in the max. There were countless weeks that I worried whether or not I would even be able to participate, let alone worrying about accessing the computers or having a safe space to study.

The actual course material never caused me stress, though I often found myself wishing that I was not involved in the program so that the prison would have nothing to constantly threaten me with. Still, readings and essays became my escape from prison reality; through Inside-Out I found a way to engage about issues that matter to me. I sat in many cells and read Freire and Foucault and felt in those moments connected to the world, not isolated, both physically and in ideas and beliefs. I continually regained confidence through Inside-Out courses. In hindsight, the contradiction of the confidence and social skills I was able to rebuild during class against the low self-worth, guardedness, and social anxieties I developed through time in max highlight how the living conditions of the max unit are entirely detrimental to human emotional and mental health. Being isolated, monitored, deprived of community, and constantly scrutinized and put down for so long was traumatic in a sense that I do not yet fully comprehend (it has presently been three months since I left max). I was extremely fortunate in my ability to use Inside-Out, aside from an opportunity to develop academically, as the tool with which I rebuilt and maintained some social skills and normalcy.

When I was finally pulled from completing my fourth course, although I was able to finish with a pass, I was devastated. This was the human rights course and it was unfortunately ironic that the only access to education that I had was being taken; that the staff would rather keep me on the unit and for all purposes — mentally and socially broken — than to be participating in a meaningful, productive social and academic experience. But such is the reality of the max unit. Such is the reality of the general attitude behind the

Canadian penal system. The Inside-Out program was and continues to be one of the only substantial opportunities available to women imprisoned at GVIW, let alone the max, and it is only available because of the prolonged determination of outside forces. Nothing similar has been developed within the institution; the majority of the women in max sit from periods of months to periods of years with absolutely nothing to do. The majority of us are not even eligible to participate. If there is any emotion expressed by an imprisoned person in max, let alone violence (which most women in max experience), the Inside-Out program would be not more than something one or two of the women's pod-mates left to do once weekly.

## Inside-Out as a Stepping Stone

The Inside-Out Prison Exchange program does and will continue to get nothing but support from me, but in praising it I will not let the system within which it exists be overshadowed. Long-term isolation is a difficult experience to express; I strongly urge anyone studying or interacting in the Canadian penal system to look at programs like Inside-Out as stepping stones away from the effects of isolation, and more generally as movement away from the development (or permanence) of a mass, industrialized imprisonment culture. Few know what women are sentenced to when shipped to any of Canada's maximum-security prisons, and I certainly did not foresee that such trauma could be inflicted upon me by the state, nor that a private organization could provide such a profound experience that my deterioration in max could be managed. I held onto the Inside-Out program for the majority of my imprisonment in the max as the reason and meaning by which I endured. Several peers of mine in max collapsed and became entirely institutionalized through the lack of dignity and opportunity we experienced, and many are still in max today as result. I do not doubt whatsoever that without my having had the ability to hang onto Inside-Out as I did, as a routine, as a source of hope for a potential future for myself, and as a healthy social setting, I too would have broken down long ago in that unit.

There is an abundance of literature on the benefits of imprisoned people studying, and surely as the Inside-Out program ages, bodies of literature will arise to support the effects of imprisoned people studying through the experiential form that the program provides. But the unfortunate reality is that in the majority of places where Inside-Out exists, the imprisoned people who could benefit the most deeply will not be institutionally supported to engage.

In Canada and in penal culture globally, there is increasing support for punitive systems. However a punitive system nearly broke me, and in sharing my experience I hope readers are imbued with the importance of programs like Inside-Out within these systems, if these systems must exist. The inclusion of maximum-security prisoners in the Inside-Out program was thankfully not overlooked at GVIW. Let it not be overlooked anywhere as the program expands and finds roots in the Canadian prison system.

13

# Enhancing the Well-Being of Criminalized Indigenous Women

A Contemporary Take on a
Traditional Cultural Knowledge Form

*Colleen Anne Dell, Jenny Gardipy, Nicki Kirlin,*
*Violet Naytowhow & Jennifer J. Nicol*

Over the past decade academic scholarship and community efforts have increasingly recognized the association between traditional cultural knowledge and well-being for First Nations, Inuit, and Métis peoples in Canada (Hopkins and Dumont 2009; McCormick and Quantz 2010; Brockman et al. 2013). This increasing recognition has been facilitated by the awareness raised through the Truth and Reconciliation Commission and other Indigenous-led health initiatives addressing Canada's colonial history. Situated at the centre of these efforts is a recognition that cultural knowledge is foundational to individuals' understandings of their self and relations with their collective community, land, and ancestors; this knowledge is fundamental to Indigenous well-being (Dell, Hopkins, and Dell 2005; Wilson 2004; Office of Ethnic Minority Affairs, American Psychological Association 2010). As Indigenous scholar Patricia Monture explains, her experiences and identity as a Mohawk woman were essential to her own health and healing (see Monture-Angus 1995; Monture-Okanee 1995).

The social, economic, and political inequities that are integral elements of colonialism have become the source of a disproportionate burden of ill health faced by Indigenous peoples (Adelson 2005; Mitchell and Maracle 2005; Lemstra and Neudorf 2008). The impacts of these inequities are particularly acute on the health status of Indigenous women. Their lives are disproportionately damaged by family violence, sexual harassment, and addiction — all of which have directly translated into disproportionate rates of criminalization (see the Introduction to Part II in this book; Niccols, Dell, and Clarke 2010; Boyer 2006). The urgency of attending to this issue is prominently illustrated in the matter of violence — which has a severe impact on the lives of Indigenous women in Canada (Beavon and Cooke 2003). Their mortality rate due to violence is five times that for non-Indigenous women, depicted most starkly in the alarming number of missing and murdered Indigenous women in Canada (Native Women's Association of Canada 2010). Amnesty International points out that poverty is a key factor "exposing Aboriginal women to a heightened risk of violence" (2009: 2). Yet, as Colleen Dell and Jennifer Kilty (2013: 53) note, "State responses to the victimization of Aboriginal women generally and drug users specifically often fail to recognize them as legitimate ... victims, in spite of their lengthy histories of intersecting trauma and victimization." Clearly, strategies for engendering Indigenous women's well-being — including healing from addictions — must attend to the trauma trails of colonialism (Atkinson 2002; Comack et al. 2013).

## Healing and Decolonization

Western approaches have been dominated by attempts to locate individualized solutions to healing from addictions. These approaches have generally overlooked the sacred relationships between Indigenous peoples and their spirit, family, community, nation, and the land. The majority of the National Native Alcohol and Drug Program centres in Canada, for example, were founded on individualized Western approaches to treatment in the 1980s, and only later began to incorporate holistic Indigenous understandings of healing and personal growth. These understandings continue to develop in their acknowledgement that healing is a way of seeing, a way of relating, a way of thinking, and a way of being (Assembly of First Nations, Health Canada, and National Native Addictions Partnership Foundation 2011). The specificity of this issue for Indigenous women remains a challenge in Canada (Niccols, Dell, and Clarke 2009).

Decolonization — the process whereby Indigenous people reclaim their traditional culture, redefine themselves as a people, and reassert their distinct identity — can take many forms. Community development, by which people participate directly or through organizations that they control in bottom-up planning and community action (Wharf and Clague 1997), is one decolonization strategy adopted by researchers and community activists alike. Jim Silver and his colleagues, for instance, report on their work with Indigenous community development workers in Winnipeg. They note how community development is about community healing, is led foremost by women, and is holistic: "It focuses on the individual, the community, the creation and operation of Aboriginal organizations, and an Aboriginal-specific, de-colonized way of understanding and interpreting the world" (Silver et al. 2006: 3). Others have applied this intricate connection between decolonization and healing in developing an Indigenous social work practice (see, for example, Hart 2002; Bruyere, Hart, and Sinclair 2009; Carriere and Strega 2009; Duran 2006).

A parallel transformation has taken place in developing research practices. Decolonizing approaches to research, as initially espoused in the work of Linda Tuhiwai Smith (1999), critically reflect on how Western scholarship has perpetuated colonizing practices. At the same time, authors such as Margaret Kovach (2009) have highlighted how Indigenous research methodologies can be a source of decolonization when they flow from tribal knowledge and are undertaken in an appropriate way; that is, with mindfulness to community connection, participation, and empowerment. As in the case of reconceptualizing healing for Indigenous peoples, we need to find alternatives to the generic and individualized Western approach to research. Failing to do so will result in a perpetuation of the status quo.

Another potentially powerful strategy of decolonization is song and music. Around the globe, song and music are recognized as traditional and sacred forms of Indigenous knowledge (Sefa Dei, Hall, and Rosenberg 2002). In Canada, song and music have held a significant place within Indigenous cultural traditions, rituals, and ceremonies (Cajete 2004). An essential plank of Canada's assimilationist policies and practices, however, was to disparage and outlaw Indigenous knowledge and culture. Colonialism resulted in significant cultural loss for First Nations, Inuit, and Métis peoples, including the demise of their languages (Papequash 2011; Arbogast 1995). Reviving traditional language and culture is, then, essential to decolonization.

The revival of traditional culture among First Nations, Inuit, and Métis peoples is strong in Canada and is key to increasing health status (Niezen 2007; Papequash 2011). Song and music have an important place in the contemporary manifestation of cultural identity. Song writers and musicians such as Buffy Sainte-Marie, Susan Aglukart, Eekwol, Violet Naytowhow, and A Tribe Called Red blend modern-day compositions with powerful lyrics and traditional sounds to educate, share stories, and connect to cultural pride (Lashua and Fox 2006).[1] While the use of song and music as therapeutic tools in Western society — such as in cancer care and dementia clinics (Daykin, McClean, and Blunt 2007; Beard 2012; De Medeiros and Basting 2013) — has been well documented, little has been written about their contemporary use as a source for Indigenous well-being and as a form of resistance to colonialism (Iwasaki et al. 2009).

Our interest in the potential for song and music to engender Indigenous well-being and contribute to a process of decolonization emerged from a study that our research team undertook to examine the role of identity and stigma in the healing journeys of criminalized First Nations, Inuit, and Métis women. Specifically, the study aimed to remedy the limited research on how the stigma linked to drug abuse, criminal involvement, and being an Indigenous woman has an impact on women's healing (Carter 2002; Razack 2000; Ridlon 1988). The research team organized interviews with sixty-five First Nations, Inuit, and Métis women in treatment for illicit drug abuse at six National Native Alcohol and Drug Abuse Program (NNADAP) treatment centres across Canada, and with twenty women who had completed treatment. The team conducted an additional thirty-eight interviews with NNADAP treatment providers, most of them First Nations.

Our study affirmed that culture is foundational for women to reclaim — and for some to claim for the first time — a healthy self-identity as Indigenous women and to respond effectually to the harmful impacts of stigma. Following the guidance of Elder Joyce Paul, our team committed to sharing this finding in a format that honoured traditional cultural knowledge in a contemporary form; and we identified a combination of song and music as a potentially far-reaching means to contribute to the cultural well-being of criminalized Indigenous women.

## Traditional Indigenous Knowledge, Cultural Identity, and Song

Traditional Indigenous knowledge is generally described as "the expression of the vibrant relationships between the people, their ecosystems, and the other living beings and spirits that share their lands" (Battiste and Henderson 2000: 42). One writer identifies it as an "extensive and valuable knowledge system" that is vital, dynamic, and capable of helping to solve contemporary problems (Battiste 2002: 7). Central to Indigenous knowledge is recognition of the historical foundation of current understanding — a foundation that can be found in ceremonies, teachings, traditions, and values, many of which contain song and music (Bicker, Pottier, and Sillitoe 2002; Larry LaLiberte, traditional cultural practitioner, personal communication, Dec. 14, 2013). It follows that the sharing of traditional Indigenous knowledge inherently revitalizes and honours Indigenous language, culture, systems, and ways of knowing at both the individual and communal levels (Smith 1999; McMaster and Martin 1992; Graveline 1998).

A First Nation woman recovering from substance abuse told how language, through her grandfather's gift of song, was central to her eventual healing:

> *It's a good thing that someone ... refreshed my thoughts in my memory in regards to where I come from, what I used to see my grandfather do when he used to pray on his own, when my mother's dad used to go to stretch on the lake, [location], and refresh my memory, because I remember my grandfather sitting in that tipi singing the songs that our Elder sang this morning. But I didn't get it, I didn't get it.... When my grandfather used to do ceremonies in sweat lodges ... (speaking Cree) ... I learned how to speak my language.* (Cited in Tempier et al. 2011: 10–12)

The origins of Indigenous knowledge are situated within an oral tradition that has been transferred from generation to generation in cultural teachings and practices. Indigenous educators are recognized as "family members, community members, and leaders who share what they know about living a good life through their actions, through apprenticeship, through spiritual guidance, and through their words" (Kaplan-Myrth and Smylie 2006: 23). Wisdom is shared by Elders, the keepers of much sacred and traditional knowledge. Historically, in some communities, women had a central role as keepers and imparters of traditional knowledge, but this role drastically deteriorated with colonization.

The relationship between traditional Indigenous knowledge and cultural identity is intricate. Pride in cultural identity is a recognized factor for well-being and is associated with traditional culture, way of life, and language (Assembly of First Nations, Health Canada and National Native Addictions Partnership Foundation 2011). A national framework published by the National Native Addictions Partnership Foundation and the Assembly of First Nations (AFN) in partnership with Health Canada states that identity for First Nations people comes "from family and, by extension, community and traditional land and clan systems" (p. 12). The loss of cultural identity has been particularly destructive to the health of Indigenous women in Canada (Office of Ethnic Minority Affairs, American Psychological Association 2010). Rooted in attempts at colonization, stereotypes of Indigenous women as substance abusers are rampant and the associated stigma has had a devastating impact on their lives and the erosion of their cultural identity (Dell and Kilty 2013). These stereotypes, unless countered, are absorbed, internalized, and reproduced. As one woman in our study shared:

> *When I came here [to the treatment centre], you know, I found my culture. 'Cause I didn't know nothing about who I was as a Micmac woman. I thought being Native was drinking, drugging, being in trouble. That's what I thought, you know, what Natives were.*

We know that interventions are needed to assist women in reclaiming their Indigenous identity by offering culturally significant healing experiences, such as the medicine wheel approach, sweat lodge, and other cultural ceremonies, as well as Aboriginal food, art, language, and traditional teachings (Wilson 2004; Poole 2000; Vinding 1998). Fostering cultural identity through traditional Indigenous knowledge offers empowering stories and discourses that can cultivate cultural identity, community connectedness, and pride (Assembly of First Nations, Health Canada & National Native Addictions Partnership Foundation 2011).

Although Western science was slow to recognize non-written forms of knowledge — as well as their linkage to cultural identity and its role in well-being — Canada has a strong oral tradition in Indigenous culture. Music and song are a near-universal means of sharing traditional Indigenous knowledge. For example, the Plains Cree (Nehiyawak) sing ceremonial songs in the traditional sweat lodge to pray, connect with the Creator, and share their values and beliefs in stories. Songs were traditionally treasured, sacred, and purposeful, and they belonged to individuals, families, or tribes; they were only shared with others if given away in ceremony or purchased (Kingman 2003). For Indigenous people, storytelling has traditionally been understood as "a means to connect the listener to the universe, to the past, to the present, and to the future; it establishes a relationship to the souls and minds of human beings, animals, and the land" (Williamson 2000: 142). Song and music, as a traditional form of storytelling, also bring with them specific duties, such as their role in healing ceremonies (Aboriginal Healing Foundation Research Series 2012: 2, 30).

Music and song have historically preserved Indigenous culture, identity, language, memory, and values. Indigenous ceremonies are most often sung in a traditional language, which not only communicates the intended meaning of the ceremony, but also helps to maintain the language, and helps others to learn it. Neal McLeod emphasizes the importance of this practice: "Language is our own vehicle for the transmission of ideas and worldviews.... Language guides a people and helps to create space wherein tribal memories linger" (2000: 29). The importance of language and song is also reflected in the words of a woman on her healing journey:

> I knew who I was but it wasn't until much later, probably into my sobriety, that I actually learned about who I was and where I come from and how important that is to me now, you know, like knowing my culture, learning my language, the songs; it means so much to me now.... Well, I come from a matrilineal society and, you know, they always talk about

*the strengths of — the women are always the backbone of the community and we don't need to be out in the front but we're always behind supporting and we're the ones who are nurturing. Yeah, I'm really proud of who I am and where I come from and, you know, I have a responsibility as an Aboriginal woman; as a mother; as a daughter; as a sister.*

Song and music offer a means of engendering the healing process. As a study by the Aboriginal Healing Foundation concluded:

Any of the music-making processes bring healing to both the listeners and the players. It is long known in our culture that drumming and traditional songs are intended to be healing. They allow clients to feel a sense of belonging and/or identity. The songs are often ways to shift energy; to wrap clients in culture; to allow them to cry sometimes; and to bring joy to others. (Aboriginal Healing Foundation Research Series 2012: 2)

Song and music are also recognized for their ability to inspire social change. For example, a song titled "Angel Street," by Inuk musician Lucy Idlout, inspired the city of Iqaluit to recognize the role of domestic violence in their community by renaming the street that their local women's shelter is on — changing it to Angel Street. The mayor of Fredericton, NB, did the same and would like to see an Angel Street in every capital city of Canada (Aboriginal Healing Foundation Research Series 2012).

## "From Stilettos to Moccasins"

As a decolonizing strategy, cultural identity is crucial to the healing process of criminalized Indigenous women. Healing from drug abuse must address the need for women to reclaim a healthy self-identity as Indigenous women. This includes understanding the negative impacts of stigma. Our team was challenged with sharing what we learned in a way that honoured traditional cultural knowledge in an accessible and contemporary form. The imagined solution, guided by the wisdom and confidence of our Elder Joyce Paul, was to produce a song and accompanying music video. It was our team's intent that "the knowledge gained in the study ... be translated through a culturally-relevant technique that would recognize, legitimize and celebrate Indigenous women's historically-silenced voices" (Dell 2012: 11). Prioritizing the often silenced voices of women with lived experience, the song and video are intended to convey the interconnection between the negative impacts of stigma and the resilient benefits of a cultural identity. What we did not fully anticipate was the positive impact that developing and distributing the song and video would have in terms of serving as a means for well-being and empowerment, thereby contributing to a process of decolonization.

Our research team gathered in February 2009 to develop the song based on the key findings of the study in relation to stigma, identity, and healing. The team collaborated with Woodland Cree singer and songwriter Violet Naytowhow. About thirty people attended the gathering, including the women we had interviewed, researchers, treatment providers, Elders, policy-makers, and government and non-government decision-makers. This compilation of individuals represented the diversity of our original research team. The goal was to collaboratively create a song portraying the healing experiences of Indigenous women who have struggled with crimi-nalization and drug abuse. The song served as a neutral means by which all our team members could work together, because the vast majority were not songwriters.

Violet initiated the song development process by introducing song-writing to our group. She started off by sharing several different genres of music and then explained how songwriting was analogous to storytelling. The songwriting process involved dividing into four groups to brainstorm lyrics for the song, which included two sets of lyrics plus the bridge/chorus. Each group was facilitated by an individual familiar with the songwriting process: Violet Naytowhow, Talla Tootoosis, Jonothon Couchman, and Douglas Purcell. Lyrics were constructed based on the themes from the study produced by the team alongside individuals' personal contributions to the lyrics. The writing took each of the groups about three hours. All four groups then met together with Violet to review and combine the lyrics. In what remains surprising to this day, the group consensus was to change only one word. This large group also discussed different ways to frame the song; for example, having the song begin with drumming and an Elder speaking, and ending with children's laughter. In the end, not only is the song a means of well-being and empowerment, as the feedback suggests, but so too is the process of its development and distribution.

Given Violet's background in traditional Indigenous song and singing, alongside her contemporary work, following the gathering she and guitarist Kevin Joseph worked with the lyrics to add a melody. The draft of the song was distributed to all team members (including those not able to attend the gathering) for feedback. It was at this point also that people from Mae Star Productions began to work on developing an accompanying music video. They attended the original songwriting gathering and went through several edits of the video based on team feedback. The video for the song, "From Stilettos to Moccasins,"[2] was formally released in May 2009.

## From Stilettos to Moccasins

I survived through the pain
Many emotions like waves
Laughing and crying again and again
Honesty, strength, friends, and devotion
Showering gifts of hopes to reclaim
Walking the streets dragging my heart
Wandering with my head held down in shame
When and how did my family fall apart
Who am I, what is my name?

BRIDGE:
Surviving the street lost and alone
I started a journey to find my way home

CHORUS:
From stilettos to moccasins
Our spirit dances within
On our way to resolution
We find our peace
And this is who I am

Broken barriers and new discoveries
My spirit I now reclaim
Coming home to who I am
Taking honour in my name
No longer a prisoner lost in this world
Look within my shell
To find that pearl

CHORUS:
From stilettos to moccasins
Our spirit dances within
On our way to resolution
We find our peace
And this is who I am.[3]

The song's development led to the creation, by the research team, of a half-day health intervention workshop, "From Stilettos to Moccasins: A Guide for Group Discussion." It is an interactive workshop intended for Indigenous women in addictions treatment centres, community-based agencies, and correctional facilities across Canada. The goals of the workshop are to discuss the role of identity and stigma in the healing journeys of Indigenous women in treatment for drug abuse; to offer hope and inspiration, gathered from over one hundred Indigenous women in substance abuse treatment who shared their healing journeys; and to reflect on participants' understandings of identity, stigma, and the healing journey and to learn from one another. The workshop, available at no cost to communities, is designed to be facilitated by community members with community members.[4]

## Responses to the Song

The "From Stilettos to Moccasins" song and music video was posted on YouTube in November 2011 and generated thousands of views. In addition to comments posted online, feedback on the impact of the song and video was collected following the delivery of service provider workshops and treatment client workshops. Our analysis of the comments posted on YouTube and the feedback from treatment clients and service providers who participated in the intervention workshops confirm that the song and music video have had a lasting impact. The YouTube comments specifically mentioned the beauty and inspirational power of the lyrics, as well as their linkage to cultural identity and healing. Overall, the feedback we received identified seven themes.

First, women and service providers said they were able to relate to the song. When relaying what they enjoyed the most about the workshop, the majority of participants noted the song and music video. One of the women said, "*The song and video was great. There was so many things I could relate to and I felt like it was written about me (I've worked the streets since I was 16).*" The song resonated with other people's lives. One woman described the music video as "*singing my song.*" Another wrote, "*It reminded me of my healing journey. I could put myself in her place.*" And yet one more said: "*This song is real. It touches your soul when you've 'walked the walk' and I made good and walked that path. I am one of the lucky ones.*" These individual stories were also understood as part of a larger fabric. Although the journey as an individual was solitary and lonely — "*I remember the song goes from feeling very lonely and lost and feeling more inspired as the journey progresses*" — continuing on one's journey meant looking to culture and a common identity as Indigenous people, and as women. One participant shared: "*Stay strong, continue the healing journey. Strong message about what Aboriginal women have and continue to go through. To keep going.*"

The workshop participants were also specifically able to relate to the song's message of transformation and change as a journey, as evident in the simple statement of one woman, "*She* [woman in music video] *was on a healing journey, you know.*" They also appreciated that hope is an important part of the journey. The journey was solitary yet shared, and the journey was one of transitions, a journey that required strength and hope. A service provider commented: "*Well my interpretation of the whole thing was one of hope. There's hope for women in our community to change their lifestyle, to go specifically from a dangerous lifestyle to one of healing and productivity.*"

The metaphor of shoes was interpreted both literally and symbolically as a journey. One woman said, "*I like the part about where you come from — talking about walking the journey. I literally walk in stilettos and moccasins because that is how my life is. I thought the song was pretty cool.*" Others reported metaphorical meanings such as "*Being in your own shoes and being yourself*" or "*Finding the shoe that represented you, thinking about who you are and what you want to become.*" Another woman simply said, "*Loved the shoe identity and self-esteem.*" A person who posted on YouTube was inspired to extend the metaphor:

> *Stilettos have no places on Mother Earth. They are only meant for hard places where we don't belong. They jolt and jar the entire body. Only sink into the dirt, poking holes in our Mother. Always Walk Softly on Mother Earth.... Leave the stilettos for those who must wear them.... Welcome home beautiful First Nations women! Ahneen!*

In addition, service providers commented that they used the song for inspirational and educational purposes, with one saying that "*the song is inspiring and something that I can use.*" Another said, "[I] *remember the song because it was so different. I have never heard a song like that before. I found it was very empowering. The whole workshop was empowering.*" A service provider spoke of sharing the song and video with colleagues and individuals from other organizations: "*We always show the song and video* [to practicum students that come here]. *It's always in our waiting area room for anyone that wants to see it.*" Similarly, a service provider talked about extending the use of the song to ceremonial occasions such as graduations and to spiritual gatherings as part of healing circles and prayer: "*We used the song in one of our women's groups — we used it as our graduation song. Used it in a healing* circle. We had prayer and then listened to the song…. It's good to wake emotion up to that song."

Specifically notable about the song, and most repeated in the YouTube comments, are its deeply felt special qualities: "Beautiful and Powerful song"; "Beautifully Done"; "beautiful song and video"; "very beautiful and had a lot of emotion in it"; "it is inspirational!"; "Inspirational, moving. I loved it"; "This song really inspires me to stay sober and clean." The journey of the women in the music video is touching and rouses feelings; some women and service providers were moved to tears.

Women who provided feedback three months after the workshop said they used the song and music video to keep inspiration alive in their daily lives. One said, "I still listen to that song on YouTube. When I'm feeling low, I just sit there and go on the computer and that is when I play that song. It is a beautiful song." Another woman commented, "I have a CD of the song. It's over at my sister's and the book with the story in it [from the workshop]. I loved it; it was so close to home. It was really good. I'm glad whoever initiated it, initiated it." A third woman talked about repeatedly listening to the CD in the first few months following the workshop:

> I don't remember the lyrics specifically but I still remember the emotions. What I took from it — it was in my car and CD player for days and days and days. It kept me going when I was feeling down. It made me cry but it also gave me strength. For the first couple of months I always had it in my head. It was very encouraging. I related to it very well and it helped me see where I wanted to be.

Yet another theme raised in the feedback related to how the shoe metaphor was a powerful way to evoke cultural identity. As one woman said, "Cultural part is the key factor for me. And that is the whole idea from the fancy high heels to moccasins." A metaphor's strength comes from its subjectivity; its use of one thing to symbolize something else. But as evidenced by one service provider's literal interpretation, metaphors can also be problematic:

> To me, it gives an inappropriate message to Aboriginal people about what health looks like. We already have a distorted perspective. Traditional Indian is really hard to attain — particularly for Urban Aboriginals. It seemed like that was the ultimate goal, and that it is set up to fail. It can give a message that you haven't reached your full potential. Seems the message is "Well, you aren't a real Indian if you don't wear Moccasins." To me, being Aboriginal means being healthy and happy — it doesn't mean to wear feathers and moccasins. [The song] suggests one extreme to another.

On the other hand, the song and music video prompted many expressions of positive cultural identification and a belief that culture can be a way of both changing and healing. One woman commented: "*Recovery can happen ... just go to culture. Things can change. They don't have to stay the same.... It really validates the human power of women.*" And another said, "*To see that women are very special and that we have a uniqueness about us. To see that I wasn't alone. Find my roots and spirituality.*"

And last, extending the theme of cultural identity, the respondents articulated a voice of connection and sisterhood. Words and phrases such as "Mother," "Mother Earth," "Sisters," "Blessings," and "Female Spirits" were used. The song was described as "*an honour to our sisters*" and as something that "*beautifully expressed the strength of the female spirit.*" YouTube was described as "*a fantastic venue to showcase our talent and tell our stories.*" The project challenged stigma and promoted cultural pride.

## Resisting Colonialism

A wealth of Indigenous culture was lost in the Canadian state's attempts at colonization, as evidenced by the lack of well-being among First Nations, Inuit, and Métis peoples today. Not lost, however, was an understanding about the importance of carrying cultural knowledge forward for future generations (Mitchell and Maracle 2005; Mundel and Chapman 2010). Equally recognized is the need to address specifically the impacts of colonization for Indigenous women. The "From Stilettos to Moccasins" song and music video attempt to honour the role of traditional cultural knowledge in well-being in a contemporary form, especially within the context of Indigenous women's efforts to (re)claim their culture and self-identity. This is particularly the case in the lives of criminalized Indigenous women who are working to heal themselves from drug addiction. Empowerment is fundamental to an individual's cultural identity and thus protects against the destructive stigma overshadowing the strengths of Indigenous culture. As the "From Stilettos to Moccasins" song says, "My spirit I now reclaim/ Coming home to who I am/ Taking honour in my name."

Traditional Indigenous knowledge and its oral origin were honoured in our team's identification of song and music as the means by which we could share knowledge. As Katherine Gordon says in *We Are Born with the Songs Inside Us: Lives and Stories of First Nations People in British Columbia*, traditional cultural knowledge is inherent to Indigenous people. Music is a keeper of Indigenous knowledge; it is used to share oral traditions and preserve memory. "For many First Nations family wealth is not held or measured in the form of material items, but in their family's own dances, songs, and stories" (Aboriginal Tourism BC, n.d.). Choosing to bring about change through a traditional cultural form — song and music — recognizes this. Music has been described as "speaking to the heart of Indigenous peoples" and "the soundtrack of humanity. Music is the soundtrack to culture. Music is to help us remember the story" (Educational CyberPlayGround n.d.).

The experiences of "From Stiletto to Moccasins" show that healing also requires giving voice to Indigenous women's stories, which colonization has tried to silence. As one of our team members commented, "When the Indian agents left our communities, 'brown patriarchy' took its place. ... Our own people learned to lead by domination and power and control relationships. The power of the church also continued to dominate our communities and a very powerful teaching was that men had to control women and children in order to be men." Smith (1999) maintains that singing is one way in which Indigenous people, including women, can have a voice. The song and music video, as an act of decolonization, gives voice to the women's stories. Although all of the women who participated in the study did not participate in the song's development, a ceremony was held to ensure that their words were honoured. Further, not all members of the song-making team were Indigenous, but they were recognized as allies (Kovach 2009; Bishop 2002).

The stories of the women in our study were developed as a collective narrative and shared with the guidance of a contemporary, inspirational Indigenous female artist. During the songwriting process itself, our Indigenous team members' voices were given priority. In the end, not only is the song a means of well-being and empowerment, as the feedback suggests, but so too is the process of its development and distribution. It also helps to address the diminished role of women in their communities as keepers and imparters of traditional knowledge due to colonization.

There was richness in the breadth of feedback received on the "From Stilettos to Moccasins" song and music video. When considered in its entirety, the feedback received was congruent with our team's goal of creating a song that offers hope and inspiration, revitalizes and honours Indigenous culture (Smith 1999), and validates Indigenous knowledge systems and philosophies (McMaster and Martin 1992; Iwasaki et al. 2009; Daykin 2004). Specifically, individuals were able to relate to the song and video and their message of cultural identity in the journey of healing. We were also influenced by the understanding that with a loss of traditional Indigenous knowledge and cultural identity among the participants in our study, we needed to develop a form of knowledge dissemination that would be meaningful to them in a contemporary sense but still drew upon traditional cultural knowledge. We attempted to bring back ceremony in a contemporary way to Indigenous women who are often far removed from it. Ultimately our team did not use traditional language in the song, but we do recognize that language is "one of the most tangible symbols of culture and group identity" and also "a link which connects people with their pasts and grounds their social, emotional and spiritual vitality" (Norris 1998: 8). The music for the song, however, does have the traditional drum beat throughout.[5]

Traditionally, Indigenous women have been honoured as the teachers, observers, life-givers, and caregivers for their children, families, and Elders in their communities. Attention needs to be refocused on these roles and their application in women's present-day lives. As Kim Anderson (2006: 23) states:

> As Aboriginal peoples, we can move forward by building on traditions that kept our people healthy in the past…. Our women were traditionally granted significant authority in recognition of their power as creators and nurturers. These core values and principles are built into our various and multiple creation stories, our traditional political and economic structures, our extended family structures, and our spiritual practices. It is up to us to retrieve these concepts and to plant them like seeds in our new world.

Decolonization is a specific process for women. Song and music video creation offers one strategy for contributing to this decolonization process. Other strategies include storytelling (Mehl-Madrona 2005), working with the land (Mundel and Chapman 2010), and dance and art (Iwasaki et al. 2009), as well as ceremonies such as sweat lodges and smudging (Aboriginal Healing Foundation 2006). Such strategies support the importance of traditional cultural knowledge, which contributes to self-identity and is foundational to well-being. This, in turn, combats stigma and the overwhelming stereotypes Indigenous people, and especially women, are subject to (Salmon 2005; Currie 2001; Poole and Isaac 2001; Padayachee 1998; Copeland 1997).

An unsolicited email to one of our team members, after the song was played at a conference for addictions service providers, captures the potential of this cultural knowledge form:

> It [the music video] was a dramatic punctuation to the end of the conference. To say that it was well received would be an understatement. It

*evoked a visceral response in many people. Dare I say that people left energized and centred, knowing why they are here, and who we serve. With much appreciation.*

The crafting of the song "From Stilettos to Moccasins" was a powerful and far-reaching way for the women to connect with the transformative stories of cultural identity, many similar to their own, and it served as a reminder of hope and inspiration for women's own personal healing journeys. It was a reminder for many that they are not alone.

## Notes

This chapter is dedicated to our team Elder, the late Joyce Paul. We also acknowledge the "From Stilettos to Moccasins" research and song team members, as well as the research assistance of Jennifer McAllister in analyzing the data for this chapter. The study was funded by the Canadian Institutes of Health Research, Institute of Aboriginal Peoples' Health. The authors' names are listed alphabetically. The idea for this chapter originated from a paper JGS wrote on the traditional role of music in Aboriginal peoples' health for a graduate class in public health. CAD and JJN extended JGS's paper, including further literature, incorporating data analysis, and crafting the chapter. NK, JGS, and VN critically reviewed and suggested revisions for the chapter and approved the final version. Correspondence concerning the chapter should be addressed to Colleen Anne Dell, Department of Sociology, University of Saskatchewan, Saskatoon, Saskatchewan, S7N 5A8. E-mail <colleen.dell@usask.ca>.

1. For more information on these artists, please visit these websites: Buffy Sainte-Marie at <creative-native.com/>; Susan Aglukart at <susanaglukark.com/>; Eekwol at <myspace.com/eekwol>; Violet Naytowhow at <myspace.com/violetnaytowhow>; A Tribe Called Red at <atribecalledred.com/>.

2. The song is available on online at <addictionresearchchair.com/creating-knowledge/national/cihr-research-project/hear-about-our-findings-through-song/>.

3. © Violet Naytowhow & the CIHR Project Research Team — Aboriginal Women Drug Users in Conflict with the Law: A Study of the Role of Self-Identity in the Healing Journey.

4. The workshop is available online at <addictionresearchchair.ca/wp-content/uploads/2011/10/On-Line-workshop-now-available-December2012.pdf>. It comes with a thirty-minute training video and all required materials, a CD of the song, and feedback forms to be returned to our project team.

5. Our team's production of a second song, "Step By Step," under the leadership of Eekwol and Joseph Naytowhow, blends traditional Indigenous and English language and cultural and contemporary Western music <tinyurl.com/StepByStepSong-Watch>.

# References

Aboriginal Healing Foundation. 2006. *Decolonization and Healing: Indigenous Experiences in the United States, New Zealand, Australia and Greenland*. Ottawa: Aboriginal Healing Foundation.

Aboriginal Healing Foundation Research Series. 2012. *Dancing, Singing, Painting, and Speaking the Healing Story: Healing through Creative Arts*. Ottawa: Aboriginal Healing Foundation.

Aboriginal Tourism B.C. n.d. The Art of Storytelling." <aboriginalbc.com/stories/the-art-of-storytelling>.

Abramovitz, M. 2001. "Everyone Is Still on Welfare: The Role of Distribution in Social Policy." *Social Work* 46, 4.

____. 1996. *Regulating the Lives of Women: Social Policy from Colonial Times to the Present* (second edition). Boston: South End Press.

Addison-Webster, M. 2013. "Ted McMeekin Talks but Who Can Act on Social Assistance Rates?" *Toronto Star*, July 17. <thestar.com/opinion/commentary/2013/07/17/ted_mcmeekin_talks_but_who_can_act_on_social_assistance_rates.html>.

Adelberg, E., and C. Currie (eds.). 1993. *In Conflict with the Law: Women and the Canadian Justice System*. Vancouver: Press Gang.

____. 1987a. *Too Few to Count: Canadian Women in Conflict with the Law*. Vancouver: Press Gang.

____. 1987b. "In Their Own Words: Seven Women's Stories." In E. Adelberg and C. Currie (eds.), *Too Few to Count: Canadian Women in Conflict with the Law*. Vancouver: Press Gang.

Adelson, N. 2005. "The Embodiment of Inequity: Health Disparities in Aboriginal Canada." *Canadian Journal of Public Health* 96 (Spring).

Adkins, L. 1992. "Sexual Work and the Employment of Women in the Service Industries." In M. Savage and A. Witz (eds.), *Gender and Bureaucracy*. Oxford: Blackwell.

Adler, F. 1975. *Sisters in Crime*. New York: McGraw-Hill.

Albrechtslund, A. 2008. "Online Social Networking as Participatory Surveillance." *First Monday* 13, 3. <firstmonday.org/htbin/cgiwrap/bin/ojs/index.php/fm/article/view/2142/1949>.

Alder, C., and A. Worrall. 2003. *Girls' Violence: Myths and Realities*. Albany: State University of New York Press.

Alexander, R. 1995. *The Girl Problem: Female Sexuality Delinquency in New York, 1900–1930*. Ithaca: Cornell University Press.

Aline. 1987. "Good Girls Go to Heaven, Bad Girls Go Everywhere." In F. Delacosta and A. Priscilla (eds.), *Sex Work: Writings by Women in the Sex Industry*. Pittsburgh: Cleis Press.

Allen, H. 1987. *Justice Unbalanced: Gender, Psychiatry and Judicial Decisions*. Milton Keynes: Open University Press.

Amir, M. 1971. *The Patterns of Forcible Rape*. Chicago: University of Chicago Press.

____. 1967. "Victim Precipitated Forcible Rape." *Journal of Criminal Law and Criminology* 58, 4.

Amnesty International. 2009. *No More Stolen Sisters*. London: Amnesty International Publications.

____. 2004. *Stolen Sisters: A Human Rights Response to Discrimination and Violence Against Indigenous Women in Canada*. (October). Ottawa: Amnesty International Canada. <amnesty.ca/sites/default/files/amr200032004enstolensisters.pdf>.

Andersen, C. 1999. "Governing Aboriginal Justice in Canada: Constructing Responsible Individuals and Communities through 'Tradition.'" *Crime, Law and Social Change* 31.

Anderson, E. 1993. *Hard Place to Do Time: The Story of Oakalla Prison, 1912–1991*. New Westminster: Hillpointe.

Anderson, K. 2006. "New Life Stirring: Mothering, Transformation and Aboriginal Womanhood." In D.M. Lavell-Harvard and J.C. Lavell (eds.), *Until Our Hearts Are on the Ground: Aboriginal Mothering, Oppression, Resistance and Rebirth*. Toronto: Demeter Press.

____. 2000. *A Recognition of Being: Reconstructing Native Womanhood.* Toronto: Sumach Press.

____. 1991. *Vancouver's Chinatown: Racial Discourse in Canada, 1875–1980.* Montreal-Kingston: McGill-Queen's University Press.

Andrejevic, M. 2005. "The Work of Watching One Another: Lateral Surveillance, Risk, and Governance." *Surveillance & Society* 2, 4.

Appignanesi, L. 2009. *Mad, Sad and Bad: A History of Women and the Mind Doctors.* New York: W.W. Norton.

Arbogast, D. 1995. *Wounded Warriors: A Time for Healing.* Omaha: Little Turtle Publications.

Arbour, The Honourable Justice Louise (Commissioner). 1996. *Commission of Inquiry into Certain Events at the Prison for Women in Kingston.* Ottawa: Solicitor General.

Armstrong, J. 2004. "'I am Not a Monster,' Ellard Says." *Globe and Mail,* July 8: A7.

Armstrong, J., and R. Matas. 2007. "More Than 'Drug Addicted Prostitutes.'" *Globe and Mail,* January 20.

Arnold, R. 1995. "The Processes of Victimization and Criminalization of Black Women." In B.R. Price and N. Sokoloff (eds.), *The Criminal Justice System and Women.* New York: McGraw Hill.

Aronowitz, S. 1992. *Politics of Identity.* New York: Routledge.

Arrigo, B. 2002. *Punishing the Mentally Ill: A Critical Analysis of Law and Psychiatry.* Albany: State University of New York Press.

Arrigo, B., and J.L. Bullock. 2007. "The Psychological Effects of Solitary Confinement on Prisoners in Supermax Units: Reviewing What We Know and Recommending What Should Change." *International Journal of Offender Therapy and Comparative Criminology* 52, 6.

Artz, S. 1998. *Sex, Power, and the Violent School Girl.* Toronto: Trifolium Books.

Assembly of First Nations, Health Canada & National Native Addictions Partnership Foundation. 2011. *Honouring Our Strengths: A Renewed Framework to Address Substance Use Issues among First Nations People in Canada.* Ottawa: Health Canada. <nnadaprenewal.ca/wp-content/uploads/2012/01/Honouring-Our-Strengths-2011_Engl.pdf>.

Atkinson, J. 2002. *Trauma Trails, Recreating Song Lines: The Transgenerational Effects of Trauma in Indigenous Australia.* Sydney: Spinifex.

Atwood, M. 1996. *Alias Grace.* Toronto: McClelland and Stewart.

Austin, J., M. Bruce, L. Carroll, P. McCall, and S. Richards. 2001. "The Use of Incarceration in the United States." *The Criminologist* 26, 3.

Australian Institute of Criminology. 2011. *Australian Crime: Facts & Figures: 2011.* <aic.gov.au/publications/current%20series/facts/1-20/2011/4_offender.html>.

AWAN (Aboriginal Women's Action Network). 2007. *Aboriginal Women's Statement on Legal Prostitution.* Vancouver: AWAN. <prostitutionresearch.com/aboriginal%20statement%20on%20legal%20prostitution.pdf>

Backhouse, C. 2002. "A Measure of Women's Credibility: The Doctrine of Corroboration in Sexual Assault Trials in Early Twentieth Century Canada and Australia." *York Occasional Working Papers in Law and Society.* Paper #1.

____. 1999. *Colour-Coded: A Legal History of Racism in Canada, 1900–1950.* Toronto: University of Toronto Press.

____. 1996. "The Shining Sixpence: Women's Worth in Canadian Law at the End of the Victorian Era." *Manitoba Law Journal* 23, 3.

____. 1994. "White Female Help and Chinese-Canadian Employers: Race, Class, Gender, and Law in the Case of Yee Clun, 1924." *Canadian Ethnic Studies/Etudes Ethniques au Canada* 26, 3.

____. 1991. *Petticoats and Prejudice: Women and Law in Nineteenth Century Canada.* Toronto: Women's Press.

Bakker, I. 1996. *Rethinking Restructuring: Gender and Change in Canada.* Toronto: University of Toronto Press.

Balfour, G. 2008. "Falling Between the Cracks of Retributive and Restorative Justice: The Victimization and Punishment of Aboriginal Women." *Feminist Criminology* 3.

Ball, K. 2006. "Organization, Surveillance and the Body: Towards a Politics of Resistance." In D. Lyon (ed.), *Theorizing Surveillance: The Panopticon and Beyond.* Cullompton: Willan Publishing.

Baluja, T. 2011. "A bumpy start for a new style of family court." *Globe and Mail,* Aug 1. <theglobeandmail.com/news/toronto/a-bumpy-start-for-a-new-style-of-family-court/article4181655/>.

Bannerji, H. 2005. "Introducing Racism: Notes towards an Anti-Racism Feminism." In B. Crow and L. Gotell (eds.), *Open Boundaries: A Canadian Women's Studies Reader* (second edition). Toronto: Pearson.

Barber, P. 1992. "Conflicting Loyalties: Gender, Class and Equality Politics in Working Class Culture." *Canadian Woman Studies* 12, 3.

Barrett, M.R., K. Allenby, and K. Taylor. 2010. *Twenty Years Later: Revisiting the Task Force on Federally Sentenced Women.* Ottawa: Correctional Service Canada.

Barron, C. 2000. *Giving Youth a Voice: A Basis for Rethinking Adolescent Violence.* Halifax: Fernwood.

Barry, K. 1979. *Female Sexual Slavery.* New York: New York University Press.

Bashevkin, S. 2002. *Welfare Hot Buttons: Women, Work, and Social Policy Reform.* Toronto: University of Toronto Press.

____. 1998. *Women on the Defensive: Living Through Conservative Times.* Toronto: University of Toronto Press.

Baskin, C. 2006. "Systemic Oppression, Violence and Healing in Aboriginal Families and Communities. In R. Alaggia, and C. Vine (eds.), *Cruel but Not Unusual: Violence in Canadian Families.* Waterloo: Wilfrid Laurier University Press.

Batacharya, S. 2004. "Racism, 'Girl Violence,' and the Murder of Reena Virk." In C. Alder and A. Worrall (eds.), *Girls' Violence: Myths and Realities.* Albany: State University of New York Press.

Battiste, M. 2002. *Indigenous Knowledge and Pedagogy in First Nations Education: A Literature Review with Recommendations.* Ottawa: National Working Group on Education and the Minister of Indian Affairs Indian and Northern Affairs Canada (INAC). <usask.ca/education/people/battistem/ikp_e.pdf>.

Battiste, M., and J. (Sa'ke'j) Youngblood Henderson. 2000. *Protecting Indigenous Knowledge and Heritage: A Global Challenge.* Saskatoon: Purich Publishing.

Bauman, Z. 2007. *Liquid Times: Living in an Age of Uncertainty.* Malden: Polity Press.

____. 1997. *Postmodernity and Its Discontents.* Cambridge: Polity Press.

BCCLA (British Columbia Civil Liberties Association). 2014a. "BCCLA: Troubling Report that CBSA Got Confidentiality Agreement from Deceased Woman's Family." <bccla.org/news/2014/01/bccla-troubling-report-that-cbsa-got-confidentiality-agreement-from-decreased-womans-family/>.

____. 2014b. "*Worm v. Canada.*" <bccla.org/our_work/worm-v-canada/>.

Beard, R.L. 2012. "Art Therapies and Dementia Care: A Systematic Review." *Dementia* 11, 5 (Fall).

Beattie, J.M. 1977. *Attitudes towards Crime and Punishment in Upper Canada, 1830–1850: A Documentary Study.* Toronto: University of Toronto, Centre of Criminology.

Beavon, D., and M. Cooke. 2003. "An Application of the United Nations Human Development Index to Registered Indians in Canada." In J.P. White, D. Beavon, and P. Maxim (eds.), *Aboriginal Conditions: The Research Foundations for Public Policy.* Vancouver: UBC Press.

Becker, D. 1997. *Through the Looking Glass: Women and Borderline Personality Disorder.* Boulder: Westview.

Becker, H. 1963. *The Outsiders.* New York: Free Press.

Beckett, K., and B. Western. 2001. "Governing Social Marginality: Welfare, Incarceration, and the Transformation of State Policy." *Punishment and Society* 3, 1.

Belknap, J. 2001. *The Invisible Woman: Gender, Crime and Justice* (second edition). Belmont: Wadsworth.

Bell, S. 2002. "Girls in Trouble." In B. Schissel and C. Brooks (eds.), *Marginality and Condemnation: An Introduction to Critical Criminology*. Halifax: Fernwood.

Benedet, J., and I. Grant. 2013. "More than an Empty Gesture: Enabling Women with Mental Disabilities to Testify on a Promise to Tell the Truth." *Canadian Journal of Women and the Law* 25.

____. 2007. "Hearing the Sexual Assault Complaints of Women with Mental Disabilities: Consent, Capacity, and Mistaken Belief." *McGill Law Journal* 52.

Bennet, T., and L. Gelsthorpe. 1996. "Public Attitudes Towards CCTV in Public Places." *Studies on Crime and Crime Prevention* 5, 1.

Benoit, C., D. Carroll, and M. Chaudry. 2003. "In Search of a Healing Place: Aboriginal Women in Vancouver's Downtown Eastside." *Social Science and Medicine* 56, 1.

Benshalom, I. 2008. "Regulating Work or Regulating Poverty: An Agenda of Inclusion or Exclusion in American Workplace Reform?" *Journal of Law and Equality* 6.

Bernier, J., and A. Cellard. 1996. "Le syndrome de la femme fatale: 'Maricide' et représentation féminine au Québec, 1898–1940." *Criminologie* 29, 2.

Bernstein, E. 2012 "Carceral Politics as Gender Justice? The 'Traffic in Women' and Neoliberal Circuits of Crime." *Theoretical Sociology* 41.

____. 2007. "The Sexual Politics of the 'New Abolitionism'." *Differences* 18, 5.

Berry, J. 1994. "Aboriginal Cultural Identity." Report Prepared for the Royal Commission on Aboriginal Peoples. Ottawa: Department of Indian and Northern Affairs.

Bertrand, M-A. 1999. "Incarceration as a Gendering Strategy." *Canadian Journal of Law and Society* 14, 1.

____. 1969. "Self-Image and Delinquency: A Contribution to the Study of Female Criminality." *Acta Criminologica* 2.

____. 1967. "The Myth of Sexual Equality Before the Law." Fifth Research Conference on Delinquency and Criminality. Montreal, Centre de Psychologies et de Pédagogie.

Berzins, L., and B. Hayes. 1987. "The Diaries of Two Change Agents." In E. Adelberg and C. Currie (eds.), *Too Few to Count: Canadian Women in Conflict with the Law*. Vancouver: Press Gang Publishers.

Bicker, A., J. Pottier, and P. Sillitoe. 2002. *Participating in Development: Approaches to Indigenous Knowledge*. New York: Taylor and Francis.

Bishop, A. 2002. *Becoming an Ally: Breaking the Cycle of Oppression in People*. Halifax and Winnipeg: Fernwood Publishing.

Bittle, S. 2006. "From Villain to Victim: Secure Care and Young Women in Prostitution." In G. Balfour and E. Comack (eds.), *Criminalizing Women: Gender and (In)justice in Neoliberal Times*. Halifax and Winnipeg: Fernwood Publishing.

Block, S. 2010. *Ontario's Growing Gap: The Role of Race and Gender*. Ottawa: Canadian Center for Policy Alternatives.

Block, S., and G.E. Galabuzi. 2011. *Canada's Colour Coded Labour Market: The Gap for Racialized Workers*. Ottawa and Toronto: Canadian Centre for Policy Alternatives and The Wellesley Institute.

Bloom, B. 2003. "A New Vision: Gender-Responsive Principles, Policy and Practices." *Gendered Justice: Addressing the Female Offender*. Durham: Carolina Academic Press.

____. 1999. "Gender-Responsive Programming for Women Offenders: Guiding Principles and Practices." *Forum on Corrections Research* 11, 3.

Bloom, B., B. Owen, and S. Covington. 2005. *Gender Responsive Strategies for Women Offenders:*

*A Summary of Research, Practice and Guiding Principles for Women Offenders*. Washington: National Institute for Corrections.

____. 2003. *Gender Responsive Strategies: Research, Practice, and Guiding Principles for Women Offenders*. Washington: National Institute of Corrections.

Bloom, H., and R.D. Schneider. 2006. *Mental Disorder and the Law: A Primer for Legal and Mental Health Professionals*. Toronto: Irwin Law.

Bordo, S. 1988. "Anorexia Nervosa: Psychopathology and the Crystallization of Culture." In I. Diamond and L. Quinby (eds.), *Feminism and Foucault: Reflections on Resistance*. Boston: Northeastern University Press.

Boritch, H. 1997. *Fallen Women: Female Crime and Criminal Justice in Canada*. Toronto: Nelson.

Bosworth, M. 1999. "Agency and Choice in Women's Prisons: Towards a Constitutive Penality." In S. Henry and D. Milovanovic (eds.), *Constitutive Criminology at Work: Applications to Crime and Justice*. Albany: State University of New York Press.

Bourdieu, P. 1998. "Utopia of Endless Exploitation: The Essence of Neoliberalism." *Le Monde Diplomatique* (December).

Bourgois, P. 2003. *In Search of Respect: Selling Crack in El Barrio* (second edition). New York: Cambridge University Press.

Boyer, Y. 2006. "First Nations, Métis and Inuit Women's Health." *Discussion Paper Series in Aboriginal Health: Legal Issues* 4. Saskatchewan: National Aboriginal Health Organization and Native Law Centre.

Bradley, H. 1996. *Fractured Identities: Changing Patterns of Inequality*. Cambridge: Polity.

Breggin, P. 1993. *Toxic Psychiatry. Drugs and Electroconvulsive Therapy: The Truth and the Better Alternatives*. London: Harper Collins.

Brennan, S. 2012. "Police-Reported Crime Statistics in Canada, 2011." *Juristat* (July 24).

____. 2011. "Canadian's Perceptions of Personal Safety and Crime, 2009." *Juristat* (December). <statcan.gc.ca/pub/85-002-x/2011001/article/11577-eng.pdf>.

Brewer, Rose M. 1997. "Theorizing Race, Class, and Gender: The New Scholarship of Black Feminist Intellectuals and Black Women's Labour." In R. Hennessy and C. Ingraham (eds.), *Materialist Feminism*. London: Routledge.

Brinkerhoff, M., and E. Lupri. 1988. "Interspousal Violence." *Canadian Journal of Sociology* 13, 4.

British Home Office. 1999. *Aim 4: The Government's Strategy for Women Offenders*. London: Home Office.

Brock, D. 2009. *Making Work, Making Trouble: The Social Regulation of Sexual Labour* (second edition). Toronto: University of Toronto Press.

____. 1998. *Making Work, Making Trouble: Prostitution as a Social Problem*. Toronto: University of Toronto Press.

Brockman, J., E. Campbell, C. Dell, B. Fornssler, C. Hopkins, L. LaLiberte, H. McKenzie, D. Mykota, Elder C. Papequash, C. Ross, S. Swampy, and T Walker. 2013. "How has Aboriginal Culture Helped You, or Someone You Know, on the Journey of Healing from Addictions?" *Qualitative Analysis Conference*. Ottawa.

Brodie, J. 1995. *Politics on the Margins: Restructuring and the Canadian Women's Movement*. Halifax: Fernwood Publishing.

Brodie, J., S. Gavigan, and J. Jenson. 1992. *The Politics of Abortion*. Toronto: Oxford University Press.

Brookes, B. 1998. "Women and Mental Health: An Historical Introduction." In S.E. Romans (ed.), *Folding Back the Shadows*. Dunedin: University of Otago Press.

Brosnahan. M. 2013. "Ashley Smith 'Could Very Easily Have Been Me.'" *CBC News*, March 1. <cbc.ca/news/canada/ashley-smith-could-very-easily-have-been-me-1.1332560>.

Brown, M. 2009. *The Culture of Punishment: Prison, Society, and Spectacle*. New York: New York University Press.

Browne, A. 1987. *When Battered Women Kill.* New York: Free Press.

Brownmiller, S. 1975. *Against Our Will: Men, Women and Rape.* New York: Simon and Schuster.

Bruckert, C. 2002. *Putting it On, Taking it Off: Women Workers in the Strip Trade.* Toronto: Women's Press.

Bruckert, C., and F. Chabot. 2010. *Challenges: Ottawa Area Sex Workers Speak Out.* Ottawa: POWER.

Bruckert, C., and T. Law. 2013. *Beyond Pimps, Procurers and Parasites: Management in the Incall/ Outcall Sex Industry.* Ottawa: Management Project.

Bruckert, C., C. Parent, and P. Robitaille. 2003. *Erotic Service/Erotic Dance Establishments: Two Types of Marginalized Labour.* Ottawa: The Law Commission of Canada.

Bruser, D. 2011. "The Kids of 311: Young Offenders Coddled by Court." *The Star,* Oct, 29. <thestar.com/news/canada/2011/10/29/the_kids_of_311_young_offenders_coddled_by_court.html>.

Brush, L.D. 2011. *Poverty, Battered Women and Work in U.S. Public Policy.* New York: Oxford University Press.

Bruyere, G., M. Hart, and R. Sinclair. 2009. *Wicihitowin: Aboriginal Social Work in Canada.* Halifax and Winnipeg: Fernwood Publishing.

Bryan, J. 1965. "Apprenticeship in Prostitution." *Social Problems* 12.

Brzozowski, J., and R. Brazeau. 2008. *What Are the Trends in Self-Reported Spousal Violence in Canada.* Ottawa: Statistics Canada.

Brzozowski, J., A. Taylor-Butts, and S. Johnson.2006. "Victimization and Offending Among the Aboriginal Population in Canada." *Juristat* 26, 3.

Buchanan, M. 1995. "The Unworthy Poor: Experiences of Single Mothers on Welfare in Chilliwack, British Columbia." M.A. thesis, Simon Fraser University, Burnaby.

Bumiller, K. 2008. *In an Abusive State: How Neoliberalism Appropriated the Feminist Movement Against Sexual Violence.* Durham: Duke University Press.

Bureau of Justice Statistics. 2000. *Prison and Jail Inmates at Mid-Year 2000.* Washington, DC: U.S. Department of Justice, #185989.

Burke, J., P. O'Campo, G. Peak, A. Gielen, K. McDonnell, and W. Trochim. 2005. "An Introduction to Concept Mapping as a Participatory Public Health Research Method." *Qualitative Health Research* 15, 10.

Burman, M., S. Batchelor, and J. Brown. 2003. "Girls and the Meaning of Violence." In E. Stanko (ed.), *The Meanings of Violence.* London: Routledge.

Busby, K. 2014. "'Sex Was in the Air': Pernicious Myths and Other Problems with Sexual Violence Prosecutions." In E. Comack (ed.), *Locating Law: Race/Class/Gender/Sexuality Connections* (third edition). Halifax and Winnipeg: Fernwood Publishing.

Busby, K., P. Downe, K. Gorkoff, K. Nixon, L. Tutty, and J. Ursel. 2002. "Examination of Innovative Programming for Children and Youth Involved in Prostitution." In H. Berman and Y. Jiwani (eds.), *In The Best Interests of the Girl Child: Phase II Report.* Ottawa: Status of Women Canada.

Butler, J. 2004. *Undoing Gender.* New York: Routledge.

CAEFS (Canadian Association of Elizabeth Fry Societies). 2005a. "More Promises to Women not Kept." Ottawa: CAEFS. <caefs.ca/wp-content/uploads/2013/05/notkepte.pdf>.

____. 2005b. *Submission of the Canadian Association of Elizabeth Fry Societies to the United Nations Human Rights Committee Examining Canada's 4th and 5th Reports Regarding the Convention Against Torture.* Ottawa: CAEFS. <caefs.ca/wp-content/uploads/2013/04/Submission-of-the-Canadian-Association-of-Elizabeth-Fry-Societies-to-the-United-Nations-Human-Rights-Committee-Examining-Canadas-4th-and-5th-Reports-Regarding-the-Convention-Against-Torture.pdf>

____. 2003. "Submission of the Canadian Association of Elizabeth Fry Societies (CAEFS) to the

Canadian Human Rights Commission for the Special Report on the Discrimination on the Basis of Sex, Race and Disability Faced by Federally Sentenced Women." Ottawa: CAEFS. <caefs.ca/wp-content/uploads/2013/04/CAEFS-Submission-to-the-Canadian-Human-Rights-Commission-for-the-Special-Report-on-the-Discrimination-on-the-Basis-of-Sex-Race-and-Disability-Faced-by-Federally-Sentenced-Women.pdf>.

____. 1998. *Another Bad Trip: CSC Malingering in the LSD Compensation Case.* Ottawa: CAEFS.

____. 1997. "Justice for Battered Women — Denied, Delayed… Diminished. Jails Are Not the Shelters Battered Women." Ottawa: CAEFS. At: <caefs.ca/wp-content/uploads/2013/04/Justice-for-Battered-Women.pdf>.

Caiazza, A. 2005. "Don't Bowl at Night: Gender, Safety, and Civic Participation." *Signs* 30, 2.

Cain, M. 1990. "Towards Transgression: New Directions in Feminist Criminology." *International Journal of the Sociology of Law* 18.

Cajete, G. 2004. "A Pueblo Story for Transformation." In E. O'Sullivan, and M. Taylor (eds.) *Learning Toward an Ecological Consciousness: Selected Transformative Practices.* New York: Palgrave.

Califia, P. 1994. *Public Sex: The Culture of Radical Sex.* Pittsburgh: Cleis.

Campaign 2000. 2012. "2012 Report Card on Child and Family Poverty: Needed: A Federal Action Plan to Eradicate Child and Family Poverty in Canada." Toronto: Family Service Toronto. <campaign2000.ca/reportCards/national/C2000ReportCardNov2012.pdf>.

Canada. 1977. *Report to Parliament by the Sub-Committee on the Penitentiary System in Canada.* Ottawa: Supply and Services.

Canada, Public Service Commission, Research Directorate. 1999. "The Future of Work: Non-Standard Employment in the Public Service of Canada." Ottawa: Policy, Research, and Communications Branch.

Canadian Advisory Council on the Status of Women. 1981. *Women in Prison: Expanding Their Options.* Ottawa.

Canadian Centre for Justice Statistics. 2000. *Juristat: Adult Correctional Services in Canada, 1998–99.* Ottawa: Statistics Canada.

____. 1997. *Uniform Crime Reporting Survey.* Ottawa: Statistics Canada.

Canadian Labour Congress. 2009. *Fair Wages and Working Conditions.* <canadianlabour.ca/action-center/municipality-matters/fair-wages-working-conditions>.

Canadian Panel on Violence Against Women. 1993. *Changing the Landscape: Ending Violence — Achieving Equality.* Ottawa: Minister of Supply and Services Canada.

Caniato, R., A. Gundabawady, B. Baune, and M. Alvarenga. 2009. "Malingered Psychotic Symptoms and Quetiapine Abuse in a Forensic Setting." *The Journal of Forensic Psychiatry & Psychology* 20, 6.

Caplan, P.J., and L. Cosgrove. 2004. *Bias in Psychiatric Diagnosis.* Lanham: Jason Aronson.

Carcach, C., and A. Grant. 2000. *Imprisonment in Australia: The Offence Composition of Australian Correctional Populations, 1998 and 1988.* Canberra: Australian Institute of Criminology, # 164 (July).

____. 1999: *Imprisonment in Australia: Trends in Prison Populations and Imprisonment Rates.* Canberra: Australian Institute of Criminology, 130 (October).

Carlen, P. 2005. "Imprisonment and the Penal Body Politic: The Cancer of Disciplinary Governance." In A. Liebling and S. Maruna (eds.), *The Effects of Imprisonment.* Cullompton: Willan Publishing.

____. 2003. "Virginia, Criminology, and the Antisocial Control of Women." In T. Bloomberg and S. Cohen (eds.), *Punishment and Social Control.* New York: Aldine De Gruyter.

____ (ed.). 2002a. *Women and Punishment: The Struggle for Justice.* Cullompton: Willan Publishing.

____. 2002b. "New Discourses of Justification and Reform for Women's Imprisonment in England." In P. Carlen (ed.), *Women and Punishment: The Struggle for Justice.* Cullompton:

Willan Publishing.

____. 1988. *Women, Crime and Poverty*. Milton Keynes: Open University Press.

____. 1983. *Women's Imprisonment: A Study in Social Control*. London: Routledge.

Carriere, J., and S. Strega. 2009. *Walking This Path Together: Anti-Racist and Anti-Oppressive Child Welfare Practice*. Halifax and Winnipeg: Fernwood Publishing.

Carrington, K. 1993. *Offending Girls: Sex, Youth and Justice*. Sydney: Allen and Unwin.

Carruthers, E. 1995. "Prosecuting Women for Welfare Fraud in Ontario: Implications for Equality." *Journal of Law and Social Policy* 11.

Carter, CS. 2002. "Perinatal Care for Women who are Addicted: Implications for Empowerment." *Health & Social Work* 27 (Fall).

Carter, V. 2004. "Prostitution and the New Slavery." In C. Stark and R. Whisnant (eds.), *Not for Sale: Feminists Resisting Prostitution and Pornography*. Sydney: Spinifex.

Cassel, J. 1987. *The Secret Plague: Venereal Disease in Canada, 1838–1939*. Toronto: University of Toronto Press.

Chan, W. 2001. *Women, Murder and Justice*. London: Palgrave.

Chan, W., D.E. Chunn, and R. Menzies (eds.) 2005.*Women, Madness and the Law: A Feminist Reader*. London: Glasshouse Press.

Chan, W., and G. Rigakos. 2002. "Risk, Crime and Gender." *British Journal of Criminology* 42.

Chapkis, W. 1997. *Live Sex Acts: Women Performing Erotic Labour*. New York: Routledge.

Chesney-Lind, M. 2004. "Feminism and Critical Criminology: Towards a Feminist Praxis." Division on Critical Criminology - American Society of Criminology. <critcrim.org/critpapers/chesney-lind1.htm>.

Chesney-Lind, M. 1999. "Review of 'When She Was Bad: Violent Women and the Myth of Innocence.'" *Women and Criminal Justice*.

____. 1988a. "Doing Feminist Criminology." *The Criminologist* 13, 1.

____. 1988b. "Girls and Status Offenses: Is Juvenile Justice Still Sexist?" *Criminal Justice Abstracts*, 20.

____. 1987. "Girls and Violence: An Exploration of the Gender Gap in Serious Delinquent Behavior." In D. Corwell, I. Evans, and C. O'Donnell (eds.), *Childhood Aggression and Violence*. New York: Plenum.

____. 1981. "Juvenile Delinquency: The Sexualization of Female Crime." *Psychology Today* (July).

____. 1978. "Chivalry Re-Examined." In L. Bowker (ed.), *Women, Crime and the Criminal Justice System*. Lexington, MA: Lexington Books.

Chesney-Lind, M., and K. Faith. 2000. "What About Feminism? Engendering Theory-Making in Criminology." In R. Paternoster (ed.), *Criminological Theories*. Los Angeles: Roxbury Press.

Chesney-Lind, M., and V. Paramore. 2001. "Are Girls Getting More Violent? Exploring Juvenile Robbery Trends." *Journal of Contemporary Criminal Justice* 17, 2.

Chesney-Lind, M., and L. Pasko. 2013. *The Female Offender: Girls, Women, and Crime* (third edition). Thousand Oaks: Sage Publications.

Chesney-Lind, M., and N. Rodriguez. 1983. "Women Under Lock and Key." *The Prison Journal* 63.

Chesney-Lind, M., and R. Sheldon. 1998. *Girls, Delinquency and Juvenile Justice*. California: Wadsworth.

Chinnery Report. 1978. *Joint Committee to Study Alternatives for Housing Federal Female Offenders*. Ottawa: Ministry of Solicitor General.

CHRC (Canadian Human Rights Commission). 2003. *Protecting Their Rights: A Systemic Review of Human Rights in Correctional Services for Federally Sentenced Women*. Ottawa: Canadian Human Rights Commission. <chrc-ccdp.ca/sites/default/files/fswen.pdf>.

Chunn, D.E. 1997. "A Little Sex can be a Dangerous Thing: Regulating Sexuality, Venereal Disease, and Reproduction in British Columbia, 1919-1945." In S. Boyd (ed.), *Challenging the Public/Private Divide: Feminism, Law and Public Policy*. Toronto: University of Toronto Press.

Chunn, D.E., S.B. Boyd, and H. Lessard (eds.). 2007. *Reaction and Resistance: Feminism, Law and Social Change*. Vancouver: UBC Press.

Chunn, D.E., and S. Gavigan. 2005. "From Mother's Allowance to 'No Mothers Need Apply': Canadian Welfare Law as Liberal and Neo-Liberal Reforms." Presented at the Thirteenth Berkshire Conference on the History of Women (June). Claremont, CA.

____. 2004. "Welfare Law, Welfare Fraud, and the Moral Regulation of the 'Never Deserving' Poor." *Social and Legal Studies* 13, 2.

Chunn, D.E., and R. Menzies. 1998. "Out of Mind, Out of Law: The Regulation of 'Criminally Insane' Women Inside British Columbia's Public Mental Hospitals, 1888–1973." *Canadian Journal of Women and the Law* 10, 3 (Fall).

____. 1994. "Gender, Madness and Crime: The Reproduction of Patriarchal and Class Relations in a Pretrial Psychiatric Clinic." In R. Hinch (ed.), *Readings in Critical Criminology*. Scarborough, ON: Prentice Hall Canada.

City of Toronto. 2010. *Toronto Municipal Code, Chapter 545 Licensing, Article XXXII*. Toronto, ON: City of Toronto.

Clark Report. 1977. *Report of the National Advisory Committee on the Female Offender*. Ottawa: Ministry of Solicitor General.

Clarke, J. 2000. "Unfinished Business? Struggles over the Social in Social Welfare." In P. Gilroy, L. Grossberg, and A. McRobbie (eds.), *Without Guarantees: In Honour of Stuart Hall*. London: Verso.

Coe, H.V., and I.S. Hong. 2012. "Safety of Low Doses of Quetiapine When Used for Insomnia." *The Annals of Pharmacotherapy* 46, 5.

Cohen, M. 1997. "From the Welfare State to Vampire Capitalism." In P. Evans and G. Wekerle, (eds.), *Women and the Canadian Welfare State: Challenges and Change*. Toronto: University of Toronto Press.

Cohen, S. 2002. *Folk Devils and Moral Panics: The Creation of Mods and Rockers*. London and New York: Routledge.

____. 1985. *Visions of Social Control*. Cambridge: Polity.

Coleman, R. 2005. "Surveillance in the City: Primary Definition and Urban Spatial Order." *Crime, Media, Culture* 1, 2.

____. 2003. "Images from a Neoliberal City: The State, Surveillance and Social Control." *Critical Criminology* 12, 1.

Coleman, R. and J. Sim. 2000. "You'll Never Walk Alone: CCTV Surveillance, Order and Neo-liberal Rule in Liverpool City Centre." *British Journal of Sociology* 51, 4.

Collier, C. 2012. "Feminist and Gender-Neutral Frames in Contemporary Child-Care and Anti-Violence Policy Debates in Canada." *Politics and Gender* 8, 3.

____. 2008. "Neoliberalism and Violence against Women: Can Retrenchment Convergence Explain the Path of Provincial Anti-Violence Policy, 1985–2005?" *Canadian Journal of Political Science* 41, 1.

____. 2005. "Do Strong Women's Movements Get Results? Measuring the Impact of the Child Care and Anti-violence Movements in Ontario 1970-2000." Paper presented at the Annual Meeting of the Canadian Political Science Association, London, Ontario, June 2-4.

Collin, C., and Hilary Jensen. 2009. *A Statistical Profile of Poverty in Canada*. Ottawa: Library of Parliament. <parl.gc.ca/content/lop/researchpublications/prb0917-e.pdf>.

Collins, A. 1988. *In the Sleep Room: The Story of the CIA Brainwashing Experiments in Canada*. Toronto: Lester and Orpen Dennys.

Comack, E. (ed.). 2014. *Locating Law: Race/Class/Gender/Sexuality Connections* (third edition). Halifax and Winnipeg: Fernwood Publishing.

____. 2012. *Racialized Policing: Aboriginal People's Encounters with the Police*. Halifax and Winnipeg: Fernwood Publishing.

____ (ed.). 2006. *Locating Law: Race/Class/Gender/Sexuality Connections* (second edition). Halifax: Fernwood Publishing.

____. 1996. *Women in Trouble*. Halifax: Fernwood.

____. 1993a. *Women Offenders' Experiences with Physical and Sexual Abuse: A Preliminary Report*. Winnipeg: Criminology Research Centre, University of Manitoba.

____. 1993b. *The Feminist Engagement with the Law: The Legal Recognition of the 'Battered Woman Syndrome.'* Ottawa: Canadian Research Institute for the Advancement of Women.

Comack, E., and G. Balfour. 2004. *The Power to Criminalize: Violence, Inequality and the Law*. Halifax: Fernwood.

Comack, E., V. Chopyk, and L. Wood. 2002. "Aren't Women Violent Too? The Gendered Nature of Violence." In B. Schissel and C. Brooks (eds.), *Marginality and Condemnation: An Introduction to Critical Criminology*. Halifax: Fernwood.

____. 2000. *Mean Streets? The Social Locations, Gender Dynamics, and Patterns of Violent Crime in Winnipeg*. Winnipeg: Canadian Centre for Policy Alternatives-Manitoba (December).

Comack, E., L. Deane, L. Morrissette, and J. Silver. 2013. *"Indians Wear Red" Colonialism, Resistance, and Aboriginal Street Gangs*. Halifax and Winnipeg: Fernwood Publishing.

Comaroff, J. 2007. "Beyond Bare Life: AIDS, (Bio)Politics, and the Neoliberal Order." *Public Culture* 19, 1.

Conrad, P. 2007. *The Medicalization of Society: On the Transformation of Human Conditions into Treatable Disorders*. Baltimore: John Hopkins University Press.

Conrad, P., and J. Schneider. 1992. *Deviance and Medicalization: From Badness to Sickness*. Columbus, Ohio: Merrill Publishing Company.

Cool, J. 2004. *Prostitution in Canada: An Overview*. Ottawa: Library of Parliament. <publications. gc.ca/collections/Collection-R/LoPBdP/PRB-e/PRB0443-e.pdf>.

Cooper, S. 1993. "The Evolution of the Federal Women's Prison." In E. Adelberg and C. Currie (eds.), *In Conflict with the Law: Women and the Canadian Justice System*. Vancouver: Press Gang.

Copeland, J. 1997."A Qualitative Study of Barriers to Formal Treatment among Women who Self-Managed Change in Addictive Behaviours." *Journal of Substance Abuse Treatment* 14 (Spring).

CORP. 1987. "Realistic Feminists." In L. Bell (ed.), *Good Girls, Bad Girls: Sex Trade Workers and Feminists Face to Face*. Toronto: Woman's Press.

Corrigan, P., and D. Sayer. 1985. *The Great Arch: English State Formation as Cultural Revolution*. London: Basil Blackwell.

____. 1981. "How the Law Rules: Variations on Some Themes in Karl Marx." In B. Fryer et al. (eds.), *Law, State, and Society*. London: Croom Helm.

Cossman, B. 2002. "Family Feuds: Neo-Liberal and Neo-Conservative Visions of the Reprivatization Project." In B. Cossman and J. Fudge (eds.), *Privatization, Law, and the Challenge to Feminism*. Toronto: University of Toronto Press.

Cossman, B., and J. Fudge (eds.). 2002. *Privatization, Law, and the Challenge to Feminism*. Toronto: University of Toronto Press.

Coulter, K. 2009. "Women, Poverty Policy and the Production of Neoliberal Politics in Ontario Canada." *Journal of Women, Politics and Policy* 30.

Cowan, D. A., and K.M. Beard Adams. 2008. "Talking Circles, Leadership Competencies, and Inclusive Learning: Expanding the Frame of Business Education." *Journal on Excellence in College Teaching* 19, 2 and 3.

Cowie, J., V. Cowie, and E. Slater. 1968. *Delinquency in Girls*. London: Heinemann.

Crenshaw, K. 1989. "Demarginalizing the Intersection of Race and Sex: A Black Feminist Critique of Antidiscrimination Doctrine, Feminist Theory and Antiracist Politics." *The University of Chicago Legal Forum* 140.

CRIAW (Canadian Research Institute for the Advancement of Women). 2005. *CRIAW Fact Sheet: Women and Poverty* (third edition). <criaw-icref.ca/WomenAndPoverty>.

Criminal Intelligence Service Canada. 2004. "2004 Annual Report on Organized Crime in Canada." <cisc.gc.ca/annual_reports/documents/2004_annual_report.pdf>.

Crookshanks, R. 2012. "Marginalization through a Custom of Deservingness: Sole-Support Mothers and Welfare Law in Canada." *Review of Current Law and Law Reform* 17.

CSC (Correctional Service Canada). 2011. *Progress Report Response to the Office of the Correctional Investigator's (OCI) Deaths in Custody Study, the Correctional Investigator's (CI) Report: A Preventable Death, and the CSC National Board of Investigation into the Death of an Offender at Grand Valley Institution for Women.* Ottawa: Correctional Service of Canada. <csc-scc.gc.ca/publications/rocidcs/grid5-eng.shtml>.

____. 2010. "Mission Statement." Ottawa: Correctional Service of Canada. <csc-scc.gc.ca/hist/mission-eng.shtml>.

____. 2006. *The Ten Year Status Report on Women's Corrections.* Ottawa: Correctional Service of Canada. <csc-scc.gc.ca/text/prgrm/fsw/wos24/tenyearstatusreport_e.pdf>.

____. 2005b. *CSC Action Plan in Response to the Report of the Canadian Human Rights Commission.* Ottawa: Correctional Service of Canada. <csc-scc.gc.ca/publications/fsw/gender4/CHRC_response_e.pdf>.

Currie, E. 2013. *Crime and Punishment in America.* New York: Picador.

Currie, J. 2001. *Best Practices: Treatment and Rehabilitation for Women with Substance Use Problems.* Ottawa: Health Canada.

Dalpy, M. 2002. "Dark Passage in Ontario's Past: Until 1958, Female Minors Deemed Incorrigible Could Be Put in Jail: Velma Demerson Was One." *Globe and Mail*, March 22.

Daly, K. 1998. "Women's Pathways to Felony Court: Feminist Theories of Lawbreaking and Problems of Representation." In K. Daly and L. Maher (eds.), *Criminology at the Crossroads: Feminist Readings in Crime and Justice.* New York: Oxford.

____. 1992. "Women's Pathways to Felony Court: Feminist Theories of Lawbreaking and Problems of Representation." *Southern California Review of Law and Women's Studies* 2.

____. 1989. "Rethinking Judicial Paternalism: Gender, Work-Family Relations, and Sentencing." *Gender and Society* 3, 1.

____. 1987. "Discrimination in the Criminal Courts: Family, Gender, and the Problem of Equal Treatment." *Social Forces* 66, 1.

Daly, K., and M. Chesney-Lind. 1988. "Feminism and Criminology." *Justice Quarterly* 5, 4.

Dauvergne, M. 2012. "Adult Correctional Statistics in Canada, 2010/2011." *Juristat* (October).

Davidson, T. 2013. "Inquest Jury Rules Ashley Smith a Homicide." *Toronto Sun*, December 19. <torontosun.com/2013/12/19/inquest-jury-rules-ashley-smith-a-homicide>.

Davies, M. 1987. "The Patients' World: British Columbia's Mental Health Facilities, 1910–1935." Unpublished M.A. thesis, University of Waterloo.

Davis, K. 1937. "The Sociology of Prostitution." *American Sociological Review* 2.5.

Dawson, D. 2012. "What Do *You* Think? International Public Opinion on Camera Surveillance." In A. Doyle, R. Lippert, and D. Lyon (eds.), *Eyes Everywhere: The Global Growth of Camera Surveillance.* New York: Routledge.

Day, S. 2008. *Prostitution: Violating the Human Rights of Poor Women.* Ottawa: Action Ontarienne contre la violence faite aux femmes.

Daykin, N. 2004. "The Role of Music in Arts-Based Qualitative Inquiry." *International Journal of Qualitative Methods* 3, 2.

Daykin, N., S. McClean, and L. Blunt. 2007. "Creativity, Identity and Healing: Participants' Accounts of Music Therapy in Cancer Care." *Health* 11, 3.

De Medeiros, K., and A. Basting. 2013. "Shall I Compare Thee to a Dose of 'Donezepil?': Cultural Arts Interventions in Dementia Care Research." *The Gerontologist* (Spring).

Dean, M. 1999. *Governmentality: Power and Rule in Modern Society.* London: Sage Publications.

___. 1994. "'A Social Structure of Many Souls': Moral Regulation, Government and Self-Formation." *Canadian Journal of Sociology* 19, 2.

DeHart, D. 2006. "Pathways to Prison: Impact of Victimization in the Lives of Incarcerated Women." *Violence Against Women* 14, 12.

DeKeseredy, W.S. 1999. "Tactics of the Anti-Feminist Backlash Against Canadian National Woman Abuse Surveys." *Violence Against Women* 5.

DeKeseredy, W., and R. Hinch. 1991. *Woman Abuse: Sociological Perspectives.* Toronto: Thompson.

DeKeseredy, W., and B. MacLean. 1998. "'But Women Do It Too': The Contexts and Nature of Female-to-Male Violence in Canadian Heterosexual Dating Relationships." In K. Bonnycastle and G. Rigakos (eds.), *Unsettling Truths: Battered Women, Policy, Politics, and Contemporary Research in Canada.* Vancouver: Collective Press.

Dell, C. 2012. "Voices of Healing: How a Research Project Is Using Music to Communicate its Findings." *Knowledge Translation Casebook.* Saskatchewan: Saskatchewan Population Health and Evaluation Research Unit.

Dell, C., C. Fillmore, and J.M. Kilty. 2009. "Looking Back 10 Years After the Arbour Inquiry: Ideology, Practice and the Misbehaved Federal Female Prisoner." *The Prison Journal* 89, 3.

Dell, C., C. Hopkins, and D. Dell. 2005. "Resiliency and Holistic Inhalant Abuse Treatment." *Journal of Aboriginal Health* 2, 1.

Dell, C., and J. Kilty. 2013. "The Creation of the Expected Aboriginal Woman Drug Offender in Canada: Exploring Relations between Victimization, Punishment, and Cultural Identity." *International Review of Victimology* 19, 1 (Special Invitation).

Demerson, V. 2004. *Incorrigible.* Waterloo: Wilfrid Laurier University Press.

___. 2001. "The Female Refuges Act." *Opening the Doors: The Newsletter of the Council of Elizabeth Fry Societies of Ontario* (Spring).

Denis, C. 1995. "'Government Can Do Whatever It Wants': Moral Regulation in Ralph Klein's Alberta." *Canadian Review of Sociology and Anthropology* 32, 3.

Devens, C. 1992. *Countering Colonization: Native American Women and Great Lake Missions, 1630–1900.* Berkeley: University of California Press.

Dhruvarajan, V. 2002. "Women of Colour in Canada." In V. Dhruvarajan and J. Vickers (eds.), *Gender, Race and Nation: A Global Perspective.* Toronto: University of Toronto Press.

DiManno, R. 2007a. "For Eastside Girls Nothing's Changed." *Toronto Star,* January 22.

___. 2007b. "Lurid Trial Reinforces Stigma." *Toronto Star,* January 27.

___. 2007c. "Women on Streets 'Still Terrified.'" *Toronto Star,* December 2.

Ditton, J. 2000. "Crime and the City: Public Attitudes towards Open-Street CCTV in Glasgow." *British Journal of Criminology* 40.

Dobash, R.E., and R. Dobash. 1992. *Women, Violence and Social Change.* London: Routledge.

___. 1979. *Violence Against Wives: A Case Against the Patriarchy.* New York: Free Press.

Dobash, R.E., R. Dobash, and S. Guttridge. 1986: *The Imprisonment of Women.* Oxford: Basil Blackwell.

Dobash, R., R.E. Dobash, M. Wilson, and M. Daly. 1992. "The Myth of Sexual Symmetry in Marital Violence." *Social Problems* 39, 1 (February).

Doe, J. 2013. "Are Feminists Leaving Women Behind? The Casting of Sexually Assaulted and Sex-Working Women." In E. van der Meulen, E. Durisin, and V. Love (eds.), *Selling Sex: Experience, Advocacy, and Research on Sex Work in Canada.* Vancouver: UBC Press.

Doob, A., and J. Sprott. 1998. "Is the 'Quality' of Youth Violence Becoming More Serious?" *Canadian Journal of Criminology* 40, 2.

Dowbiggin, I.R. 1997. *Keeping American Sane: Psychiatry and Eugenics in the United States and Canada, 1880–1940.* Ithaca: Cornell University Press.

Doyle, A., R. Lippert, and D. Lyon (eds.). 2012. *Eyes Everywhere: The Global Growth of Camera*

*Surveillance.* New York: Routledge.

Dubinsky, K., and F. Iacovetta. 1991. "Murder, Womanly Virtue, and Motherhood: The Case of Angelina Napolitano, 1911–1922." *Canadian Historical Review* 72, 4 (December).

Dubois, E., and L. Gordon. 1983. "Seeking Ecstasy on the Battlefield: Danger and Pleasure in Nineteenth-Century Sexual Thought." *Feminist Studies* 9.

DuBois, T. 2012. "Police Investigations of Sexual Assault Complaints: How Far Have We Come Since *Jane Doe*?" In E. Sheehy (ed.), *Sexual Assault in Canada: Law, Legal Practice and Women's Activism.* Ottawa: University of Ottawa Press.

Duncan, K. 1965. "Irish Famine Immigration and the Social Structure of Canada West." *Canadian Review of Sociology and Anthropology* 1.

Duran, Eduardo. 2006. *Healing the Soul Wound: Counseling with American Indians and Other Native Peoples.* New York: Teachers College Press.

Durazo, A.C.R. 2007. "'We Were Never Meant to Survive': Fighting Violence Against Women and the Fourth World War." In INCITE! Women of Color Against Violence (eds.), *The Revolution Will Not Be Funded: Beyond the Non-Profit Industrial Complex.* Cambridge, MA: South End Press.

Dutton, D. 1994. "Patriarchy and Wife Assault: The Ecological Fallacy." *Violence and Victims* 9.

Eden, Dr. D.S. 2003. *Letter to Chief Coroner of Ontario re: Inquest into the Death of Kimberly Rogers.* (letter on file with D.E. Chunn and S.A.M. Gavigan).

*Educational CyberPlayGround.* n.d. "Learn About Story Telling: The Folk Tradition of Story Telling." <edu-cyberpg.com/Arts/Story_telling.html>.

Edwards, S. 1985. "Gender Justice? Defending Defendants and Mitigating Sentence." In S. Edwards (ed.), *Gender, Sex and the Law.* London: Croom Helm.

Ehrenreich, B., and D. English. 1973. *Complaints and Disorders: The Sexual Politics of Sickness.* Old Westbury: FeministPress.

Ericson, R., P. Baranek, and J. Chan. 1991. *Representing Order: Crime, Law, and Justice in the News Media.* Buffalo and Toronto: University of Toronto Press.

____. 1987. *Visualizing Deviance: A Study of News Organization.* Buffalo and Toronto: University of Toronto Press.

Ericson, R.V., and K.D. Haggerty. 1997. *Policing the Risk Society.* Toronto: University of Toronto Press.

Evans, P., and K. Swift. 2000. "Single Mothers and the Press: Rising Tides, Moral Panic, and Restructuring Discourses." In Sheila M. Neysmith (ed.), *Restructuring Caring Labour.* Toronto: Oxford University Press.

Ewing, P., and S. Silbey. 1995. "Subversive Stories and Hegemonic Tales: Toward a Sociology of Narrative." *Law and Society Review* 29, 2.

Faith, K. 1995. "Aboriginal Women's Healing Lodge: Challenge to Penal Correctionalism?" *Journal of Human Justice* 6, 2.

____. 1993. *Unruly Women: The Politics of Confinement and Resistance.* Vancouver: Press Gang Publishers.

Faith, K., and D. Currie. 1993. *Seeking Shelter: A State of Battered Women.* Vancouver: Collective Press.

Faith, K., and K. Pate. 2000. "Personal and Political Musings on Activism." In K. Hannah-Moffat and M. Shaw (eds.), *An Ideal Prison? Critical Essays on Women's Imprisonment in Canada.* Halifax: Fernwood.

Farley, M. 2004. "'Bad for the Body, Bad for the Heart': Prostitution Harms Women Even if Legalized or Decriminalized." *Violence Against Women* 10, 10.

____. 2003. "Prostitution and the Invisibility of Harm." *Women & Therapy* 26, 3/4.

Feldberg, G. 1997. "Defining the Facts of Rape: The Uses of Medical Evidence in Sexual Assault Trials." *Canadian Journal of Women & the Law* 9.

Feree, M. 1990. "Between Two Worlds: German Feminist Approaches to Working-Class Women." In J. Nielsen (ed.), *Feminist Research Methods*. Boulder: Westview Press.

____. 1984. "Sacrifice, Satisfaction and Social Change: Employment and the Family." In K. Sacks, and D. Remy (eds.), *My Troubles Are Going to Have Trouble with Me*. New Brunswick: Rutgers University Press.

Ferenbok, J., and A. Clement. 2012. "Hidden Changes: From CCTV to 'Smart' Video Surveillance." In A. Doyle, R. Lippert, and D. Lyon (eds.), *Eyes Everywhere: The Global Growth of Camera Surveillance*. New York: Routledge.

Ferrao, V. 2010. "Paid Work." *Women in Canada: A Gender-Based Statistical Report*. Ottawa: Statistics Canada.

Fillmore, C., and C.A. Dell. 2000. "A Study of Prairie Women: Violence and Self Harm." *The Canadian Women's Health Network* 4 (Spring). <pwhce.ca/pdf/self-harm.pdf>.

Finn, A., S. Trevethan, G. Carriere, and M. Kowalski. 1999. "Female Inmates, Aboriginal Inmates, and Inmates Serving Life Sentences: A One Day Snapshot." *Juristat* 19, 5.

Finnane, M. 1985. "Asylums, Families and the State." *History Workshop Journal* 20 (Autumn).

Flexner, A. 1920. *Prostitution in Europe*. New York: Century Co.

Flowers, A. 1998. *The Fantasy Factory: An Insider's of the Phone Sex Industry*. Philadelphia: University of Pennsylvania Press.

Follett, K. 2012. "Embodied Awareness and the Complexities of Power and Privilege." Presentation at Congress 2012 of the Humanities and Social Sciences, University of Waterloo, Waterloo, Ontario, May 27.

Fortin, D. 2004. *Program Strategy for Women Offenders*. Ottawa: Correctional Service of Canada.

Fortune, D., J. Thompson, A. Pedlar, and F. Yuen. 2010. "Social Justice and Women Leaving Prison: Beyond Punishment and Exclusion." *Contemporary Justice Review: Issues in Criminal, Social and Restorative Justice* 13, 1.

Foucault, M. 1983. "The Subject and Power." In H. Dreyfus and P. Rabinow (eds.), *Michel Foucault: Beyond Structuralism and Hermeneutics* (second edition). Chicago: University of Chicago Press.

____. 1979. *History of Sexuality: An Introduction* (Vol. 1). London: Penguin.

____. 1978a [1991]. "Governmentality." In G. Burchell, C. Gordon, and P. Miller (eds.), *The Foucault Effect: Studies in Governmentality*. Chicago: University of Chicago Press.

____. 1978b. "Politics and the Study of Discourse." *Ideology and Consciousness* (Spring).

____. 1977. *Discipline and Punish: The Birth of the Prison*. New York: Vintage.

Fournier-Ruggles, L. 2011. "The Cost of Getting Tough on Crime: Isn't Prevention the Policy Answer?" *Journal of Public Policy, Administration and Law* 2 (October).

Frank, L.R. 1978. *The History of Shock Treatment*. San Francisco: Self-published.

Fraser, N. 1997. *Justice Interruptus: Critical Reflections on the "Postsocialist" Condition*. New York: Routledge.

____. 1994. "A Genealogy of Dependency: Tracing a Keyword of the U.S. Welfare State." *Signs* 19, 2.

Freedman, E.B. 1981: *Their Sister's Keepers: Women's Prison Reform in America, 1830–1930*. Ann Arbor: University of Michigan Press.

Freire, Paulo. 2003. *Pedagogy of the Oppressed* (30th anniversary edition). New York: Continuum.

Freund, M. 2002. "The Politics of Naming: Constructing Prostitutes and Regulating Women in Vancouver, 1939–45." In J. McLaren, R. Menzies, and D.E. Chunn (eds.), *Regulating Lives: Historical Essays on the State, Society, the Individual, and the Law*. Vancouver: UBC Press.

Fudge J. 2002. "From Segregation to Privatization: Equality, the Law and Women Public Servants 1908–2001." In B. Cossman, and J. Fudge (eds.), *Privatization, Law and the Challenge to Feminism*. Toronto: University of Toronto Press.

Fudge, J., and B. Cossman. 2002. "Introduction: Privatization, Law and the Challenge to

Feminism." In B. Cossman, and J. Fudge (eds.), *Privatization, Law and the Challenge to Feminism*. Toronto: University of Toronto Press.

Funk, W. 1999.*What Difference Does It Make? The Journey of a Soul Survivor*. Vancouver: Wild Flower Publishers.

Fyfe, N., and J. Bannister. 1996. "City Watching: Closed Circuit Television Surveillance in Public Spaces." *Area* 28, 1.

Galloway, G. 2004. "Liberals Scrap Lifetime Ban for Those Who Cheat Welfare System." *Globe and Mail*, January 10.

Galton, F. 1907 [1883]. *Inquiries into Human Faculty and its Development*. New York: Dent and Dutton.

Gannon, M. 2005. *General Social Survey on Victimization, Cycle 18: An Overview of Findings*. Ottawa: Statistics Canada.

Gardner, C. 1995. *Passing By: Gender and Public Harassment*. Berkeley: University of California Press.

Garland, D. 2001. *The Culture of Control: Crime and Social Order in Contemporary Society*. Chicago: University of Chicago Press.

____. 1990. *Punishment and Modern Society: A Study in Social Theory*. Chicago: University of Chicago Press.

Gaskell, J. 1986. "Conceptions of Skill and Work of Women: Some Historical and Political Issues." In R. Hamilton, and M. Barrett (eds.), *The Politics of Diversity: Feminism, Marxism and Nationalism*. London: Verso.

Gavigan, S.A.M. 2012. *Hunger, Horses, and Government Men: Criminal Law on the Aboriginal Plains*. Vancouver: UBC Press.

____. 1999. "Poverty Law, Theory and Practice: The Place of Class and Gender in Access to Justice." In E. Comack (ed.), *Locating Law: Race/Class/Gender Connections*. Halifax: Fernwood.

____. 1993. "Women's Crime: New Perspectives and Old Theories." In E. Adelberg and C. Currie (eds.), *In Conflict with the Law: Women and the Canadian Justice System*. Vancouver: Press Gang Publishers.

Gavigan, S.A.M., and D.E. Chunn (eds.). 2010. *The Legal Tender of Gender: Law, Welfare, and the Legal Regulation of Women's Poverty*. Oxford: Hart Publishing.

____. 2007. "From Mothers' Allowance to Mothers Need Not Apply: Canadian Welfare Law as Liberal and Neo-Liberal Reforms." *Osgoode Hall Law Journal* 45.

Gazso, A. 2012. "Moral Codes of Mothering and the Introduction of Welfare-to-Work in Ontario." *Canadian Review of Sociology* 49.

Gazso, A., and I. Waldron. 2009. "Fleshing Out the Racial Undertones of Poverty for Canadian Women and Their Families: Re-envisioning a Critical Integrative Approach." *Atlantis* 34.

Geller, J.L., and M. Harris. 1994. *Women of the Asylum: Voices From Behind the Walls, 1840–1945*. New York: Anchor Doubleday.

Gelsthorpe, L. 1989. *Sexism and the Female Offender*. Aldershot: Gower.

____. 1988. "Feminism and Criminology in Britain." *British Journal of Criminology* 23.

Gilfus, M. 1992. "From Victims to Survivors to Offenders: Women's Routes of Entry and Immersion into Street Crime." *Women and Criminal Justice* 4, 1.

Gill, A. 2002. "Prostitutes, Addicts, Too Strung Out to Care." *Globe and Mail*, Feburary 9.

Gillies, K. 2013. "A Wolf in Sheep's Clothing: Canadian Anti-Pimping Law and How It Harms Sex Workers." In E. van der Meulen, E. Durisin, and V. Love (eds.), *Selling Sex: Experience, Advocacy, and Research on Sex Work in Canada*. Vancouver: UBC Press.

Gilliom, J., and T. Monahan. 2013. *SuperVision: An Introduction to the Surveillance Society*. Chicago: University of Chicago Press.

Gilmore, J. 2002. "Creeping Privatization in Health Care: Implications for Women as the State

Redraws its Role." In B. Cossman and J. Fudge (eds.), *Privatization, Law and the Challenge to Feminism*. Toronto: University of Toronto Press.

Girard, A. 2009. "Backlash or Equality? The Influence of Men's and Women's Rights Discourses on Domestic Violence Legislation in Ontario." *Violence Against Women* 15, 1.

Girard, D. 2002a. "Despair Stalks Hookers on Mean Streets. *Toronto Star*, February 10.

____. 2002b. "The Little Sister Behind the Statistic." *Toronto Star*, February 15.

____. 2002c. "All We Can Do Is Keep Waiting." *Toronto Star*, February 9.

Glasbeek, A. 2009. *Feminized Justice: The Toronto Women's Court, 1913–34*. Vancouver: UBC Press.

____. 2006a. *Moral Regulation and Governance in Canada*. Toronto: Canadian Scholars' Press.

____. 2006b. "'My Wife Has Endured a Torrent of Abuse': Gender, Safety, and Anti-Squeegee Discourses in Toronto, 1998–2000." *Windsor Yearbook of Access to Justice* 24, 1.

Glasbeek, H. 2002. *Wealth by Stealth: Corporate Crime, Corporate Law, and the Perversion of Democracy*. Toronto: Between the Lines.

*Globe and Mail*. 2007. "The Victims." December 10.

Glover, E. 1969 [1943]. *The Psychopathology of the Prostitute*. London: Institute for the Study and Treatment of Delinquency.

Glueck, S., and E. Glueck. 1934. *Five Hundred Delinquent Women*. New York: Alfred A. Knopf.

Golding, P., and S. Middleton. 1982. *Images of Welfare: Press and Public Attitudes to Poverty*. Oxford: Martin Robertson.

Gonzales, J. 2010. "Booth Rental: Is It Right for You?" Hairdresser Career Development Systems. <hcds4you.com/blog/booth-rental-is-it-right-for-you/>.

Gordon, A. 2010. *Self-Injury Incidents in CSC Institutions over a Thirty-Month Period*. Ottawa: Correctional Service of Canada.

Gordon, K. 2013. *We Are Born with the Songs Inside Us: Lives and Stories of First Nations People in British Columbia*. Maderia Park: Harbour Publishing.

Gordon, L. 1994. *Pitied But Not Entitled: Single Mothers and the History of Welfare*. Cambridge: Harvard University Press.

Goring, C. 1913. *The English Convict: A Statistical Study*. London: His Majesty's Stationery Office.

Gotell, L. 2008. "Rethinking Affirmative Consent in Canadian Sexual Assault Law: Neoliberal Sexual Subjects and Risky Women." *Akron Law Review* 41.

____. 2007. "The Discursive Disappearance of Sexualized Violence: Feminist Law Reform, Judicial Resistance, and Neo-Liberal Sexual Citizenship." In D.E. Chunn, S. Boyd, and H. Lessard (eds.), *Reaction and Resistance: Feminism, Law, and Social Change*. Vancouver: UBC Press.

Gottfredson, M., and T. Hirschi. 1990. *General Theory of Crime*. Stanford: Stanford University Press.

Graveline, J. 1998. *Circle Works: Transforming Eurocentric Consciousness*. Halifax: Fernwood Publishing.

Greenwald, H. 1958. *The Call Girl: A Social and Psychoanalytic Study*. New York: Ballantine.

Greenwood, F.M., and B. Boissery. 2000. *Uncertain Justice: Canadian Women and Capital Punishment 1754–1954*. Toronto: Dundurn Press.

Greer, C., and Y. Jewkes. 2005. "Extremes of Otherness: Media Images of Social Exclusion." *Social Justice* 32, 1.

Gunn, R., and C. Minch. 1988. *Sexual Assault: The Dilemma of Disclosure, The Question of Conviction*. Winnipeg: University of Manitoba Press.

Gunn Allen, P. 1992. *The Sacred Hoop: Recovering the Feminine in American Indian Traditions*. Boston: Beacon Press.

Gustafson, K. 2009. "The Criminalization of Poverty." *Journal of Criminal Law and Criminology* 99.

Hagan, J., A.R. Gillis, and J. Simpson. 1985. "The Class Structure of Gender and Delinquency: Toward a Power-Control Theory of Common Delinquent Behavior." *American Journal of Sociology* 90.

Hagan, J., J. Simpson, and A.R. Gillis. 1987. "Class in the Household: A Power-Control Theory of Gender and Delinquency." *American Journal of Sociology* 92, 4 (January).
____. 1979. "The Sexual Stratification of Social Control: A Gender-Based Perspective on Crime and Delinquency." *British Journal of Sociology* 30.
Hagedorn, J. (ed.). 2007. *Gangs in the Global City: Alternatives to Traditional Criminology.* Chicago: University of Chicago Press.
Haggerty, K.D. 2009. "Forward: Surveillance and Political Problems." In S.P. Hier and J. Greenberg (eds.), *Surveillance: Power, Problems, and Politics.* Vancouver: UBC Press.
____. 2006. "Tear Down the Walls: On Demolishing the Panopticon." In D. Lyon (ed.), *Theorizing Surveillance: The Panopticon and Beyond.* Cullompton: Willan Publishing.
Haggerty, K.D., and R.V. Ericson. 2000. "The Surveillant Assemblage." *British Journal of Sociology* 51, 4.
Haggerty, K.D. and M. Samatas (eds.). 2010. *Surveillance and Democracy.* New York: Routledge.
Hall, S. 1988. "The Toad in the Garden: Thatcherism among the Theorists." In C. Nelson and L. Grossberg (eds.), *Marxism and the Interpretation of Culture.* Champaign: University of Illinois Press.
____. 1980. "Reformism and the Legislation of Consent." In National Deviancy Conference (ed.), *Permissiveness and Control: The Fate of the Sixties Legislation.* London: Macmillan.
Hall, S., C. Critcher, T. Jefferson, J. Clarke, and B. Robert. 1978. *Policing the Crisis: Mugging, The State, and Law and Order.* London: MacMillan Press.
Hallgrimsdottir, H., R. Phillips, and C. Benoit. 2006. "Fallen Women and Rescued Girls: Social Stigma and Media Narratives of the Sex Industry in Victoria, B.C. from 1980 to 2005." *Canadian Review of Sociology and Anthropology* 43, 3.
Hamilton, A.C., and C.M. Sinclair. 1991. *The Justice System and Aboriginal People: Report of the Aboriginal Justice Inquiry of Manitoba.* Vol. 1. Winnipeg: Queen's Printer.
Haney, C. 2003. "Mental Health Issues in Long-Term Solitary and 'Supermax' Confinement." *Crime & Delinquency* 49, 1.
Hannah-Moffat, K. 2010. "Sacrosanct or Flawed: Risk, Accountability, and Gender-Responsive Penal Politics." *Current Issues in Criminal Justice* 22, 2.
____. 2008. "Re-Imagining Gendered Penalties: The Myth of Gender Responsivity." In P. Carlen (ed.), *Imaginary Penalties.* Cullompton: Willan Publishing.
____. 2006. "Pandora's Box: Risk/Need and Gender-Responsive Corrections." *Criminology and Public Policy* 5, 1.
____. 2004. "Gendering Risk at What Cost: Negotiations of Gender and Risk in Canadian Prisons." *Feminism and Psychology* 14, 2.
____. 2002. "Creating Choices: Reflecting on Choices." In P. Carlen (ed.), *Women and Punishment: The Struggle for Justice.* Cullompton: Willan Publishing.
____. 2001. *Punishment in Disguise: Penal Governance and Federal Imprisonment of Women in Canada.* Toronto: University of Toronto Press.
____. 2000. "Prisons that Empower: Neo-Liberal Governance in Canadian Women's Prisons." *British Journal of Criminology* 40, 3 (Summer).
Hannah-Moffat, K., and P. Maurutto. 2012. "Shifting and Targeted Forms of Penal Governance: Bail, Punishment and Specialized Courts." *Theoretical Criminology,* 16, 2.
Hannah-Moffat, K., and M. Shaw. 2001. *Taking Risks: Incorporating Gender and Culture into the Assessment and Classification of Federally Sentenced Women in Canada.* Ottawa: Status of Women Canada.
____ (eds.). 2000. *An Ideal Prison? Critical Essays on Women's Imprisonment in Canada.* Halifax: Fernwood.
Hannah-Moffat, K., and C. Yule. 2011. "Gaining Insight, Changing Attitudes and Managing 'Risk': Parole Release Decisions for Women Convicted of Violent Crimes." *Punishment*

*& Society* 13, 2.

Harding, S. 1990. "Feminism, Science, and the Anti-Enlightenment Critiques." In L. Nicholson (ed.), *Feminism/Postmodernism*. London: Routledge.

Harell, A., S. Soroka, and K. Ladner. 2013. "Public Opinion, Prejudice and the Racialization of Welfare in Canada." *Ethnic and Racial Studies*.

Harris, R. 1989. *Murders and Madness: Medicine, Law, and Society in the Fin de Siècle*. Oxford: Clarendon Press.

Hart, M. 2002. *Seeking Mino-Pimitisawin: An Aboriginal Approach to Helping*. Halifax and Winnipeg: Fernwood Publishing.

Hartman, M. 1985. *Victorian Murderesses: A True History of Thirteen Respectable French and English Women Accused of Unspeakable Crimes*. London: Robson.

Hartnagel, T. 2004. "Correlates of Criminal Behaviour." In R. Linden (ed.), *Criminology: A Canadian Perspective* (fifth edition). Toronto: Harcourt Brace.

____. 2000. "Correlates of Criminal Behaviour." In R. Linden (ed.), *Criminology: A Canadian Perspective* (fourth edition). Toronto: Harcourt Brace.

Hawthorn, T. 2007. "Still so Many Questions about Lillian O'Dare." *Globe and Mail*, December 12.

Hayman, S. 2006. *Imprisoning Our Sisters: The New Federal Women's Prisons in Canada*. Montreal and Kingston: McGill-Queen's University Press.

____. 2000. "Prison Reform and Incorporation: Lessons from Britain and Canada." In K. Hannah-Moffat and M. Shaw (eds.), *An Ideal Prison? Critical Essays on Women's Imprisonment in Canada*. Halifax: Fernwood.

Hazelwood, R., J. Warren, and P. Dietz. 1993. "Compliant Victims of the Sexual Sadist." *Australian Family Physician* 22, 4 (April).

Health Canada. 2012. *Honouring Our Strengths: A Renewed Framework to Address Substance Use Issues among First Nations People in Canada*. <nnadaprenewal.ca/wp-content/uploads/2012/01/Honouring-Our-Strengths-2011_Eng1.pdf>.

____. 1999. *The Health of Aboriginal Women*. Ottawa: Health Canada.

Healy, D. 2004. *Let Them Eat Prozac*. New York: New York University Press.

Hearn, J., and W. Parkin. 1995. *Sex at Work: The Power and Paradox of Organization Sexuality*. New York: St. Martin's Press

Heidensohn, F. 1994. "From Being to Knowing: Some Issues in the Study of Gender in Contemporary Society." *Women and Criminal Justice* 6, 1.

____. 1985. *Women and Crime*. London: Macmillan.

____. 1968. "The Deviance of Women: A Critique and an Enquiry." *British Journal of Sociology* 19, 2.

Heimer, K. 1995. "Gender, Race and Pathways to Delinquency." In J. Hagan and R. Peterson (eds.), *Crime and Inequality*. Stanford: Stanford University Press.

Heney, J. 1990. *Report on Self-Injurious Behaviour in the Kingston Prison for Women*. Ottawa: Solicitor General.

Henry, F., C. Tator, W. Mattis, and T. Rees. 2000. *The Colour of Democracy* (second edition). Toronto: Harcourt Brace.

Herd, D., A. Mitchell, and E. Lightman. 2005. "Rituals of Degradation: Administration as Policy in the Ontario Works Programme." *Social Policy and Administration* 39.

Hermer, J., and J. Mosher (eds.). 2002. *Disorderly People: Law and the Politics of Exclusion in Ontario*. Halifax: Fernwood Publishing.

Heyl, B. 1979. *The Madam as Entrepreneur: Career Management in House Prostitution*. New Brunswick, NJ: Transaction Books.

____. 1977. "The Training of House Prostitutes." *Social Problems* 24.

Hier, S.P. 2010. *Panoptic Dreams: Streetscape Video Surveillance in Canada*. Vancouver: UBC Press.

____. 2004. "Risky Spaces and Dangerous Faces: Urban Surveillance, Social Disorder and CCTV."

*Social and Legal Studies* 13, 4.

Hier, S.P., and J. Greenberg (eds.). 2009. *Surveillance: Power, Problems, and Politics,* Vancouver: UBC Press.

Hirschi, T. 1969. *Causes of Delinquency.* Berkeley: University of California Press.

Hochschild, A. 1983. *The Managed Heart: Commercialization of Human Feeling.* Berkeley: University of California Press.

Hogeveen, B. 2003. "Can't You Be a Man? Rebuilding Wayward Masculinities and Regulating Juvenile Deviance in Ontario, 1860–1930." Ph.D. thesis, University of Toronto.

Hogeveen, B., and J. Minaker. 2009. *Youth, Crime, and Society: Issues of Power and Justice.* Toronto: Pearson.

Holsopple, K. 1999. "Pimps, Tricks, and Feminists." *Women's Studies Quarterly* 27, 1/2.

hooks, b. 1994. *Teaching to Transgress: Education as the Practice of Freedom.* New York: Routledge.

Hooton, E.A. 1939. *The American Criminal: An Anthropological Study.* Cambridge: Harvard University Press.

Hopkins, C., and J. Dumont.2009. "Cultural Healing Practice within National Native Alcohol and Drug Abuse Program/Youth Solvent Addiction Program Services." Ottawa: Health Canada. <nnadaprenewal.ca/wp-content/uploads/2012/01/summary-cultural-healing-practicemedicine-within-nnadapysap.pdf>.

Houtman, I., and M. Kompier. 1995. "Risk Factors and Occupational Risk Groups for Work Stress in the Netherlands." In S. Sauter and L. Murphy (eds.), *Organizational Risk Factors for Job Stress.* Washington: American Psychological Association.

Howarth, D. 2000. *Discourse.* Buckingham: Open University Press.

Howe, A. 1994. *Punish and Critique: Towards a Feminist Analysis of Penality.* London: Routledge.

Hubbard, P. 1999. *Sex and the City: Geographies of Prostitution in the Urban West.* Aldershot: Ashgate.

Hudson, B. 2002. "Gender Issues in Penal Policy and Penal Theory." In P. Carlen (ed.), *Women and Punishment: The Struggle for Justice.* Cullompton: Willan Publishing.

Huey, L. 2010. "False Security or Greater Social Inclusion? Exploring Perceptions of CCTV Use in Public and Private Spaces Accessed by the Homeless." *British Journal of Sociology* 61, 1.

Huey, L., R.V. Ericson, and K.D. Haggerty. 2005. "Policing Fantasy City." In D. Cooley (ed.), *Re-imagining Policing in Canada.* Toronto: University of Toronto Press.

Hugill, D. 2010. *Missing Women, Missing News: Covering Crisis in Vancouver's Downtown Eastside.* Halifax and Winnipeg: Fernwood Publishing.

Human Rights Watch International. 2013. *Those Who Take Us Away: Abusive Policing and Failures in Protection of Indigenous Women and Girls in Northern British Columbia, Canada.* (February). New York: Human Rights Watch. <hrw.org/sites/default/files/reports/canada0213webwcover_0.pdf>.

Hume, M. 2007. "The Downtown Eastside: A Haunting Ground for Many, A Hunting Ground for One." *Globe and Mail*, December 10.

Hunt, A. 2002. "Regulating Heterosocial Space: Sexual Politics in the Early Twentieth Century." *Journal of Historical Sociology* 15, 1.

____. 1999a. "The Purity Wars: Making Sense of Moral Militancy." *Theoretical Criminology* 13, 4.

____. 1999b. *Governing Morals: A Social History of Moral Regulation.* Cambridge: Cambridge University Press.

____. 1997. "Moral Regulation and Making-up the New Person: Putting Gramsci to Work." *Theoretical Criminology* 1, 3.

Hunt, S. 2013. "Decolonizing Sex Work: Developing an Intersectional Indigenous Approach." In E. van der Meulen, E. Durisin, and V. Love (eds.), *Selling Sex: Experience, Advocacy and Research on Sex Work in Canada.* Vancouver: UBC Press.

Hutchinson, B. 2013. "The Abuse Excuse: Were Courts Right to Drop Case against Woman

Who Hired Hit Man to Kill Her Husband?" *National Post*, June 21.

_____. 2007. "Not Much Has Changed in the Downtown Eastside." *National Post*, February 9.

Income Security Advocacy Centre. 2013. *Budget 2013 Analysis: Moving Forward on Social Assistance Reform*. Toronto.

_____. 2008. *Rethinking the Role of Social Assistance within a Poverty Reduction Strategy: A Submission to the Cabinet Committee for Poverty Reduction*. Toronto.

_____. 2005. *The Matthews Report: Moving Towards Real Income Security*. Toronto.

Iwasaki, Y., J. Bartlett, B. Gottlieb, and D. Hall. 2009. "Leisure-Like Pursuits as an Expression of Aboriginal Cultural Strengths and Living Actions." *Leisure Sciences*, 31.

Jackson, Margaret. 1999. "Canadian Aboriginal Women and Their 'Criminality': The Cycle of Violence in the Context of Difference." *The Australian and New Zealand Journal of Criminology* 32, 2.

Jackson, Michael. 1988. *Justice Behind the Walls*. Ottawa: Canadian Bar Association.

James, J. 1977. "The Prostitute as Victim." In J. Chapman and M. Gates (eds.), *The Victimization of Women*. Beverly Hills: Sage Publications.

Järvinen, M. 1993. *Of Vice and Women: Shades of Prostitution* (translated by K. Leeander). Oslo: Scandinavian University Press.

Jarvis, E. 1979. "Mid-Victorian Toronto: Panic, Policy and Public Response, 1857–1873." Ph.D. thesis, University of Western Ontario.

Jeffords, S. 2014. "Transgendered Woman Transferred from Men's Prison." *Toronto Sun*, February 11. <torontosun.com/2014/02/11/transgender-woman-avery-edison-in-toronto-area-mens-prison>.

Jeffrey, L., and G. MacDonald. 2006. *Sex Workers in the Maritimes Talk Back*. Vancouver: UBC Press.

Jeffreys, S. 2005. "Different Word, Same Dangers from Trade in Women." *Sydney Morning Herald*, April 20.

_____. 1985. "Prostitution." In D. Rhodes and S. McNeil (eds.), *Women Against Violence Against Women*. London: Onlywomen Press.

Jiwani, E., R. Sydie, and C. Krull. 1999. "Images of Prostitution: The Prostitute and Print Media." *Women and Criminal Justice* 10, 4.

Jiwani, Y. 2006. *Discourses of Denial: Mediations of Race, Gender, and Violence*. Vancouver: UBC Press.

_____. 2002. "Erasing Race: The Story of Reena Virk." In K. McKenna and J. Larkin (eds.), *Violence Against Women: New Canadian Perspectives*. Toronto: Inanna Publications.

Jiwani, Y., and M. Young. 2006. "Missing and Murdered Women: Reproducing Marginality in News Discourse." *Canadian Journal of Communication* 31.

Johnson, H. 2006. *Measuring Violence Against Women: Statistical Trends 2006*. Ottawa: Statistics Canada. <ywcacanada.ca/data/research_docs/00000043.pdf>.

_____. 1996. *Dangerous Domains*. Toronto: Nelson.

Johnson, H., and M. Dawson. 2011. *Violence against Women in Canada*. Don Mills, Ontario: Oxford University Press.

Johnson, H., and K. Rodgers. 1993. "A Statistical Overview of Women and Crime in Canada." In E. Adelberg and C. Currie (eds.), *In Conflict with the Law: Women and the Canadian Justice System*. Vancouver: Press Gang Publishers.

Johnson, M. 2002. "Jane Hocus, Jane Focus." In M. Johnson (ed.), *Jane Sexes It Up*. New York: Thunders Mouth Press.

Jones, A. 1999. "The Limits of Cross-Cultural Dialogue: Pedagogy, Desire, and Absolution in the Classroom." *Educational Theory* 49.

_____. 1996. *Women Who Kill*. Boston: Beacon Press.

_____. 1994. *Next Time She'll Be Dead: Battering and How to Stop It*. Boston: Beacon Press.

Jones, H. 2005. "Visible Rights: Watching Out for Women." *Surveillance and Society* 2, 4.

Joseph, J. 2006. "Intersectionality of Race/Ethnicity, Class and Justice: Women of Color." In A. Merlo and J. Pollock (eds.), *Women, Law and Social Control.* Boston: Pearson.

Kaiser-Derrick, E. 2012. "Listening to What the Criminal Justice System Hears and the Stories it Tells: Judicial Sentencing Discourses about the Victimization and Criminalization of Aboriginal Women." Master of Laws thesis, University of British Columbia.

Kane, M., and W. Trochim. 2007. *Concept Mapping for Planning and Evaluation.* London: Sage Publications.

Kaplan-Myrth, N., and J. Smylie. 2006. *Sharing What We Know About Living a Good Life: Summit Report.* Indigenous Knowledge Translation Summit. Regina: First Nations University of Canada. <iphrc.ca/assets/Documents/Final_Summit_Report_Sept_30.pdf>.

Keck, J. 2002. "Remembering Kimberly Rogers." *Perception* 25.

Kelly, L. 1988. *Surviving Sexual Violence.* Minneapolis: University of Minnesota Press.

Kelm, M.E. 1992. "'The Only Place Likely to Do Her Any Good': The Admission of Women to British Columbia's Provincial Hospital for the Insane." *BC Studies* 96 (Winter).

Kendall, K. 2002. "Time to Think Again About Cognitive Behavioural Programmes." In P. Carlen (ed.), *Women and Punishment: The Struggle for Justice.* Cullompton: Willan Publishing.

____. 2000. "Psy-ence Fiction: Governing Female Prisons through the Psychological Services." In K. Hannah-Moffat and M. Shaw (eds.), *An Ideal Prison? Critical Essays on Women's Imprisonment in Canada.* Halifax: Fernwood.

____. 1999. "Beyond Grace: Criminal Lunatic Women in Victorian Canada." *Canadian Woman Studies* 19.

____. 1993. *Program Evaluation of Therapeutic Services at the Prison for Women.* Ottawa: Correctional Service Canada.

____. 1992. "Dangerous Bodies." In D. Farrington and S. Walklate (eds.), *Offenders and Victims: Theory and Policy.* London: British Society of Criminology.

____. 1991. "The Politics of Premenstrual Syndrome: Implications for Feminist Justice." *Journal of Human Justice* 2, 2 (Spring).

Kennedy, L., and D. Dutton. 1989. "The Incidence of Wife Assault in Alberta." *Canadian Journal of Behavioural Science* 21.

Kerr, L. 2013. "Solitary Confinement and the Question of Judicial Control of Punishment." J.S.D. dissertation, New York University School of Law.

Kershaw, A., and M. Lasovich. 1991. *Rock-A-Bye Baby: A Death Behind Bars.* Toronto: Oxford University Press.

Kerwin, S. 1999. "The Janet Smith Bill of 1924 and the Language of Race and Nation in British Columbia." *BC Studies* 121 (Spring).

Kilty, J.M. 2012a. "'It's Like They Don't Want You to Get Better': Psy Control of Women in the Carceral Context." *Feminism & Psychology* 22, 2.

____. 2012b. "Slashing and Managing the Stigma of a Scarred Body." In S. Hannemand and C. Bruckert (eds.), *Stigma Revisited: Negotiations, Resistance and the Implications of the Mark.* Ottawa: University of Ottawa Press.

____. 2012c. "Aux prises avec les restrictions et les bandages: la production discursive de l'autoblessure chez les détenues." In Sylvie Frigon (ed.), *Corps suspect, corps deviant.* Montreal, QC: Les Éditions du Remue-Ménage.

____. 2008. "Governance through Psychiatrization: Seroquel and the New Prison Order." *Radical Psychology* 2, 7.

____. 2006. "Under the Barred Umbrella: Is There Room for Women Centred Self-Injury Policy in Canadian Corrections?" *Criminology & Public Policy* 5, 1.

Kilty, J.M., and S. Frigon. 2006. "From a Woman in Danger to a Dangerous Woman, the Case of Karla Homolka: Chronicling the Shifts." *Women and Criminal Justice* 17, 4.

Kimmel, E. 2007. "Welfare Law, Necessity and Moral Judgment." *Rutgers Journal of Law and Public Policy* 4.

King, R. 1999. "The Rise and Rise of Supermax: An American Solution in Search of a Problem?" *Punishment & Society* 1, 2.

Kingman, D. 2003. *American Music: A Panorama* (second edition). Belmont: Wadsworth/ Thomson Learning.

Kinnell, H. 2002. *Why Feminists Should Rethink on Sex Workers' Rights.* UK Network of Sex Work Projects, Beyond Contract Seminar Series. <nswp.org/sites/nswp.org/files/KINNELL-FEMINISTS.pdf>.

Klein, D. 1982. "The Dark Side of Marriage: Battered Wives and the Domination of Women." In N. Rafter and E. Stanko (eds.), *Judge, Lawyer, Victim, Thief: Women, Gender Roles and Criminal Justice.* Boston: Northeastern University Press.

____. 1973. "The Etiology of Female Crime: A Review of the Literature." *Issues in Criminology* 8, 3.

Kline, M. 1997. "Blue Meanies in Alberta: Tory Tactics and the Privatization of Child Welfare." In S.B. Boyd (ed.), *Challenging the Public Private Divide: Feminism, Law and Public Policy.* Toronto: University of Toronto Press.

____. 1994. "The Colour of Law: Ideological Representations of First nations in Legal Discourse." *Social & Legal Studies* 3.

Klein, S., and A. Long. 2003. *A Bad Time to Be Poor: An Analysis of British Columbia's New Welfare Policies.* Vancouver: Canadian Centre for Policy Alternatives-B.C.

Knelman, J. 1998. *Twisting in the Wind: The Murderess and the English Press.* Toronto: University of Toronto Press.

Kong, R., and K. AuCoin. 2008. "Female Offenders in Canada." *Juristat* 28, 1.

Konopka, G. 1966. *The Adolescent Girl in Conflict.* Englewood Cliffs: Prentice Hall.

Koshan, J. 2013. "Teaching Bedford: Reflections on the Supreme Court's Most Recent Charter Decision." The University of Calgary Faculty of Law Blog on Developments in Alberta Law. <ablawg.ca/wp-content/uploads/2013/12/Blog_JK_Canada_Attorney_General_v_Bedford_December-2013.pdf>.

Koshan, J., and W. Wiegers. 2007. "Theorizing Civil Domestic Violence Legislation in the Context of Restructuring: A Tale of Two Provinces." *Canadian Journal of Women and the Law* 19.

Koskela, H. 2012. "'You Shouldn't Wear that Body': The Problematic of Surveillance and Gender." In D. Lyon, K. Haggerty, and K. Ball (eds.), *Routledge Handbook of Surveillance Studies.* London: Routledge.

____. 2002a. "'Cam Era'—The Contemporary Urban Panopticon." *Surveillance & Society* 1, 3.

____. 2002b. "Video Surveillance, Gender, and the Safety of Public Urban Space: 'Peeping Tom' Goes High Tech?" *Urban Geography* 23, 3.

____. 2000. "The Gaze without Eyes: Video Surveillance and the Changing Nature of Urban Space." *Progress in Human Geography* 24, 2.

Kovach, M. 2009. *Indigenous Methodologies: Characteristics, Conversations, and Contexts.* Toronto: University of Toronto Press.

Koyama E. 2002. *Instigations from the Whore Revolution.* Portland: Confluere Publications.

Kramar, K. 2005. *Unwilling Mothers, Unwanted Babies: Infanticide in Canada.* Vancouver: UBC Press.

Kramer, R., and T. Mitchell. 2002. *Walk Toward the Gallows: The Tragedy of Hilda Blake, Hanged 1899.* Don Mills: Oxford University Press.

Krishnamurti, S. 2013. "Queue-Jumpers, Terrorists, Breeders: Representations of Tamil Migrants in Canadian Popular Media." *South Asian Diaspora* 5, 1.

Kruttschnitt, C. 1982. "Women, Crime and Dependency." *Criminology* 19, 4.

____. 1980–81. "Social Status and Sentences of Female Offenders." *Law and Society Review* 15, 2.

Laberge, D. 1991. "Women's Criminality, Criminal Women, Criminalized Women? Questions in and for a Feminist Perspective." *Journal of Human Justice* 2, 2.

Labrum, B. 2005. "The Boundaries of Femininity: Madness and Gender in New Zealand, 1870–1910." In W. Chan, D.E. Chunn, and R. Menzies (eds.), *Women, Madness and the Law: A Feminist Reader*. London: Glasshouse Press.

Laframboise, D. 1999. "Men and Women Are Equals in Violence." *National Post*, July 10.

____. 1997. "Sugar and Spice Not So Nice." *Globe and Mail*, October 11.

____. 1996. *The Princess at the Window*. Toronto: Penguin.

Laishes, J. 2002. *The 2002 Mental Health Strategy for Women Offenders*. Ottawa: Correctional Services of Canada: Mental Health Services. <csc-scc.gc.ca/publications/fsw/mhealth/toc-eng.shtml>.

Lakeman, L., A. Lee, and S. Jay. 2004. "Resisting the Promotion of Prostitution in Canada: A View from the Vancouver Rape Relief and Women's Shelter." In C. Stark and R. Whisnant (eds.), *Not for Sale: Feminists Resisting Prostitution and Pornography*. Melbourne Australia: Spinifex Press.

Lalonde, L. 1997. "Tory Welfare Policies: A View from the Inside." In D. Ralph et al. (eds.), *Open for Business, Closed for People: Mike Harris's Ontario*. Halifax: Fernwood.

Landsberg, M. 2001. "Plight of 'Incorrigible' Women Demands Justice." *Toronto Star*, May 6.

Laner, M. 1974. "Prostitution as an Illegal Vocation." In C. Bryant (ed.), *Deviant Behaviour*. Chicago: Rand McNally.

Langner, N., J. Barton, D. McDonough, C. Noel, and F. Bouchard. 2002. "Rates of Prescribed Medication Use by Women in Prison." *Forum on Corrections Research* 4, 2.

LaPrairie, C. 1994. *Seen But Not Heard: Native People in the Inner City*. Ottawa: Aboriginal Justice Directorate, Minister of Justice and Attorney General of Canada.

LaRocque, E. 2002. "Violence in Aboriginal Communities." In K. McKenna and J. Larkin (eds.), *Violence Against Women: New Canadian Perspectives*. Toronto: Inanna.

Lashua, B., and K. Fox. 2006. "Rec Needs a New Rhythm Cuz Rap Is Where We're Livin'." *Leisure Sciences: An Interdisciplinary Journal* 28, 3 (Winter).

Law, T. 2011. "Not a Sob Story: Transitioning Out of Sex Work." M.A. thesis, University of Ottawa.

Law, V. 2012. "Where Abolition Meets Action: Women Organizing Against Gender Violence." *Contemporary Justice Review* 14, 1.

LeBlanc, N., and J.M. Kilty. 2013. "Prison — A Predictable Death." *Policy Options* 34, 1.

LeFrançois, B.A., R. Menzies, and G. Reaume (eds.). 2013. *Mad Matters: A Critical Reader in Canadian Mad Studies*. Toronto: Canadian Scholars' Press.

Leman-Langlois, S. 2009. "Public Perceptions of Camera Surveillance." In *A Report on Camera Surveillance in Canada: Part One*. Kingston: Surveillance Camera Awareness Network. <sscqueens.org/sites/default/files/SCAN_Report_Phase1_Final_Jan_30_2009.pdf>.

____. 2002. "The Myopic Panopticon: The Social Consequences of Policing Through the Lens." *Policing and Society* 13, 1.

Lemstra, M., and C. Neudorf. 2008. *Health Disparity in Saskatoon: Analysis to Intervention*. Saskatoon: Saskatoon Health Region.

Leonard, E.D. 1982. *Women, Crime and Society: A Critique of Theoretical Criminology*. New York: Longman.

Lett, D., S.P. Hier, and K. Walby. 2012. "Policy Legitimacy, Rhetorical Politics, and the Evaluation of City-Street Video Surveillance Monitoring Programs in Canada." *Canadian Review of Sociology* 49, 2.

Levi, L., M. Frankenhauser, and B. Gardell. 1986. "The Characteristics of the Workplace and the Nature of Its Social Demands." In S. Wolf and A. Finestone (eds.), *Occupational Stress: Health and Performance at Work*. Littleton: PSG.

Lewis, J., and E. Maticka-Tyndale. 2000. "Licensing Sex Work: Public Policy and Women's Lives."

*Canadian Public Policy* XXVI, 4.

Lewis, J., and F. Shaver. 2006. *Safety, Security and the Well-Being of Sex Workers: A Report Submitted to the House of Commons Subcommittee on Solicitation Laws.* Windsor: Sex Trade Advocacy and Research.

Liebling, A. 2011. "Moral Performance, Inhuman and Degrading Treatment and Prison Pain." *Punishment & Society* 13, 5.

____ (assisted by H. Arnold). 2004. *Prisons and Their Moral Performance: A Study of Values, Quality, and Prison Life.* Oxford: Oxford University Press.

____. 1992. *Suicides in Prison.* London: Routledge.

Liebling, A., and T. Ward (eds.). 1994. *Deaths in Custody: International Perspectives.* London: Whiting & Birch.

Liebling, A., L. Durie, A. Stiles, and S. Tait. 2005. "Revisiting Prison Suicide: The Role of Fairness and Distress." In A. Liebling and S. Maruna (eds.), *The Effects of Imprisonment.* Cullompton: Willan Publishing.

Little, M. 2005. *If I Had a Hammer: Retraining That Really Works.* British Columbia: UBC Press.

____. 2003. "The Leaner, Meaner Welfare Machine: The Ontario Conservative Government's Ideological and Material Attack on Single Mothers." In D. Brock, (ed.), *Making Normal: Social Regulation in Canada.* Scarborough: Nelson Thompson Learning.

____. 2001. "A Litmus Test for Democracy: The Impact of Ontario Welfare Changes on Single Mothers." *Studies in Political Economy* 66.

____. 1998. *No Car, No Radio, No Liquor Permit: The Moral Regulation of Single Mothers in Ontario, 1920–1997.* Toronto: Oxford University Press.

Lloyd, A. 2005. "The Treatment of Women Patients in Secure Hospitals." In W. Chan, D.E. Chunn, and R. Menzies (eds.), *Women, Madness and the Law: A Feminist Reader.* London: Glasshouse Press.

Lobel, S. 1993. "Sexuality at Work." *Journal of Vocational Behavior* 42.

Lombroso, C., and E. Ferrero. 1885 [1985]. *The Female Offender.* New York: Appleton.

Lopez, S.H. 2006. "Emotional Labor and Organized Emotional Care: Conceptualizing Nursing Home Care Work." *Work and Occupations* 33, 2.

Lös, M. 1990. "Feminism and Rape Law Reform." In L. Gelsthorpe and A. Morris (eds.), *Feminist Perspectives in Criminology.* Milton Keynes: Open University Press.

Lowman, J. 2011. "Deadly Inertia: A History of Constitutional Challenges to Canada's *Criminal Code* Sections on Prostitution." *Beijing Law Review* 2.

____. 2000. "Violence and the Outlaw Status of (Street) Prostitution in Canada." *Violence Against Women* 6, 9.

Luckhaus, L. 1985. "A Plea for PMT in the Criminal Law." In S. Edwards (ed.), *Gender, Sex and the Law.* Kent: Croom Helm.

Luxton, M., and J. Corman. 2001. *Getting By in Hard Times: Gendered Labour at Home and on the Job.* Toronto: University of Toronto Press.

Lyon, D. 2007. *Surveillance Studies: An Overview.* Cambridge: Polity Press.

____ (ed.). 2006. *Theorizing Surveillance: The Panopticon and Beyond.* Cullompton: Willan Publishing.

____ (ed.). 2003. *Surveillance as Social Sorting: Privacy, Risk, and Digital Discrimination.* New York: Routledge.

MacCharles, T. 2012. "Federal Prison Population in Canada Growing." *Toronto Star*, October 23. <thestar.com/news/canada/2012/10/23/federal_prison_population_in_canada_growing.html>.

MacDonald, I., and B. O'Keefe. 2000. *Canadian Holy War: A Story of Clans, Tongs, Murder, and Bigotry.* Surrey: Heritage House.

MacDonald, M., and M.P. Connelly. 1989. "Class and Gender in Fishing Communities in Nova

Scotia." *Studies in Political Economy* 30.

MacGuigan Report. 1977. *Report to Parliament: Subcommittee on the Penitentiary System in Canada*. Ottawa: Ministry of Supply and Services.

MacKay, R.D. 1995. "Insanity and Unfitness to Stand Trial in Canada and England: A Comparative Study of Recent Developments." *Journal of Forensic Psychiatry* 6.

MacKinnon, C. 1987. *Feminism Unmodified: Discourses on Life and Law*. Cambridge: Harvard University Press.

MacKinnon, M., and K. Lacey. 2001. "Bleak House." *Globe and Mail*, August 18.

Macklin, A. 2002. "Public Entrance/Private Member." In B. Cossman and J. Fudge (eds.), *Privatization, Law and the Challenge to Feminism*. Toronto: University of Toronto Press.

MacLeod, J. 2000. *Beginning Postcolonialism*. Manchester and New York: Manchester University Press.

MacLeod, L. 1980. *Wife Battering in Canada: The Vicious Circle*. Ottawa: CACSW.

Mahony, T. 2011. *Women in Canada: A Gender-Based Statistical Report Women and the Criminal Justice System*. Ottawa: Statistics Canada. <statcan.gc.ca/pub/89-503-x/2010001/article/11416-eng.pdf>.

Mahood, L. 1990. *The Magdalenes: Prostitution in the Nineteenth Century*. London: Routledge.

Maidment, M. 2006. *Doing Time on the Outside: Deconstructing the Benevolent Community*. Toronto: University of Toronto Press.

Maki, K. 2011. "Neoliberal Deviants and Surveillance: Welfare Recipients under the Watchful Eye of Ontario Works." *Surveillance and Society* 9.

Mallea, P. 2012. *Fearmonger: Stephen Harper's Tough on Crime Agenda*. Toronto: Lorimer.

____. 2010. *Fear Factor: Stephen Harper's Tough on Crime Agenda*. Ottawa: Canadian Centre for Policy Alternatives.

Malloch, M., and G. McIvor. 2011. "Women and Community Sentences." *Criminology and Criminal Justice* 11, 4.

Mann, R. 2012. "Invisibilizing Violence Against Women." In W. Antony and L. Samuelson (eds.), *Power and Resistance: Critical Thinking about Canadian Social Issues* (fifth edition). Halifax and Winnipeg: Fernwood Publishing.

____. 2003. "Violence Against Women or Family Violence? The 'Problem' of Female Perpetration in Domestic Violence." In L. Samuelson and W. Antony (eds.), *Power and Resistance: Critical Thinking About Canadian Social Issues* (third edition). Halifax: Fernwood.

____. 2000. *Who Owns Domestic Abuse? The Local Politics of a Social Problem*. Toronto: University of Toronto Press.

Maracle, B. 1993. *Crazywater: Native Voices on Addiction and Recovery*. Toronto: Penguin.

~~Marleau, J. 1999. "Demanding to Be Heard: Women's Use of Violence." *Humanity and Society* 23, 4.~~

Marsh J., A. Geist, and N. Caplan. 1982. *Rape and the Limits of Law*. Boston: Auburn House.

Martin, D. 2002. "Both Pitied and Scorned: Child Prostitution in an Era of Privatization." In B. Cossman and J. Fudge (eds.), *Privatization, Law and the Challenge to Feminism*. Toronto: University of Toronto Press.

____. 1992. "Passing the Buck: Prosecution of Welfare Fraud; Preservation of Stereotypes." *Windsor Yearbook of Access to Justice* 12.

Martin, D., and J. Mosher. 1995. "Unkept Promises: Experiences of Immigrant Women with the Neo-Criminalization of Wife Abuse." *Canadian Journal of Women and the Law* 8.

Martinson, D., M. MacCrimmon, I. Grant, and C. Boyle. 1991. "A Forum on *Lavallee* v. *R*: Women and Self-Defence." *University of British Columbia Law Review* 25, 1.

Marx, K. 1974 [1859]. *Capital* (Volume 1). New York: International.

Mason, C.L., and S. Magnet. 2012. "Surveillance Studies and Violence Against Women." *Surveillance & Society* 10, 2.

Masuch, C. 2004. "Man-Haters, Militants and Aggressive Women: Young Women, Media

Representations and Feminist Identity." Unpublished M.A. thesis, Queen's University, Kingston.

Matas, R. 2002. "Sister Was a Prostitute but so Much More." *Globe and Mail*, February 27.

Mathiesen, T. 1997. "The Viewer Society: Michel Foucault's Panopticon Revisited." *Theoretical Criminology* 1, 2.

Matthews, D. 2004. *Review of Employment Assistance Programs in Ontario Works and Ontario Disability Support Program*. Report to The Honourable Sandra Pupatello, Minister of Community and Social Services. <mcss.gov.on.ca/documents/en/mcss/social/publications/EmploymentAssistanceProgram_Matthews_eng1.pdf>.

Matthews, N. 1994. *Confronting Rape*. London: Routledge.

Mawani, R. 2002. "Regulating the 'Respectable' Classes: Venereal Disease, Gender, and Public Health Initiatives in Canada, 1914–35." In J. McLaren, R. Menzies and D.E. Chunn (eds.), *Regulating Lives: Historical Essays on the State, Society, the Individual, and the Law*. Vancouver: UBC Press.

McClintock, A. 1993. "Maid to Order: Commercial Fetishism and Gender Power." *Social Text* 37.

McCormick, R., and D. Quantz. 2010. *Improving Mental Health Services and Supports in the National Native Alcohol and Drug Abuse Program*. Ottawa: National Native Alcohol and Drug Abuse Program. <nnadaprenewal.ca/wp-content/uploads/2012/01/improving-mental-health-services-and-supports-national-native-alcohol-and-drug-abuse-program.pdf>.

McDermott, M.J., and J. Garofalo. 2004. "When Advocacy for Domestic Violence Victims Backfires: Types and Sources of Victim Disempowerment." *Violence Against Women* 10.

McEvoy, M., and J. Daniluk. 1995. "Wounds to the Soul: The Experiences of Aboriginal Women as Survivors of Sexual Abuse." *Canadian Psychology* 36.

McGillivray, A. 1998. "'A Moral Vacuity in Her Which Is Difficult if Not Impossible to Explain': Law, Psychiatry and the Remaking of Karla Homolka." *International Journal of the Legal Profession* 5, 2/3.

McGovern, C. 1998. "Sugar and Spice and Cold as Ice: Teenage Girls Are Closing the Gender Gap in Violent Crime with Astonishing Speed." *Alberta Report* 25.

McInturff, K. 2013. *Closing Canada's Gender Gap: Year 2240 Here We Come!* Ottawa: Canadian Centre for Policy Alternatives. <policyalternatives.ca/publications/reports/closing-canadas-gender-gap>.

McIntyre, M. 2011. "Rape Victim 'Inviting,' So No Jail: Judge Rules Woman's Clothes, Conduct Ease Blame on Attacker." *Winnipeg Free Press*, February 24. <winnipegfreepress.com/local/rape-victim-inviting-so-no-jail--rape-victim-inviting-so-no-jail-116801578.html>.

McIvor, S., and T. Nahanee. 1998. "Aboriginal Women: Invisible Victims of Violence." In K. Bonnycastle and G. Rigakos (eds.), *Unsettling Truths: Battered Women, Policy, Politics, and Contemporary Research in Canada*. Vancouver: Collective Press.

McKeever, G. 1999. "Detecting, Prosecuting, and Punishing Benefit Fraud: The Social Security Administration (Fraud) Act 1997." *Modern Law Review* 62, 2.

McKim, A. 2008. "Getting Gut-Level: Punishment, Gender and Therapeutic Governance." *Gender and Society* 22.

McLaren, A. 1993. "Illegal Abortions: Women, Doctors, and Abortion, 1886–1939." *Journal of Social History* 26, 4.

____. 1990. *Our Own Master Race: Eugenics in Canada, 1885–1945*. Toronto: McClelland and Stewart.

McLaren, A., and A. McLaren. 1997. *The Bedroom and the State: The Changing Practices and Politics of Contraception and Abortion in Canada, 1880–1997* (second edition). Toronto: Oxford University Press.

McLaren, J. 1987. "White Slavers: The Reform of Canada's Prostitution Laws and Patterns of Enforcement, 1900–1920." *Criminal Justice History* 8.

____. 1986. "Chasing the Social Evil: Moral Fervour and the Evolution of Canada's Prostitution Laws, 1867–1917." *Canadian Journal of Law and Society* 1.

McLeod, H. 2004. "A Glimpse at Aboriginal-Based Street Gangs." A Report for the Royal Canadian Mounted Police "D" Division, Winnipeg, Manitoba for the National Aboriginal Policing Forum held in Ottawa, ON. Hosted by Pacific Business and Law Institute, September 22 and 23.

McLeod, N. 2000. "Indigenous Studies: Negotiating the Space between Tribal Communities and Academia." *Expressions in Canadian Native Studies.* Saskatoon: University Extension Press.

McMahon, M., and E. Pence. 2003. "Making Social Change: Reflections on Individual and Institutional Advocacy with Women Arrested for Domestic Violence." *Violence Against Women* 9.

McMaster, G., and L-A. Martin. 1992. *Indigena: Contemporary Native Perspectives.* Vancouver: Douglas & McIntyre.

McMullin, J., L. Davies, and G. Cassidy. 2002 "Welfare Reform in Ontario: Tough Times in Mothers' Lives." *Canadian Public Policy* 28, 2.

McQuaig, L. 1993. *The Wealthy Banker's Wife: The Assault on Equality in Canada.* Toronto: Penguin.

Mehl-Madrona, Lewis. 2005. *Coyote Wisdom: The Power of Story in Healing.* Rochester, Vermont: Bear and Company.

Mensah, M.N. 2006. "Débat feminist sur la prostitution au Québec: Points de vue des travailleuses du sexe." *The Canadian Review of Sociology and Anthropology, Special Issue: Casting a Critical Lens on the Sex Industry in Canada* 43, 3.

Menzies, R. 2007. "Virtual Backlash: Representing Men's 'Rights' and Feminist 'Wrongs' in Cyberspace." In D.E. Chunn, S.B. Boyd, and H. Lessard (eds.), *Reaction and Resistance: Feminism, Law and Social Change.* Vancouver: UBC Press.

____. 2001. "Contesting Criminal Lunacy: Narratives of Law and Madness in West Coast Canada, 1874–1950." *History of Psychiatry* 7.

____. 1989. *Survival of the Sanest: Order and Disorder in a Pre-Trial Psychiatric Clinic.* Toronto: University of Toronto Press.

Menzies, R., and D.E. Chunn. 2013. "Mapping the Intersections of Psycho-Legal Power: A Tale of Murder, Madness, and Motherhood from British Columbia History." *Australasian Canadian Studies* 30, 1/2.

____. 1999. "The Gender Politics of Criminal Insanity: 'Order-in-Council' Women in British Columbia, 1888–1950." *Histoire sociale/Social History* 31, 62.

Menzies, R., D.E. Chunn, and C.D. Webster. 1992. "Female Follies: The Forensic Psychiatric Assessment of Women Defendants." *International Journal of Law and Psychiatry* 15, 1 (January).

Merton, R. 1938. "Social Structure and Anomie." *American Sociological Review* 3 (October).

Mignard, A. 1976. "Propos élémentairessur la prostitution." *Les Temps Modernes* 356.

Miller, E. 1986. *Street Woman.* Philadelphia: Temple University Press.

Miller, J. 2001. *One of the Guys: Girls, Gangs, and Gender.* New York: Oxford University Press.

Millett, K. 1971. *The Prostitution Papers: A Candid Dialogue.* New York: Avon.

Minaker, J. 2014. "Marginalized Young Mothering." In J. Minaker and B. Hogeveen (eds.), *Criminalizing Mother(ing).* Toronto: Demeter Press.

____. 2003. "Censuring the Erring Female: Governing Female Sexuality at the Toronto Industrial Refuge, 1853–1939." Ph.D. thesis, Queen's University, Kingston.

Minaker, J., and L. Snider. 2006. "Husband Abuse: Equality with a Vengeance?" *Canadian Journal of Criminology and Criminal Justice* 48, 5.

Ministry of Justice. 2013. Story of the Prison Population: 1993–2012. London: Ministry of Justice (January). <gov.uk/government/uploads/system/uploads/attachment_data/

file/218185/story-prison-population.pdf>.

Mirchandani, K., and W. Chan. 2007. *Criminalizing Race, Criminalizing Poverty.* Halifax: Fernwood Publishing.

Misra, J., S. Moller, and M. Karides. 2003. "Envisioning Dependency: Changing Media Depictions of Welfare in the 20th Century." *Social Problems* 50, 4.

Mitchell, T. 2008. "Traditional vs. Critical Service Learning: Engaging the Literature to Two Different Models." *Michigan Journal of Community Service Learning* (Spring).

Mitchell, T., and D. Maracle. 2005. "Healing the Generations: Post-traumatic Stress and the Health Status of Aboriginal Populations in Canada." *Journal of Aboriginal Health* 2, 1 (Spring).

Mohr, R., and J. Roberts. 1994. "Sexual Assault in Canada: Recent Developments." In J. Roberts and R. Mohr (eds.), *Confronting Sexual Assault: A Decade of Legal Change.* Toronto: University of Toronto Press.

Molinier, P. 2003. *L'énigme de la femme active. Égoïsme, sexe et compassion.* Paris: Payot.

Monture-Angus, P. 2002. *The Lived Experience of Aboriginal Women Who Are Federally Sentenced.* Submission of the Canadian Association of Elizabeth Fry Societies to the Canadian Human Rights Commission. Ottawa: Canadian Association of Elizabeth Fry Societies.

____. 1995. *Thunder in My Soul: A Mohawk Woman Speaks.* Halifax: Fernwood.

Monture-Okanee, P. 1995. "Self-Portrait: Flint Woman." In L. Jaine and D.H. Taylor (eds.), *Voices: Being Native in Canada* (second edition). Saskatoon: University Extension Press.

Moore, D., and K. Hannah-Moffat. 2005. "The Liberal Veil: Revisiting Canadian Penality." In J. Pratt, D. Brown, M. Brown, S. Hallsworth, and W. Morrison (eds.), *The New Punitiveness: Trends, Theories, Perspectives.* Cullompton: Willan Publishing.

Moore-Gilbert, B. 1997. *Postcolonial Theory: Contexts, Practices, Politics.* London and New York: Verso.

Moran, R. 1981. *Knowing Right From Wrong: The Insanity Defense of Daniel McNaughtan.* New York: Free Press.

Morris, A. 1987. *Women, Crime and Criminal Justice.* London: Blackwell.

Morrisey, B. 2003. *When Women Kill: Questions of Agency and Subjectivity.* London: Routledge.

Morrison, I. 1998. "Ontario Works: A Preliminary Assessment." *Journal of Law and Social Policy* 13.

____. 1995. "Facts About the Administration of Social Assistance/UI that Criminal Lawyers Need to Know." In *Charged with Fraud on Social Assistance: What Criminal Lawyers Need to Know.* Department of Continuing Legal Education, Law Society of Upper Canada, March 25 [unpublished].

Morrison, I., and G. Pearce. 1995. "Under the Axe: Social Assistance in Ontario in 1995." *Journal of Law and Social Policy* 11.

Morrow, M., O. Hankivsky, and C. Varcoe. 2004. "Women and Violence: The Effects of Dismantling the Welfare State." *Critical Social Policy* 24, 3.

Mortenson, M. 1999. "B.C. Benefits Whom? Motherhood, Poverty, and Social Assistance Legislation in British Columbia." M.A. thesis, Simon Fraser University, Burnaby.

Moscovitch, A. 1997. "Social Assistance in the New Ontario." In D. Ralph, A. Régimbald, and N. St-Amand (eds.), *Mike Harris's Ontario: Open for Business, Closed to People.* Halifax: Fernwood Publishing.

Mosher, J. 2014. "The Construction of 'Welfare Fraud' and the Wielding of the State's Iron Fist." In E. Comack (ed.), *Locating Law: Race/Class/Gender/Sexuality Connections* (third edition). Halifax and Winnipeg: Fernwood Publishing.

____. 2006. "The Construction of 'Welfare Fraud' and the Wielding of the State's Iron Fist." In E. Comack (ed.), *Locating Law: Race/Class/Gender/Sexuality Connections* (second edition). Halifax: Fernwood.

____. 2000. "Managing the Disentitlement of Women: Glorified Markets, the Idealized Family, and the Undeserving Other." In S.M. Neysmith (ed.), *Restructuring Caring Labour*. Toronto: Oxford University Press.

Mosher, J., P. Evans, M. Little, E. Morrow, J. Boulding, and N. Vanderplaats. 2004. *Walking on Eggshells; Abused Women's Experiences of Ontario's Welfare System: Final Report on the Research Findings on the Woman and Abuse Welfare Research Project*. Toronto: Osgoode Hall Law School. <yorku.ca/yorkweb/special/Welfare_Report_walking_on_eggshells_final_report.pdf>.

Mosher, J., and J. Hermer. 2005. *Welfare Fraud: The Constitution of Social Assistance as Crime*. A Report Prepared for the Law Commission of Canada (July). Ottawa: Law Commission of Canada.

Moyer, S. 1992. "Race, Gender and Homicide: Comparisons between Aboriginals and Other Canadians." *Canadian Journal of Criminology* 34.

Moynihan, R., I. Health, and D. Henry. 2002. "Selling Sickness: The Pharmaceutical Industry and Disease Mongering." *British Medical Journal* 324.

Mundel, E., and G. Chapman. 2010. "A Decolonizing Approach to Health Promotion in Canada: The Case of the Urban Aboriginal Community Kitchen Garden Project." *Health Promotion International* 25, 2.

Murray, C., 1990. *The Emerging Underclass*. London: Institute of Economic Affairs.

Myers, A., and S. Wight (eds.). 1996. *No Angels: Women Who Commit Violence*. London: Pandora.

Myers, T. 1999. "The Voluntary Delinquent: Parents, Daughters and the Montreal Juvenile Delinquents' Court in 1918." *Canadian Historical Review* 80, 1.

____. 1998. "Qui t'à debauchee? Female Adolescent Sexuality and the Juvenile Delinquent's Court in Early Twentieth-Century Montreal." In L. Chambers and E.-A. Montigny (eds.), *Family Matters: Papers in Post-Confederation Canadian Family History*. Toronto: Canadian Scholars' Press.

Naffine, N. 1997. *Feminism and Criminology*. Sydney: Allen and Unwin.

____. 1987. *Female Crime: The Construction of Women in Criminology*. Sydney: Allen and Unwin.

Namaste, V. 2005. *Sex Change, Social Change: Reflections on Identity, Institutions and Imperialism*. Toronto: Women's Press.

National Post. 2007. "These are Our Sisters, Our Mothers, Our Daughters." *National Post*, January 23.

NCW (National Council of Welfare). 2010. *Welfare Incomes 2009*. Ottawa: Minister of Public Works and Government Services Canada (NCW Reports #123).

____. 2007. *First Nations, Métis and Inuit Children and Youth: Time to Act*. Ottawa: Minister of Public Works and Government Services Canada (NCW Reports # 127).

____. 2006. *Poverty Profile: Special Edition*. Ottawa: Minister of Public Works and Government Services Canada.

____. 2005. *Welfare Incomes 2004*. Ottawa: Minister of Public Works and Government Services Canada. (NCW Reports #123)

Needham Report. 1978. *Report of the National Planning Committee on the Female Offender*. Ottawa: Ministry of Solicitor General.

Neve, L., and K. Pate. 2005. "Challenging the Criminalization of Women Who Resist." In J. Sudbury (ed.), *Global Lockdown: Race, Gender, and the Prison-Industrial Complex*. London: Routledge.

Niccols, A., C. Dell, and S. Clarke. 2010. "Treatment Issues for Aboriginal Mothers with Substance Use Problems and Their Children." *International Journal of Mental Health and Addiction* 8, 2 (Winter).

Niezen, R. 2007. "Revival of Aboriginal Culture and Practices Key to Suicide Intervention Programs." *Canadian Psychiatry* 3, 1.

Noonan, S. 1993. "Moving Beyond the Battered Woman Syndrome." In E. Adelberg and C. Currie (eds.), *In Conflict with the Law: Women and the Canadian Justice System*. Vancouver: Press Gang Publishers.

Norris, C. 2012. "There's No Success like Failure and Failure's No Success at All: Some Critical Reflections on the Global Growth of CCTV Surveillance." In A. Doyle, R. Lippert, and D. Lyon (eds.), *Eyes Everywhere: The Global Growth of Camera Surveillance*. New York: Routledge.

Norris, C., and G. Armstrong. 1999. *The Maximum Surveillance Society: The Rise of CCTV*. New York: Berg.

Norris, M.J. 1998. "Canada's Aboriginal Languages." *Canadian Social Trends: Statistics Canada* (Winter).

NWAC (Native Women's Association of Canada). 2010a. *What Their Stories Tell Us: Research Findings from the Sisters in Spirit Initiative*. Ottawa: NWAC. <nwac.ca/sites/default/files/imce/2010_NWAC_SIS_Report_EN.pdf>.

____. 2010b. "NWAC Responds to $10M Announcement from the Department of Justice Canada (Press Release)." Ottawa: NWAC. <nwac.ca/sites/default/files/imce/Press%20 Release_NWAC%20responds%20to%20%2410M_9%20November%202010.pdf>.

____. n.d. "Fact Sheet: Missing and Murdered Aboriginal Women and Girls." Ottawa: NWAC. <nwac.ca/files/download/NWAC_3D_Toolkit_e_0.pdf>

O'Doherty, T. 2011." Criminalization and Off-street Sex Work in Canada." *Canadian Journal of Criminology and Criminal Justice* 53, 2.

O'Donnell, V., and S. Wallace. 2011. "First Nations, Métis and Inuit Women." *Women in Canada: A Gender-Based Statistical Report*. Ottawa: Statistics Canada.

O'Hara, M. 1985. "Prostitution Towards a Feminist Analysis and Strategy." In D. Rhodes and S. McNeil (eds.), *Women Against Violence Against Women*. London: Onlywomen Press.

O'Malley, P. 2010. *Crime and Risk*. Los Angeles: Sage.

____. 1996. "Risk and Responsibility." In A. Barry, T. Osborne and N. Rose (eds.), *Foucault and Political Reason: Liberalism, Neo-Liberalism and Rationalities of Government*. Chicago: University of Chicago Press.

____. 1992. "Risk, Power and Crime Prevention." *Economy and Society* 21, 3.

O'Neill, M., R. Campbell, P. Hubbard, J. Pitcher, and J. Scoular. 2008. "Living With the Other: Street Sex Work, Contingent Communities and Degrees of Tolerance." *Crime Media Culture* 4, 1.

OCI (Office of the Correctional Investigator). 2013. *A Case Study of Diversity in Corrections: The Black Inmate Experience in Federal Penitentiaries*. Ottawa: The Correctional Investigator Canada.

Odem, M. 1995. *Delinquent Daughters: Protecting and Policing Adolescent Female Sexuality in the United States, 1885–1920*. Chapel Hill: University of North Carolina Press.

Office of Ethnic Minority Affairs, American Psychological Association. 2010. "Special Section — Indigenous Peoples: Promoting Psychological Healing and Well-Being." <apa.org/pi/oema/resources/communique/2010/08/august-special.pdf>.

Offman, A., and P. Kleinplatz. 2004. "Does PMDD Belong in the DSM? Challenging the Medicalization of Women's Bodies." *Canadian Journal of Human Sexuality* 13, 1.

Oliver, P. 1994. "'To Govern by Kindness': The First Two Decades of the Mercer Reformatory for Women." In J. Phillips, T. Loo, and S. Lewthwaite (eds.), *Essays in the History of Canadian Law* (Volume V). Toronto: Osgoode Society.

Ombudsman of Ontario. 2011. *Ombudsman's Report: The Code*. Ontario: Ombudsman's Office. <ombudsman.on.ca/Resources/Reports/The-Code.aspx>.

Ontario. 2013. *News Release: Improving Social Assistance*. Toronto: Ministry of Community and Social Services.

_____. 2012. *Brighter Prospects: Transforming Social Assistance in Ontario*. Commission for the Review of Social Assistance in Ontario. Toronto: Queen's Printer.

_____. 2009. *Ontario Works Policy Directives*. Toronto: Queen's Printer.

_____. 2003. *Welfare Fraud Control Report 2001–2002*, Table 1. Ministry of Community, Family and Children's Services. Toronto: Queen's Printer.

_____. 2002. Verdict of the Coroner's Jury into the Death of Kimberly Ann Rogers, held at Sudbury, Ontario. Office of the Chief Coroner.

_____. 2000a. *Welfare Fraud Control Report, 1998–99*. Ministry of Community and Social Services. Toronto: Queen's Printer.

_____. 2000b. *Making Welfare Work: Report to Taxpayers on Welfare Reform*. Ministry of Community and Social Services. Toronto: Queen's Printer.

_____. 1999. *Welfare Fraud Control Report, 1997–98*. Ministry of Community and Social Services. Toronto: Queen's Printer.

_____. 1988. *Transitions: Report of the Social Assistance Review Committee* (SARC Report). Toronto: Queen's Printer.

Ontario Ministry of Labour. 2010. *Workplace Violence and Workplace Harassment*. Ontario: Queen's Printer. <labour.gov.on.ca/english/hs/topics/workplaceviolence.php>.

Ontario Native Women's Association. 1989. "Breaking Free: A Proposal for Change to Aboriginal Family Violence." Thunder Bay: Ontario Native Women's Association. <onwa.ca/upload/documents/breaking-free-report-final_1989-pdf.doc.pdf>.

Oppal, Wally T. (Commissioner). 2012. *Forsaken: The Report of the Missing Women Commission of Inquiry*. Victoria: Distribution Centre — Victoria. <missingwomeninquiry.ca/obtain-report/>.

Orenstein, M. 2011. "Pension Privatization in Crisis: Death or Rebirth of a Global Policy Trend?" *International Social Security Review* 64, 3.

Osborne, J. 1989. "Perspectives on Premenstrual Syndrome: Women, Law and Medicine." *Canadian Journal of Family Law* 8.

Padayachee, A. 1998. "The Hidden Health Burden: Alcohol-Abusing Women, Misunderstood and Mistreated." *International Journal of Drug Policy* 9, 1.

Pain, R. 2001. "Gender, Race, Age and Fear in the City." *Urban Studies* 38, 5–6.

Palmer, P. 2008. *A Hidden Wholeness: The Journey Toward and Undivided Life*. San Francisco: Jossey-Bass.

Papequash, C. 2011. *The Yearning Journey: Escape from Alcoholism*. Norquay: Seven Generation Helpers Publishing.

Parent, C. 2005. "Le Travail du Sexe dans les Établissement de Service Érotiques: Une Forme de Travail Marginalisé." *Déviance et Société* 29, 1.

_____. 2001. "Les Identités Sexuelles et les Travailleuses de l'Industrie du Sexe à l'Aube du Nouveau Millénaire." *Sociologie et Sociétés* 33, 1.

_____. 1994. "La Prostitution ou le Commerce des Services Sexuels." In L. Langlois, Y. Martin, and F. Dumont (eds.), *Traité de Problèmes Sociaux*. Québec: Institut québécois de recherche sur la culture.

Parent, C., and C. Bruckert. 2010. "Le Travail du Sexe Comme Métier." In C. Parent, C. Bruckert, P. Corriveau, M.N. Mensah, and L.Toupin (eds.), *Mais Oui C'est un Travail! Penser le Travail du Sexe au-delà de la Victimisation*. Québec: Presses de l'Université du Québec.

_____. 2006. "Répondre aux besoins des Travailleuses du Sexe de Rue: Un objectif qui passé par la décriminalisation de leurs activités de travail." *Reflets* 11.

Pate, K. 2003. "Prisons: The Latest Solution to Homelessness, Poverty and Mental Illness." Women Speak Series, Calgary, September 18.

_____. 2002. "Labelling Young Women as Violent: Vilification of the Most Vulnerable." In K. McKenna and J. Larkin (eds.), *Violence Against Women: New Canadian Perspectives*.

Toronto: Inanna.

____. 1999a. "csc and the 2 Per Cent Solution." *Canadian Women's Studies* 19, 1 and 2.

____. 1999b. "Young Women and Violent Offences." *Canadian Women's Studies* 19.

Paules, G. 1991. *Dishing It Out.* Philadelphia: Temple University Press.

Pearce, F., and S. Tombs. 1998. *Toxic Capitalism: Corporate Crime and the Chemical Industry.* Aldershot: Ashgate and Dartmouth.

Pearson, P. 1997. *When She Was Bad: Women's Violence and the Myth of Innocence.* Toronto: Random House.

____. 1995. "Behind Every Successful Psychopath." *Saturday Night* 110 (October).

Penney, J. 1983. *Hard Earned Wages: Women Fighting for Better Work.* Toronto: Women's Press.

Perreault, I. 2012. "Esprits Troublés et Corps Déviants: Les Fonctions de la Psychochirurgie à Saint-Jean-de-Dieu, 1948–1956." In S. Frigon (ed.), *Corps Suspect, Corps Déviant.* Montréal: Éditions du Remue-ménage.

Perreault, S. 2012. "Homicide in Canada, 2011." *Juristat* (December 4).

____. 2011. "Violent Victimization of Aboriginal People in the Canadian Provinces, 2009." *Juristat* (March).

____. 2009. "The Incarceration of Aboriginal People in Adult Correctional Services." *Juristat* 29, 3.

Pheterson, G. 1989. *A Vindication of the Rights of Whores.* Seattle: Seal Press.

Philips, L. 2002. "Tax Law and Social Reproduction: The Gender of Fiscal Policy in an Age of Privatization." In B. Cossman and J. Fudge (eds.), *Privatization, Law and the Challenge to Feminism.* Toronto: University of Toronto Press.

Phillips, J. 1986. "Poverty, Unemployment and the Administration of Criminal Law: Vagrancy in Halifax, Nova Scotia, 1864–1890." In P. Girard and J. Phillips (eds.), *Essays in the History of Canadian Law.* Toronto: University of Toronto Press.

Phillips, P. 1997. "Labour in the New Canadian Political Economy." In W. Clement (ed.), *Understanding Canada: Building the New Canadian Political Economy.* Montreal: McGill-Queen's University Press.

Phoenix, J. 2002. "Youth Prostitution Police Reform: New Discourse, Same Old Story." In P. Carlen (ed.), *Women and Punishment: The Struggle for Social Justice.* Portland: Willan Publishing.

Piche, J. 2011. "Tracking the Politics of 'Crime' and Punishment in Canada." <tpcp-canada.blogspot.ca/>.

Piche, J., and M. Larsen. 2010. "The Moving Targets of Penal Abolitionism: ICOPA, Past, Present, and Future." *Contemporary Justice Review* 13, 4.

Pizzey, E. 1974. *Scream Quietly or the Neighbours Will Hear You.* London: Penguin.

Platt, M. 2012. "Canada's Criminal Sitting Pretty as Price Tag for Prisoners Soars." *Calgary Sun,* February 28. <calgarysun.com/2012/02/28/canadas-criminal-sitting-pretty-as-price-tag-for-prisoners-soars>.

Pollack, S. 2012. "An Imprisoning Gaze: Practices of Gendered, Racialized and Epistemic Violence." *International Review of Victimology* 19, 1.

____. 2010. "Labelling Clients 'Risky': Social Work and the Neo-Liberal Welfare State." *British Journal of Social Work* 40, 4.

____. 2009. "You Can't Have It Both Ways: Punishment and Treatment of Imprisoned Women." *Journal of Progressive Human Services* 20, 2.

____. 2008. *Locked In, Locked Out: Imprisoning Women in the Shrinking and Punitive Welfare State.* Faculty of Social Work, Wilfrid Laurier University.

____. 2007. "I'm Just Not Good in Relationships: Victimization Discourses and the Gendered Regulation of Criminalized Women." *Feminist Criminology* 2, 2.

____. 2006. "Therapeutic Programming as Regulatory Practice in Women's Prisons." In G. Balfour and E. Comack (eds.), *Criminalizing Women: Gender and (In)justice in Neo-Liberal Times.*

Halifax and Winnipeg: Fernwood Publishing.

____. 2004. "Anti-Oppressive Practice with Women in Prison: Discursive Reconstructions and Alternative Practices." *British Journal of Social Work* 34, 5.

____. 2000a. "Dependency Discourse as Social Control." In K. Hannah-Moffat and M. Shaw (eds.), *An Ideal Prison? Critical Essays on Women's Imprisonment in Canada.* Halifax: Fernwood Publishing.

____. 2000b. "Reconceptualizing Women's Agency and Empowerment: Challenges to Self-Esteem Discourse and Women's Lawbreaking." *Women and Criminal Justice* 12, 1.

Pollack, S., M. Battaglia, and A. Allspach. 2005. "Women Charged in Domestic Violence Situations in Toronto: The Unintended Consequences of Mandatory Charge Policies." Toronto: Woman Abuse Council of Toronto.

Pollack. S., and K. Kendall. 2005. "'Taming the Shrew': Regulating Prisoners through 'Women-Centred' Mental Health Programming." *Critical Criminology: An International Journal* 13, 1.

Pollak, O. 1950. *The Criminality of Women.* Philadelphia: University of Philadelphia Press.

Poole, N. 2000. *Evaluation Report of the Sheway Project for High-Risk and Parenting Women.* Vancouver: BC Centre of Excellence for Women's Health.

Poole, N., and B. Isaac. 2001. *Apprehensions: Barriers to Treatment for Substance-Using Mothers.* Vancouver: BC Centre of Excellence for Women's Health.

Poulin, R. 2004. *La Mondialisation des Industries du Sexe: Prostitution, Pornographie et Traite des Enfants.* Ottawa: L'Interligne.

Power, J., J. Beaudette, and A. Ussher. 2012. *A Qualitative Study of Self-Injurious Behaviour in Male Offenders.* Ottawa: Correctional Service of Canada.

Power, J., and S. Brown. 2010. *Self-Injurious Behaviour: A Review of the Literature and Implications for Corrections.* Ottawa: Correctional Service of Canada.

Power, J., and D. Riley. 2010. *A Comparative Review of Suicide and Self-Injury Investigative Reports in a Canadian Federal Correctional Population.* Ottawa: Correctional Service of Canada.

Power, J., and A. Usher. 2011a. *A Descriptive Analysis of Self-Injurious Behaviour in Federally Sentenced Women.* Ottawa: Correctional Service of Canada.

____. 2011b. *Correlates and Trajectories to Self-Injurious Behaviour in Federally Sentenced Men.* Ottawa: Correctional Service of Canada.

____. 2011c. *Correlates and Trajectories to Self-Injurious Behaviour in Federally Sentenced Women.* Ottawa: Correctional Service of Canada.

____. 2011d. *Self-injurious Behaviour in Federally Sentenced Women: An Archival Study.* Ottawa: Correctional Service of Canada.

____. 2010. *A Qualitative Study of Self-Injurious Behaviour in Women Offenders.* Ottawa: Correctional Service of Canada.

Powers, E. 2005. "The Unfreedom of Being Other: Canadian Lone Mothers' Experiences of Poverty and Life on the Cheque." *Sociology* 39.

Pratt, G. 2005. "Abandoned Women and Spaces of the Exception." *Antipode* 37, 5.

Pratt, J. 2007. *Penal Populism.* London: Routledge.

Pruegger, V., D. Cook, and S. Richter-Salomons. 2009. *Inequality in Calgary: The Racialization of Poverty.* Calgary: City of Calgary Community and Neighbourhood Services—Social Research Unit.

Pringle, R. 1988. *Secretaries Talk.* London: Verso.

Quadagno, J. 2000. "Another Face of Inequality: Racial and Ethnic Exclusion in the Welfare State." *Social Politics* 7.

Quan, D. 2011. "Prisons to End Rare Solitary-Confinement Protocol for Women." *Postmedia News*, March 14. <canada.com/health/Prisons+rare+solitary+confinement+protocol+w omen/4435512/story.html>.

Rachert, J. 1990. "Welfare Fraud and the State: British Columbia 1970–1977." M.A. thesis,

Simon Fraser University, Burnaby.

Rafter, N.H. 1985a. *Partial Justice: Women in State Prisons, 1900–1935.* Boston: Northeastern University Press.

____. 1985b. "Gender, Prisons, and Prison History." *Social Science History* 9, 3.

Raftner, N.H., and E.M. Natalazia. 1981. "Marxist Feminism: Implications for Criminal Justice." *Crime and Delinquency* 27.

Raitt, F., and S. Zeedyk. 2000. *The Implicit Relation of Psychology and Law: Women and Syndrome Evidence.* London: Routledge.

Raphael, J., and B. Myers-Powell. 2010. *From Victims to Victimizers: Interviews with 25 Ex-Pimps in Chicago.* Chicago: Schiller DuCanto & Fleck Family Law Center of DePaul University College of Law. <newsroom.depaul.edu/pdf/family_law_center_report-final.pdf>.

Raphael, J., J.A. Reichert, and M. Powers. 2010. "Pimp Control and Violence: Domestic Sex Trafficking of Chicago Women and Girls." *Women & Criminal Justice* 20, 1.

Ratushny, L. 1997. *Self-Defence Review: Final Report.* Ottawa: Minister of Justice and Solicitor General Canada. <publicsafety.gc.ca/lbrr/archives/ke%208839%20r3%201997-eng.pdf>.

Razack, S. 2007. "When Place Becomes Race." In T. Das Gupta, C.E. James, R. Maaka, G.-E. Galabuzi, and C. Andersen (eds.), *Race and Racialization: Essential Readings.* Toronto: Canadian Scholars' Press.

____. 2002. *Race, Space and the Law: Unmapping a White Settler Society.* Toronto: Between the Lines.

____. 2000. "Gendered Racial Violence and Spatialized Justice: The Murder of Pamela George." *Canadian Journal of Law and Society* 15, 2.

____. 1998. "Race, Space and Prostitution: The Making of the Bourgeois Subject." *Canadian Journal of Women and the Law* 10.

RCAP (Royal Commission on Aboriginal Peoples). 1996. *Report of the Royal Commission on Aboriginal Peoples.* Ottawa: Department of Indian and Northern Affairs. <collections-canada.gc.ca/webarchives/20071115053257/http://www.ainc-inac.gc.ca/ch/rcap/sg/sgmm_e.html>.

RCMP (Royal Canadian Mounted Police). 2014. *Miissing and Murdered Aboriginal Women: A National Operational Overview.* <rcmp-grc.gc.ca/pubs/mmaw-faapd-eng.pdf>.

Reaume, G. 2000. *Remembrance of Patients Past: Patient Life at the Toronto Hospital for the Insane, 1870–1940.* Don Mills: Oxford University Press.

Rebick, J. 2005. *Ten Thousand Roses: The Making of a Feminist Revolution.* Toronto: Penguin.

Reiter, E. 1991. *Making Fast Food.* Kingston: McGill-Queen's University Press.

Reitsma-Street, M. 1999. "Justice for Canadian Girls: A 1990s Update." *Canadian Journal of Criminology* 41, 3.

Renzetti, C. 1999. "The Challenge to Feminism Posed by Women's Use of Violence in Intimate Relationships." In S. Lamb (ed.), *New Versions of Victims: Feminists Struggle with the Concept.* New York: New York University Press.

____. 1998. "Violence and Abuse in Lesbian Relationships: Theoretical and Empirical Issues." In R. Bergen (ed.), *Issues in Intimate Violence.* Thousand Oaks: Sage.

Rice, M. 1989. "Challenging Orthodoxies in Feminist Theory: A Black Feminist Critique." In L. Gelsthorpe and A. Morris (eds.), *Feminist Perspectives in Criminology.* Milton Keynes: Open University Press.

Richard, B. 2008. *The Ashley Smith Report.* Fredericton NB: Office of the Ombudsman and Child and Youth Advocate.

Richie, B. 1996. *Compelled to Crime: The Gender Entrapment of Battered Black Women.* New York: Routledge.

Rickard, W., and M. Storm. 2001. "Sex Work Reassessed." *Feminist Review* 67.

Ridlon, Florence. 1988. *A Fallen Angel: The Status Insularity of the Female Alcoholic.* Toronto:

Associated University Press.

Rios, V. 2011. *Punished: Policing the Lives of Black and Latino Boys*. New York: New York University Press.

Ripa, Y. 1990. *Women and Madness: The Incarceration of Women in Nineteenth-Century France*. Minneapolis: University of Minnesota Press.

Ritzer, G. 2004. *The McDonaldization of Society*. Thousand Oaks: Pine Forge.

Roach Pierson, R. 1990. *'They're Still Women After All': The Second World War and Canadian Womanhood*. Toronto: McClelland and Stewart.

Roberts, D. 1997. *Killing the Black Body: Race, Reproduction, and the Meaning of Liberty*. New York: Pantheon.

Roberts, J. 1991. *Sexual Assault Legislation in Canada: An Evaluation Report*. Vols. 1–9. Ottawa: Department of Justice, Ministry of Supply and Services.

Roberts, J., and C. La Prairie. 2000. *Conditional Sentencing in Canada: An Overview of Research Findings*. Ottawa: Department of Justice Canada. <dppc.gc.ca/eng/rp-pr/csj-sjc/jsp-sjp/rr00_6/rr00_6.pdf>.

Robinson, M. 2004. "Cam Girls are the New 'It' Girls of the Sex Industry." *Fulcrum* 65, 13.

Rolph, C. 1955. *Women of the Streets: A Sociological Study of the Common Prostitute*. London: Secker and Warburg.

Rosen, R. 1982. *The Lost Sisterhood*. Baltimore: Johns Hopkins University Press.

Ross, B.L. 2006. "'Troublemakers' in Tassels and C-Strings: Striptease Dancers and the Union Question in Vancouver, 1965–1980." *Canadian Review of Sociology and Anthropology* 43, 3.

Ross, R., and E. Fabiano. 1985. *Correctional Alternatives: Programmes for Female Offenders*: Ottawa: Ministry of Solicitor General Programmes Branch.

Ruddick, S. 1996. "Constructing Difference in Public Spaces: Race, Class, and Gender as Interlocking Systems." *Urban Geography* 17, 2.

Ruebsaat, G. 1985. *The New Sexual Assault Offences: Emerging Legal Issues*. Ottawa: Ministry of Supply and Services.

Ruppert, E. 2006. *The Moral Economy of Cities: Shaping Good Citizens*. Toronto: University of Toronto Press.

Said, E. 1979. *Orientalism*. New York: Vintage.

Salmon, A. 2005. "Beyond Guilt, Shame, and Blame to Compassion, Respect, and Empowerment: Young Aboriginal Mothers and the First Nations and Inuit Fetal Alcohol Syndrome/Fetal Alcohol Effects Initiative." Ph.D. dissertation, University of British Columbia.

Salzinger, L. 1991. "A Maid by Any Other Name." In M. Burnaway (ed.), *Ethnography Unbound*. Berkeley: University of California Press.

Sangster, J. 2002. *Girl Trouble: Female Delinquency in English Canada*. Toronto: Between the Lines.

____. 2001. *Regulating Girls and Women: Sexuality, Family, and the Law in Ontario, 1920–1960*. Toronto: Oxford University Press.

____. 2000. "Girls in Conflict with the Law: Exploring the Construction of 'Female Delinquency' in Ontario, 1940–60." *Canadian Journal of Women and the Law* 12.

____. 1999. "Criminalizing the Colonized: Ontario Native Women Confront the Criminal Justice System, 1920–1960." *The Canadian Historical Review* 80, 1.

____. 1996. "Incarcerating 'Bad Girls': The Regulation of Sexuality through the Female Refuges Act in Ontario, 1920–1945." *History of Sexuality* 7.

Sapers, H. 2013. *Annual Report of the Office of the Correctional Investigator, 2012–2013*. Ottawa: The Correctional Investigator Canada.

____. 2012. *Annual Report of the Office of the Correctional Investigator, 2011–2012*. Ottawa: Office of the Correctional Investigator. <oci-bec.gc.ca/cnt/rpt/pdf/annrpt/annrpt20112012-eng.pdf>.

____. 2011. *Annual Report of the Office of the Correctional Investigator, 2010–2011*. Ottawa: Office of the Correctional Investigator. <oci-bec.gc.ca/cnt/rpt/pdf/annrpt/annrpt20102011-eng.pdf>.

____. 2008. *A Preventable Death.* Ottawa: Office of the Correctional Investigator. <oci-bec.gc.ca/cnt/rpt/pdf/oth-aut/oth-aut20080620-eng.pdf>.

Saunders, R. 2003. "Defining Vulnerability in the Labour Market." Paper presented at cprn/lcc Roundtable on Vulnerable Workers. June 17. Ottawa.

Savaraese, J., and B. Morton. 2005. *Women and Social Assistance Policy in Saskatchewan and Manitoba.* Winnipeg: Prairie Women's Health Centre of Excellence.

Scambler, G. 2007. "Sex Work Stigma: Opportunist Migrants in London." *Sociology* 21, 6.

Schissel, B. 2001. "Youth Crime, Moral Panics and the News: The Conspiracy Against the Marginalized in Canada." In R. Smandych (ed.), *Youth Crime: History, Legislation, and Reform.* Toronto: Harcourt Canada.

____. 1997. *Blaming Children: Youth Crime, Moral Panics and the Politics of Hate.* Halifax: Fernwood.

Schramm, H. 1998. *Young Women Who Use Violence — Myths and Facts.* Calgary: Elizabeth Fry Society of Alberta.

Schrecker, T. 2001. "From the Welfare State to the No-Second-Chances State." In S. Boyd, D.E. Chunn, and R. Menzies (eds.), *(Ab)Using Power: The Canadian Experience.* Halifax: Fernwood Publishing.

Schur, E. 1984. *Labeling Women Deviant: Gender, Stigma, and Social Control.* New York: Random House.

Scott, K. 2011. "Society, Place, Work: The BC Public Hospital for the Insane, 1872–1902." *BC Studies* 171.

Scutt, J. 1979. "The Myth of the 'Chivalry Factor' in Female Crime." *Australian Journal of Social Issues* 14, 1.

Seccombe, K., D. James, and K. Walters. 1998. "'They Think You Ain't Much of Nothing': The Social Construction of the Welfare Mother." *Journal of Marriage and the Family* 60.

Sefa Dei, G., B. Hall, and D. Rosenberg. 2002. *Indigenous Knowledges in Global Contexts: Multiple Readings of Our Worlds.* Toronto: University of Toronto Press.

Segal, L. 1999. *Why Feminism? Gender, Psychology, Politics.* New York: Columbia University Press.

Sentencing Project. 2012. *Incarcerated Women Fact Sheet.* Washington DC: The Sentencing Project. <sentencingproject.org/doc/publications/cc_Incarcerated_Women_Factsheet_Sep24sp.pdf>.

Seshia, Maya. 2005. *The Unheard Speak Out.* Winnipeg: Canadian Centre for Policy Alternatives–Manitoba.

Shadd, A. 1991. "Institutionalized Racism and Canadian History: Notes of a Black Canadian." In O. McKague (ed.), *Racism in Canada.* Saskatoon: Fifth House.

Sharma, U., and P. Black. 2001. "Look Good, Feel Better: Beauty Therapy as Emotional Labour." *Sociology* 35, 4.

Sharpe, A. 2005. "Sex Work Research: Methodological and Ethical Challenges." *Journal of Interpersonal Violence* 20, 3.

Shaver, F. 1996. "Traditional Data Distort Our View of Prostitution." <walnet.org/csis/papers/shaver-distort.html>.

Shaw, M. 2000. "Women, Violence, and Disorder in Prisons." In K. Hannah-Moffat and M. Shaw (eds.), *An Ideal Prison? Critical Essays on Women's Imprisonment in Canada.* Halifax: Fernwood Publishing.

____. 1994a. *Ontario Women in Conflict with the Law: Community Prevention Programmes and Regional Issues.* Toronto: Ministry of the Solicitor General and Correctional Services.

____. 1994b. "Women in Prison: Literature Review." *Forum* 6, 1 (Special Issue on Women in Prison). <csc-scc.gc.ca/publications/forum/e061/061d_e.pdf>.

____. 1993. "Reforming Federal Women's Imprisonment." In E. Adelberg and C. Currie (eds.), *In Conflict With the Law: Women and the Canadian Justice System*. Vancouver: Press Gang.

____. 1991. *The Female Offender: Report on a Preliminary Study*. User Report 1991–3. Ottawa: Solicitor General, Ministry Secretariat.

Shaw, M., K. Rodgers, J. Blanchette, T. Hattem, L.S. Thomas, and L.Tamarack. 1991. *Survey of Federally Sentenced Women: Report of the Task Force on Federally Sentenced Women*. User Report 1991–4. Ottawa: Corrections Branch, Ministry of Solicitor General of Canada.

Sheehy, E. 2014. *Battered Women on Trial*. Vancouver: UBC Press.

Sheehy, E., J. Stubbs, and J. Tolmie. 2012. "Battered Women Charged with Homicide in Australia, Canada and New Zealand: How Do They Fare?" *Australian & New Zealand Journal of Criminology* 4.

Shipley, S.L., and B.A. Arrigo. 2004. *The Female Homicide Offender: Serial Murder and the Case of Aileen Wuornos*. Upper Saddle River: Pearson Education/Prentice Hall.

Shostak, A. 1980. *Blue Collar Stress*. Menlo Park: Addison-Welsley.

Sibley, D. 1995. *Geographies of Exclusion: Society and Difference in the West*. New York: Routledge.

Silver, J. 2010. "Segregated City: A Century of Poverty in Winnipeg." In P. Thomas and C. (eds.), *Voices from the Prairies*. Regina: Canadian Plains Research Centre.

____. 2006. *In Their Own Voices: Building Aboriginal Communities*. Halifax and Winnipeg: Fernwood Publishing.

Silver, J., P. Ghorayshi, J. Hay, and D. Klyne. 2006. *In a Voice of Their Own: Urban Aboriginal Community Development*. Winnipeg: Canadian Centre for Policy Alternatives–Manitoba.

Simon, R. 1975. *Women and Crime*. Lexington: D.C. Heath.

Sjostrom, S. 1997. *Party or Patient: Discursive Practices Relating to Coercion in Psychiatric and Legal Settings*. Umea: Borea Bokforlag.

Skrapec, C. 1994. "The Female Serial Killer: An Evolving Criminality." In H. Birch (ed.), *Moving Targets: Women, Murder and Representation*. Berkeley: University of California Press.

Smart, C. 1995. *Law, Crime and Sexuality*. London: Sage.

____. 1990. "Feminist Approaches to Criminology or Postmodern Woman Meets Atavistic Man." In L. Gelsthorpe and A. Morris (eds.), *Feminist Perspectives in Criminology*. Milton Keynes: Open University Press.

____. 1989. *Feminism and the Power of the Law: Essays in Feminism*. London: Routledge.

____. 1977. "Criminological Theory: Its Ideology and Implications Concerning Women." *British Journal of Sociology* 28, 1.

____. 1976. *Women, Crime and Criminology: A Feminist Critique*. London: Routledge and Kegan Paul.

Smith, L.T. 1999. *Decolonizing Methodologies: Research and Indigenous Peoples*. London: Zed Books.

Snider, L. 2006. "Relocating Law: Making Corporate Crime Disappear." In E. Comack (ed.), *Locating Law: Race/Class/Gender/Sexuality Connections* (second edition). Halifax: Fernwood Publishing.

____. 2004. "Female Punishment: From Patriarchy to Backlash?" In C. Sumner (ed.), *The Blackwell Companion to Criminology*. Oxford: Blackwell.

____. 2003. "Constituting the Punishable Woman: Atavistic Man Incarcerates Postmodern Woman." *British Journal of Criminology* 43, 2.

____. 2002. "The Sociology of Corporate Crime: An Obituary (or, Whose Knowledge Claims Have Legs?)" *Theoretical Criminology* 4.

____. 1999. "Relocating Law: Making Corporate Crime Disappear." In Elizabeth Comack (ed.), *Locating Law: Race/Class/Gender Connections*. Halifax: Fernwood Publishing.

____. 1998. "Towards Safer Societies: Punishment, Masculinities and Violence Against Women." *British Journal of Criminology* 38, 1.

____. 1994. "Feminism, Punishment and the Potential of Empowerment." *Canadian Journal of Law and Society* 9, 1.

____. 1991. "The Potential of the Criminal Justice System to Promote Feminist Concerns." In E. Comack and S. Brickey (eds.), *The Social Bias of Law: Critical Readings in the Sociology of Law* (second edition). Halifax: Fernwood Publishing.

____. 1985. "Legal Reform and Social Control: The Dangers of Abolishing Rape." *International Journal of the Sociology of Law* 13, 4.

Snyder, H. 2012. *Arrest in the United States, 1990–2010.* Washington: Bureau of Justice Statistics. <bjs.gov/content/pub/pdf/aus9010.pdf>.

Sommers, J., and N. Blomley. 2002. "The Worst Block in Vancouver." In R Shier (ed.), *Stan Douglas: Every Building on 100 West Hastings.* Vancouver: Contemporary Art Gallery and Arsenal Pulp Press.

Sossin, L. 2004. "Boldly Going Where No Law Has Gone Before: Call Centres, Intake Scripts, Database Fields and Discretionary Justice in Social Assistance." *Osgoode Hall Law Journal* 42.

Spivak, G. 1988. "Can the Subaltern Speak?" In C. Nelson and L. Grossberg (eds.), *Marxism and the Interpretation of Culture.* Basingstoke: MacMillan.

Spohn, C., and K. Tellis. 2012. "The Criminal Justice System's Response to Sexual Violence." *Violence Against Women* 18, 2.

Stanko, E. 1997. "Conceptualizing Women's Risk: Assessment as a Technology of the Soul." *Theoretical Criminology* 1, 4.

____. 1990. *Everyday Violence.* London: Pandora.

____. 1985. *Intimate Intrusions: Women's Experience of Male Violence.* London: Routledge and Kegan Paul.

Statistics Canada. 2011. *Family Violence in Canada: A Statistical Profile.* <statcan.gc.ca/pub/85-224-x/85-224-x2010000-eng.pdf>.

____. 2009a. *Perspectives on Labour and Income: Minimum Wage.* <statcan.gc.ca/pub/75-001-x/topics-sujets/pdf/topics-sujets/minimumwage-salaireminimum-2008-eng.pdf>.

____. 2009b. *Homicide in Canada, 2008.* Catalogue no. 85-002-X. Ottawa: Minister of Industry.

____. 2005. *General Social Survey, Cycle 18 Overview: Personal Safety and Perceptions of the Criminal Justice System.* Ottawa: Statistics Canada.

____. 1993. "The Violence Against Women Survey." *The Daily,* 18 November.

Steffensmeier, D. 1980. "Sex Differences in Patterns of Adult Crime, 1965–1977." *Social Forces* 58, 4.

Steffensmeier, D., and J. Kramer. 1982. "Sex-Based Differences in the Sentencing of Adult Criminal Defendants." *Sociology and Social Research* 663.

Steinmetz, S. 1981. "A Cross-cultural Comparison of Marital Abuse." *Journal of Sociology and Social Welfare* 8.

Steinstra, D. 2010. *Fact Sheet: Women and Restructuring in Canada.* Ottawa: CRIAW/ICREF.

Stenson, K., and P. Watt. 1999. "Governmentality and 'the Death of the Social'? A Discourse Analysis of Local Government Texts in South-East England." *Urban Studies* 36, 1.

Stephen, J. 1995. "The 'Incorrigible,' the 'Bad,' and the 'Immoral': Toronto's 'Factory Girls' and the Work of the Toronto Psychiatric Clinic." In L. Knafla and S. Binnie (eds.), *Law, Society and the State: Essays in Modern Legal History.* Toronto: University of Toronto Press.

Strange, C. 1996. "The Lottery of Death: Capital Punishment, 1867–1976." *Manitoba Law Journal* 23.

____. 1995. *Toronto's Girl Problem: The Perils and Pleasures of the City, 1880–1930.*Toronto: University of Toronto Press.

Strange, C., and T. Loo. 1997. *Making Good: Law and Moral Regulation in Canada.* Toronto: University of Toronto Press.

Straus, M. 1979. "Measuring Intrafamily Conflict and Violence: The Conflict Tactics (CT) Scales."

*Journal of Marriage and the Family* 41, 1.

Straus, M., and R. Gelles. 1986. "Societal Changes and Change in Family Violence from 1975 to 1985 as Revealed by Two National Surveys." *Journal of Marriage and the Family* 48.

Straus, M., R. Gelles, and S. Steinmetz. 1980. *Behind Closed Doors: Violence in the American Family*. New York: Doubleday.

Strega, S. 2006. "Failure to Protect: Child Welfare Interventions When Men Beat Mothers." In R. Alaggia and C. Vine (eds.), *Cruel but Not Unusual: Violence in Canadian Families*. Waterloo: Wilfrid Laurier University Press.

Stubbs, J., and J. Tolmie. 1999. "Falling Short of the Challenge? A Comparative Assessment of the Australian Use of Expert Evidence on the Battered Woman Syndrome." *Melbourne University Law Review* 23, 3.

Sudbury, J. (ed.). 2005a. *Global Lockdown: Race, Gender, and the Prison-Industrial Complex*. London: Routledge.

____. 2005b. "Introduction: Feminist Critiques, Transnational Landscapes, Abolitionist Visions." In J. Sudbury (ed.), *Global Lockdown: Race, Gender, and the Prison-Industrial Complex*. New York: Routledge.

Sugar, F., and L. Fox. 1989. "Nistem Peyako Seht'wawin Iskwewak: Breaking the Chains." *Canadian Journal of Women and the Law* 3, 2.

Sumner, C. 1990. "Foucault, Gender and the Censure of Deviance." In L. Gelsthorpe and A. Morris (eds.), *Feminist Perspectives in Criminology*. Milton Keynes: Open University Press.

Sutherland, E. 1949. *Principles of Criminology* (fourth edition). Philadelphia: J.B. Lippincott.

Swainger, J. 1995. "A Distant Edge of Authority: Capital Punishment and the Prerogative of Mercy in British Columbia, 1872–1880." In H. Foster and J. McLaren (eds.), *Essays in the History of Canadian Law. Vol. VI: British Columbia and the Yukon*. Toronto: Osgoode Society and University of Toronto Press.

Swan, R., Linda L. Shaw, S. Cullity, J. Halpen, J. Humphrey, W. Limbert, and M. Roche. 2008. "The Untold Story of Welfare Fraud" *Journal of Sociology & Social Welfare* 35.

Swift, K., and M. Birmingham. 2000. "Location, Location, Location: Restructuring and the Everyday Lives of 'Welfare Moms.'" In S.M. Neysmith (ed.), *Restructuring Caring Labour*. Toronto: Oxford University Press.

Sykes, G. 1958. *The Society of Captives: A Study of a Maximum Security Prison*. Princeton: Princeton University Press.

Taillon, J. 2006. "Offences against the Administration of Justice." *Juristat* 26, 1.

Tartaro, C., and D. Lester. 2009. *Suicide and Self-Harm in Prisons and Jails*. Lanham: Lexington Books.

Taylor, I., P. Walton, and J. Young. 1973. *The New Criminology*. London: Routledge and Kegan Paul.

Tcheremissine, O. 2008. "Is Quetiapine a Drug of Abuse? Re-examining the Issue of Addiction." *Expert Opinion on Drug Safety* 7, 6.

Tempier, A., C. Dell, Elder C. Papaquash, R. Duncan, and R. Tempier. 2011. "Awakening: 'Spontaneous Recovery' from Substance Abuse among Aboriginal Peoples in Canada." *The International Indigenous Policy Journal* 2, 1.

Teotonio, I. 2009. "6,000 Homes Canvassed for Mariam Clues." *Toronto Star*, November 10.

TFFSW (Task Force on Federally Sentenced Women). 1990. *Creating Choices: The Task Force Report of the Task Force on Federally Sentenced Women*. Ottawa: Correctional Service of Canada.

Thanh Ha, Tu. 2012. "Karla Homolka Lives in Guadeloupe and Has Three Children, New Book Reveals." *Globe and Mail*, June 21. <theglobeandmail.com/news/national/karla-homolka-lives-in-guadeloupe-and-has-three-children-new-book-reveals/article4360378>.

Thomas, W.I. 1923 [1967]. *The Unadjusted Girl*. New York: Harper and Row.

Tombs, S. 2002. "Understanding Regulation?" *Social and Legal Studies* 11.

Tong, R. 1996. "Maternal-Fetal Conflict: The Misguided Case for Punishing Cocaine-Using Pregnant and/or Postpartum Women." In C. Sistare (ed.), *Punishment: Social Control and Coercion*. New York: Peter Lang.

____. 1984. *Women, Sex and Law*. Savage: Rowman and Littlefield.

Turnbull, S., and K. Hannah-Moffat. 2009, "Under These Conditions: Gender, Parole and the Governance of Reintegration." *British Journal of Criminology* 49.

Tyrer, P., and T. Kendall. 2009. "The Spurious Advance of Antipsychotic Drug Therapy." *The Lancet* 373, January 3. <psychrights.org/research/Digest/NLPs/SpuriousAdvanceofNeurolepticsLancetTurner2008.pdf>.

UFCW Canada. 2013. "By the Numbers: Minimum Wage in Canada by Province for 2011." <ufcw.ca/index.php?option=com_content&view=article&id=2359%3Aby-the-numbers-cpi&Itemid=306&lang=en>.

Ursel, J. 1991. "Considering the Impact of the Battered Women's Movement on the State: The Example of Manitoba." In E. Comack and S. Brickey (eds.), *The Social Basis of Law: Critical Readings in the Sociology of Law* (second edition). Halifax: Fernwood.

Usher, A., J. Power, and G. Wilton. 2010. *Assessment, Intervention and Prevention of Self-injurious Behaviour in Correctional Environments*. Ottawa: Correctional Service of Canada.

Ussher, J. M. 2011. *The Madness of Women: Myth and Experience*. London, UK: Taylor and Francis.

____. 2010. "Are We Medicalizing Women's Misery? A Critical Review of Women's Higher Rates of Reported Depression." *Feminism & Psychology* 20, 9.

____. 1992. *Women's Madness: Misogyny or Mental Illness?* Amherst: University of Massachusetts Press.

Valentine, G. 1989. "The Geography of Women's Fear." *Area* 21, 4.

Valverde, M. 1998. *Diseases of the Will: Alcohol and the Dilemmas of Freedom*. Cambridge: Cambridge University Press.

____. 1995. "The Mixed Social Economy as a Canadian Tradition." *Studies in Political Economy* 47.

____. 1994. "Moral Capital." *Canadian Journal of Law and Society* 9.

____. 1991. *The Age of Light, Soap, and Water: Moral Reform in English Canada 1885–1925*. Toronto: McClelland and Stewart.

Valverde, M., and L. Weir. 1988. "The Struggles of the Immoral: Preliminary Remarks on Moral Regulation." *Resources for Feminist Research* 17.

Van Brunschot, E., R. Sydie, and C. Krull. 1999. "Images of Prostitution: The Prostitute and Print Media." *Women and Criminal Justice* 10, 4.

van der Meulen, E., and E. Durisin. 2008. "Why Decriminalize? How Canada's Municipal and Federal Regulations Increase Sex Workers' Vulnerability." *Canadian Journal of Women and the Law* 20, 2.

van der Meulen, E., E. Durisin, and V. Love. 2013. *Selling Sex: Experience, Advocacy, and Research on Sex Work in Canada*. Vancouver: UBC Press.

van der Meulen, E., and A. Glasbeek. 2013. *The Gendered Lens: A Report on Women's Experiences with Video Surveillance and Urban Security in Toronto*. Toronto. <jdawncarlson.files.wordpress.com/2013/08/1-gendered-lens-report-april-2013.pdf>.

van der Meulen, E., and M. Valverde. 2013. "Beyond the Criminal Code: Municipal Licensing and Zoning By-laws." In E. van der Meulen, E. Durisin, and V. Love (eds.), *Selling Sex: Experience, Advocacy, and Research on Sex Work in Canada*. Vancouver: UBC Press.

Velarde, A. 1975. "Becoming Prostituted." *British Journal of Criminology* 15, 3.

Vinding, D. 1998. *Indigenous Women: The Right to a Voice*. Copenhagen: International Work Group for Indigenous Affairs.

Wacquant, L. 2009a. *Prisons of Poverty*. Minnesota: University of Minnesota Press.

____. 2009b. *Punishing the Poor: The Neoliberal Government of Social Insecurity*. Durham: Duke

University Press.

Walker, L. 1987. *Terrifying Love: Why Battered Women Kill and How Society Responds.* New York: Harper Collins.

____. 1979. *The Battered Woman.* New York: Harper and Row.

Walkowitz, J. 1992. *City of Dreadful Delight: Narratives of Sexual Danger in Late Victorian London.* Chicago: University of Chicago Press.

____. 1980. "The Politics of Prostitution." *Signs* 6, 1.

Walmsley, R. 2007. *World Female Imprisonment List* (second edition). London: International Centre for Prison Studies. <prisonstudies.org/sites/prisonstudies.org/files/resources/downloads/wfil_2nd_edition.pdf>.

Weir, L. 1986. "Studies in the Medicalization of Sexual Danger: Sexual Rule, Sexual Politics, 1830–1930." Ph.D. dissertation, York University, Toronto.

Weiss, J. 1976. "Liberation and Crime: The Invention of the New Female Criminal." *Crime and Social Justice* 6.

Weldon, J. 2006. "Show Me the Money: A Sex Worker Reflects on Research into the Sex Industry." *Research for Sex Work* 9.

Welsh, B., and D. Farrington. 2007. "Closed Circuit Television Surveillance and Crime Prevention: A Systemic Review." Report prepared for the Swedish National Council for Crime Prevention. Stockholm: Swedish Council for Crime Prevention.

____. 2003. *Crime Prevention Effects of Closed Circuit Television: A Systemic Review.* London: Home Office.

Wesley, M. 2012. *Marginalized: The Aboriginal Women's Experience in Federal Corrections.* Ottawa: Public Safety Canada and the Wesley Group. <publications.gc.ca/collections/collection_2012/sp-ps/PS4-120-2012-eng.pdf>.

Westwood, S. 1984. *All Day Every Day.* London: Pluto Press.

Wharf, B., and M. Clague (eds.). 1997. *Community Organizing: Canadian Experiences.* Toronto: Oxford University Press.

Whitaker, R. 2010. *Mad in America: Bad Science, Bad Medicine, and the Enduring Mistreatment of the Mentally Ill* (second edition). New York: Basic Books.

White, K. 2008. *Negotiating Responsibility: Law, Murder, and States of Mind.* Vancouver: UBC Press.

Williams, C. 2010. "Economic Well-Being." *Women in Canada: A Gender-Based Statistical Report.* Ottawa: Statistics Canada.

Williams, K., and C. Johnstone. 2000. "The Politics of the Selective Gaze: Closed Circuit Television and the Policing of Public Space." *Crime, Law, and Social Change* 34, 2.

Williams, R. 2012. "Are CEO Salaries Out of Control?" *Psychology Today* (April 21). <psychologytoday.com/blog/wired-success/201204/are-ceo-salaries-out-control>.

Williams, T. 2009. "Intersectionality Analysis in the Sentencing of Aboriginal Women in Canada: What Difference Does It Make?" In E. Grabham, D. Cooper, J. Krishnadas, and D. Herman (eds.), *Intersectionality and Beyond: Law, Power and the Politics of Location.* New York: Routledge-Cavendish.

Williamson, K. 2000. "Celestial and Social Families of the Inuit." In R. Laliberte, P. Settee, J. Waldram, R. Innes, B. MacDougall, L. McBain, and F.L. Barron (eds.), *Expressions in Canadian Native Studies.* Saskatoon: University Extension Press.

Wilson, A. 2004. *Living Well: Aboriginal Women, Cultural Identity and Wellness.* Winnipeg: Manitoba Aboriginal Women's Health Community Committee and Prairie Women's Health Centre of Excellence.

Wilson, E. 1983. *What Is To Be Done About Violence Against Women.* Harmondsworth: Penguin.

Winnifrith, T. 1994. *Fallen Women in the Nineteenth Century Novel.* London: MacMillan.

Wolfe, P. 2006. "Settler Colonialism and the Elimination of the Native." *Journal of Genocide Research* 8, 4.

Women's Court Watch Project. 2006. *Court Watch IV, Annual Report*. Toronto: Woman Abuse Council of Toronto.

Wong, J. 2002. "Prisoner of Love, Sixty Years Ago, Velma Demerson was a Teenager Caught Up in a Great Romance, then She Discovered how Harsh Canadian Law Can Be." *Globe and Mail*, October 26.

Wood, D. 2004. "House Rules." *Vancouver Magazine*, April. <telus.net/public/pace9/media_files/House_Rules_Vancouver_Magazine-April_2004.pdf>.

Wood, E. 2002. "Working in the Fantasy Factory." *Journal of Contemporary Ethnograpy* 29, 1.

Wood, T. 2001. "The Case Against Karla." *Elm Street Magazine*, April.

Woolf Report. 1991. *Prison Disturbances April 1990*. Report of an Inquiry by the Rt. Hon. Lord Justice Woolf (Parts I and II) and His Honour Judge Stephen Tumin (Part II). Cmnd 1456. London: HMSO.

Worrall, A. 2002. "Rendering Women Punishable: The Making of a Penal Crisis." In P. Carlen (ed.), *Women and Punishment: The Struggle for Justice*. Cullompton: Willan Publishing.

____. 1990. *Offending Women: Female Lawbreakers and the Criminal Justice System*. New York: Rutledge and Keagan Paul.

Wright, M.-E. 1987. "Unnatural Mothers: Infanticide in Halifax, 1850–1875." *Nova Scotia Historical Review* 7.

Wynter, S. 1987. "Whisper." In F. Delacoste and P. Alexander (eds.), *Sex Work: Writings by Women in the Sex Industry*. Pittsburgh: Cleis Press.

Yalkin, T., and M. Kirk. 2012. *The Fiscal Impacts of Changes to Eligibility for Conditional Sentences of Imprisonment in Canada*. Ottawa: Office of the Parliamentary Budget Officer.

Yalnizyan, A. 2013. *Study of Income Inequality in Canada — What Can Be Done*. Ottawa: Canadian Centre for Policy Alternatives. <policyalternatives.ca/sites/default/files/uploads/publications/National%20Office/2013/05/Armine_Inequality_Presentation_HOC_Finance_Committee.pdf>.

Young, C. 2000. *Women, Tax and the Gendered Impact of Funding Social Programs Through the Tax System*. Ottawa: Status of Women Canada.

Zedner, L. 2003. "Too Much Security?" *International Journal of the Sociology of Law* 31, 3.

____. 1998. "Wayward Sisters." In N. Morris and D. Rothman (eds.), *The Oxford History of Prison*. New York: Oxford University Press.

Zinger, I., C. Wichmann, and D.A. Andrews. 2001. "The Psychological Effects of 60 Days in Administrative Segregation." *Canadian Journal of Criminology* 43, 1.

Zingraff, M., and R. Thomson. 1984. "Differential Sentencing of Women and Men in the U.S.A." *International Journal of the Sociology of Law* 12.

## Cases Cited

*Bedford v Canada (Attorney General)* [2013] SCC 72.

*Broomer v Ontario (Attorney General)*, [2002] O.J. No 2196 (Ont. Sup Ct), online QL (OJ)

*Falkiner v Ontario (Ministry of Community and Social Services, Income Maintenance Branch)*, [2002] 59 OR (3d) 481, [2002] OJ No 1771 (Ont CA), online QL (OJ)

*Masse v Ontario (Ministry of Community and Social Services, Income Maintenance Branch)*, [1996] OJ No 363 (Ont Ct J (Gen Div)), online QL (OJ), leave to appeal denied, [1996] OJ No. 1526 (Ont CA), online (QL (OJ)

*R v Ahmed*, [2005] ABPC 38, [2005] AJ No 1112 (Alta Pro Ct), online QL

*R v Allan*, [2008] OJ No 2794 (Ont Supt Ct J), online QL (OJ)

*R v Bedford*, [2000] SCCA No 328

*R v Bjorn*, [2004] BCPC 127, [2004] BCJ No 1073 (BC Pro Ct) online QL

*R v Bond*, [1994] OJ No 2185 (Ont Ct J (Gen Div)), online QL (OJ)

*R v Brandes*, [1997] OJ No 5443

*R v Caringi*, [2002] OJ No 2367

*R v Collins*, [2011] ONCA 182, [2011] 2 CNLR 256 (Ont CA), online QL (OJ)

*R v Gladue*, [1999] 1 SCR 699

*R v Ipeelee*, [2012] SCC 13

*R v Jantunen*, [1994] OJ No 889 (Ont Ct (Gen Div)), online QL (OJ)

*R v Lalonde*, [1995] 22 OR (3d) 275; [1995] OJ (Ont Ct (Gen Div))

*R v Lavallee*, 1990. SCR 852

*R v McCloy*, [2008] ABPC 212, [2008] AJ No 1509 (Alta Pro Ct), online QL

*R v Plemel*, [1995] OJ No 4155 (Ont Ct (Gen Div)), online QL (OJ)

*R v Ryan*, [2013] SCC 3

*R v S.L.N.* [2010] BCSC 405

*R v Sim*, [1980] 63 CCC (2d) 376 (Ont Co Ct J (Cr Ct))

*R v Slaght* [1995] OJ No 4192 (Ont Ct (Gen Div)), online QL (OJ)

*R v Thurrott*, [1971] 5 CCC (2d) 129 (Ont CA)

*R v Wilson*, [2005] ONCJ 21, [2005] OJ No 382 (Ont Ct J), online QL (OJ)

*Rogers v Sudbury*, [2001] 57 OR (3d) 460 (Ont Sup Ct)

*Bobby Lee Worm v Attorney General of Canada*, [2011] BCSC. Notice of Civil Claim. <bccla.org/wp-content/uploads/2012/03/20110303-BCCLA-Legal-Case-BobbyLee-Worm.pdf>.

## Legislation Cited

*An Act Respecting Industrial Refuges for Females [Female Refuges Act]*. [1919] RSO c 84

*Canadian Criminal Code*, RSC 1985, c C-46

*Corrections and Conditional Release Act*, [1992] SC c 20

*General Welfare Assistance Act*, RSO 1990, c G.6, as rep. by *Social Assistance Reform Act*, 1997, SO 1997, c 25 enacting *Ontario Works Act*, 1997, SO 1997, c 25, s.1 [OWA] and *Ontario Disability Support Program Act*, 1997, SO 1997 c. 25, s. 2 [ODSPA].

*Safe Streets Act*, 1999, SO 1999, c 8

*Ontario Works Act*, 1997, SO 1997, c 25

*Protection of Children Involved in Prostitution Regulation*, Alta Reg 5/1999

## Legal Facta

*Bedford v Attorney General of Canada and Attorney General of Ontario*, [2011]. (Factum of the Intervener Women's Coalition) OCA C52799 and C52814.

*Bedford v Attorney General of Canada and Attorney General of Ontario*, [2009]. (Factum of The Christian legal Fellowship, REAL Women of Canada and The Catholic Civil Rights League) OSCJ 07-CV-329807 PDI.

# Index